Disasters and the American State

Disasters and the American State offers a thesis about the trajectory of federal government involvement in preparing for disaster, shaped by contingent events. Politicians and bureaucrats claim credit for the government's successes in preparing for and responding to disaster, and they are also blamed for failures outside of government's control. New interventions have created precedents and established organizations and administrative cultures that accumulated over time and produced a general trend in which citizens, politicians, and bureaucrats expect the government to provide more security from more kinds of disasters. The trend reached its peak when the Federal Emergency Management Agency adopted the idea of preparing for "all hazards" as its mantra. Despite the rhetoric, however, the federal government's increasingly bold claims and heightened public expectations are disproportionate to the ability of the federal government to prevent or reduce the damage caused by disaster.

Patrick S. Roberts is an associate professor in the Center for Public Administration and Policy (CPAP) in the School of Public and International Affairs at Virginia Polytechnic and State University (Virginia Tech). He is the associate chair and program director for CPAP, Northern Virginia. Roberts holds a PhD in government from the University of Virginia and spent two years as a postdoctoral Fellow, one at the Center for International Security and Cooperation at Stanford University and one at the Program on Constitutional Government at Harvard University. He spent 2010–2011 as the Ghaemian Scholar-in-Residence at the University of Heidelberg Center for American Studies in Germany. He has also been a reporter for the Associated Press. Roberts's work has been published in a variety of scholarly and popular journals including *Studies in American Political Development, Public Administration Review, Journal of Policy History, Political Science Quarterly, Publius, Presidential Studies Quarterly, Administration & Society, Public Organization Review, National Affairs, Policy Review, American Interest,* and *USA Today.* His research has been funded by the National Science Foundation, the United States Naval Laboratories, the Federal Emergency Management Agency, and the Social Science Research Council.

Disasters and the American State

How Politicians, Bureaucrats, and the Public Prepare for the Unexpected

PATRICK S. ROBERTS

Virginia Polytechnic Institute and State University

CAMBRIDGE
UNIVERSITY PRESS

32 Avenue of the Americas, New York, NY 10013-2473, USA

Cambridge University Press is part of the University of Cambridge.

It furthers the University's mission by disseminating knowledge in the pursuit of education, learning, and research at the highest international levels of excellence.

www.cambridge.org
Information on this title: www.cambridge.org/9781107025868

First published 2013

Printed in the United States of America

A catalog record for this publication is available from the British Library.

Library of Congress Cataloging in Publication data
Roberts, Patrick S., 1975–
Disasters and the American state : how politicians, bureaucrats, and the public prepare for the unexpected / Patrick S. Roberts, Virginia Polytechnic Institute and State University.
  pages cm
Includes bibliographical references and index.
ISBN 978-1-107-02586-8 (hardback)
1. Disaster relief – Government policy – United States. 2. Emergency management – Government policy – United States. 3. Civil defense – United States. I. Title.
HV555.U6R625 2013
363.34′70973–dc23   2013000570

ISBN 978-1-107-02586-8 Hardback

Contents

List of Figures   *page* vi
Acknowledgments   vii

1. From Disaster Relief to Disaster Management   1
2. The Origins of the Disaster State, 1789–1914   16
3. Civil Defense and the Foundations of Disaster Policy, 1914–1979   41
4. The Rise of Emergency Management and FEMA, 1979–2001   70
5. Terrorism and the Creation of the Department of Homeland
    Security, 1993–2003   113
6. "Where the Hell Is the Army?": Hurricane Katrina Meets the
    Homeland Security Era   127
7. Administrative Evil and Elite Panic in Disaster Management   146
8. Government's Increasing Role in Disaster Management   174

Bibliography   195
Index   215

Figures

2.1. Selected major U.S. natural disasters from 1755 to 1920   *page* 18

3.1. Organization of federal disaster functions, 1950–2010   51

3.2. Civil defense appropriations from 1952 to 1982   60

4.1. Major disaster declarations from 1953 to 2007   76

4.2. Presidential disaster spending by year from 1953 to 2008   77

4.3. Presidential disaster declarations by year from 1950 to 2009   77

4.4. Presidential disaster declarations by type from 1953 to 2009   78

4.5. Percentage of declaration requests turned down between 1953 and 2009, by administration   79

4.6. Tone of major newspaper editorials' coverage of FEMA from 1982 to 2008   89

4.7. Major professional emergency management associations and their founding dates   93

4.8. Growth of emergency management higher education programs from 1983 to 2004   95

4.9. Federal Emergency Management Agency administrators   98

4.10. Interview summary   99

8.1. Population growth in major U.S. cities from 1870 to 1990   183

8.2. Billion-dollar disaster losses from 1980 to 2009   184

8.3. Natural-disaster-related deaths from 1920 to 2009   185

8.4. Major Atlantic hurricane damages from 1900 to 1995   186

Acknowledgments

Long before social media shout-outs, the acknowledgments section of a book was the place to publicly recognize friends and colleagues who have been enormously helpful, and this section is no exception. My interest in the federal government's expanding role in disaster management began while I was a graduate student at the University of Virginia, writing a dissertation under the guidance of James Ceaser, Sidney Milkis, Eric Patashnik, and Edmund Russell. My interest in disasters and security organizations deepened during a formative year as a postdoctoral Fellow at Stanford University's Center for International Security and Cooperation, under the guidance of Scott Sagan, Lynn Eden, and Charles Perrow, and with the encouragement of my fellow CISAC Fellows. I began writing this manuscript during my year as a Fellow in the Program on Constitutional Government at Harvard University under the supervision of Harvey C. Mansfield, Jr., and Shep Melnick. I appreciate their gracious hospitality, and I also benefited from the spirited criticism of Paul Peterson and the government department's American Politics workshop. Steve Kelman kindly allowed me to observe his course on public management, which challenged some of my notions about the civil service.

I completed the bulk of the manuscript during a memorable year as the Ghaemian Scholar in Residence at the Heidelberg Center for American Studies at the University of Heidelberg in Germany. I am grateful to the faculty and staff including Manfred Berg, Mischa Honeck, Dorothea Fischer-Hornung, Detlef Junker, Günter Leypoldt, Wilfried Mausbach, Dietmar Schloss, Anja Schüler, and Martin Thunert for making the HCA a shining example of what a scholarly community can be. Many other staff members, students, and friends made my stay both enjoyable and productive. Not least, I thank the HCA's dedicated benefactors, including Soheyl Ghaemian, for providing support for a year of research, writing, and transatlantic exploration.

I have accrued many debts to the faculty, staff, and students at Virginia Tech, which has been my home since graduate school. The Center for Public Administration and Policy and the School of Public and International Affairs have been stimulating communities for research and teaching. My colleagues Brian Cook, Matt Dull, Laura Jensen, Gerry Kearns, Anne Khademian, and John Rohr commented on parts of the manuscript.

Notions and arguments that found their way into this manuscript have been presented at conferences and invited talks on two continents. My arguments benefited from comments and criticism at meetings of the American Political Science Association, the Midwest Political Science Association, the Western Political Science Association, the Policy History Conference, and the Academy of Management. Over the past few years, I presented my research on disaster and security organizations at the University of Heidelberg; the Peace Research Institute Frankfurt; the Congressional Research Service; the City University of New York Graduate Center; Grand Valley State University; Harvard University; Boston College; Virginia Tech's Blacksburg and Alexandria campuses; the Annual Natural Hazards Research and Applications Workshop organized by the University of Colorado, Boulder's, Natural Hazards Center; the FEMA Emergency Management Institute; and the Transatlantic Dialog at Bocconi University organized by the American and European public administration societies. The dynamic community of disaster researchers across social science, natural science, and engineering fields encouraged me to go beyond the confines of my own discipline. The Next Generation of Hazards and Disasters Researchers Fellowship, sponsored by the National Science Foundation, was particularly helpful – and challenging – and I owe thanks to my mentor there, Tom Birkland.

A number of people read and commented on parts of the manuscript in its earliest stages. Among those who were generous in receiving my ideas, taking them seriously, and steering me in the right direction or at least away from the most wrong directions are: Ben Bateman, Tom Birkland, Wayne Blanchard, Dan Carpenter, Andrew Coffey, Don Critchlow, Bill Cumming, Gareth Davies, Daniel DiSalvo, Lynn Eden, Saunji Fyffe, Holly Goerdel, Laura Helper-Ferris, Ruth Homrighaus, Kevin Kosar, Marc Landy, Eli Lehrer, Jerry Passannante, Charles Perrow, Claire Rubin, Andrew Schlewitz, Susan Sterett, Paul Stockton, Rick Sylves, Karen Till, and Gary Wamsley. Parts of chapter 7 appear in the article "Discrimination in a Disaster Agency's Security Culture," in the May 2013 (45:4) issue of *Administration & Society*.

At the final stages of the manuscript's development, a number of friends, colleagues, and critics were generous enough with their time to read the manuscript and point out sections where I could buff and polish sentences and in a few cases refinish chapters. Jaimy Alex, Frank Blazich, Robert Cole, Alexander Hamilton, Elvin Lim, Andrew Novak, Barry Pump, Vikram Raghavan, Rob Saldin, Anim Sampong, Travis St. Clair, and Kris Wernstedt deserve special thanks for this task. Meaghan Dee and the FourDesign team transformed my rudimentary figures into informational graphic art.

At Cambridge University Press, Lew Bateman's patient stewardship of the manuscript was vital to ensuring its publication. Lew and the reviewers and editors at Cambridge have been a pleasure to work with. Throughout the project and during several household moves, I benefited from the support, encouragement, and sometimes gentle prodding of my family, my mom, dad, grandmother, Donna, Ann, and Stuart. I would like to thank everyone mentioned immensely.

I

From Disaster Relief to Disaster Management

From late August 1926 through the spring of 1927, unusually heavy rain fell in the Mississippi River Valley. The rain-swollen river flowed over its banks and spilled onto the land, much of which had been stripped of natural barriers because of heavy logging. Rain overtopped some levees and burst others, and floodwaters did not recede until July 1927.[1] The water's rush was so quick and violent that it left new lakes in its wake. Some people drowned in their homes; others were found dead in the fields.

Only a year before, the Army Corps of Engineers' chief had blithely asserted that the levee system "is now in condition to prevent the destructive effects of floods."[2] Congress started working to tame the river in 1879, when it created the Mississippi River Commission, which worked with the Army Corps to build levees along the river's path. By the spring of 1927, the levees had failed. The river swelled over its banks, and governors of states along the river asked for federal help. Mississippi Governor Dennis Murphree sent an urgent wire to the president: "[U]nprecedented floods have created a national emergency. This territory will be water covered one to twenty feet in twenty four hours contains population 150,000 highways covered railroad operations suspended beyond capacity local and state agencies to relieve control."[3]

President Calvin Coolidge dispatched Commerce Secretary Herbert Hoover to lead the response. On April 22, 1927, Coolidge named Hoover as chairman of a special committee of five cabinet secretaries and a Red Cross representative,

[1] John M. Barry, *Rising Tide: The Great Mississippi Flood of 1927 and How It Changed America* (New York: Simon & Schuster, 1997), 279.
[2] Kevin Kosar, *Disaster Response and the Appointment of a Recovery Czar: The Executive Branch's Response to the Flood of 1927* (Washington, DC: Congressional Research Service, October 25, 2005), 2; United States Army Corps of Engineers, *Annual Report of the Chief of Engineers for 1926: Mississippi River Commission* (Washington, DC: Government Printing Office, 1926), 1793; cited in Kosar, *Disaster Response and the Appointment of a Recovery Czar*, 6.
[3] Barry, *Rising Tide*, 262.

and Hoover spent most of the next two and a half months in the region deluged by the Mississippi River. Hoover had near-absolute authority to organize a response, and his efforts dominated national headlines.[4] His group and the Army began spending money for relief almost immediately. Meanwhile, the president asked the public to donate $5 million to the Red Cross to pay for relief.[5]

Hoover centralized relief policy and decentralized implementation.[6] This was the only way he thought that an ad hoc response could meet the needs of as many as 500,000 refugees. He and the Red Cross were in contact with representatives from every relevant federal agency, but he gave relief workers in the field a great deal of autonomy. For example, Hoover gave Henry Baker, the Red Cross relief director in Memphis, the authority "to use such government equipment as necessary and charter any private property needed."[7] Historian John Barry reports that "a Red Cross purchasing agent conducted a nearly continuous reverse auction as he stood on a platform and shouted out supplies and quantities needed, and dozens of suppliers shouted back bids."[8]

Few of the 105,000 people in danger along the Louisiana Cajun portion of the Mississippi River country heeded Hoover's call to evacuate.[9] By May 9, levees crumbled, and sandbags could not hold back the floodwaters. Yet Hoover's organization was prepared. Thousands of trucks carrying boats, motors, experienced rescuers, and room for evacuees entered the area as the first waves of the swollen river overtopped the levees. Everyone in danger was evacuated, along with their livestock, and there were few injuries or deaths.

During the May–June 1927 flooding, rescuers saved 330 people from land that was underwater. The Red Cross housed and fed 325,554 displaced, mostly African-American people in camps for as long as four months.[10] An additional 311,922 mostly white people received food and clothing outside the camps. Approximately 300,000 fled the flood-ravaged areas on their own. It is impossible to know how many people died or were buried in mud washed out to sea, but estimates range from 246 to more than 1,000.[11] The U.S. Weather Bureau put losses at $355,147,000, but indirect loss estimates approached $1 billion. The speed and scale of the recovery was unprecedented. The Red

---

[4] Barry, *Rising Tide*, 262.
[5] Kosar, *Disaster Response and the Appointment of a Recovery Czar*, 5; "Text of the President's Flood Relief Appeal," *New York Times*, May 3, 1927, A2.
[6] William Holmes, "William Alexander Percy and the Bourbon Era in Mississippi Politics," *Mississippi Quarterly* 26 (Winter 1972–1973): 71–87; William Alexander Percy, *Lanterns on the Levee: Recollections of a Planter's Son* (Baton Rouge: Louisiana State University Press, 1942), 1–2, 18–20, 259.
[7] Barry, *Rising Tide*, 273.
[8] Barry, *Rising Tide*, 274.
[9] Barry, *Rising Tide*, 282.
[10] Barry, *Rising Tide*, 286.
[11] Barry, *Rising Tide*, 286; The American National Red Cross, *The Mississippi Valley Flood Disaster of 1927* (Washington, DC: Red Cross, 1929), 5.

Cross delivered $21 million in aid, and the federal government provided approximately $10 million in resources and personnel.[12]

Contemporaries regarded the relief efforts as a success, but historians have criticized abuses stemming from a lack of federal oversight. In the camps, relief workers abused the displaced, particularly African Americans, and forced some African-American workers to carry out relief efforts at gunpoint.[13] Hoover formed a Colored Advisory Commission composed of influential African Americans to investigate the abuses.[14]

Furthermore, the government's best efforts were in response rather than in mitigation or recovery. Displaced persons whose property was destroyed found few public resources to help get them back on their feet after Hoover left, and some were dismayed at Coolidge's refusal to provide for long-term recovery.[15]

Nonetheless, the response to the Mississippi River flood was remarkable for the lack of disputes among federal agencies or between federal and state agencies. There was relatively little federal government involvement to begin with, compared with contemporary disaster relief, and states and localities generally welcomed federal assistance when Hoover arrived. Hoover created what one historian called an "administrative machine" with enormous centralized policy-making authority and precedents for decentralized execution.[16] The widely regarded successful government response to the disaster gave Hoover, never before mentioned as a presidential contender, a national stage and catapulted him to the presidency.[17]

---

[12] Bruce Lohof, *Hoover and the Mississippi Valley Flood of 1927: A Case Study of the Political Thought of Herbert Hoover* (Syracuse, NY: Syracuse University Press, 1968), 170–173; Kosar, *Disaster Response and the Appointment of a Recovery Czar*, 8.

[13] Lohof, "Herbert Hoover, Spokesman of Humane Efficiency: The Mississippi Flood of 1927," *American Quarterly* 22 (1970): 690–700, 692; Lohof, *Hoover and the Mississippi Valley Flood of 1927*, 365, 395; Kosar, *Disaster Response and the Appointment of a Recovery Czar*, 9, 10; Wesley A. Sturges, "The Legal Status of the Red Cross," *Michigan Law Review* 56 (1957): 1–32.

[14] Walter White, "The Negro and the Flood," *The Nation* 124 (1927): 688–689; The Final Report of the Colored Advisory Commission Appointed to Cooperate with The American National Red Cross and the President's Committee on Relief Work in the Mississippi Valley Flood Disaster of 1927, Dr. Robert R. Moton, Chairman, May 21, 1929, available at: http://www.pbs.org/wgbh/amex/flood/filmmore/ps_cac.html (accessed January 12, 2013).

[15] "Victims of Flood Still Plead for Aid," *New York Times*, July 3, 1927, E1.

[16] Lohof, "Herbert Hoover, Spokesman of Humane Efficiency: The Mississippi Flood of 1927," 692; Richard Hofstadter, "Herbert Hoover and the Crisis of American Individualism," in *The American Political Tradition and the Men Who Made It* (New York: Vintage, 1948), 367–409.

[17] Calvin Coolidge believed that the federal government had a responsibility to assist the public during disaster but noted in an address to Congress that the government's responsibility had limits: "The Government is not the insurer of its citizens against the hazards of the elements. We shall always have flood and drought, heat and cold, earthquake and wind, lightning and tidal wave, which are all too constant in their afflictions. The Government does not undertake to reimburse citizens for loss and damage incurred under such circumstances. It is chargeable, however, with the rebuilding of public works and the humanitarian duty of relieving its

The Mississippi River Flood of 1927 might have been unprecedented, but like most disasters, it was no surprise. The river ebbs and flows according to a natural cycle, usually flooding in the spring and summer and receding to its bed by August. People who live along the river judge time not simply by calendar years, but by flood years.[18] Mark Twain wrote that if the Mississippi were a "little European river it would just be a holiday job to wall it, and pile it, and dike it, and tame it down, and boss it around.... But this ain't that kind of a river."[19]

Just as the Mississippi River Flood was the seminal disaster of its age, Hurricane Katrina became the archetypical natural disaster for Americans in the twenty-first century because, paradoxically, it was so severe. How could such a devastating event occur in the modern, scientific, expertly organized United States?[20] The answer was that while much had changed since 1927, essential features of how the United States prepared for disasters remained startlingly similar. People built buildings and towns in low-lying areas, flood barriers were irregular and did not offer complete security, and the federal government had to work with and sometimes against state and local governments and nonprofits to mount a sufficiently large response. By the twenty-first century, moreover, it was increasingly difficult to claim that the federal government *could* coordinate disaster response like a puppet master. Instead of a Hoover-like czar with a central office, the government managed disasters through an array of loosely connected agencies responsible for insurance, shelter, transportation, and relief spending requests, usually working through states. Even the meaning of disaster had changed. At the federal level, concern about terrorism so reorganized all manner of organizations and legal authorities that there was considerable confusion in Katrina.

Hurricane Katrina struck a swath of land along the Gulf Coast from south-central Louisiana through Mississippi to Mobile, Alabama, but the complications of government involvement in disaster revealed themselves

citizens of distress." President Calvin Coolidge, "President's Annual Message," as reprinted in 69 *Congressional Record* 107 (1927), and cited in Kosar, *Disaster Response and the Appointment of a Recovery Czar*, 7.

[18] Pete Daniel, *Deep'n As It Come: The 1927 Mississippi River Flood* (New York: Oxford University Press, 1977), 4–5.

[19] Mark Twain, *Life on the Mississippi* (New York: Harper and Brothers, 1901), 208.

[20] In Spike Lee's HBO documentary about Hurricane Katrina, *After the Levees Broke*, a Louisiana resident asks why the government failed to deliver aid to New Orleans quickly when it had responded so efficiently to a tsunami in Aceh, Indonesia, eight months before. The U.S. aircraft carrier *Abraham Lincoln* took about a week to respond to the tsunami, but the differences between the two situations highlight the difference between domestic and foreign disasters and the difficulties the president has in responding to domestic disasters. Legal and organizational barriers prevent the president from sending the military to respond immediately to domestic disasters or even from appointing a Hoover-like relief-and-recovery czar. I take up these barriers in later chapters.

most starkly in New Orleans. The city is sandwiched between a river and two shallow lakes; ever since it was first settled in 1699, New Orleans has required elaborate drainage systems to make it inhabitable. For the first 200 years of its existence, people built on high ground and drained standing water into lower-lying areas and swamps. As the city developed, an elaborate system of canals and drainage devices kept the city dry.

This was a system in name only, however. It was a mix of levees, dams, and canals, each with different standards and authorities. Local levee boards used the levees as a way of creating new land to develop rather than as a tool to reduce the severity of floods.[21] The city's first major airport was one of the earliest boondoggles built on land that otherwise might have been used as a buffer or for drainage.

At a Senate hearing investigating the causes of post-Katrina disaster, Senator Susan Collins of Maine would conclude: "There has been confusion about the basic question of who is in charge of the levees. Key officials at the Army Corps [of Engineers] and the Orleans Levee District have demonstrated this confusion by telling Committee staff one thing during interviews and then another later."[22] Numerous experts had warned of New Orleans's vulnerability to a hurricane, and a training exercise in the spring of 2004 had exposed gaps in government plans for a catastrophic storm.[23] Despite the warnings, officials failed to address the shortcomings in preparation.

Katrina made landfall in Louisiana on August 29, 2005, and it became the costliest and one of the five deadliest storms in U.S. history.[24] More than 1,800 deaths are attributable to the storm, and estimates place damages at $81 billion. The storm sent waves as high as 27 feet crashing against barriers, sandbags, and levees. Eventually water poured into the city. Journalists John McQuaid and Mark Schleifstein described the scene:

In the space of a few hours, the storm stripped away the security blanket. Floodwalls were breached in dozens of places, their concrete and steel components bent, broken, and scattered into the backyards they had once protected. Floodgates were ripped from their hinges.... In the aftermath, only a narrow rim along the natural high ground of

---

[21] Christopher Cooper and Robert Block, *Disaster: Hurricane Katrina and the Failure of Homeland Security* (New York: Times Books, 2006).

[22] Susan M. Collins, "Opening Statement, Senator Susan M. Collins, Chairman, Homeland Security and Governmental Affairs Committee, Hearing on 'Hurricane Katrina: Who's In Charge of the New Orleans Levees?'" Washington, DC: U.S. Senate, December 15, 2005, 11 pages. Available at: http://hsgac.senate.gov/index.cfm?Fuseaction=Hearings.Detail&HearingID=300 (accessed October 12, 2011).

[23] There were many other warnings of impending disaster in New Orleans. In August 2000, the former deputy director of emergency preparedness in Louisiana wrote to FEMA director James Lee Witt requesting money to prepare for a hurricane. "We believe that the level of response required to sustain, protect, and rescue survivors during such post-hurricane devastation is well beyond what we conceptualize as 'the worst-case scenario,'" he wrote. See Cooper and Block, *Disaster*, 7.

[24] See Figure 2.1 in Chapter 2.

the riverbank was still inhabited and functioning – the approximate boundaries of New
Orleans in the mid-1800s. The city was once again open to the sea.[25]

The storm overwhelmed government at all levels. The federal government's
primary disaster agency, the Federal Emergency Management Agency (FEMA),
is small relative to cabinet-level departments. During Katrina, it had only 2,500
full-time positions, of which 15–20 percent were vacant.[26] Because of its small
size and limited authority, the agency functioned (and continues to function) as
a disaster clearinghouse, receiving requests for aid from states and localities and
seeking assistance from federal agencies, such as the departments of defense or
transportation, with the resources and manpower to help. FEMA did not and
does not own most of the resources it uses to respond to disasters.

Politicians created FEMA to avoid ad hoc disaster responses such as the
government's actions in the 1927 Mississippi River Flood, but in practice
the agency's performance in Katrina had characteristics of the worst of ad
hoc responses: poor communication, uncertainty about resources and capacity, vague plans, and clear plans on the books that were ignored in practice.
FEMA's performance was hampered by several factors. The agency was swept
up in a reorganization that created the Department of Homeland Security. As a
result, FEMA lost direct access to the president. Morale at FEMA sank, and the
agency lost experienced professionals to retirement or to other agencies.[27]

The government's response was not a complete failure, however. Without
waiting for FEMA's direction, the Coast Guard and the Louisiana Department
of Wildlife and Fisheries rescued stranded people from rooftops, and ad hoc
local groups organized to care for the sick and elderly.[28] The evacuation
exceeded expectations; an estimated 1–1.2 million people out of 1.4 million
evacuated safely, largely because of previous experience with evacuations,
repeated warnings, and the use of contraflow, a technique to reverse traffic on
major highways so that all lanes flow out of the city.[29]

The conditions for those left behind, however, were notoriously inadequate.
There were no workable plans to evacuate citizens who could not or would
not leave on their own. FEMA director Michael Brown eagerly told state and
local officials, "If there's one thing FEMA's got, it's buses," but FEMA did not
actually know where the buses were, and they did not arrive until days later.[30]
The primary shelter, the Superdome, became uninhabitable because of storm
damage, overcrowding, and failed plumbing. An alternate site, the convention

[25] John McQuaid and Mark Schleifstein, *Path of Destruction: The Devastation of New Orleans
and the Coming Age of Superstorms* (New York: Little, Brown, 2006), 7–8, 246.
[26] U.S. Senate Committee of Homeland Security and Government Affairs, *Hurricane Katrina:
A Nation Still Unprepared* (Washington, DC, 2006), 210–231.
[27] Cooper and Block, *Disaster*, 4–8.
[28] Rebecca Solnit, *A Paradise Built in Hell: The Extraordinary Communities That Arise in Disaster*
(New York: Viking, 2009).
[29] U.S. Senate, *Hurricane Katrina*, 243; Cooper and Block, *Disaster*, 122.
[30] U.S. Senate, *Hurricane Katrina*, 70; Cooper and Block, *Disaster*, 172, 184–187, 210.

center, had not been stocked with supplies. While there was blame enough to go around, the federal government bore the brunt of the criticism. The debacle led to the end of Brown's tenure at FEMA, and no Hoover figure earned renown or was propelled to higher office.[31]

The Mississippi River Flood of 1927 and Hurricane Katrina in 2005 are bookends to a period of increasing federal government involvement in disaster. In the former, the federal government responded to pleas from state leaders with a recovery effort of unprecedented scale. In the latter, the federal government mounted a large response but drew criticism for providing too little, too late. The intervening century witnessed a social construction of disaster in which citizens (especially through voting), members of Congress, disaster management professionals, presidents, and the media inadvertently created new ideas about what counts as a disaster and how much responsibility the government bears in addressing it, all while pursuing their own various interests. This book maps changes in relationships between official and popular understandings of natural disasters, internal and external threats, and response to and mitigation of natural disasters and catastrophic attacks. Taken as a whole, it shows how ad hoc disaster response became institutionalized and bureaucratized as disaster management.

Disaster management today is full of apparent contradictions. The same plans and personnel are used to prepare for fires, floods, and hurricanes as for nuclear attacks and sometimes for terrorism. States and localities blame the federal government for lackluster disaster response, but the law generally allows the federal government to intervene after a disaster only at the request of governors. Finally, modern presidents appoint political cronies to lead disaster agencies, even though the media and the public blame presidents for poor federal government responses to disasters that can sometimes be attributed to the inexperience of the president's appointed managers.

Disasters and the American State shows how the changing social construction and contestation of disaster has increased expectations of government's responsibility for responding to and preparing for disasters, even as it shapes what counts as a disaster. The arc of social construction begins with politicians and the public debating what counts as a disaster worthy of national rather than merely local attention. Nineteenth-century Americans learned how to marshal collective resources to respond to fires (and, eventually, to mitigate or prevent them through insurance schemes and building codes), how to recognize earthquakes, and how to tame rivers and shorelines to prevent flooding (even as cities and towns expanded further into flood-prone areas). People eventually included security threats such as attack and war in their

---

[31] Kosar, *Disaster Response and the Appointment of a Recovery Czar*; Daniel Schorr, "What Would Herbert Hoover Do?" *Christian Science Monitor*, September 16, 2005, 9; Timothy Walch, "We Could Use Another Man Like Herbert Hoover," *History News Network*, October 17, 2005.

understanding of disaster, and disaster managers juggled attention to acute fears of terrorist attacks, nuclear war, and technological accidents with attention to perennial natural disasters. Finally, in the late twentieth and twenty-first centuries, debates in emergency management and homeland security turned on who counted as a citizen and who required special surveillance. In the realm of natural disasters, politicians and the public negotiated who deserved special assistance, given that the poor, the elderly, and other marginalized groups bore the brunt of disasters. The end result is the system we have today, in which disaster managers claim to protect the public from a range of hazards and emergencies in a system that is a patchwork of state, local, and federal authorities. Understanding disasters as the product of social construction and contestation sheds light on the paradox of how an expanded disaster state exists alongside the sober reality of dashed hopes. The arc of social construction also shows how a major expansion of federal government involvement in disaster took place through "small-'c' constitutionalism" – the incremental development of statutes, administrative action, and political interpretation – rather than through "big-'C' constitutionalism" of amendments and major legislative action.[32]

THE DRIVERS OF CHANGE OVER TIME

Mark Twain wrote, "History never repeats itself, but the Kaleidoscopic combinations of the pictured present often seem to be constructed out of the broken fragments of antique legends."[33] More pithily, he is often quoted as saying, "History doesn't repeat itself, but it rhymes." Like most people, Twain sensed that events occurring in sequence are connected, but he was skeptical of claims about grand laws or a priori patterns that determine those connections. The history of disaster policy follows something more concrete than the music of a rhyme but something less rigid than the necessary cause and effect implied by the social science term "mechanism."[34] In the simplest terms possible, one process shapes disaster policy – social construction. Three institutions – elections, federalism, and bureaucracy – set the boundaries. Political leaders, bureaucrats, and the public have a great deal of freedom to shape what disaster policy means, but they are constrained by the institutions of U.S. government. Social construction encompasses political choices about elections

---

[32] This book confirms the basic thesis of Eskridge and Ferejohn while adding a focus on administrative politics and the pressures that disasters impose on politicians and administrators. See William N. Eskridge, Jr. and John Ferejohn, *A Republic of Statutes: The New American Constitution* (New Haven, CT: Yale University Press, 2010).

[33] Mark Twain and Charles Dudley Warner, *The Gilded Age* (Stillwell, KS: Digireads.com Publishing, 2007 [1873]), 199.

[34] Peter Hedström and Petri Ylikoski, "Causal Mechanisms in the Social Sciences," *Annual Review of Sociology* 36 (2010): 49–67; John Gerring, "Causal Mechanisms: Yes, But ..." *Comparative Political Studies* 43 (2010): 1499–1526.

and governing institutions straight out of a U.S. government textbook.[35] Yet social construction also includes lower-level phenomena that shape the choices people make, from organizational routines, as in the construction of FEMA, to what is inside people's heads, including stereotypes about who is likely to be a victim and who is likely to be a perpetrator.

In the United States, government agencies are created to solve public problems: the government builds armies to provide security from enemies, and it establishes regulatory agencies in the wake of financial crisis to promote stability and consumer protection. At the same time, there remain many problems that people believe *should* be solved but nevertheless are unaddressed by coordinated federal government action. The total cost of strokes in the United States is estimated to be about $1 billion per year, a sum so large that it could merit the term "crisis" or "disaster." The average annual flood loss in the United States over the past decade was $2.7 billion, a total that ranks next to medium-sized hurricanes.[36] Either of these conditions could be addressed by coordinated government action, but responses largely remain in the hands of private actors, nongovernmental organizations, and small, ad hoc government efforts.

The social part of social construction occurs when a broad segment of society agrees on the definition of a problem. In the nineteenth century, some politicians and citizens suffering the effects of fires, floods, and earthquakes argued that the federal government should provide disaster relief. After the Civil War, the accumulated precedents of federal government intervention, once considered exceptions, overcame constitutional arguments about the limits of federal power. Federal government disaster relief became the status quo. Amid the expansion of the American state in the second half of the twentieth century, disaster policy found a home in new government agencies, often next to civil defense programs to prepare for the worst.[37]

Often, the term "social construction" begs the question of who performs the construction – a limitation this book seeks to avoid by using historically specific analysis.[38] In disaster policy, who performs the construction changes over time. In the nineteenth century, members of Congress were important, arguing for more aid after disaster despite few precedents. By the twentieth century, the president and bureaucrats took center stage, establishing permanent programs to prepare for disaster. Judges decide cases that set the boundaries for the debate,

[35] Anne Schneider and Helen Ingram, "The Social Construction of Target Populations: Implications for Politics and Policy," *American Political Science Review* 87 (1993): 334–348.

[36] National Flood Insurance Program, http://www.floodsmart.gov (accessed May 16, 2011).

[37] Scholars from the fields of history and U.S. political development prefer the term "political construction," whereas "social construction" is the more common term in sociology, anthropology, critical theory, and public policy. The basic meaning of the terms is the same here.

[38] Ian Hacking, *The Social Construction of What?* (Cambridge, MA: Harvard University Press, 2000); Hacking offers a criticism, largely addressed to studies of science rather than politics. An example of overly casual forms of social construction argument is Eric Hobsbwam and Terence Ranger, eds. *The Invention of Tradition* (New York: Cambridge University Press, 1992).

and the public is important in demanding help during and after disaster, and in extending sympathy to victims portrayed in the media. The national electronic news media was especially important in recent years, apportioning credit and blame after disaster. The constructional structure of the United States was also important in setting the boundaries of social construction. Federalism provides for constitutionally separate powers for states and the national government, and the Constitution protects local and state spheres of influence and power, even as nationalizing rhetoric and programs grow.[39]

Articulating a claim is not enough for social construction to occur; the claim must be sold through symbols, arguments, stories, debate, and repetition. Which claims prevail varies according to the social, political, ideological, and institutional structures of a given period. Some analysts of social construction stress the role of traditions of ideas in shaping policy. For example, the United States has a tradition of individual responsibility and limited government, which may explain its more limited welfare state when compared to European counterparts.[40] While it is true that Americans are more suspicious of state activity than citizens of many other countries, ideology does not seem to be the primary driver of disaster policy. Politicians of the left and the right in the United States have contributed to expanding the government's role in disaster, particularly in the last half-century.

Rather than focus on the role of ideology, this book casts disaster policy as the result of a political process in which different groups – politicians, bureaucrats, and the public – make claims for greater involvement.[41] The book's central claim is that politicians, bureaucrats, and the public engaged in a process of social construction that increased expectations of the federal government's role in disaster policy, constrained chiefly by electoral politics, federalism, and bureaucracy. Over the course of U.S. history, however, many more actors played

[39] For example, federal mandates to account for race, disability, and performance have eroded state and localities' prerogatives in education policy to a greater degree than in emergency management, which arrived at a more harmonious, albeit still at times strained, relationship. See Gareth Davies, *See Government Grow: Education Politics from Johnson to Reagan* (Lawrence: University Press of Kansas, 2007). On the tensions in federalism in disaster management, see Paul Stockton and Patrick Roberts, "Findings from the Forum on Homeland Security After the Bush Administration: Next Steps in Building Unity of Effort," *Homeland Security Affairs* 4 (2008): 1–11.

[40] John Kingdon, *America the Unusual* (New York: Worth Publishers, 1999).

[41] The agenda-setting literature in public policy asks similar questions, typically according to a narrower timeframe of years or decades. With a constrained timeframe, the agenda-setting literature can assume the relative stability of basic institutions of the policy process, such a federalism, congressional lawmaking, parties, and administrative processes. My project is more squarely in the U.S. political development tradition, which examines the emergence of these basic institutions and their changes over time. For examples of the agenda-setting and related problem definition literature, see Frank R. Baumgartner and Bryan D. Jones, *Agendas and Instability in American Politics* (Chicago: The University of Chicago Press, 1995); Bryan D. Jones, *Politics and the Architecture of Choice: Bounded Rationality and Governance* (Chicago: University of Chicago Press, 2001).

a role, from political parties to the media to even the disasters themselves.[42] Disasters are actors insofar as disaster policy rarely changes without them, and disasters shape people and places in ways that would not have occurred without a catastrophic event.[43]

On one hand, the book's explanation has the same character as many others in the social sciences. Think, for example, of the cottage industry about the industrial revolution and markets as an explanation for the rise of the West. This book explains the development of disaster policy by making mid-range causal claims about institutions and mechanisms that increase federal government involvement in disasters, defined as a particular and historically contingent set of events. On the other hand, no one ever predicted in advance that the combination of credit and blame games of politicians and bureaucrats plus a democratic electoral system and federalism would lead to the contemporary FEMA and Department of Homeland Security. Ex post facto, the features of U.S. disaster policy are somewhat of an accident, contingent on the more muscular state that emerged after the Union victory in the Civil War, the rise of civil defense in the twentieth century, the emergence of a terrorist threat, and the spread of electronic media.[44] This book explains the development of disaster policy, but the contemporary disaster state is more of an accident than is normally acknowledged.

One of the ironies of disaster management in the United States is that as government brazenly claims that it can protect the public from "all hazards," it is increasingly incapable of assuring protection against new catastrophic technologies and protean terrorist attack or of limiting vulnerable development in risky locations. Disaster managers and politicians first made claims to protect citizens from all hazards as part of civil defense practices during the Cold War under the heading of "dual use," which meant that plans and equipment used to prepare for nuclear attack could be used to prepare for a range of events from fires to floods, tornadoes, and hurricanes. The all-hazards claims became enshrined in formal missions and in emergency managers' professional identities during the 1980s and 1990s.

As disaster management became more centralized in the federal government and more bureaucratized, government contributed to worsening the effects of some disasters, as in Chapter 6's account of the Mississippi River Gulf Outlet prior to Hurricane Katrina and Chapter 7's analysis of discriminatory security practices. The shift from disaster policy as ad hoc deliberation in Congress to

---

[42] Actor network theory conceives of nonhuman phenomena such as disasters as "actants." For an overview, see Anne Taufen Wessells, "Reassembling the Social: An Introduction to Actor-Network-Theory by Bruno Latour," *International Public Management Journal* 10 (2007): 351–356.

[43] John Law and John Hassard, *Actor Network Theory and After* (Hoboken, NJ: Wiley-Blackwell, 1999); Bruno Latour, *Reassembling the Social: An Introduction to Actor-Network-Theory* (New York: Oxford University Press, 2007).

[44] Chapter 2 engages debates over the role of the Civil War in nineteenth-century state-building.

bureaucratized disaster management on the whole saved lives and property, but it also created blind spots in unintended consequences and in routinizing security practices that ideally should be exceptional.

This book offers evidence of the limits of government's ability to prepare for disaster as well as evidence that good governance depends on the expertise of competent, nonelected public officials as an important part of democratic decision making, even though democracy is most often understood in terms of elections and voting.[45] The book focuses on disaster policy, but it offers a window into how government prepares for the unexpected.

DISASTER MANAGEMENT AND THE STUDY OF PUBLIC ORGANIZATIONS

While this project provides a history of state response to disaster at the national government level, it also contributes to three debates in social science. First, this book clarifies the foundations of *bureaucratic autonomy* in professional networks and expertise. The term "bureaucratic autonomy" has been used to describe both instances of independent action by bureaucracies and long periods in which nonelected public organizations exert independent force on the political system. Most studies have examined the foundation of bureaucratic autonomy in progressive-era social movements, but these social movements are less prominent in the late twentieth century, having been replaced by interest groups and professions.[46] Cohesive lobbies and citizens' groups are relatively weak in the disaster field, however. (The civil defense and emergency management professions are two possible exceptions taken up later in the book, but these reinforce the claim that professions, not citizens' groups, support contemporary bureaucratic autonomy.)

Much of the recent work in bureaucratic politics has focused on the importance of mid-level civil servants, but my analysis highlights the strategic role of appointees in shaping an agency's long-term direction and their leadership role during crises such as Hurricanes Andrew and Katrina.[47] Appointees play a crucial role as actors in the social and political construction process, steering an agency between the concerns of politicians and the public on one hand

---

[45] For one line of research that examines the ways in which nonelected administrators can practice democratic virtues, see Martha Feldman and Anne Khademian, "The Role of the Public Manager in Inclusion: Creating Communities of Participation," *Governance* 20 (2007): 305–324. While contemporary political science understands democracy in terms of voting and elections, nineteenth- and early-twentieth-century accounts of democracy were more likely to feature constitutionalism or administrative expertise as essential features of democracy. See Ido Oren, *Our Enemies and US: America's Rivalries and the Making of Political Science* (Ithaca, NY: Cornell University Press, 2003).

[46] Carpenter, Daniel P. *The Forging of Bureaucratic Autonomy* (Princeton, NJ: Princeton University Press, 2001).

[47] Carpenter, *The Forging of Bureaucratic Autonomy*; Marissa Martino Golden, *What Motivates Bureaucrats? Politics and Administration during the Reagan Years* (New York: Columbia University Press, 2000).

and the scientific consensus of expert professionals on the other.[48] Too often, critics assume politicization is an unmitigated evil because a greater number of appointed positions incorporate more political agendas and less expertise into public organizations.[49] FEMA's most successful director, however, was politically appointed. James Lee Witt used his political connections to the agency's advantage and drew on expert professional networks.[50]

Second, rather than focusing on brief snapshots of organizational failure, my analysis considers how public organizations shape their environment over time according to political ambition, security threats, and the demands of electoral politics and federalism. Classic theories of organizational failure (many of which were deployed as explanations after September 11 and Hurricane Katrina) examine shortcomings of institutional design or immediate problems inside an organization.[51] My analysis, however, considers how disaster organizations relate to their external environments.[52] Bureaucrats, politicians, and the public have encouraged FEMA, civil defense, and homeland security organizations to claim credit for successes for which they are not fully responsible. They have blamed these same organizations for the damage caused by disaster. Claiming credit for successful response and relief is associated with a growing perception of how much the federal government can and should do to limit the damage caused by disaster.

The most striking example of how public organizations interact with their environment occurs in agencies that juggle natural disasters and security missions. These agencies, most notably the Department of Homeland Security, are responsible for reducing public risk for a number of hazards and disasters. Yet in recent times, there have been relatively few coordinated efforts to invest in mitigation, prevention, and protection related to natural disasters compared to man-made disasters or deliberate attack.[53]

[48] Philip B. Heymann, *The Politics of Public Management* (New Haven, CT: Yale University Press, 1987).

[49] For a summary, see Matthew Dull and Patrick S. Roberts, "Continuity, Competence, and the Succession of Senate-Confirmed Agency Appointees, 1989–2009," *Presidential Studies Quarterly* 39 (September 2009): 432–453.

[50] On the development of emergency management professional networks, see Scott Gabriel Knowles, *The Disaster Experts: Mastering Risk in Modern America* (Philadelphia: University of Pennsylvania Press, 2011).

[51] Stephen Ackroyd, "Organizational Failure," in *Blackwell Encyclopedia of Sociology*, Ritzer, ed. (Blackwell, 2007).

[52] Organizational psychologists and sociologists have not paid much attention to how the external environment shapes organizations. These scholars study complex environments, uncertainty, and institutionalization, but not the political and governmental factors that influence organizations. See Hal G. Rainey, "Goal Ambiguity and the Study of American Bureaucracy," in Robert Durant, ed., *The Oxford Handbook of American Bureaucracy*, Oxford, UK: Oxford University Press, 2010: 231–252, 244.

[53] Patrick S. Roberts, "A Capacity for Mitigation as the Next Frontier in Homeland Security," *Political Science Quarterly* 124 (Spring 2009): 127–142.

Third, this book highlights the contestability of security missions that are constructed over time by politicians, bureaucrats, the media, and the public. Some scholarship portrays agency missions as fixed either in law or common understanding, and therefore agencies have a narrow range of possible action.[54] Recent legal theory, however, focuses on the mutability of legal commands and common understandings.[55] The history of civil defense and emergency management offers fascinating material for testing out ideas about the mutability of missions, goal ambiguity, and the ways in which politicians and bureaucrats shape missions and tasks over time.[56] During the civil defense era, politicians at the national level supported civil defense programs in order to shore up support for the Cold War, while state and local officials reluctantly lent support in order to secure resources to respond to natural disasters. By the 1980s, emergency management grew out of the fragments of civil defense, as bureaucrats identified a need for government intervention to prepare for disaster but had to contend with politicians who wanted to use emergency management organizations for security purposes. Similar confusion and contestation over missions characterize the homeland security era. Security missions to protect against an external threat sometimes crowd out efforts to prepare for natural disasters.

With a few notable exceptions, scholarship in U.S. political development separates the domestic and national security spheres.[57] In practice, experience in preparing for natural disasters, industrial accidents, and nuclear or terrorist attack can be mutually reinforcing, especially under a policy to be prepared for all hazards. How politicians and professional groups define the government's security responsibilities says as much about political agendas as it does about the nature of the event. (Franklin Roosevelt's attempt to fuse health care and civil defense missions in the Federal Security Agency is one such example).[58] This book offers evidence for how bureaucratic entrepreneurs and administrative politicians shape their political environment over time, and evidence of how their ambitions are inflected by elections, public opinion, federalism,

[54] Matthew D. McCubbins and Thomas Schwartz, "Congressional Oversight Overlooked: Police Patrols versus Fire Alarms." *American Journal of Political Science* 28 (1984): 165–179; Barry R. Weingast and Mark J. Moran, "Bureaucratic Discretion of Congressional Control?: Regulatory Policymaking by the Federal Trade Commission." *Journal of Political Economy* 91 (1983): 765–800.

[55] Sanford Levinson, *Constitutional Faith* (Princeton, NJ: Princeton University Press, 1989); Ronald R. Krebs and Patrick T. Jackson, "Twisting Tongues and Twisting Arms. The Power of Political Rhetoric," *European Journal of International Relations* 13 (2007): 35–66.

[56] Young Han Chun and Hal G. Rainey, "Goal Ambiguity in U.S. Federal Agencies," *Journal of Public Administration Research and Theory* 15 (2005): 1–30.

[57] Exceptions include: Andrew D. Grossman, *Neither Dead nor Red: Civilian Defense and American Political Development During the Early Cold War* (New York: Routledge, 2001); *Shaped by War and Trade: International Influences on American Political Development*, Ira Katznelson and Martin Shefter, eds. (Princeton, NJ: Princeton University Press, 2002).

[58] Mariano-Florentino Cuéllar, "'Securing' the Nation: Law, Politics, and Organization at the Federal Security Agency, 1939–1953," *University of Chicago Law Review* 76 (2009): 587–717.

and disasters themselves. The cumulative result is a "durable shift in governing authority" toward a national state capacity to prepare for and respond to many kinds of disasters, both natural and man-made.[59] Politicians and disaster managers hope for something like the Mississippi Flood of 1927 if they can claim credit for a successful response, but they fear a future with more Katrinas – events in vulnerable locations over which disaster managers have little regulatory authority to guide preparedness or response.

[59] Karen Orren and Stephen Skowronek, *The Search for American Political Development* (New York: Cambridge University Press, 2004), 123.

2

The Origins of the Disaster State, 1789–1914

The U.S. government has provided ad hoc disaster aid since the early days of the republic, but the nature and extent of that aid have expanded.[1] What was an event, a condition to be tolerated, or a largely local responsibility in the early nineteenth century became by the late twentieth century a disaster that requires federal government intervention long before and after the event itself. How and why did the U.S. government begin delivering more aid for more kinds of disasters? Finding the answer to this question requires an investigation into the very earliest examples of government intervention after disaster. Arguments for relief first found a voice when members of Congress advocated for disaster relief for their geographically specific districts. Although the Constitution is silent about the permissibility of disaster relief, the gradual accumulation of precedent for federal government aid before and after disaster made disaster relief a regular function of government by the twentieth century.

The constitutional structure of Congress in the U.S. system of government set the bounds for the process of social construction whereby individual politicians pursuing their own interests inadvertently contributed to building a *disaster state* – the collection of relief agencies, programs, professionals, and budgets that became a routine part of the federal government. Congressional representatives conceived of their job as representing a geographic constituency by, in part, securing resources to solve public problems. (In some other countries, legislative representatives have a less geographically specific orientation and instead represent large regions, parties, ideologies, or the entire polity.) As the Constitution was read through layers of interpretation over time, members of Congress saw fewer and fewer reasons to deny disaster relief to other

[1] Despite an emerging consensus that the federal government should provide disaster relief, in many individual cases the federal government would not intervene, and in other cases localities did not want federal intervention. See Theodore Steinberg, *Acts of God: The Unnatural History of Natural Disasters in America* (New York: Oxford University Press, 2000).

districts when they might receive the same benefits for their own districts in the future. After a pause in regular government activity during the Civil War, Reconstruction and subsequent partisan and legal developments further broke down resistance to federal government intervention in what were once state and local matters.[2] Advocates for expanding the amount and frequency of federal aid to states and localities cited the rare pre–Civil War precedents and the less rare postwar ones, and they outnumbered and outlobbied the opposition over time. Most but not all advocates for disaster relief after the Civil War were Republicans, who prevailed in Congress from 1861 to 1932 with minor exceptions.

These congressional advocates provided arguments taken up more boldly by presidents and bureaucrats in the twentieth century. The presidency of Theodore Roosevelt, in particular, marked a transition. Before Roosevelt, presidents were generally not involved in responding to disasters in which the Red Cross provided relief, such as the Great Fire of 1881 in Michigan, which left 5,000 homeless, or the 1889 Johnstown, Pennsylvania flood, in which 2,209 people died.[3] The Johnstown flood of 1889 provides a convenient case for comparison with later large-scale disasters. Presidents were more directly involved in relief efforts and made more pronouncements after subsequent Johnstown floods in 1936 and 1977 than in the earlier Johnstown flood.[4] The increase in presidential involvement correlates with the rise of the institutional presidency seeking control over the levers of government and policy.[5] Politicians, bureaucrats, and citizens built what Stephen Skowronek describes as "politically negotiated" structures that define what a disaster is and what the federal government bears responsibility for – another way of describing the process of social construction. Together, congressional committees, executive agencies, White House staff, and nonprofits composed a nascent disaster state within the United States by the early twentieth century.[6]

---

[2] For instance, before the Civil War, the incorporation doctrine firmly subordinated state law to federal authority, and a legal and constitutional firewall separated federal and state governments to a degree we would find astonishing today. (The Fourteenth Amendment transformed federalism by subjecting state governments to the protections of the Constitution's Bill of Rights after the amendment was adopted in 1868).

[3] David McCullough, *The Johnstown Flood* (Gloucester, MA: Peter Smith Publisher, 1968).

[4] National Science Foundation, "Report on Flood Hazard Mitigation," Washington, DC, September 1980; Benjamin Radford, *Media Mythmakers* (New York: Prometheus Books, 2003), 163–164, 176.

[5] James W. Ceaser, *Presidential Selection* (Princeton, NJ: Princeton University Press, 1979); Elvin T. Lim, *The Anti-Intellectual Presidency* (New York: Oxford University Press, 2008); Terry Moe, "The Politicized Presidency," in *The New Direction in American Politics*, edited by John E. Chubb and Paul E. Peterson, (Washington, DC: Brookings, 1995), 235–272; Daniel Galvin and Colleen Shogan, "Executive Authority and the Bureaucracy: The Analytical Shortcomings of the Modern Presidency Construct," *Polity* 36 (April 2004): 477–504.

[6] Stephen Skowronek, *Building a New Administrative State: The Expansion of National Administrative Capacities, 1877–1920* (Cambridge: Cambridge University Press, 1982).

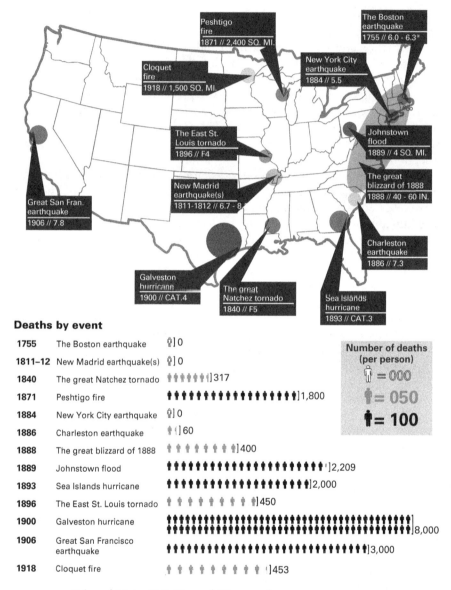

Deaths by event

Year	Event	Deaths
1755	The Boston earthquake	0
1811–12	New Madrid earthquake(s)	0
1840	The great Natchez tornado	317
1871	Peshtigo fire	1,800
1884	New York City earthquake	0
1886	Charleston earthquake	60
1888	The great blizzard of 1888	400
1889	Johnstown flood	2,209
1893	Sea Islands hurricane	2,000
1896	The East St. Louis tornado	450
1900	Galveston hurricane	8,000
1906	Great San Francisco earthquake	3,000
1918	Cloquet fire	453

Number of deaths (per person)

= 000
= 050
= 100

FIGURE 2.1. Selected Major U.S. Natural Disasters from 1755 to 1920.

Note: The severity measurement is taken from the Saffir-Simpson Scale for hurricanes (as well as the number of buildings destroyed), the Fujita Scale for tornadoes, and the Richter Scale for earthquakes. Only a rough estimate is available for the Boston earthquake and the New Madrid earthquakes. The severity of fires and floods is measured in the number of square miles affected.

Sources: The United States Geological Survey (USGS), "Earthquake Hazards Program," http://www.earthquake.usgs.gov; Myron Fuller, *The New Madrid Earthquake*, Prospect, KY: Care Publications, 1995; *The Free Trader*, Sunday, May 10, 1840; The Tornado

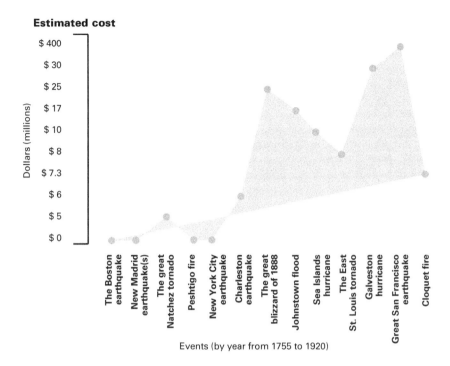

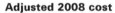

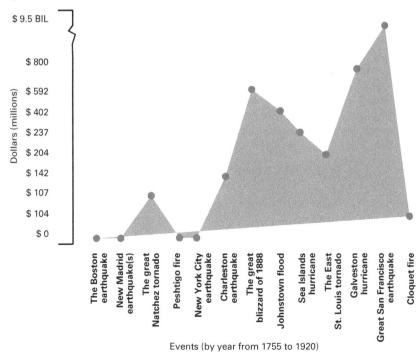

FIGURE 2.1. (*cont.*)

Cost

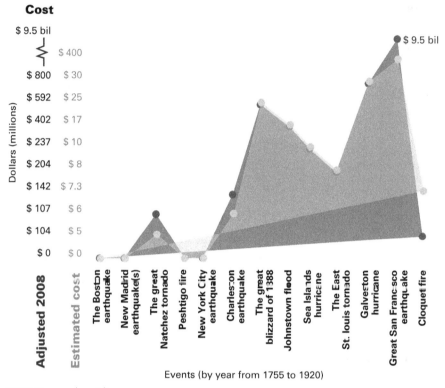

FIGURE 2.1. (*cont.*)

Project, "Top Ten U.S. Killer Tornadoes," http://www.tornadoproject.com; "The Great
Peshtigo Fire of 1871," http://www.peshtigofire.info; University of South Carolina,
"Lithospheric Seismology: The Charleston Earthquake of 1886," http://www.seis.
sc.edu; Borgna Brunner, "The Great White Hurricane: The Blizzard of 1888," http://
www.infoplease.com; The National Weather Service (NWS), "Biggest Snowstorms in the
United States," and NWS Eastern Region Headquarters, "Major Winter Storms," http://
www.erh.noaa.gov; Johnstown Flood Museum, "The Compelling Story of the 1889
Disaster: Facts and Figures," www.jaha.org; South Carolina State Climatology Office,
http://www.dnr.sc.gov/climate/sco/; William and Fran Marscher, *The Great Sea Island
Storm of 1893*, Macon, GA: Mercer University Press, 2004; The National Oceanic and
Atmospheric Administration (NOAA), National Hurricane Center, "Hurricane History:
Galveston 1900," http://www.nhc.noaa.gov; "The 1900 Storm," www.1900storm.com;
Gladys Hansen and Emmet Condon, *Denial of Disaster*, San Francisco: Cameron and
Co., 1989; United States Geological Survey (USGS) Earthquake Hazards Program,
"Casualties and Damage after the 1906 Earthquake," http://earthquake.usgs.
gov; NOAA Report for the Office of Emergency Preparedness: U.S. Department of
Commerce, *A Study of Earthquake Losses in the San Francisco Bay Area – Data and
Analysis*(Washington, DC: National Oceanic and Atmospheric Administration, 1972);
"South and Middle West Visited by Numerous Violent Storms in Last 25 years," *The
New York Times*, March 25, 1913; Kate Roberts, *Minnesota 150: The People, Places,
and Things That Shape Our State*, St. Paul: Minnesota Historical Society, 2007.

FIRES, FLOODS, AND EARTHQUAKES

In the eighteenth and nineteenth centuries, fires and floods were the most common major disasters, and Congress passed private bills to compensate particular individuals for property lost or damaged during these events (See Figure 2.1).[7] Congress passed its first ad hoc relief bills to compensate victims of a tax protest in 1789 called the Whiskey Rebellion and, later, a slave insurrection in Haiti (St. Domingo). Eventually, Congress administered aid for communities struck by natural disasters through relief agencies established within the executive branch or through the War Department.[8] Congress delivered aid to Portsmouth, New Hampshire, after a massive fire in 1802 and passed general relief bills for victims of an expanding array of natural disasters and violent revolts. Both violent attacks and extreme weather events were considered disasters. Members of Congress invoked similar arguments in both kinds of events for the justice of federal government assistance to restore order and critical economic functions, and military or ad hoc executive branch organizations delivered aid for both.

Initially, aid from Congress was most often issued as compensation for property losses rather than as supplies for rescue and relief. Congress's interventions were limited as much by nineteenth-century communications and transportation technology as by a tradition of limited national government. It might take days for news of an earthquake or flood to reach Washington, DC, and if Congress wanted to intervene, its aid would arrive only weeks later. The immediate response was, by necessity, a local matter, and the federal government usually stepped in only after the earth's trembling ceased, flood waters receded, or fires burned down to embers.

Despite these limits on how quickly government could act, members of Congress assumed from the beginning that the national government had an obligation to restore basic functions in disaster-stricken communities. This was not the same as providing disaster relief to suffering victims, which would require more aid for larger groups of people. Nevertheless, Congress's interventions were real. After a second Portsmouth fire in 1806, Congress suspended the collection of bonds in order to relieve the financial burden on the town.[9] In

---

[7] For example, in 1790, Congress passed two private relief bills, An Act for the Relief of Thomas Jenkins & Company (ch. 20, 6 stat. 2 [1790]), and An Act for the Relief of John Stewart and John Davidson (ch. 37, 6 Stat. 3 [1790]). The bills concerned flood and storm relief, respectively. Quoted and cited in Michele Landis Dauber, *Helping Ourselves: Disaster Relief and the Origins of the American Welfare State*, (Ph.D. diss., Northwestern University, 2003), 12.

[8] Michele Landis Dauber, "The War of 1812, September 11, and the Politics of Compensation," *DePaul Law Review* 53 (2003): 289–354.

[9] "House Journal – FRIDAY, JANUARY 14, 1803" in *Journal of the House of Representatives of the United States, 1801–1804*, available at: http://memory.loc.gov/ (accessed December 4, 2011). "Bills and Resolutions, House of Representatives, 9th Congress, 2nd Session, Read the first and second time, and committed to a committee of the whole House, to-morrow. A Bill, For the relief of the sufferers by fire, in the tow of Portsmouth, New Hampshire." January 22, 1807, available at: http://memory.loc.gov/ (accessed December 4, 2011).

an age before the income tax, the tariffs collected from Portsmouth and other major ports were an important source of revenue for the new nation, and members of Congress recognized that it was in the national interest to restore the port's operational capacity over the long term. Congress had passed a similar act after a fire in the ports of Norfolk, Virginia, in 1804 (and would again in New York City in 1835).

The dislocation and damage caused by earthquakes provided another opportunity for Congress to act in the public interest. After a 9.6 magnitude earthquake struck Venezuela in 1812 and leveled Caracas, killing at least 20,000 people, Congress passed what is usually regarded as the first foreign aid bill providing $50,000 in assistance to victims.[10] Disaster aid sent abroad became enshrined as precedent for relief to victims, and not just funds to restore critical infrastructure.

How did Congress shift from narrowly targeted aid to restore commercial ports at home to aid for victims abroad? The preeminent legal scholar of the nineteenth century, Joseph Story, cited the Venezuela earthquake case approvingly two decades later (along with another bill for aid for refugees in Santo Domingo) as evidence of a newly broad interpretation of the Constitution's general welfare clause.[11] The words "general welfare" appear twice in the Constitution.[12] Defenders of Congress's power to provide disaster relief cite the mention in Article I, Section 8, which reads, "The Congress shall have power to lay and collect taxes, duties, imposts and excises, to pay the debts and provide for the common defense and general welfare of the United States." The text links general welfare to the taxing power of Congress, but nothing is said explicitly about the spending power.[13] While taxing without spending might seem absurd

[10] Gaines Foster, *The Demands of Humanity: Army Medical Disaster Relief* (Washington, DC: Center of Military History, United States Army, 1983), 9–10; David Stewart and Ray Knox, *The Earthquake America Forgot* (Marble Hill, Mo.: Gutenberg-Richter Publications, 1995), 252; "Earthquake Destroyed Many Lives; Eighteen Venezuelan Villages Badly Damaged," *New York Times*, May 27, 1894, 1. Stewart is a controversial figure among seismologists for his use of narrative accounts and for the urgency with which he encourages citizens of the mid-continent U. S. to prepare for earthquakes. On the controversy surrounding him, see Conevery Bolton Valencius, "Accounts of the New Madrid Earthquakes: Personal Narratives across Two Centuries of North American Seismology" *Science in Context*, 25 (2012): 17–48, 32–33.

[11] Joseph Story, *Commentaries on the Constitution of the United States* (Boston: Hilliard, Gray & Co., 1833), 457.

[12] The other use is in the preamble: "We the People of the United States, in Order to form a more perfect Union, establish Justice, insure domestic Tranquility, provide for the common defence, promote the general Welfare, and secure the Blessings of Liberty to ourselves and our Posterity, do ordain and establish this Constitution for the United States of America." The Supreme Court has found that the use of the phrase "the general Welfare" in the Preamble is not justiciable and is not the source of any substantive power. See *Jacobson v. Massachusetts*, 197 U.S. 11, 22 (1905).

[13] "To pay the debts" follows "collect taxes," which might be said to imply spending. Article I, Section 9 also implies a spending power: "No Money shall be drawn from the Treasury, but in Consequence of Appropriations made by Law; and a regular Statement and Account of the Receipts and Expenditures of all public Money shall be published from time to time."

today, the ability of the national government to decide what constituted a common purpose for which it could spend was in dispute when the Constitution was drafted. The Constitution replaced the Articles of Confederation, which relied on a requisition system of taxation in which states had a greater role in deciding on the objects of spending for national purposes. Arguably, the Constitution could have returned tax revenues to the states for further deliberation about how and whether to spend. The Constitution's ambiguity about the extent of the national government's taxing and spending powers reflects the dispute between the Federalists and Anti-Federalists that surfaced during the ratification debates and continued long after.[14] The sides of the debate were fluid, as prominent Anti-Federalists such as Melancton Smith came to vote for the Constitution in their state ratifying conventions, while Federalists including, most famously, James Madison, an author of the *Federalist Papers*, ultimately left the movement. The text of the Constitution is considered more Federalist than not, but it reflects some of the Anti-Federalist concerns through the limits it places on the national government.

Judicial interpretations have upheld Congress's power to appropriate funds under the general welfare and common defense headings so that the power to spend was never seriously in dispute. Whether disaster relief constituted an appropriate object for national government spending was, however. Even though the general welfare clause refers to the welfare *of the United States*, not necessarily to other countries throughout the world, members of Congress might have been thinking more about national security strategy than humanitarianism when they sent aid abroad. With Latin America in the grip of revolutionary fervor, disaster aid strengthened U.S. ties with the region and helped stabilize its governments.

Whatever the motivation, Congress's aid for earthquake victims in Latin America was soon taken up as precedent by residents of the Missouri territory. Three of the strongest earthquakes in U.S. history erupted near sparsely populated New Madrid, Missouri, in 1811 and 1812. The tremors were reportedly strong enough to ring church bells 1,000 miles away in Boston.[15] Subsequent

[14] Elvin T. Lim, *The Lovers' Quarrel: The Two Foundlings in American Political Development* (New York: Oxford University Press, 2013); Martin Diamond, "The Federalist's View of Federalism," in *Essays in Federalism*, edited by George C. Benson (Claremont, CA: Institute for Studies in Federalism, 1962), 21–64. On the Anti-Federalist arguments to limit the national government's taxing and spending powers, see, for example, Melancton Smith's comments in *The Debate on the Constitution: Federalist and Antifederalist Speeches, Articles, and Letters During the Struggle over Ratification Part Two: January to August 1788*, edited by Bernard Bailyn (New York: Literary Classics of the United States, 1993), 817.

[15] The precise strength of the earthquakes is still the subject of debate. The United States Geological Survey (USGS) lists the quakes as 7.7 and 7.5 magnitude, ranking them fourth among earthquakes in the continental United States. See: http://earthquake.usgs.gov/earthquakes/states/10_largest_us.php (accessed June 24, 2009). Some seismologists estimate that the earthquake was smaller than reported, and even USGS estimates have been downgraded from estimates of more than 8 magnitude. Many seismologists criticize the revisionist view of downgrading the

liquefaction, subsidence, landslide, and changes in the water table ravaged the land of Missouri homesteaders, and residents successfully petitioned Congress to pass a law permitting landholders to relocate on other public lands if the earthquake had rendered their property unproductive.[16]

By 1820, then, Congress had given aid to return a port to operation, had sent aid abroad as part of its foreign policy, and had intervened after disaster in the western territories where there were no state governments. If these places could receive aid, why not eastern cities? One city pressed that argument. In 1827, a fire broke out by accident in the workshop of a cabinetmaker in downtown Alexandria, Virginia, destroying fifty-three homes, warehouses, and stables, plus personal property.[17] Members of Congress proposed passing a bill to provide $20,000 to be spent for the relief of victims of the fire.[18] Even though Alexandria was at the time part of the District of Columbia and thus under the jurisdiction of Congress rather than the state of Virginia, several members of Congress disputed the constitutionality of the relief measure, claiming that it lacked precedent and diverged from the spirit of the Constitution, which left disaster relief as a local or private matter. Other members countered that disaster relief had precedent in the government's ability to spend for internal improvements such as roads and canals. The urgent demands of the moment

earthquake's magnitude as too extreme, however. See Seth Stein, *Disaster Deferred: How New Science Is Changing Our View of Earthquake Hazards in the Midwest* (New York: Columbia University Press, 2010); Christine A. Powell, "Review of Disaster Deferred: How New Science is Changing Our View of Earthquake Hazards in the Midwest," *Seismological Research Letters* 82 (March/April 2011), 238–239. Whether the earthquake actually shook the ground enough to ring church bells in Boston is open to debate. Newspaper accounts of the quake report church bells ringing after the tremors in Boston and New York, but some seismologists conclude that the reports were exaggerations and that the earthquake rang bells in Charleston, South Carolina, rather than the Charlestown neighborhood of Boston. See Jay Feldman, *When the Mississippi Ran Backwards: Empire, Intrigue, Murder, and the New Madrid Earthquakes* (New York: Free Press, 2005); Eugene Schweig, Joan Gomberg, and James W. Hendley II, *The Mississippi Valley – Whole Lotta Shakin' Goin' On* (Washington, DC: U.S. Geological Survey Fact Sheet, 1995), 168–195.

[16] When individuals took Congress up on the offer, they claimed new land and gave their old land to the federal government, which then redistributed the property. Congress's humanitarian gesture led to acrimonious disputes over land titles that continued for generations after shrewd investors bought the abandoned land and then traded it for more valuable property. James Penick, *The New Madrid Earthquakes* (Columbia: University of Missouri Press, 1982), 49–50; also Foster, *The Demands of Humanity*; Stewart and Knox, *The Earthquake America Forgot*, 255–262; 254–255.

[17] Alexandria has a port, but it did not expand to become a shipping hub until after the fire in 1828. The committee tallied the destruction at: "53 buildings consisting of dwellings, ware and storehouses, exclusive of a number of stables and other outbuildings; all of which are valued at sixty thousand nine hundred and twenty dollars; and personal property which we have estimated at forty-six thousand, three hundred and fifty-seven dollars..." *Alexandria Gazette*, January 23, 1827.

[18] "Sufferers by Fire at Alexandria," Register of Debates in Congress, January 19, 1827, 2nd Sess, 19th Cong., Vol. III (Washington, DC: Gales & Seaton, 1829), 752–753.

also swayed members. In a frequently quoted line, Churchill C. Cambreleng, a Jacksonian from New York, said, "This was not the time nor the occasion to fight the battles of the Constitution."[19] The relief bill prevailed, but its opponents recognized that federal government intervention in Alexandria opened the door to intervention in other cases where Congress might provide relief to compensate victims of disasters outside of their control, and not merely to restore critical national infrastructure.[20] "What then is it that prevents Congress from administering to the relief of sufferers by fire, everywhere?" asked Francis Johnson, a Republican from Kentucky. "Because the Constitution confines the appropriation of public money to public purposes."[21] What counted as public purposes, however, could – and did – grow.[22]

Between the Portsmouth fire of 1802 and 1947 – the beginning of the Cold War – Congress enacted 128 pieces of disaster-specific legislation to fund relief workers and compensate property owners.[23] How these aid bills were implemented depended on the highly variable capacity of local organizations. "When army (or beginning in the 1880s, Red Cross) representatives arrived on the scene of a disaster, they generally found ad hoc local or regional relief committees collecting funds and relief supplies, and performing recovery efforts," writes Peter May.[24] Reducing vulnerability before disaster struck – what is today referred to as mitigation – was accomplished by individuals or localities, if at all.[25]

Given the lack of institutionalized federal support for disaster preparation or relief, Congress debated what to do after each calamity. The debate over whether to provide relief usually turned on two factors: precedent and constitutionality. Arguments from precedent cited previous aid for victims of fires, floods, insurrection, or other disasters, and arguments from the Constitution were at first invoked as reason to deny a request for relief

---

[19] Cambreleng, "Sufferers by Fire at Alexandria," *Register of Debates in Congress*, January 1827, 2nd Sess, 19th Cong., Vol. III (Washington, DC: Gales & Seaton, 1829), 764.
[20] Cited in *In Re Sugar Bounty* (Washington, DC: Comptroller of the Treasury, 1895).
[21] "Sufferers by Fire at Alexandria," in *Abridgement of the Debates of Congress, from 1789 to 1856*, January 19, 1827, 2nd Sess, 19th Cong., 891, vol. IX (New York: D. Appleton & Company, 1858), 391.
[22] Historian Michele Landis Dauber counts twenty-seven claims for disaster relief passed by Congress as private bills and administered through the executive branch by the time of the Alexandria fire. (These were for smaller events, however, and the aid was directed toward specific individuals or institutions). See Michele Landis Dauber, "The War of 1812, September 11, and the Politics of Compensation," *DePaul Law Review* 53 (2003): 289–354. Members of Congress debated whether victims of the Alexandria fire should be compensated, and those members opposed suffered the electoral consequences. Democrat James K. Polk voted against aid to victims of the Alexandria fire, and a majority of voters in Alexandria and neighboring Fairfax County supported Henry Clay for president in 1844 rather than Polk.
[23] Peter J. May, *Recovering From Catastrophes* (Westport, CO: Greenwood Press, 1985), 18.
[24] May, *Recovering From Catastrophes*, 18.
[25] Rutherford H. Platt, *Disasters and Democracy: The Politics of Extreme Natural Events* (Washington, DC: Island Press, 1999), 1.

because of the limits of federal power over local matters. Before the Civil War, people on both sides of the debate understood the Constitution to be silent about disaster relief. Some opponents of relief argued that relief was therefore unconstitutional.

It was more common in the antebellum period, however, for members of Congress to object to aiding victims on the grounds that such matters must be left to states and localities. Fiercely independent states and a reluctance to further deepen divisions between national and subnational governments over slavery gave credence to arguments for Congress's limited authority in all spheres, including relief. For example, in 1827, frontiersman Davy Crockett served in the House and refused to approve $10,000 in compensation for the widow of a naval officer. He told Congress: "We must not permit our respect for the dead nor our sympathy for the living to lead us into an act of injustice to the balance of the living. I will not attempt to prove that Congress has no power to appropriate this money as an act of charity. Every member upon this floor knows it. We have the right as individuals to give away as much of our own money as we please in charity; but as members of Congress we have no right to appropriate a dollar of the public money."[26] After Crockett's speech, the bill was defeated. In this period, members of Congress proposed bills to compensate individuals for losses and misfortunes, especially in connection with federal government service. Sometimes bills for individual aid succeeded, and sometimes they failed, depending on factors particular to each instance, such as partisan control, legislative skill, or even an impassioned speech like Crockett's. Bills to compensate entire communities for charitable reasons alone – rather than to restore a critical function, such as a port – were rare.

Legal scholar David P. Currie wrote that in these few cases, "the refusal of an early Congress to provide disaster relief for a single community after debate had raised serious constitutional doubts tends to support Hamilton's insistence that 'the object to which an appropriation of money is ... made [must] be *General* and not *local*; its operation extending in fact, or by possibility, throughout the Union, and not being confined to a particular spot.'"[27] In one such case, the New York City fire of 1835 destroyed a large swath of Manhattan, including the New York Stock Exchange, but Congress failed to approve a disaster assistance bill despite the fire's impact on the nation's economy and the lives of New Yorkers.[28] The fire destroyed 570 buildings, caused $15 million in property

[26] "Davy Crockett's Electioneering Tour," *Harper's New Monthly Magazine*, December 1866 to May 1867, Vol. 34 (New York: Harper and Brothers, 1867), 607.

[27] David P. Currie, "The Constitution in the Supreme Court: The New Deal, 1931–1940," *University of Chicago Law Review* 54 (1987): 504, at n. 136; quoted in Howard Gillman, "Disaster Relief, 'Do Anything' Spending Powers, and the New Deal," *Law and History Review* 23 (2005) 443–450, fn 7.

[28] A. E. Costello, *Our Firemen: A History of the New York Fire Departments* (New York: Costello, 1887), "The Great Conflagration of 1835," ch. 18, Part I. Available online at: http://www.usgen-net.org/usa/ny/state/fire/11–20/ch18pt1.html (accessed June 3, 2010). Even in 1835, New York

damage, and decimated the city's fire insurance industry.[29] Twenty-three of the city's twenty-six fire insurance companies exhausted their capital by paying losses, which totaled $11.45 million by one estimate.[30]

Advocates for aid to New York City deployed arguments about economic necessity and compassion, but these fell on deaf ears because Congress was tied up with other business. Without a permanent bureaucracy responsible for distributing aid, disaster-stricken communities depended on the smooth functioning of Congress for timely aid. In the two decades leading up to the Civil War, Congress actually provided less disaster recovery aid than in the preceding years because factions in Congress feared that extending federal power even in disaster policy might exacerbate the tensions that eventually led to war.[31] The slowdown in disaster relief in the immediate antebellum period shows the degree to which disaster policy is at the mercy of larger trends in U.S. politics and state-building.

The effect of the Civil War on disaster policy sheds light on a debate among historians and political scientists over how to describe the character of the nineteenth-century state. That debate, in turn, sheds light on the degree to which disaster policy followed other trends in U.S. government. The reigning consensus among historians is that the United States had a weak state before and after the Civil War.[32] Morton Keller describes the government of that era as a state of parties and courts, without the large bureaucracy that is normally associated with the term "state" today. Keller finds that increases in spending and government employment reflected shifting partisan control, not efforts to build a state apparatus. Pensions for veterans and new post offices and customs houses were intended to secure party loyalty, not usher in the welfare state. There was no equivalent of the Federal Emergency Management Agency in the

was a hub of the national economy. See Edward L. Glaeser, "Urban Colossus: Why Is New York America's Largest City?" *FRBNY Economic Policy Review* (December 2005): 7–24.

[29] Albert S. Bolles writes that "the re-action after the fire of 1835 was consequently dreadful. The whole country stood aghast. Public confidence in the joint-stock companies was profoundly shaken." Bolles, *Industrial History of the United States* (Norwich, CT: The Henry Bill Publishing Company, 1879), 827.

[30] Bolles, 827.

[31] Congress passed some bills for disaster and humanitarian relief, however. These include aid to the Irish famine victims. See *Resolution of March 3, 1847* (9 Stat. 207, No. 10); *Congressional Globe*, 29th Cong., 2d sess., 1847, 16, pt. 1:505. In addition, Congress approved $200,000 in relief paid to victims of the Sioux Indian depredations in Minnesota. See *Act of February 16, 1863* (12 Stat. 652, ch. 37); *Congressional Globe*, 37th Cong., 3d sess., 1863, 34, pt. 1:179, 192, 440–445, 509–518.

[32] Beyond Keller, other accounts support the idea of continuity before and after the Civil War. See Joel H. Silbey, *The American Political Nation, 1838–1893* (Stanford, CA: Stanford University Press, 1991); Stephen Skowronek, *Building a New American State* (Cambridge: Cambridge University Press, 1982), 20–26; Richard F. Bensel, *The Political Economy of American Industrialization 1870–1900* (New York: Columbia University Press, 2000). Bensel shows that rather than reshaping politics, American industrialization occurred in response to an existing political order.

nineteenth century, and Congress delivered most aid on an ad hoc basis without a significant bureaucracy. If Keller's thesis is true for disaster policy, then the disaster state did not begin until Roosevelt's New Deal reforms in 1932.[33]

More recently, scholars have challenged Keller's account of discontinuity between the centuries, arguing that nineteenth-century U.S. government engaged in significant state-building that had more in common with the twentieth-century state than previous historians recognized. William Novak analyzes the interventions of the nineteenth-century state in moral regulation and public health, whereas John Larson focuses on internal improvements, and Richard John shows the surprising reach of the U.S. Post Office.[34] Brian Balogh's claim is the most general among members of this school of thought. He portrays the nineteenth-century state as working behind the scenes across many policy areas by setting the rules of the private market and offering services through nongovernmental organizations. For Balogh, it was no less a state for being behind the scenes; it was a government "out of sight," as the title of his book puts it. [35] Other accounts suggest that the coming of the Civil War forestalled state-building. Historian John Majewski's study of the economy of the Confederacy implies that the United States limited federal government power longer than it would have without a north-south division and the resulting disagreement over what government should be doing.[36]

Rather than occur "out of sight," nineteenth-century federal government involvement in disaster was periodic and political, punctuated by the Civil War and then, later, bureaucratization in the twentieth century. This differs from what Balogh and others have argued. Disaster relief grew during the nineteenth century without becoming bureaucratized. Disaster policy was not an issue for party platforms in the nineteenth century, so it does not fit neatly into periodizations based on partisan and electoral coalitions.[37] Instead, increasing

---

[33] Morton Keller, *America's Three Regimes: A New Political History* (New York: Oxford University Press, 2007); Morton Keller, *Affairs of State: Public Life in Late Nineteenth Century America* (Cambridge, MA: Harvard University Press, 1977).

[34] William J. Novak, *People's Welfare: Law and Regulation in Nineteenth-Century America* (Chapel Hill: University of North Carolina Press, 1996); Richard John, *Spreading the News: The American Postal System from Franklin to Morse* (Cambridge, MA: Harvard University Press, 1998); John Larson, *Internal Improvement: National Public Works and the Promise of Popular Government in the Early United States* (Chapel Hill: University of North Carolina Press, 2000).

[35] Brian Balogh, *A Government Out of Sight: The Mystery of National Authority in Nineteenth-Century America* (New York: Cambridge University Press, 2009); Balogh, "Americans Love Government, as Long as They Can't See It," History News Network, June 15, 2009, available at: http://www.hnn.us/articles/88154.html (accessed November 17, 2012).

[36] John Majewski, *Modernizing a Slave Economy: The Economic Vision of the Confederate Nation* (Chapel Hill: University of North Carolina Press, 2009).

[37] Richard Bensel, "Sectionalism and Congressional Development," *Oxford Handbook of the American Congress*, edited by Eric Schickler and Frances E. Lee (New York: Oxford University Press, 2011), 761–786. Crockett's comments and others show ideological coalitions in Congress, chiefly variants of nationalizing northern Federalists and more states' rights-oriented southern groups. Disaster relief was never a central issue for these coalitions, however.

requests for disaster relief came from members of Congress seeking aid for their districts, and from community leaders seeking help.

The Civil War greatly expanded the federal government's power over matters once reserved to the states, and therefore the power of the federal government to administer disaster relief. As historian James McPherson notes, the Union government enacted "an astonishing blitz" of laws that "did more to reshape the relation of the government to the economy than any comparable effort except perhaps the first hundred days of the New Deal."[38] Between 1861 and 1863, Congress created a single national currency, began bank charters, established a land grant college system, and created new and durable national administrative agencies.[39] Proponents of disaster relief after the Civil War had a wealth of new precedents for federal action from which to draw. Between 1860 and 1903, Congress issued more than ninety relief measures for fires, floods, earthquakes, and droughts, roughly twice the number of disaster measures that were issued between 1790 and 1860.[40]

RECONSTRUCTION AS A TURNING POINT

A more self-assured union emerged after the Civil War led by pro-Union Republicans who assembled a remarkably cohesive coalition at least until the twentieth century.[41] The federal government resumed its increasing interventions after disaster that, for the first time, took a bureaucratic form. From Reconstruction onward, the government's legal authority to issue disaster relief to communities was never in dispute, but some factions questioned whether Congress should provide aid to marginalized victims or for marginally sized disasters. President Andrew Johnson vetoed the first attempt to extend Freedmen's Bureau aid to famine victims in the former Confederate states after widespread crop failures because the disaster was outside the Bureau's original mission, and because the victims might have been disloyal to the Union.[42] The second attempt at a bill passed in 1867, however, and the Bureau of Refugees,

---

[38] James M. McPherson, *Lincoln and the Second American Revolution* (New York: Oxford University Press, 1991), 39–42.

[39] Elvin Lim adds evidence for the Civil War's transformation of the federal government's relationship to the states in *The Lovers' Quarrel: The Two Foundlings in American Political Development* (New York: Oxford University Press, 2013), 133.

[40] Michele Landis, "'Let Me Next Time Be Tried by Fire': Disaster Relief and the Origins of the American Welfare State 1789–1874," *Northwestern University Law Review* 92 (1998): 967–1034; Michele Landis, "Fate, Responsibility, and Natural Disaster Relief: Narrating the American Welfare State," *Law and Society Review* 33 (1999): 257–318.

[41] Bensel, "Sectionalism and Congressional Development," 769–771.

[42] *Congressional Globe*, 39th Cong., 1st sess., 1866, 37, pt. 1:916. The Freedmen's Bureau, more officially the Bureau of Refugees, Freedmen, and Abandoned Lands, delivered aid to freed slaves from 1865 to 1871. The bureau provided food, housing, education, and health care to freed slaves, including those suffering the effects of natural disasters or environmental devastation. See Chad Allen Goldberg, *Citizens and Paupers: Relief, Rights, and Race, from the Freedmen's Bureau to Workfare* (Chicago: University of Chicago Press, 2007).

Freedmen, and Abandoned Lands distributed aid to freed slaves from 1865 to 1871. The Bureau was lodged in the Department of War, but it distributed a range of aid for peacetime, including legal assistance, food, housing, education, health care, and disaster relief until Congress disbanded the Bureau. Law professor Michele Landis Dauber characterizes the Bureau as a proto-welfare state because for the first time the U.S. government distributed aid to civilians over several years through administrative processes.[43]

Congress continued to distribute aid ad hoc following major disasters. More and more, citizens and the media applauded Congress for its interventions, which presumably helped raise members' stature in the eyes of voters. After the Mississippi Valley Floods in 1897, a *New York Daily Tribune* headline read, "Congress to the rescue."[44] Before the president forged closer ties with individual citizens in the twentieth century, the executive was the most likely branch of government to issue objections to disaster aid, so Congress most often received credit for help. In one such example, Grover Cleveland vetoed a bill providing relief to victims of a Texas drought in 1887.[45] "I feel obligated to withhold my approval of the plan to indulge in benevolent and charitable sentiment through the appropriation of public funds for that purpose," he wrote in his veto. "I can find no warrant for such an appropriation in the Constitution."

Cleveland was no principled strict constructionist, however. Instead, he saw few reasons why federal government disaster relief would benefit him or the nation in an age before widespread national media and without much precedent for presidential involvement in disaster. Cleveland justified not acting because of the Constitution's textual ambiguity about federal government authority when it suited him. When a powerful constituency pressed him to use the federal government's coercive power to protect them, Cleveland was not so careful to adhere to the Constitution's text. In 1886, dairy farmers convinced Congress to pass a bill imposing a 2-cent-per-pound tax on margarine and requiring expensive licensing for manufacturers and sellers of margarine or "counterfeit butter" as they labeled it. Cleveland, from the dairy state of New York, signed the bill even while recognizing its dubious constitutional foundations and the particularly brazen and self-interested efforts of the butter lobby. The Margarine Tax Act of 1886 is one of the first instances of an industry successfully lobbying for the coercive power of government to disadvantage its competitors.[46]

---

[43] Congressional Record, 40th cong. 2nd sess. 1867, pt. I: 40, 42, 45. Quoted in Dauber, *Helping Ourselves*, 104.

[44] "Congress to the Rescue: Appeal from the President in Behalf of the Flood Sufferers," *New York Daily Tribune*, April 8, 1897, 1.

[45] *Congressional Record*, 49th Cong., 2d sess., February 16, 1887, 18, pt. 2:1875.

[46] Geoffrey P. Miller, "Public Choice at the Dawn of the Special Interest State: The Story of Butter and Margarine, *California Law Review* 77 (January 1989): 83–131, 125–127; Henry C. Bannard, "The Oleomargarine Law: A Study of Congressional Politics," *Political Science Quarterly* 2 (December 1887): 545–557.

While the number of areas open to federal government intervention gradually increased, not all of the expansion of federal authority in disaster relief occurred through direct legislation. The partially private and indirect character of disaster relief supports Balogh's characterization of parts of state activity as "out of sight." Allowing private organizations – whether nonprofit or for-profits – to provide disaster relief permitted even conservative politicians suspicious of the expansion of the central state to lend their support. In 1900, Congress chartered the Red Cross as a private, independent organization that would distribute federal relief dollars. During the Coolidge administration, which had a famously limited approach to government, Commerce Secretary Herbert Hoover attempted to persuade the Red Cross to provide relief for drought, floods, and unemployment even though he was considered an opponent of state intervention.[47] The Red Cross initially hesitated because drought was "one of the many hazards of farming – like the boll weevil or a bad harvest."[48] The Red Cross insisted that unemployment (and other slow-onset disasters) were outside its mission and legislative charter because they could too easily blend into other social ills such as poor health care and education.[49] Despite this early resistance, the Red Cross expanded its mission when given substantial federal government funds, foreshadowing how disaster organizations would respond to new civil defense and homeland security money in the next century – at first resisting, then incorporating new missions into their organizations when the government tied those new missions to new funding.

New opportunities for quasi-governmental organizations opened up during the nineteenth century as arguments that federal aid violated the Hamiltonian standard of general, not local, concerns became less common. If fires, floods, hurricanes, earthquakes, and violent insurrections took a similar toll on citizens, supporters of federal aid argued, why restrict aid for any single category of calamitous event that takes citizens by surprise? Congress members' pleas for aid emphasized victims' lack of responsibility for their own woes, whereas opponents claimed that victims should have seen the disaster coming or that disaster relief was a local responsibility – two arguments against federal aid deployed to the present day. Yet contentious debates over the constitutionality of federal aid for disasters were rare after the Civil War, and most appropriations

[47] At the time, Herbert Hoover was Calvin Coolidge's commerce secretary, and he tried to persuade the Red Cross to provide relief for both drought and unemployment. Hoover was one of the earliest prominent officials who favored private aid for disaster victims while opposing state intervention. After the Mississippi flood of 1927, Hoover oversaw a massive Red Cross relief effort. Nan Elizabeth Woodruff, *As Rare as Rain: Federal Relief in the Great Southern Drought of 1930–31* (Urbana: University of Illinois Press, 1985), 9; Congressional Record 1931, 74, pt2: 2152–2154; John M. Barry, *Rising Tide: The Great Mississippi Flood of 1927 and How It Changed America* (New York: Simon & Schuster, 1997).

[48] Woodruff, *As Rare as Rain: Federal Relief in the Great Southern Drought of 1930–31*, 9.

[49] Foster Rhea Dulles, *The American Red Cross* (New York: Harper and Brothers, 1950).

for relief were made by unanimous joint resolutions from the Reconstruction period to the early twentieth century.[50]

DISASTER RELIEF AND THE EMERGENCE OF THE MODERN PRESIDENCY

Accounts of presidential restraint and congressional largesse in distributing disaster aid support Jeffrey Tulis's description of a limited constitutional presidency in the nineteenth century.[51] That period provides scant evidence of presidents making public speeches after disasters or of distributing aid in the name of the public, even though major disasters received national news coverage. Scholars dispute exactly when a president's direct appeals to the public became routine – some say they began with William McKinley, others Theodore Roosevelt, and still others Franklin D. Roosevelt – but in any case, presidential appeals have become a key characteristic of the modern presidency.[52] At the very least, Theodore Roosevelt is a transitional figure between the limited constitutional presidency and the modern presidency.

At the dawn of the twentieth century, several relatively autonomous relief organizations vied for control, and the presidency was one institution among many in the government's emerging arsenal of emergency response. The 1906 San Francisco crisis would test that arsenal, and Theodore Roosevelt's limited response, mediated by other organizations, illustrates how the presidency is shaped by doctrine, institutional powers, technology, and popular expectations. The earthquake that struck San Francisco on April 16 and the subsequent fires are estimated to have killed more than 3,000 people and caused massive structural and economic damage.[53] Roosevelt sent a telegram to California Governor George Pardee: "Hear rumors of great disaster through an earthquake at San Francisco, but know nothing of the real facts. Call upon me for any assistance I can render."[54] The next morning, the president called a

[50] Michele Landis Dauber, "The Sympathetic State," *Law and History Review* 23 (2005): 387–442.

[51] Jeffrey K. Tulis, *The Rhetorical Presidency* (Princeton, NJ: Princeton University Press, 1987); Terri Bimes and Stephen Skowronek, "Woodrow Wilson's Critique of Popular Leadership: Reassessing the Modern-Traditional Divide," in *Speaking for the People: The Rhetorical Presidency in Historical Perspective, edited by Richard Ellis* (Amherst: University of Massachusetts Press, 1998), 134–161; Fred I. Greenstein, *The Presidential Difference: Leadership Style from FDR to Clinton* (New York: The Free Press, 2000).

[52] Tulis, *The Rhetorical Presidency*; David K. Nichols, *The Myth of the Modern Presidency* (State College: Pennsylvania State University Press, 1994); Lewis Gould, *The Presidency of William McKinley* (Lawrence: University of Kansas Press, 1981); Lewis Gould and Richard Norton Smith, *The Modern American Presidency* (Lawrence: University of Kansas Press, 2004).

[53] Philip L. Fradkin, *The Great Earthquake and Firestorms of 1906* (Berkeley: University of California Press, 2005), 305–338; The earthquake has been rated between 7.7 and 8.3 magnitude. See U.S. Geological Survey, "1906 Earthquake: What Was the Magnitude?" USGS Earthquake Hazards Program, Northern California, undated, available at: http://earthquake. usgs.gov/regional/nca/1906/18april/magnitude.php (accessed October 6, 2009).

[54] "Roosevelt Offers Aid," *New York Times*, April 19, 1906, 8. His first telegram to Pardee read: "Hear rumors of great disaster through an earthquake at San Francisco, but know nothing of

cabinet meeting to discuss the earthquake, even though little news from San Francisco had reached the east coast. Eventually, Roosevelt sent Secretary of Commerce (and former congressman) Victor Metcalf to San Francisco to represent the federal government.[55] Metcalf did not have as much authority as Herbert Hoover would later have in his czar position, but did act as the eyes and ears of the president.

On April 22, four days after the earthquake, Roosevelt announced that the Red Cross would distribute $2.5 million in aid to victims. The announcement seemed to be aimed at foreign governments whose assistance Roosevelt had declined in an attempt to prove the United States could handle its own affairs (an "ethical Monroe doctrine" as one German newspaper put it at the time) rather than at the U.S. public.[56] This tradition continues today: the U.S. government still politely declines international assistance in domestic disasters.[57]

Roosevelt's interventions after the San Francisco earthquake appear mild compared to the involvement of other semiautonomous public organizations. The Army was actively engaged from the beginning of the crisis with apparently little direction from the commander-in-chief. With little communication possible with Washington, Brigadier General Frederick Funston, a San Francisco resident, responded to citizen requests for law and order by marshaling troops

the real facts. Call upon me for any assistance I can render"; *The Letters of Theodore Roosevelt*, edited by Elting E. Morison, vol. 5: *The Big Stick, 1905–1907* (Cambridge, MA: Harvard University Press, 1952), 213.

[55] Metcalf, a former member of Congress, wrote a memo to the president on April 26, 1906 (available at: http://www.sfmuseum.org/1906/metcalf.html (accessed September 8, 2009) that praised the cooperation between levels of government and concluded: "It is almost impossible to describe the ruin wrought by the earthquake and especially the conflagration.... The people however, are confident and hopeful for the future and have not in any sense lost their courage. They feel under deep obligation to you and the national Government for the prompt and efficient assistance rendered them."

[56] Roosevelt was more involved in corruption investigations among San Francisco government and businesses and in questions about the status of foreign labor in California than in quake relief. Quoted in: *Die Katastrophe von San Francisco: Mit einer kurzen illustrierten Vorgeschichte der Stadt* (St. Louis, MO: Louis Lange, 1906), 54. Also quoted in: Christoph Stupp. *Dealing with Disaster: The San Francisco Earthquake of 1906.* (Berkeley, CA: Institute of European Studies, 2006). Available at eScholarship Repository, University of California, http://repositories.cdlib.org/ies/060322 (accessed November 12, 2011). See also John Castillo Kennedy, *The Great Earthquake and Fire, San Francisco, 1906* (New York: Morrow, 1963), 173–174; Charles Morris, *The San Francisco Calamity* (Champaign: University of Illinois Press, 2002 [1906]), 147. For an overview of the messages Roosevelt received from foreign heads of state and government leaders, see Richard Linthicum, Trumbull White, and Samuel Fallows, *Complete Story of the San Francisco Horror* (Chicago: n.p., 1906), 215–217.

[57] Following Hurricane Katrina, the U.S. government refused to allow search and rescue teams from the UN Office for the Coordination of Humanitarian Assistance into the disaster area. For a review of how the U.S. government handles international disaster assistance, see "Comprehensive Policies and Procedures Are Needed to Ensure Appropriate Use of and Accountability for International Assistance," GAO-06-460, April 6 (Washington, DC: Government Accountability Office, 2006).

from the Presidio, an Army post on the edge of the city. Army soldiers based
in California also took responsibility for feeding, sheltering, and clothing displaced residents. By the time civil authorities assumed responsibility for relief
and recovery on July 1, 4,000 Army troops had contributed to relief efforts in
San Francisco. The Army saved lives, but it also shot citizens on suspicion of
looting.[58]

War Secretary William Howard Taft was in communication with Funston
by telegram, but the content of his messages shows the limits of the president's
reach.

> April 18, 1906
>
> To Funston, Commanding Dept. California, San Francisco, Cal.
>
> The Associated Press reports to me that you have charge of San Francisco,
> Oakland and the Bay. I wish that you would report to me at once what you
> have done, the measures you have taken, under what authority you are act-
> ing, how many people need your assistance and supplies, and that you will
> give passes to the Associated Press representatives and those of other press
> associations. Wire as soon as possible.
>
> (Signed) W. H Taft, Secretary of War. [59]

Taft worked through a chain of command, constrained by the limitations of
the telegraph and bureaucratic hierarchy. By the twentieth century, the telegraph spurred the spread of news, and canals and railroads reduced travel time,
yet it still took days for details about the earthquake to reach the rest of the
country. And it was impractical for Washington, DC to send relief resources
across the country with any haste. Funston wrote back by telegram, either on
the nineteenth or the twentieth, advising the War Department that Fort Mason
was intact and some looters had been shot, but that most people in the "better
portions" of the city had been saved.[60]

While the Army provided much of the food and shelter in the immediate
aftermath of the crisis, the Red Cross organized much of its relief effort independently of Washington, DC, or the Army. Congress and the president had
authorized it to be the chief disaster relief agency, but the Red Cross took

---

[58] Media reports at the time fixed on fear of looting. Jane Gray and Elizabeth Wilson, "Looting in
Disaster: A General Profile of Victimization," Disaster Research Center, Ohio State University,
August 1984, available at: http://dspace.udel.edu:8080/dspace/bitstream/19716/1295/1/WP71.
pdf (accessed December 2, 2012).

[59] Frederick Funston, "How the Army Worked to Save San Francisco," *Cosmopolitan Magazine*,
61 July 1906, available at: http://www.sfmuseum.net/1906/cosmo.html (Museum of the city of
SF) and at: http://www.sfmuseum.org/1906.2/apress.html (accessed November 16, 2012).

[60] Timeline of the San Francisco Earthquake, April 18–23, 1906, Virtual Museum of San Francisco:
The Great 1906 Earthquake and Fire: http://www.sfmuseum.net/hist10/06timeline.html
(accessed November 11, 2012); Christoph Strupp, "Dealing with Disaster: The San Francisco
Earthquake of 1906" (Berkeley, CA: Institute of European Studies, 2006), available at: http://
escholarship.org/uc/item/9gd2v192 (accessed November 12, 2012).

weeks to find its niche in San Francisco.[61] The city had already established a committee to lead the relief effort, and the *San Francisco Chronicle* criticized the Red Cross for interfering with matters best left to the city.[62] Eventually, the Red Cross negotiated an arrangement with city leaders to share disaster relief funds (aside from the funds specifically appropriated to the relief organization). The Red Cross eventually distributed $8.5 million in aid from public donations and congressional appropriations.

Thus, although federally sponsored organizations participated in the relief effort, Roosevelt exercised little direct authority and made few appeals to the public despite being a figure who in other circumstances, such as campaigns and international diplomacy, was known for exercising his charisma and making direct appeals to the public.[63] The president was still a relatively minor figure in disaster relief. Still, in the response to the San Francisco earthquake there were hints of the presidency to come. It was Roosevelt, not Congress, who took the initiative. With the emergence of a national news media, the president received coverage each time he appealed to Congress for additional aid for earthquake victims.[64] In a limited way, Roosevelt used disaster to shape his image as a figure responsible for the smooth and benevolent functioning of government.

THE RATCHETING UP OF DISASTER RELIEF THROUGH PRECEDENT

The American public and public officials accepted limited government in most cases throughout the nineteenth century, and exceptions such as aid to victims of fires or earthquakes, or the Freedman's Bureau were just that – exceptions. The gradual increase in government aid to disaster victims occurred in fits and starts. The government's role in disaster aid increased by the gradual accumulation of precedents for intervention and the weakening of arguments that the federal government lacked authority to provide aid for humanitarian purposes or intervene in matters reserved to the states. The structure of argument in U.S. politics makes precedent through repetition an important tool in policy change.

[61] Dulles, *The American Red Cross* (American Red Cross Museum, http://www.redcross.org/museum/history/sanfranquake.asp (accessed November 12, 2012).

[62] Edward T. Devine, *The Principles of Relief* (New York, London: Macmillan, 1904), 58; Kennedy, *The Great Earthquake*, 211–214; Gordon Thomas and Max M. Witts, *The San Francisco Earthquake* (New York: Stein and Day, 1971), 163–164; William Bronson, *The Earth Shook, the Sky Burned* (Garden City, NY: Doubleday, 1959), 195–197; on Roosevelt's motives, see his letter of April 22, 1906 to Mabel T. Boardman of the National Relief Board of the Red Cross, in *Letters of Theodore Roosevelt, The Big Stick*, Vol. 5 (Cambridge, MA: Harvard University Press, 1954), 216; also the "Telegram to Schmitz," April 25, 1906, ibid., 219–220.

[63] Elizabeth Sanders, *Roots of Reform: Farmers, Workers, and the American State, 1877–1917* (Chicago: University of Chicago Press, 1999), 76–99; H. W. Brands, *TR: The Last Romantic* (New York: Perseus, 1997).

[64] For example, see "President Asks $500,000, Recommends New Congressional Appropriation for San Francisco," *New York Times*, May 9, 1906.

Although the focus of disaster policy shifted to the executive branch in the twentieth century, Congress still mattered for the accumulation of precedent. The U.S. Congress can encounter opposition from states, the Supreme Court, and even members of its own body if it does not cite a constitutional foundation for its actions. Appealing to precedent through creative interpretations time and time again made it easier for members of Congress to accept government intervention as permissible.

The accumulation of precedent for federal government intervention before and after disasters formed the core of social construction. Sometimes members of Congress opposed disaster aid under any circumstances, but they were countered by advocates for aid who appealed to constitutional duty, not just charitable impulse. Members who advocated aid liberally interpreted the Constitution's "general welfare" clause.[65] By the mid-nineteenth century, Congress had appropriated funds from the Treasury for the relief of hundreds of fires, floods, earthquakes, Indian raids, and other disasters, giving disaster relief a constitutional foundation in precedent.[66] Initially, relief was limited to earthquakes and conflagrations, and it came in the form of debt forgiveness. But once the logic of disaster relief as general welfare was in place as a precedent, there were few good reasons not to expand the range of disasters for which the government provided relief, and to extend the means of relief to include direct aid to victims.

By the early twentieth century, members of Congress (and affected citizens) began asking for a greater variety of aid, including bonds and direct payments for a greater variety of calamities, which included prolonged economic hardship exacerbated by weather conditions. The collapse of the world cotton markets in 1914 during World War I led to a depression in the U.S. South and drew appeals from southern legislators for relief. Some southern senators demanded price supports for cotton farmers, but other members of Congress objected that such aid constituted paternalism. Senator William Borah replied to such charges by invoking the logic of an expansive federal government authority to provide relief from many kinds of sudden calamities:

The cry of paternalism should not deter us from the discharge of a plain duty of government in case of great emergencies. It is not paternalism to protect the people against the sufferings of earthquakes and great fires. It is not paternalism to provide in so far

---

[65] Gaines Foster, "The Demands of Humanity: Army Medical Disaster Relief," (Washington, DC: Center of Military History, United States Army, 1983), 15.

[66] Howard Gillman, "Disaster Relief, 'Do Anything' Spending Powers, and the New Deal," *Law and History Review*, Summer 2005, available at: http://www.historycooperative.org/journals/lhr/23.2/gillman.html (accessed May 19, 2009); *Frothingham v. Mellon*, 262 U.S. 447 (1923). The case stands for the proposition that individual taxpayers have no standing to challenge the constitutionality of congressional spending because of article III limits to standing, not because of a consensus about the powers of Congress. Individual citizens who might have objected to Congress spending their tax dollars for disaster relief lacked standing to challenge the government's legislation.

as possible against the baneful fruits of war.... Paternalism is fostered often by the failure of government to exercise with wisdom and discretion the just and sane powers of government.[67]

But what was the root of those powers of government, and what were their limits? Advocates of price supports for cotton farmers cited congressional aid for disasters abroad as evidence that Congress could act for humanitarian purposes. These arguments failed to persuade a majority to provide price supports, but these same arguments would be deployed again for other disasters. Eventually, popular consensus would hold that the federal government had a duty to provide relief for disaster-stricken Americans for economic *and* humanitarian reasons.[68]

Despite the failure to secure price supports for Southern cotton farmers, the logic of ratcheting up of disaster relief was intact. All sides acknowledged that Congress could determine the meaning of "the general welfare," and therefore could decide what policies were in keeping with the Constitution. Princeton constitutional law professor Edward Corwin's claim in 1922 that "the General Welfare is what Congress finds it to be" sums up the conventional wisdom of the early twentieth century.[69]

Corwin's declaration echoes other post–Civil War statements that equate congressional deliberation about the general welfare with the will of the people and assume that the legislative product of such deliberation is constitutional. Consider this statement from Illinois Republican Joseph Cannon in support of relief following a flood on the Rio Grande in 1897: "In matters of this kind, involving the appropriation of money, Congress has unlimited power. Gentlemen on one side or the other may say that measures of this kind violate the Constitution; yet when we make an appropriation we are the judges of the propriety of the appropriation, and there is no power to withhold the money when it is appropriated."[70]

---

[67] Senator William Borah (D-Idaho), *Cong. Rec.*, 63d Cong, 1st sess., 1914, 51, pt. 16:1677. Also Dauber, *The Sympathetic State.*

[68] Dauber in *The Sympathetic State* argues that these cases constituted precedent for Congress to appropriate funds on humanitarian grounds to relieve suffering. There is some evidence for her view. For instance, in his 1935 law review article, McGuire discussed the citation of disaster relief appropriations in the Sugar Bounty cases and concluded that the Court had relinquished judicial review over appropriations decisions by Congress. O. R. McGuire, "The New Deal and the Public Money," *Georgetown Law Journal* 23 (1935): 155, 190. Similarly, in an article published the same year, Cathcart discussed the Sugar Bounty and *Butler* decisions and concluded that Congressional power to spend out of the general revenues, including for the "relief of human suffering" is essentially unlimited. Arthur Cathcart, "The Supreme Court and the New Deal," *Southern California Law Review* 9 (1935): 328–330.

[69] Cited widely, including in Charles Warren, *Congress as Santa Claus* (Charlottesville, VA: Michie Company, 1932), 142. Original: Edward Corwin, "The Spending Power of Congress – Apropos the Maternity Act," *Harvard Law Review* 36 (1922–1923): 548–582.

[70] Quoted in Dauber, *The Sympathetic State*, fn 5. *Cong. Rec.*, 55th Cong., 1st sess., pt. 2, 30 1897:1470.

By the dawn of the twentieth century, then, Congress assumed a central role in deciding what kind of aid to deliver for which disasters because of the legislature's constitutional duty to promote the general welfare. Throughout U.S. history, other branches of government have exercised authority based on normative claims to their centrality to the democratic process. Thomas Jefferson famously argued that the president alone can "command a view of the whole ground" because he alone is elected by all the people.[71] The Supreme Court claimed the authority to decide which legislation is constitutional based on the body's expertise and relative neutrality.[72] Arguments for bureaucratic authority ranged from Woodrow Wilson's claims for the value of scientific neutrality and administrative separation from politics to the more provocative claims of some administrative theorists that the bureaucracy is more representative of the public than elected branches of government and, therefore, more legitimate.[73] (Members of the bureaucracy, the argument goes, are more equally distributed among a range of economic classes, races, ethnicities, and genders than members of the elected branches.) In more recent times, some democratic theorists have argued that a market-based price system more accurately reflects the general welfare than legislative deliberation.[74] These last claims support efforts to privatize disaster response functions.

Claims for the authority of Congress (and later the president) to expand the disaster state eventually prevailed, but not necessarily because of their normative superiority. Rather, members of Congress and later presidents who pursued their reelection interests and looked for problems to solve on behalf of constituents were able to deploy new and increasingly available arguments for the federal government's authority to respond to and even prepare for disaster. Congress's authority to provide disaster relief existed from the first time the gavel struck, but at the beginning disaster relief was far from a central concern of the government. Political science scholars of Congress prefer to explain how members of Congress behave with reference to electoral incentives rather than rhetoric.[75] While members of Congress have many goals, assuming that they

[71] Thomas Jefferson, First Inaugural Address, March 4, 1801.

[72] John Hart Ely, *Democracy's Distrust, A Theory of Judicial Review* (Cambridge, MA: Harvard University Press, 1980).

[73] Woodrow Wilson, "The Study of Administration," November 1, 1886, available at: http://teachingamericanhistory.org/library/index.asp?document=465 (accessed December 10, 2012); J. D. Kingsley, *Representative Bureaucracy: An Interpretation of the British Civil Services* (Yellow Springs, OH: Antioch Press, 1944); Paul P. Van Riper, *History of the United States Civil Service* (White Plains, NY: Row Peterson, 1958).

[74] Stephen P. Croley, *Regulation and Public Interests: The Possibility of Good Regulatory Government* (Princeton, NJ: Princeton University Press, 2008); Bryan Caplan, *The Myth of the Rational Voter: Why Democracies Choose Bad Policies* (Princeton, NJ: Princeton University Press, 2007).

[75] I thank Barry Pump for his explanation of the incentive-based perspective. For a classic scholarly account, see Morris P. Fiorina, *Congress: Keystone of the Washington Establishment*, 2nd

want to win reelection above all else works reasonably well as a rule of thumb given that members who seek reelection will win reelection more often than those who do not. Using an incentive-based explanation, the president would not become involved in nineteenth-century disasters because there was little electoral incentive to do so. The president has a wide-angle lens, and unless the disaster was large enough or politically sensitive, the costs to federal government involvement in increased debt decrease the incentives for presidential involvement. Members of Congress, facing reelection by a local constituency, face the opposite pressures. As each member begins to understand his situation, there are incentives for a quid pro quo in which members allow aid packages to pass with the expectation that other members will do the same for them in the future. The electoral-incentive argument in its strongest form considers the expansion of the disaster state completely independent of rhetorical claims.

While acknowledging electoral incentives, a social (and political) construction argument recognizes how claims frame issues and make arguments available for future use. Arguments matter because they shape what politicians and citizens should expect from one another, and they can be taken up in the future in new and creative ways. As disasters receive more attention in the media, and as Americans expect more of their government, members of Congress face more pressure from citizens to do something – anything – in response to disaster. No reliable public opinion polls from the nineteenth century exist to gauge citizens' perceptions of the federal government's responsibility after disaster. Nevertheless, the gradual weakening of constitutional arguments against disaster relief and the increase in aid from Congress rather than other parts of government suggests that members of Congress pursuing their jobs, seeking new ways to deliver benefits for their constituents, has led to a gradual increase in disaster relief.

Framing the federal government's job as disaster relief rather than disaster prevention or mitigation shapes policy. Members of Congress claim credit for large aid packages after disasters while very rarely attempting to pass comprehensive legislation to prevent disaster. Over time, legislators are increasingly willing to offer relief following a major disaster, and even to expand the definition of disaster to encompass more kinds of events – a dynamic that gives rise to scholarly depictions of disaster policy as ad hoc and "event-driven."[76] The collective and inadvertent nature of disaster aid, far from following a plan, reflects the process of social construction rather than pure agency or deliberation in which members of government discuss an explicit policy change.

ed. (New Haven, CT: Yale University Press, 1989), 32–36; R. Douglas Arnold, *The Logic of Congressional Action* (New Haven, CT and London: Yale University Press, 1990).

[76] Thomas Birkland, *After Disaster: Agenda Setting, Public Policy, and Focusing Events* (Washington, DC: Georgetown University Press, 1997); Claire Rubin, ed., *Emergency Management: The American Experience 1900–2010* (Boca Raton, FL: Taylor & Francis, 2012).

FROM RESTORING CRITICAL FUNCTIONS TO DISASTER RELIEF

Putting the central focus of this book – disaster management in the twentieth century – in historical relief helps provide a truer account of the government's role in disaster relief than is found in the popular press or in general
interest scholarship. Whereas some critics portray disasters as constructed by
corporate profiteering, others describe disaster policy as event-driven, and still
others claim disaster aid is a distortion of constitutional government used for
short-term political advantage, none of these explanations provide the whole
truth.[77] This chapter shows that the federal government intervened after disaster from the beginning. The nature of the government's interventions was
driven by the claims of members of Congress and their constituents that the
government exists to preserve critical economic functions and, increasingly, to
provide relief for blameless victims of calamity.

What began as money to forgive debts, compensate individuals, or rebuild
critical national infrastructure was extended to become disaster relief owed
to citizens who were victims. While during the nineteenth century Congress
was the chief advocate for disaster relief, by the early twentieth century the
president began issuing orders for relief; Theodore Roosevelt's interventions
after the San Francisco earthquake are prime examples. The Civil War marked
a pause in the issuance of relief, but soon after relief continued apace, and a
nascent aid bureaucracy in the Freedman's Bureau foreshadowed relief agencies that would become more entrenched and self-assured in the twentieth century. The United States did not have a "disaster state" in the contemporary
sense of a bureaucracy populated by civil servants charged with administering
aid, but it did develop a nascent state in a softer version of the term – a set of
expectations and obligations for aid, usually funded by the federal government
and carried out by cabinet members, the military, nonprofits, and various existing programs for financial transfers to states and individuals. The period before
World War I was a period without a significant national-level bureaucracy and
without consensus that the national government existed to direct disaster preparation and relief.

---

[77] For example, Naomi Klein's *The Shock Doctrine: The Rise of Disaster Capitalism* (New York:
Picador, 2007) portrays disasters themselves as being constructed and manipulated by corporate
interests that profit from a close relationship with government in the disaster business. From
an opposite perspective, James Bovard claims that disaster aid and disaster organizations are
created for political advantage, and assumes that they are pathologies of contemporary government. See, for example, James Bovard, "FEMA Money! Come & Get It!," *The American
Spectator*, September, 1996, 24–31.

3

Civil Defense and the Foundations of Disaster Policy, 1914–1979

In contrast to the ad hoc responses of the nineteenth century, throughout the twentieth century the federal government created lasting programs to prepare ahead of time for real and imagined disasters. The twentieth century witnessed the beginning of a strange marriage between federal government's preparations for natural disasters and for attack from abroad. The union began in the period of the Springfield Rifle and World War I among hastily assembled domestic mobilization agencies. During World Wars I and II, the United States developed civil defense programs to prepare citizens for attacks from conventional, chemical, and biological weapons.[1] After World War II, these programs receded until the Korean War in 1950 and related developments in the Soviet Union and China. In civil defense, many of the same plans, policies, and organizations addressed both security threats and natural disasters, but it is not obvious why preparing for strategic bombing and nuclear war should have much to do with preparing for fires, floods, and hurricanes. Understanding the links among these scenarios requires understanding the emergence and surprising durability of civil defense agencies and programs.

---

[1] For examples of federal government assistance with civil defense manuals that offered advice for preparing for chemical and bomb attacks, see, for example, the *Civilian Defense Manual of Ohio State University*, Columbus, OH, November 1, 1942, 9–14. Truman disbanded the Office of Civilian Defense in 1945. Between 1945 and 1950, civil defense in the federal government was limited to planning efforts in the Office of Civil Defense Planning and the National Security Resources Board. A YouTube search produces footage from dozens of World War II films advising U.S. citizens how to protect themselves from poison gas. The films instruct viewers that household items, such as baking soda and bleach, can be used as a defense. This advice resembles homeland security advisories that instructed citizens to protect themselves with another household item – duct tape. For example, see "What to Do in A Gas Attack" (New York: Prelinger Archives, 1943), available at: http://www.archive.org/details/WhattoD01943 (accessed August 2, 2010).

The history of civil defense sheds light on how politics and world events shaped what counted as a disaster for which the national government bore responsibility. The locus of social and political construction during the civil defense period shifted from Congress to the bureaucracy to its executive, the president, who as commander-in-chief bore responsibility for national security. The threat of attack from abroad during two world wars and the lingering Cold War cast security threats, not wind and water, as the worst imaginable disasters. Citizens increasingly looked to the national government for guidance, and ambitious politicians and bureaucrats were eager to provide it.

Natural disaster preparations were subsumed under civil defense organizations at the national level first, and then states and localities followed. Politicians created federal programs to prepare for a Soviet attack, but state and local governments used some of these programs for their own purposes, to address problems ranging from social ills to floods and tornadoes. Hurricane-, earthquake-, fire-, and tornado-prone cities and counties pressured the federal government to allow civil defense programs to be used for protection against natural disasters. A shelter could just as easily protect citizens from a tornado or hurricane as from a bomb, and evacuation worked even better when given a few days warning about an impending hurricane than it did when given a few minutes to empty a city in the sights of a nuclear missile. But disputes over the place of civil defense and the role of the federal government were part of the social construction of what counted as a disaster for which the federal government bore responsibility. Because civil defense agencies had a high degree of goal ambiguity, presidents' national aims and state and local power were particularly important in shaping disaster management.

The civil defense period was a time of contests over the priority of security concerns versus disasters, but the period saw a clear increase in the role of the federal government. The Cold War's urgency and the patriotic fervor it spawned were turning points in breaking down deep-seated resistance to federal government intervention in disaster preparation and relief.

THE ROOTS OF CIVIL DEFENSE

The Cold War was its apogee, but civil defense originally grew out of much earlier threats from abroad.[2] After the poor performance of militia-style forces during the Spanish-American War, the U.S. Army's structure evolved toward a

---

[2] See Edward M. Coffman, *The Regulars, The American Army, 1989–1941* (Cambridge, MA: Belknap Press, 2004); for an account of early civil defense, see Thomas J. Kerr, *Civil Defense in the US, Band-Aid for a Holocaust?* (Boulder, CO: Westview Press, 1983), 10, 13. For the creation of a Council of National Defense charged with "coordinating resources and industries for national defense" and "stimulating civilian morale," see "Records of the Council of National Defense," National Archives, http://www.archives.gov/research/guide-fed-records/groups/062.html#62.1 (accessed July 8, 2010), Record Group 62, 1915–37.

more professionalized civil defense that was first tested during World War I.[3] After that war, the nation slid into an economic depression, and social welfare functions emerged as part of what was arguably the advent of combined civil defense and early disaster management.

During the Depression, politicians employed arguments about aid for disaster victims in new ways, and later they linked the provision of aid to civil defense organizations. Advocates for the New Deal claimed that the economic turmoil of the Depression was a disaster that merited relief just as Congress had provided relief to victims of fires, floods, and earthquakes in the past. The Depression as natural disaster, advocates argued, warranted the same effort as civil defense against a national security disaster. Historian Michele Landis Dauber describes how a narrative of disaster that portrayed blameless victims of random events helped advocates for revolutionary federal aid during the Depression appear to be not so revolutionary. Members of Congress such as the Republican (and later Progressive) Robert LaFollette paved the way by arguing that the devastation from hundreds of local droughts or spikes in unemployment added up to a collective crisis, the Depression, and that it was as much a disaster as other natural disasters. The cumulative effect of LaFollette's comments, along with those of other politicians and attorneys for President Franklin D. Roosevelt, led Solicitor General Stanley Reed to tell the Supreme Court in 1936 that the Depression was a disaster for which it could be "safely assumed" that federal relief was constitutional because of a history of precedent for federal government disaster relief.[4]

Roosevelt's shaping of the disaster state was not merely rhetorical, however. New Deal agencies were central in responding to floods in 1936 and 1937 and to the New England Hurricane of 1938. Responding to disasters and helping communities recover was a small but very real part of the mandate of many of these agencies. In 1933, President Roosevelt granted the Reconstruction Finance Corporation the "authority to provide loans for the repair and reconstruction of certain public facilities that had been damaged by earthquakes."[5]

---

[3] The Army Appropriations Act of 1916 authorized the president to create a National Council of Defense to mobilize the home front for war. William J. Breen, *Uncle Sam at Home: Civilian Mobilization, Wartime Federalism, and the Council of National Defense, 1917–1919* (Westport, CT: Greenwood Press, 1984).

[4] Michele Landis Dauber, "The Real Third Rail of American Politics," *Catastrophe: Law, Politics, and the Humanitarian Impulse*, edited by Austin Sarat and Javier Lezau (Amherst, MA: University of Massachusetts Press, 2009), 60–82; Michele Landis Dauber, "The Sympathetic State," *Law and History Review* 23 (2005): 387–442; Michele Landis, "Let Me Next Time Be 'Tried by Fire': Disaster Relief and the Origins of the American Welfare State, 1789–1874," *Northwestern Law Review* 92 (1998): 967–1034; Solicitor General's Notes for Oral Argument, 1936-October Term, B-C-2, Stanley Reed Papers, Solicitor General Series, Box 13, University of Kentucky Libraries, Lexington, Kentucky.

[5] Thomas E. Drabek, "The Evolution of Emergency Management," in *Emergency Management: Principles and Practice for Local Government*, edited by Thomas E. Drabek and Gerard J. Hoetmer (Washington, DC: International City Management Association, 1991), 3–29; 6–7.

Other disasters were later included within this authority. In 1934, the Bureau of Public Roads was given authority to provide grants to repair federal highways damaged by natural disasters. In 1936, Roosevelt signed the Flood Control Act, which granted the Army Corps of Engineers the authority to build dams, dikes, and levees to reduce vulnerability to floods.

In one of his most ambitious attempts to broaden the definition of security, Roosevelt created the Federal Security Agency in 1939, which centralized responsibility for an array of programs for health, education, and welfare, as well as domestic and international security.[6] Ultimately, however, preparations for war lifted security concerns to the top of security agencies' priorities and overcame broader attempts to fuse security and social welfare, as in the programs of the Federal Security Agency.

After the outbreak of World War II in Europe in 1939, President Roosevelt's executive order created the Office of Emergency Management, which included programs to coordinate preparations for attack on the United States. In 1941, Roosevelt created the Office of Civilian Defense, which included a Division of State and Local Cooperation housed in the executive branch and intended to encourage subnational governments to cooperate with civil defense aims.[7] Big-city mayors opposed the new division as a bottleneck and called for a new federal government civil defense agency to address local problems directly rather than work through fiscally strapped state governments.[8] To placate governors and mayors, the president appointed New York Mayor Fiorello LaGuardia as the first head of the Office of Civil Defense. In eight months, LaGuardia created thousands of local defense councils and programs to involve citizens as auxiliary police, air raid wardens, and medical staff. There was even a program for messengers sixteen to twenty-one years of age who carried news among civil defense organizations.[9] Total participation when LaGuardia departed was, by one estimate, 5,601,920 volunteers through 8,500 civil defense councils, but critics in the Roosevelt administration thought participation was not high enough and that LaGuardia neglected the social welfare function of civil defense promoted by Eleanor Roosevelt.[10] Little Flower, as he was known, both

---

[6] "WPA Expands Aid for Flooded Zone," *New York Times*, February 13, 1937, 28; Mariano-Florentino Cuéllar, "'Securing' the Nation: Law, Politics, and Organization at the Federal Security Agency, 1939–1953," *University of Chicago Law Review* 76 (2009): 587–717; Cuéllar, *Governing Security, The Hidden Origins of American Security Agencies* (Stanford, CA: Stanford University Press, 2013).

[7] Kerr, *Civil Defense in the US*, 13.

[8] Elwyn A. Mauck, "Civilian Defense in the United States: 1940–1945" (Unpublished manuscript by the Historical Officer of the Office of Civilian Defense, July 1946), 55; Augustin M. Prentiss, *Civil Air Defense* (New York: McGraw Hill, 1941).

[9] *A Handbook for Fire Watchers* (Washington, DC: United States Office of Civil Defense, 1941).

[10] V. R. Cardoszier, *The Mobilization of the United States in World War II: How the Government, Military, and Industry Prepared for War* (Jefferson, NC: McFarland, 1995), 185; Keith E. Eiler, *Mobilizing America: Robert P. Patterson and the War Effort, 1940–1945* (Ithaca, NY: Cornell University Press, 1997); Elwyn A. Mauck, "Civilian Defense in the United States: 1940–1945"

because Fiorello is Italian for "little flower" and because he stood only five feet tall, also drew criticism for dealing directly with mayors and city governments and bypassing state offices.[11]

Eleanor Roosevelt, who held a position in the Office of Civilian Defense (OCD), sometimes clashed with LaGuardia's views by emphasizing the welfare possibilities of her office. She maintained that "better nutrition, better housing, better day-by-day medical care, better education, better recreation for every age" should be part of civil and national defense, as she told a radio audience.[12] Social welfare, in this view, went beyond helping the poor to encompass home front morale, recreation, health, and civic participation. Like LaGuardia, she drew complaints from politicians for bypassing state offices. The loudest public complaints, however, came after a scandal.

Mrs. Roosevelt hired two friends from the entertainment industry to work in the OCD, actor Melvyn Douglas and dancer Mayris Chaney, who had charmed the first lady by naming a dance after her, the Eleanor Glide. Someone in the OCD, perhaps a LaGuardia partisan, provided Congress with information about Douglas and Chaney. A member of Congress then complained that the renowned General Douglas MacArthur's salary was the same as Melvyn Douglas, and yet no one could figure out what the actor was contributing to the defense of the nation, while the other Douglas was busy fighting the war. The OCD issued half-hearted explanations about Chaney's value to the nation in teaching physical fitness, but the media frenzy surrounded the OCD, and Chaney and Douglas resigned. Mrs. Roosevelt's resignation followed soon after the scandal in 1942 as wartime concerns eclipsed economic worries.[13]

LaGuardia had left his position just before Mrs. Roosevelt, replaced by outspoken New Dealer James Landis, who created the Civil Defense Corps, which recruited 10 million volunteers by the end of 1943.[14] Over the next two years, volunteers engaged in blackout drills by covering streetlights, learned basic emergency techniques, and practiced cleaning up chemical spills. As the war progressed, public support for civil defense grew along with the number of volunteers. At the same time, however, some members of Congress believed that the OCD should turn all of its protective duties over to the Army. The War Department, occupied with the war abroad, rebuffed these efforts by establishing the Civilian Defense Board (formally created through presidential executive order 9134) to advise government civil defense activities.[15] Meanwhile, a

---

(Unpublished manuscript by the Historical Officer of the Office of Civilian Defense, July 1946), 13–14.

[11] Robert Earnest Miller, "The War That Never Came: Civilian Defense, Mobilization, and Morale During World War II" (Ph.D. diss., University of Cincinnati, 1991), 82–94.

[12] Joseph P. Lash, *Eleanor and Franklin* (New York: W.W. Norton & Company, 1971), 842.

[13] Miller, "The War That Never Came," 93–162; Thomas Fleming, *The New Dealers' War: FDR and the War within World War II* (New York: Basic Books, 2001), 104–107.

[14] Kerr, *Civil Defense in the US*, 13.

[15] Stetson Conn, Rose Engelman, and Byron Fairchild, *Guarding the United States and Its Outposts* (Washington, DC: Center of Military History: The United States Army, 2000).

nongovernmental organization, the American Legion, campaigned for a robust civil defense to mobilize civilians and increase industrial production. The American Legion proposed that FDR designate the organization to lead civil defense, but the president refused, convinced that civil defense was an inherently governmental police power and not merely propaganda.[16] During World War II, civilian defense meant participating in blackout drills, refugee relief, and conserving resources. Wartime civil defense, however, was never put to a truly serious test in the United States, and planners never solved the problem of how to provide accurate, specific, and timely advice to localities in the event of a strike.[17] Civil defense was seen by many, including President Harry Truman, as a wartime function, and not intended to remain postwar. Therefore, postwar civil defense assumed a character distinct from its wartime manifestation. FDR created the Office of *Civilian* Defense in 1941, and during World War II people continued to use the term "civilian." After the war, however, planners switched to "civil" defense, specifically in 1946 with the Provost Marshal General's Study 3B-1, Defense Against Enemy Action Directed at Civilians. The term "civil" emphasizes the protection of people, the economy, and government, not just the citizenry.[18]

Efforts during World War II laid the foundation, but civil defense programs that emerged during the Cold War were more far-reaching and more deeply institutionalized than those of earlier eras because of two elements: the fear of nuclear war and the deteriorating relationship between the United States and the Soviet Union. The first element, fear, was especially palpable during the early years. The 1950s are remembered in popular culture as a decade of American innocence and consumer culture – cars with fins, soda fountains, and sock hops. But this was also a period of anxiety and fear of Armageddon. The problem of preventing or recovering from nuclear war generated consequences far beyond the field of national security.[19] Imagining how to prepare for war required fixing into place governmental structures that increased the role of the federal government in directing subnational governments and the public. As for the second element, the Soviet nuclear and conventional attack threat was potentially more destructive than the threat to the domestic United States posed by Germany or Japan during World War II. A robust civil defense program appeared to be a strategic necessity during

[16] B. Franklin Cooling, "US Army Support of Civil Defense: The Formative Years," *Military Affairs* 35 (February 1971), 7–11; 8.

[17] Cooling, "US Army Support of Civil Defense: The Formative Years," 7–11.

[18] Lyon G. Tyler, Jr., "Civil Defense: The Impact of the Planning Years, 1945–1950" (Ph.D. diss., Duke University, Durham, NC, 1967).

[19] Aaron Wildavsky, "Practical Consequences of the Theoretical Study of Defense Policy," *Public Administration Review* 25 (March 1965), 90–103; 90; Bruce Kuklick, *Blind Oracles: Intellectuals and War from Kennan to Kissinger* (Princeton, NJ: Princeton University Press, 2006); John Lukacs, *George Kennan: A Study of Character* (New Haven, CT: Yale University Press, 2007).

the Cold War, even though the most ambitious civil defense plans were never fully implemented.

EXPERT STUDIES AND THE CREATION OF CIVIL DEFENSE AGENCIES

The justification for a national civil defense effort lies in the U.S. Strategic Bombing Surveys (USSBS). These reports, first released in 1945, examined the Allied air war against Germany and Japan during World War II.[20] President Roosevelt commissioned the 200-volume studies, which drew on the efforts of 1,150 civilians, officers, and enlisted men. The military delegated leadership of the studies to Wall Street finance executives and professors recruited for their lack of preconceived notions about air power.[21] Among other findings, the studies concluded that some famous, bloody battles were less effective in weakening Germany than more targeted attacks on energy production facilities.[22] The survey led to a recommendation to reduce fire bombing and strategically target critical infrastructure such as energy and transportation hubs. The recommendation had implications for civil defense: protect critical infrastructure and, eventually, prepare for large geographic devastation, given that nuclear weapons lacked precision targeting.[23]

War department study groups used the Bombing Survey to plan for reorganizing the defense establishment and concluded that a consolidated civil defense program at the national level was even more important in a nuclear age for building morale in a war effort, reducing damage, and persuading the enemy of the country's seriousness about war.[24] Subsequent studies reinforced the conclusions of the survey. The most influential of these, the Bull Board, led

---

[20] The studies have stood the test of time. For example, the authors of the 1992 Gulf War Airpower Survey took the studies "as their standard." Rebecca Grant, "The Long Arm of the US Strategic Bombing Survey," *Air Force Magazine* (February 2008), 64–67; 64; *The Effects of Atomic Bombs on Hiroshima and Nagasaki, United States Strategic Bombing Survey* (Washington, DC: Government Printing Office, 1946), available at: http://www.ibiblio.org/hyperwar/AAF/USSBS/AtomicEffects/index.html (accessed September 9, 2010).

[21] Nehemiah Jordan, *US Civil Defense Before 1950: The Roots of Public Law 920*, Study S-212, Washington, DC, May 1966, 56–57.

[22] Grant, "The Long Arm of the US Strategic Bombing Survey," 66.

[23] Nitze and others made the unlikely assumption that that the United States could fight and win a limited nuclear war; if attacked, the Soviets planned an all-out response. Nicholas Thompson, *The Hawk and the Dove: Paul Nitze, George Kennan, and the History of the Cold War* (New York: Henry Holt, 2009).

[24] "Under the assumptions of 'total war,' every individual throughout the nation must be trained in the principles of civil defense." From an influential study group, in a study dated June 30, 1945, from the War Department's Provost Marshal General, PMG 3B-1 study (Provost Marshal General, "Defense against Enemy Action Directed at Civilians," Study 3B-1, April 30, 1946, copy in General Reference Branch Library, Office, Chief of Military History, Department of the Army, Washington, DC). The Strategic Bombing Survey showed that repeated bombings of Germany did not greatly reduce workers' morale (which led to the peak of German fighter plane production coming in November 1944, much later than is popularly assumed). Civil defense efforts appear to improve the morale of the country being defended, however.

by Major General Harold Bull, met from 1946 until 1948. It heard approximately sixty witnesses and reviewed documents from the wartime experiences of Great Britain, Germany, and Japan. The Board's report concluded: "It is apparent, in retrospect, that civil defense organization, in spite of the noteworthy patriotic response of the civilian volunteers, was inadequate to cope with a heavy attack."[25] The report proposed creating a permanent national-level agency to plan for civil defense.

The Bull Board concluded that civil defense is the responsibility of civilian authorities, but that the military should be involved.[26] The report's publication in 1948 sparked a reaction among government officials. Military planners feared that civilians would want the military to take over all civil defense but concluded that it was in the military's best interest to keep civil affairs at arm's length for fear of the budgetary impact and the danger that civil defense would sap combat effectiveness.[27] The military did continue to be involved in civil defense and later emergency management and homeland security, but it also continued to insist that ultimate responsibility for these functions rest with civilian agencies such as state and local departments of civil defense and emergency management, the National Guard, and local emergency services. Military leaders believed that the armed services were organized to fight wars abroad, not engage in something as amorphous as civil defense at home. The military's refusal to sit atop a civil defense and disaster management hierarchy (as found in other countries) contributed to the decentralized character of emergency management in the United States. The military would offer much-needed resources and logistical support during crisis, but it would not take responsibility for disaster preparation or response. Instead, civilian agencies much smaller and weaker than the Department of Defense would be blamed for the government's shortcomings in preparing for disaster.

The Bull Board also reinforced the notion that if it was to be effective, civil defense had to be led from Washington, DC. The Board's report concluded that "adherence to the principle of States' rights and traditional municipal individuality" had hindered civil defense in World War II.[28] The Board heard from experts who stressed the need to preserve a role for states in order to achieve

---

[25] Office of the Secretary of Defense, Press Release Number 15-48, for morning papers of February 15, 1948. Quoted in Charles Fairman, "The President as Commander-in-Chief," *The Journal of Politics* 11 (February 1949): 145–170; 159.

[26] Kerr, *Civil Defense in the US*, 21, available at: http://www.openwifinyc.com/classic/freewifi-hotspot.php?id=190 (accessed September 9, 2010); National Military Establishment, Office of Secretary of Defense, Study of Civil Defense (Bull Board Report), Washington, 1948, 7.

[27] Tyler, Jr., "Civil Defense," 241–284; Stephen J. Collier and Andrew Lakoff, "Distributed Preparedness: The Spatial Logic of Domestic Security in the United States," *Environment and Planning D: Society and Space* 26 (2008): 7–28.

[28] Cited in Charles Fairman, "Government Under Law in Time of Crisis," in *Government Under Law*, edited by Arthur E. Sutherland (Cambridge, MA: Harvard University Press, 1956), 249; original is *A Study of Civil Defense* (Washington, DC: The Office of the Secretary of Defense), 9.

buy-in from governors and mayors, but the thrust of the Board's report was greater consolidation in the federal government.[29]

The position of the postwar National Guard epitomized the partially decentralized, partially nationalized, push-and-pull character of disaster federalism. The Guard responded to natural disasters at the request of state governors, but the president could also assign it to overseas military service or domestic security.[30] In 1957, President Dwight Eisenhower federalized the Arkansas National Guard to provide protection for African-American children entering Little Rock Central High School.

The paradox of postwar civil defense planning was that the creation of federal civil defense programs expanded the authority of states and localities to implement them. The Bull Board recommended using states as organizing structures, finding that "the state government must accept the responsibility of civil defense for its people and communities." At the same time, the General's Board recognized that "the great burden of operation falls on the civilian communities."[31] The Board recommended a system based on the experience of World War II to confront a range of uncertain emergencies in the future. The civil defense and emergency management system would evolve through fits and starts, built on tension between state prerogatives that prevented national standardization and a lack of commitment from the national government to the civil defense and disaster management enterprise.

The Bull Board also laid the foundation for thinking about civil defense and emergency management in terms of periods in time. It concluded that civil defense consisted of two periods: pre-attack, which involved mobilization and planning, and post-attack, which involved recovery and restoration. The same pre- and post-event thinking undergirded emergency management, whose playbook was drawn from the earliest civil defense documents. Conceptualizing disaster in terms of periods on a time line offers the benefits of specialization by placing experts with relevant information about each time period close to one another. When reified, however, the time line neglects the interconnectedness of each period. For example, mitigation – or efforts to reduce the damage caused by disasters – is both a pre- and post-event activity.

Along with the Strategic Bombing Survey and the Bull report, the Hopley report stands as the third leg of the stool of the conceptual foundation for civil defense and emergency management. An ambitious plan published in 1948 and written by the first director of the Office of Civil Defense Planning, the Hopley report emphasized the importance of state and local offices in public communication: "How to allay fears and control the panic that could come with attacks

[29] Benet D. Gellman, "Planning for a National Nuclear Emergency: The Organization of Government and Federal- State Relations," *Virginia Law Review* 52 (April 1966): 435–462; 448.

[30] Norman Beckman, "Limiting State Involvement in Foreign Policy: The Governors and the National Guard in Perpich v. Defense," *Publius* 21 (1991): 109–123.

[31] Quoted in Charles Fairman, "The President as Commander-in-Chief," *The Journal of Politics* 11 (February 1949): 145–170.

by modern weapons, and yet to keep the public informed on the dangers and the means of protecting against them – these are the basic functions requiring the attention in Civil Defense organizations not only in the national office but in the state and local organizations."[32] President Truman refused to officially endorse the Hopley report, but its ideas lingered and formed the foundation for postwar civil defense thinking. National-level governing documents recognized that state and local offices were important, but the authoritative civil defense plans did not specify what precisely they were to do.

While the federal authorities pushed civil defense requirements to state and local governments, some localities pulled in federal involvement because they wanted assistance with a nebulous threat of nuclear attack that was outside their control. After a civilian bombing campaign in Europe and fear of attacks in the United States, LaGuardia wrote a letter to President Franklin Roosevelt, stating:

There is a need for a strong Federal Department to coordinate activities, and not only to coordinate but to initiate and get things going. Please bear in mind that up to this war and never in our history has the civilian population been exposed to attack. The new technique of war has created the necessity for developing new techniques of civilian defense.[33]

LaGuardia's plea was hyperbole – it omitted the Civil War – but it is characteristic of letters sent by mayors and governors. State and local leaders requested federal government involvement in civil defense, and they would request more federal government involvement during the 1970s, which led to the creation of FEMA.

The tension among state and local offices between social welfare and militaristic functions that first emerged during World War II continued during the Cold War. Some civil defense organizations at the local level engaged communities through art, community gatherings, and health assistance. LaGuardia, who became director of the OCD, called these local nonprotective functions "sissy stuff," and instead wanted to build neighborhood militias.[34] Politicians who opposed the OCD's social welfare programs called it "pink" and complained that the country needed bombers, not dancers and social programs.[35]

---

[32] Office of Civil Defense Planning, *Civil Defense for National Security (Report to the Secretary of Defense)* (Washington, DC: OCDP, National Military Establishment, October 1, 1948), 13. (Known as the Hopley Report.); Tyler, Jr., "Civil Defense," 117–161.

[33] Elwyn A. Mauck, *Civilian Defense in the United States, 1940–1945* (Unpublished manuscript by the Historical Officer of the Office of Civilian Defense, July 1946), 55.

[34] Laura McEnaney, *"Civil Defense Begins at Home": Militarization Meets Everyday Life in the Fifties* (Princeton, NJ: Princeton University Press, 2000), 17; Julia Siebel, "Soldiers on the Homefront," in *Franklin D. Roosevelt and the Formation of the Modern World*, edited by Thomas Howard and William Pederson (Armonk, NY: M.E. Sharpe, 2003), 172; Elwyn A. Mauck, "History of Civil Defense in the United States," *Bulletin of Atomic Scientists* 6 (August 1950): 268–269.

[35] Kerr, *Civil Defense in the US*, 16–17.

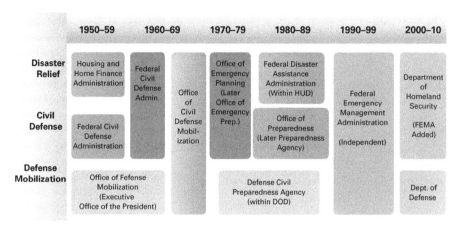

	1950–59	1960–69	1970–79	1980–89	1990–99	2000–10
Disaster Relief	Housing and Home Finance Administration	Federal Civil Defense Admin.	Office of Civil Defense Mobil-ization	Office of Emergency Planning (Later Office of Emergency Prep.)	Federal Disaster Assistance Administration (Within HUD)	Federal Emergency Management Administration (Independent)	Department of Homeland Security
Civil Defense	Federal Civil Defense Administration				Office of Preparedness (Later Preparedness Agency)		(FEMA Added)
Defense Mobilization	Office of Fefense Mobilization (Executive Office of the President)			Defense Civil Preparedness Agency (within DOD)		Dept. of Defense

FIGURE 3.1. Organization of Federal Disaster Functions, 1950–2010.
Source: Adapted from National Research Council, *Facing Hazards and Disasters: Understanding Human Dimensions* (Washington, DC: National Academy Press, 2006), 51.

Eleanor Roosevelt, the object of some of the criticism, believed that social welfare needs were more urgent than defense against attack. Proponents of social welfare functions of the OCD thought that the federal government's amped up civil defense capacity was a waste when it sat dormant waiting for an uncertain event. Mrs. Roosevelt led the social welfare functions of the OCD's neighborhood volunteers, and she helped nominate LaGuardia's successor, James Landis, who was more sympathetic to the office's social welfare functions.[36] Newer social programs challenged core defense tasks, and bureaucrats and politicians who favored the latter were determined to limit new missions.

In addition to the tension between security and social welfare, policy makers debated how long civil defense organizations should last. Landis recommended that the OCD, which he directed, be only temporary and be abolished at the end of the war.[37] Contrary to popular belief, federal agencies are not immortal. Of agencies in existence from 1946 to 1997, 62 percent were terminated, usually after shifts in party control of the White House and Congress.[38] As Figure 3.1 shows, civil defense agencies expired, too, but the federal government's role in preparing for attack and disaster remained once it became institutionalized in defense strategy and federal-state-local relations.

[36] Doris Kearns Goodwin, *No Ordinary Time* (New York: Simon & Schuster 1995), 326–345.
[37] Kerr, *Civil Defense in the US*, 18.
[38] David Lewis, "The Politics of Agency Termination: Confronting the Myth of Agency Immortality," *Journal of Politics* 64 (2002): 89–107.

The tensions between militaristic and non-militaristic civil defense functions, combined with debates about the permanence of civil defense organizations, constrained the development of centralized, top-down civil defense (and later emergency management). Civil defense lacked clear and lasting agreement about what its mission should be. With limited federal government involvement after World War II, the basic principle was self-help. The federal government provided infrastructure – shelters, stockpiles, warning systems, support for fire-fighting and rescue training – and individuals planned for themselves and their families. Self-help suited the American tradition of limited government as well as a federal government that was unwilling to shift massive resources from offensive preparations for war to defensive measures.[39]

THE STATE PUSH AND FEDERAL PULL RELATIONSHIP
OF DISASTER FEDERALISM

Structurally, early civil defense documents created a national government authority to issue preparedness plans, but not a large bureaucracy to implement them.[40] Implementation depended on state and local officials who were more concerned with the threats for which they bore responsibility: fires, floods, hurricanes, tornadoes, and industrial accidents that occur in every jurisdiction.[41] In order to win state and local cooperation, federal authorities allowed regional civil defense organizations to prepare for natural disasters while also preparing for a nuclear attack.[42]

The federal government also recognized the need for greater coordination after disaster. The Disaster Relief Act of 1950 marked a shift in the federal government's legal authority. The Act replaced ad hoc, event-specific aid packages with general law governing who in the federal government was to distribute relief and how they were to do it. The underlying idea behind the Act was to supplement, not supplant state and local resources. Thus, the Act provided that relief funds would be sent only to state and local governments, not to individuals. Meanwhile, the Red Cross continued to manage relief efforts directed toward private citizens and businesses. The Act also formalized the president's broad, discretionary authority to declare what constituted a disaster eligible for federal aid.[43]

[39] Aaron Friedberg, *In the Shadow of the Garrison State: America's Anti-Statism and Its Cold War Grand Strategy* (Princeton, NJ: Princeton University Press, 2000), 245–296.
[40] "U.S. Civil Defense" (Washington, DC: National Security Resources Board, 1950).
[41] Wayne Blanchard, "American Civil Defense 1945–1975" (PhD diss., University of Virginia, 1980).
[42] E. L. Quarantelli, "Disaster Planning, Emergency Management and Civil Protection: The Historical Development of Organized Efforts to Plan for and Respond to Disasters," *Preliminary Paper* (Newark, DE: University of Delaware Disaster Research Center, University of Delaware, 2000), 1–33. Copy on file with author. Earlier 1998 version available here: http://dspace.udel.edu:8080/dspace/bitstream/handle/19716/635/PP227.pdf?sequence=1 (accessed February 8, 2013).
[43] Birkland, *After Disaster*, 49.

The federal government expanded the authority of the 1950 Act piecemeal. For example, the 1951 Kansas-Missouri floods led Congress to authorize funds to provide emergency housing for victims.[44] After Hurricane Diane in 1955, the Federal Civil Defense Administration began to coordinate assistance to states to cope with flooding.[45] Federal money and oversight gradually institutionalized emergency management functions at the state and local level that before the 1950 Act were performed ad hoc.[46] With federal money came federal regulations, and the central government began to prescribe how to organize local disaster functions.

Natural disaster management and defense against attack were incorporated into federal government organizations in related but distinct ways. The federal government expanded piecemeal natural disaster programs in the 1940s and 1950s, such as levee construction and forest management, and it created the category "federal disaster area" to designate regions eligible for relief funds. Programs to prepare for response and relief at the federal level were limited during the 1950s, however, while programs at the state and local level endured – as did federal preparation for nuclear attack.[47]

In some cases, local governments wanted more civil defense than the federal government was capable of delivering. For example, local organizations in New Jersey sent a deluge of requests to Governor Alfred Driscoll for federal civil defense help to train watchmen, exercise leaders, and other civil defenders. During the Korean War, the federal government received a spike in inquiries from communities seeking to begin their own civil defense organizations.[48]

---

[44] David Moss, "Courting Disaster? The Transformation of Federal Disaster Policy since 1803," *The Financing of Catastrophe Risk*, edited by Kenneth A. Froot (Chicago: University of Chicago Press, 1999), 307–362; 315.

[45] Arthur S. Fleming, "The Impact of Disasters on Readiness for War," *The ANNALS of the American Academy of Political and Social Science* 309 (1957): 65–70.

[46] "At the national level, a civil defense system developed earlier than any comparable disaster planning or emergency management system. However, at the local level, the prime concern after World War II became to prepare for and respond to disasters." Quarantelli, "Disaster Planning, Emergency Management and Civil Protection 1–33." Also see Claire B. Rubin, "Local Emergency Management: Overview of its Origins and Evolution," in *Emergency Management: Principles and Practice for Local Government*, edited by William Waugh and Kathleen Tierney (Washington, DC: International City/County Management Association, 2007), 25–38; Peter J. May and Walter Williams, *Disaster Policy Implementation: Managing Programs under Shared Governance* (New York: Plenum Press, 1986); Peter J. May, *Recovering from Catastrophes: Federal Disaster Relief Policy and Politics* (Westport, CT: Greenwood Press, 1985); National Research Council, Committee on Disaster Research in the Social Sciences, *Facing Hazards and Disasters: Understanding Human Dimensions* (Washington, DC: National Academies Press, 2006).

[47] Quarantelli, "Disaster Planning, Emergency Management and Civil Protection" 10, 14, 18; William Waugh, Jr., "Terrorism, Homeland Security, and the National Emergency Management Network," *Public Organization Review* 3 (2003): 373–385.

[48] National Archives, Records Group 304, Office of Civil Defense Mobilization, box 5, civil defense comments and queries file.

There is evidence of substantial enthusiasm on the part of localities in these early days of civil defense, but it is hard to measure the extent of the enthusiasm precisely. At a minimum, political scientist Andrew Grossman writes, "The willingness of local communities to mobilize in the late 1940s and early 1950s is a rare example, in American history at least, of the local community demanding more from a federal line agency than it could quickly deliver."[49]

WHAT CIVIL DEFENSE MEANT IN PRACTICAL TERMS

Although civil defense began earlier, many associate it with the Cold War.[50] The most prominent of an alphabet soup of agencies in this period was the Federal Civil Defense Administration (FCDA), created in 1951, which consolidated functions of wartime civil defense agencies (see Figure 3.1). In addition to shelters, the FCDA sponsored local civil defense organizations, worked with public schools to distribute educational materials and syllabi, and used a warden-and-spotter system to mobilize communities. By the end of 1952, the FCDA had sponsored civil defense training in 87.4 percent of all elementary schools.[51] The warden program generated solidarity around civil defense and engendered a mix of fear and protection in communities. Some wardens were paid while others were volunteers, but all were civil defenders. They were generally businessmen, housewives, or emergency services personnel rather than the former military officers that led most civil defense agencies, but their local knowledge was invaluable to implementing civil defense.

Meanwhile, the spotter system, or Ground Observers Corps, was a joint FCDA and Department of Defense effort to enlist volunteers to watch for invading aircraft.[52] The federal government encouraged these programs, but they grew mainly through the efforts of state and local governments, the practical men and women who staffed civil defense agencies, and citizens who responded to the call of duty. To take one relatively obscure example, Montana Governor John W. Bonner called for "at least 4000 patriotic Montanans" to man spotting stations around the clock to record potential enemy aircraft flights that might be missed by radar.[53] By 1951, approximately 750–1,000 Montanans had volunteered. In New Jersey, more than 50,000 people had enrolled as wardens by 1952.[54] Commercial and private flights overhead kept spotters busy, but the programs did not produce a single confirmed sighting of a Soviet flight.

[49] Andrew Grossman, *Neither Dead Nor Red: Civil Defense and American Political Development during the Early Cold War* (New York: Routledge, 2001), 70.
[50] Spencer R. Weart, *Nuclear Fear* (Cambridge, MA: Harvard University Press, 1989).
[51] Grossman, *Neither Dead Nor Red*, 81; *FCDA Annual Report for 1952* (Washington, DC: GPO, 1952), 66.
[52] L. C. Guthman, ed., *Warplane Spotter's Manual* (Washington, DC: GPO, 1943); Kenton Clymer, "U.S. Homeland Defense in the 1950s: The origins of the Ground Observer Corps," *Journal of Military History* 75 (July 2011): 835–859.
[53] "Plane Spotter Need Stressed," *The Spokesman-Review*, August 31, 1951, A18.
[54] Grossman, *Neither Dead Nor Red*, 81.

Beyond the volunteer realm, universities maintained a symbiotic relationship with civil defense through sponsored research. Major foundations, including Rockefeller, Carnegie, Russell Sage, and Paul Lazarsfeld's Bureau of Applied Social Research at Columbia, received grants for various domestic security projects from the FCDA.[55] In the private sector, the FCDA funded a remarkably effective advertising campaign through the Ad Council that employed cutting-edge marketing techniques.[56] The agency developed the "Duck and Cover" film in 1951, in which "Bert the Turtle" and singing schoolchildren from New York advise that nuclear war could happen at any time without warning, and the citizens should be mindful and be prepared to "duck and cover." The agency also promoted civil defense volunteers in the homefront with the progressive claim that "the categories open to women volunteers run across the whole field of operational services" – an idea that was in tension with the social norms in more conservative states and localities.[57]

Legislation supported this arrangement of national coordination and state and local implementation. The Civil Defense Act of 1950 provided that the FCDA would spur participation and coordinate local programs only loosely. The Civil Defense Act, passed during the Korean War, provided that states have primary responsibility for civil defense. Section 201(i) of the law mandated that the federal government's contribution would not be used for state and local personnel or equipment, meaning that states and localities would shoulder most of the financial burden for civil defense.[58] The Act encouraged states to use interstate compacts for civil defense problems that extended across state lines. The reliance on interstate compacts persisted through 1955, when the FCDA reasoned in its 1955 Annual Statistical Report that "the interstate compact was considered necessary by the Congress to avoid Federal centralization of civil defense operations which might result if each State could operate in civil defense matters only as a separate entity."[59] Whether civil defenders could respond to natural disasters was up to the states. By 1955, thirty-nine states and the District of Columbia permitted dual use, which is the use of civil defense plans, personnel, and equipment to prepare for attack and for natural disasters. (The term "dual use" did not become widespread until the Defense Civil Preparedness Agency adopted it in the 1970s, however.) The goal of civil defense was ambiguous to begin with: was it to protect Americans

---

[55] Christopher Simpson, *Science of Coercion: Communication Research and Psychological Warfare, 1945–1960* (New York: Oxford University Press, 1994), 4.

[56] Grossman, *Neither Dead Nor Red*, 79–80; "Preliminary Report on Public Attitudes towards Civil Defense," Survey Research Center, University of Michigan, 1951.

[57] Federal Civil Defense Administration, "Women Expected to Form Major Part of CD Force," *The Civil Defense Alert*, April 1952, 2.

[58] Wilbur J. Cohen and Evelyn F. Boyer, "Federal Civil Defense Act of 1950: Summary and Legislative History," *Social Security Bulletin* (April 1951): 11–16; 14.

[59] Federal Civil Defense Administration, "Annual Statistical Report," Battle Creek, Michigan, June 30, 1955, available at: http://training.fema.gov/EMIWeb/edu/docs/HistoricalInterest/FCDA1955AnnualStatisticalReport.pdf (accessed May 27, 2010).

from nuclear attack, an impossible goal, or to project an image of confidence and seriousness about war preparations to the Soviet Union? The true aims were never clear, although policy makers' confidence in civil defense's defensive capabilities waned over time. Dual use added another layer of goal ambiguity, because civil defense could be aimed at the wildly different threats of nuclear war and more routine threats such as tornadoes and floods.

A closer look at one city's civil defense office shows how national government military planning and local neighborhood organizations sometimes clashed. While states and localities bore the brunt of civil defense duties, the local leaders of civil defense organizations often had national-level military experience. General Norman D. Cota, the first executive director of the Philadelphia Civil Defense Council, was an archetypal civil defender.[60] If governors and mayors assumed that people would panic and that disaster bred chaos, military officers offered a sense of order and control.[61] Like other early civil defenders who were celebrated as war heroes, General Cota served in World War II and was assistant division commander of the 29th Infantry at Normandy on D-Day. Cota landed on Omaha Beach and, according to legend, he quickly realized the danger Americans faced and led the landing party to safety. Cota's leadership was memorialized in the 1962 film, *The Longest Day*. He retired from the Army at the war's end as major general and settled in Philadelphia and became director of the Philadelphia office of the War Assets Administration, an agency responsible for army surplus goods. The agency's work ended by 1948, however, and two years later Cota was offered the job of executive director for civil defense in Philadelphia, then the nation's third-largest city.

The opportunity arose for Cota because civil defense plans devolved implementation to localities. The FCDA created planning requirements, and governors developed civil defense plans for their states.[62] Pennsylvania Governor James Duff created a civil defense office in 1950 to build air raid sirens and recruit volunteers to watch for suspicious aircraft. The governor left local planning to counties, and because Philadelphia's county is coterminous with the city, the mayor created a civil defense office with a $500,000 initial appropriation from the city council.

Like other civil defenders, Cota took the threat of foreign attack seriously. During World War II, the federal OCD had developed programs for a range of hazards, including social ills. Cota's office, however, like most of the civil

[60] The case of Cota is reported in Scott Knowles's excellent account of Philadelphia's civil defense program. Scott Gabriel Knowles, "Defending Philadelphia: A Historical Case Study of Civil Defense in the Early Cold War," *Public Works Management & Policy* 11 (January 2007): 1–16. Also see Scott Knowles, *The Disaster Experts: Mastering Risk in Modern America* (Philadelphia: University of Pennsylvania Press, 2011).
[61] Russell Dynes, "Community Emergency Planning: False Assumptions and Inappropriate Analogies," *International Journal of Mass Emergencies and Disasters* 12 (1994): 141–158.
[62] Kerr, *Civil Defense in the US*, 1–28.

defense offices staffed by former military offices, carried these programs into peacetime. Cota explained his initial plans for civil defense:

Now, here in Philadelphia we had to act, we couldn't wait for the formulation of an overall planning by the Government nor by the State. We had to do first things first, or at least we had to begin to do first things first, and we had to establish an efficient Air Raid Warning System. Certainly if you cannot get the warning, all your other problems don't amount to very much. Secondly, we had to organize a sound Civil Defense organization with necessary control and communication facilities.... Third, we had to put in effect a thorough and sound training program based on sound warden organization, and number four, we had to introduce a modest training program [with] the auxiliary police and auxiliary fire organization, trained to control traffic and fight fires, and also to guard against the destruction of vital property, and lastly, we had to have a foresighted plan for the future.[63]

In Philadelphia, as elsewhere, the heart of local civil defense were wardens who organized neighborhoods, planned evacuations, recruited volunteers, and knew the geographies and peculiarities of the areas they were responsible for. While the warden system was surprisingly large compared with public participation in contemporary homeland security programs, it was much smaller than civil defense agencies had hoped. In Philadelphia's Region 1, only 417 of the 12,000 wardens that were planned for had signed on by 1952. The numbers were similar for other regions and for the auxiliary fire and police units that were part of local civil defense.

Cota resigned from the Philadelphia office in 1952 because of management challenges in organizing what amounted to local militias during peacetime on a small budget. Historian Scott Knowles quips that Cota found the landing at Omaha Beach easier to organize than civil defense. Cota's successors in Philadelphia came to civil defense from similar military backgrounds, and they produced similar results. Philadelphia Mayor Samuel concluded that his city had only "paper plans," and not real resources or infrastructure that would protect his city from nuclear attack.[64] Civil defenders at the local level produced what sociologist Lee Clarke calls "fantasy documents."[65] These are plans designed to reassure the public that dangers are under control, when in fact authorities have no experience with and little understanding of the dangers. The brittle nature of local civil defense plans contributed to a skepticism among observers about whether civil defense would ever really work.

One way to deal with divergent needs of a national government threatened by war and local governments threatened by natural disasters was to enshrine

---

[63] City Council of Philadelphia, "Special Committee to Investigate Civil Defense Program," Philadelphia City Archives, February 25, 1952, 13.

[64] Knowles, "Defending Philadelphia," 3.

[65] Lee Clarke, *Mission Improbable, Using Fantasy Documents to Tame Disaster* (Chicago: University of Chicago Press, 1999).

a policy of dual use. In 1955, the FCDA encouraged states to broaden their dual use policies:

> The advantages of having natural and enemy-caused disaster functions combined in the same forces have been demonstrated many times within the past few years. Natural disaster operations have afforded excellent training in organization, leadership, and the use of technical skills to those individuals in civil defense whose responsibility it would be to act in an enemy-caused disaster. On the other hand, previous organization and training in civil defense has resulted in increased capability to provide assistance in natural disasters.[66]

Just two years later, however, the tide shifted toward federal government primacy in civil defense because the national government sought control and state and local governments sought clarity. Val Peterson, the FCDA administrator, wrote in a letter to House Speaker Sam Rayburn:

> The question of the appropriate division of responsibility for the Nation's civil defense has been thoroughly studied .... The majority of the recommendations resulting from such studies urge that civil defense be made primarily a Federal responsibility.

> However, the Federal Civil Defense Administration considers State and local efforts of such vital importance to the development of a true civil defense operational capability for the Nation that the better course is to amend section 2 of the Act to declare civil defense to be the joint responsibility of the Federal Government and the States and their political subdivisions. Under such joint responsibility the Federal Government, while exerting positive leadership, can properly exercise its partnership role by encouraging and requiring the maximum civil defense effort on the part of the States and their political subdivisions.[67]

Peterson's letter echoed beyond his communication to the Speaker; it was included in the Congressional Record and cited as precedent up until the present-day FEMA.[68] His assertions reflected the conclusions of groups at the state and national levels, including the Commission on Intergovernmental Relations and a 1956 governors' conference. In fact, many groups proposed that civil defense be primarily a national responsibility because of the national character of the threat of attack, and in order to reduce confusion for states (and presumably inject more federal dollars). Congress amended the FCDA, however, to make civil defense officially a joint federal-state responsibility. What "joint" actually meant, however, was left open, and congressional attempts at clarity tended to confuse matters. Civil defense after 1957 was more of a

---

[66] Annual Statistical Report, 1955, 13.

[67] Letter from Val Peterson to Sam Rayburn, February 8, 1957, appended to Sen. Rep. No. 1831, 85th Cong., 2nd sess., printed in 1958 U.S. Code, Congress and Ad. News 3311, 3317.

[68] For an example of Peterson's letter as precedent, see: letter to Hon. Edward J. Markey, from Congressional Research Service American Law Division, "Whether the Federal Emergency Management Agency May Assume 'Command and Control' Functions in the Event of a Nuclear Incident," February 7, 1989.

shared responsibility than was planned in 1950, but the boundaries between state and national government responsibility were opaque.[69]

Federal government involvement often came reluctantly, at the request of localities that lobbied their members of Congress for more resources and guidance, or from federal officials concerned that states and localities were focusing on other priorities rather than preparing for attack. According to one of the most thorough histories of the period, "Congressional committees soon joined the ranks of those who felt that fear of infringement of States' rights and local prerogatives were only a smokescreen for evasion of federal responsibility for civil defense."[70] In 1958, Congress amended the 1950 Act to reflect "joint" responsibility and "partnership" among levels of government.[71] Despite the change in wording, civil defense always comprised unfunded mandates at the state and local level, in addition to scattered grants.[72]

The shelter program was one example of a civil defense effort that received national government support and directions but was largely funded by local governments or private individuals with the exception of occasional federal grants.[73] Cold War spending priorities favored appropriations for military and diplomatic programs rather than shelters. Congress appropriated $32 million for shelter construction and improvement in 1951, $75 million at the peak in 1952, but $43 million in 1953 and much less thereafter.[74] In other ways, the shelter program reached its apex in the 1970s, as an increasing number of existing structures were identified and labeled as shelters. The National Fallout Shelter Survey lasted from 1948 until 1986, and was responsible for surveying and documenting the location and conditions of shelters.[75]

---

[69] States attempted to clarify the governor's authority over civil defenders in times of crisis, following a recommendation from Congress. The first such act was The Post-Attack Resource Management Act, passed in Virginia on February 26, 1966. Va. H.D. No. 164 was introduced January 26, 1966; see Benet D. Gellman, "Planning for a National Nuclear Emergency: The Organization of Government and Federal-State Relations," *Virginia Law Review* 52 (April 1966): 435–462.

[70] Harry B. Yoshpe, *Our Missing Shield: The US Civil Defense Program in Historical Perspective* (Washington, DC: FEMA 1981), 27, available at: http://oai.dtic.mil/oai/oai?verb=getRecord& metadataPrefix=html&identifier=ADA099634 (accessed March 12, 2011).

[71] Public Law 85–602, approved August 8, 1958, 72. Stat. 532. See also Office of Civil and Defense Mobilization, Legislative History – Amendments to the Federal Civil Defense Act of 1950, n.d., Vol. IV

[72] Dee Garrison, *Bracing for Armageddon: Why Civil Defense Never Worked* (New York: Oxford University Press, 2006), 35; James M. Landis, "The Central Problem of Civilian Defense: An Appraisal," *State Government* 23 (November 1950): 236–257.

[73] For an example of how national government programs relied on state and local funding, see Federal Civil Defense Act of 1950 (64 Stat. 1245).

[74] "Activities and Status of Civil Defense in the United States, Department of the Army, October 26, 1971" (Washington DC: General Accounting Office, 1971), 8.

[75] "National Fallout Shelter Survey, 1948–1986," Washington, DC. Portions available at: http:// csudigitalhumanities.org/exhibits/exhibits/show/shelter-survey (accessed January 7, 2011).

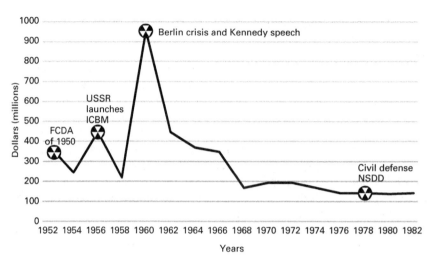

FIGURE 3.2. Civil Defense Appropriations from 1952 to 1982.

*Constant FY 1982 dollars

Sources: Wayne Blanchard, "American Civil Defense 1945–1975" (Ph.D. diss., University of Virginia, 1980); "American Civil Defense 1945–1984," NETC Monograph, Emmitsburg, MD, 1985.

As Figure 3.2 shows, shelter spending diminished before civil defense spending as a whole. The height of civil defense spending came in 1961, when President Kennedy, spurred by the Berlin crisis, stressed the need for a comprehensive civil defense program. Civil defense spending fell off sharply after the crisis, however.

Meanwhile, the shelter program had one cost unaccounted for: the danger that nuclear attack would be seen as just another hazard to be mitigated, like a flood, and the emergence of a generation that accepted nuclear war as just another risk. By the late 1960s, civil defense plans and funding supported the design of fortress-like schools that became fashionable for presumably educational reasons as well as for minimizing the effects of a different kind of crisis – anti–Vietnam War student protests.

GOAL AMBIGUITY IN CIVIL DEFENSE ORGANIZATIONS

The Cold War spawned the creation of a class of large, permanent organizations in government and business dedicated to securing the home front.[76] These permanent organizations had ambiguous goals, however. Were they intended to prepare for disasters, respond to them, or reduce their consequences? And was civil defense intended to protect against airplanes dropping conventional

---

[76] Friedberg, *In the Shadow of the Garrison*.

bombs, against nuclear missiles, against tornadoes and hurricanes, or even against social ills? At various times, "civil defense" referred to all of these things in the minds of some people.

The missions and formal goals of an organization establish the rules of the game, but sometimes missions and goals are ambiguous, especially in public organizations.[77] Public agencies produce public goods and pursue value-driven goals for which objective performance measures (such as profit, in private organizations) are hard to identify.[78] In an organization with ambiguous goals, decentralized groups below the layer of top management can shape what an organization does, even moving it in a different direction than the organization's formal superiors intend.

"Organizational goal ambiguity" is the degree to which goals are open to multiple interpretations. In a study of decision making in the policy shops of federal agencies, Martha Feldman defines "ambiguity" as "the state of having many ways of thinking about the same circumstances or phenomena."[79] In standard management texts, ambiguous goals are a vice to be remedied.[80] Business consultants help private organizations formalize mission statements and clarify goals as a way to achieve objectives. For public organizations, however, goal clarification is often managerially sound but politically unwise. Public organizations depend on multiple constituencies for funding and authority, and goals that are too clear can alienate a powerful constituency or reveal that an organization has outlasted its raison d'être – both problems that plagued civil defense agencies.

The president and Congress did not resolve ambiguities about the goals of civil defense, which could mean, variously, programs to defend against nuclear attack, programs to show the Soviet Union that the United States was prepared for war, and programs to increase civic capacity to meet a range of needs, including disaster preparedness. Faced with goal ambiguity, public administrators and state and local officials competed to define the goals of civil defense. During the Cold War and beyond, coalitions that favored addressing the threat of nuclear attack battled for resources and authority with coalitions

---

[77] Robert A. Dahl and Charles E. Lindblom, *Politics, Economics, and Welfare* (New York: Harper & Row, 1958); James Q. Wilson, Jr. *Bureaucracy: What Government Agencies Do and Why They Do It* (New York: Basic Books, 1989); Charles Perrow, "The Analysis of Goals in Complex Organizations." *American Sociological Review* 26 (1961): 854–866.

[78] Young Han Chun and Hal G. Rainey, "Goal Ambiguity and Organizational Performance in U.S. Federal Agencies," *Journal of Public Administration Research and Theory* 15.4 (2005): 529–557; James L. Perry and Hal G. Rainey, "The Public-Private Distinction in Organization Theory: A Critique and Research Strategy," *Academy of Management Review* 13 (1988): 182–201.

[79] Martha Feldman, *Order Without Design: Information Production and Policymaking* (Stanford, CA: Stanford University Press, 1989), 5.

[80] For a review of the literature, see Lisa D. Ordóñez, Maurice E. Schweitzer, Adam D. Galinsky, and Max H. Bazerman, "Goals Gone Wild: How Goals Systematically Harm Individuals and Organizations," *Academy of Management Perspectives* 23 (2009): 6–16.

concerned about natural disasters. Security and disaster cultures often perceived themselves as locked in a zero sum game, though at times they had a symbiotic relationship. The federal government was more concerned with nuclear attack, which was an existential threat to the country, and devoted resources to similar natural disaster concerns to achieve buy-in from states and localities. Subnational government agencies used civil defense programs to obtain additional resources and to cloak their work in patriotism. Both defense against attack and preparation against natural disaster appealed to the public's instinctive sense of risk and dread, but what government agencies were supposed to do about these protean enemies was unclear. In the memorable and perhaps apocryphal phrase of sociologist Michael Crozier, "the problem is the problem." The federal government did what governments do best by attempting to make the murky problem of how to defend against foreign attack appear rational and coordinated.

Social scientists sometimes call this process "legibility," describing how governments impose transparent simplifications on citizens in a range of domains through techniques ranging from the convention of last names to scientific forestry.[81] In imposing legibility, however, governments sometimes lose local, context-specific knowledge. The clarity the federal government attempted to impose on civil defense had lasting effects by nationalizing emergency management, but the nationalizing did not go very deep. Civil defense began with military concerns, which were themselves ambiguous. At a national and international level, calculating the effects of nuclear war involved a great deal of uncertainty.[82] At a local level, cities, states, and nonprofits retained control over implementation, a fragmentation built into the U.S. constitutional structure and antistatist tradition that would continue after the Cold War threat subsided.[83]

Ambiguity about the goals of civil defense lent power to lower-level units beyond the federal government politicians and bureaucrats who wrote formal mission statements and goals. Normally the architects of institutional rules and forms wield substantial power because they set the rules of the game.[84]

[81] James Scott, *Seeing Like a State: How Certain Schemes to Improve the Human Condition Have Failed* (New Haven, CT: Yale University Press, 1998).

[82] On the high degree of uncertainty and miscalculation involved in planning for nuclear attack, see Lynn Eden, *Whole World on Fire, Organizations, Knowledge, and Nuclear Weapons Devastation* (Ithaca, NY: Cornell University Press, 2004).

[83] Aaron Friedberg, "American Antistatism and the Founding of the Cold War State," in *Shaped by War and Trade: International Influences on American Political Development*, edited by Ira Katznelson and Martin Shefter (Princeton, NJ: Princeton University Press, 2002), 239–267; Friedberg, *In the Shadow of the Garrison State*, 9–33.

[84] A substantial literature in political science emphasizes the power wielded by the architects of rules among presidents and congressional committees. This chapter shows how lower-level groups, too, can shape policies to suit their needs when goals and missions are ambiguous. Politicians can benefit from ambiguous and mutable goals. For examples of the literature emphasizing the importance of governing rules, see: Terry M. Moe, "Interests, Institutions,

Sometimes, however, lower-level groups use discretion to their advantage. In civil defense and disaster management, lower-level groups took advantage of ambiguous goals and used their knowledge of local needs and power over implementation to shape what their organizations did. To take just one example, a high school in Oklahoma boasted of a new underground theater that, in addition to serving an academic purpose, helped in "protecting the community against possible fallout hazards and probable tornadoes."[85] Existing civil defense structures also served double duty in the event of natural disasters, which became more salient as civil defense reached its peak. During the 1950s, the United States experienced a spate of highly publicized hurricanes, tornadoes, and ice storms. During one 24-hour period in March 1952, 31 tornadoes in six states killed 315 and left many more injured. When pressed to find more money for shelters from tornadoes, mayors invoked civil defense to receive federal grants and generate new revenue from local sources.

Robert Moses, the master planner responsible for reshaping the urban design of New York City, denounced civil defense as a farce, but the fact that he wrote an article in a prominent national magazine critical of civil defense is proof that civil defense was important enough in politics and culture for Moses to notice. Moses summed up his evaluation in 1957: "There is presently no effective civil defense agency. People who have been running what little there is in Washington and in most of our states and cities have not been competent or persuasive, and they don't seem to have much public standing anywhere."[86] Despite looking a gift horse in the mouth, Moses acknowledged that he would use civil defense money from the federal government for his own purposes – to build underground tunnels connecting major landmarks to improve commerce and to bolster fire departments and emergency preparedness.

STRENGTHS AND SHORTCOMINGS OF CIVIL DEFENSE

Civil defense fluctuated between a focus on foreign attack and natural disasters, and between state and national government control. The multiple possibilities for what civil defense could be illustrate the degree of social and political construction involved. Politicians and citizens groups choose what the government should address as a problem. The existence of competing claims

and Positive Theory: The Politics of the NLRB," *Studies in American Political Development* 2 (1987): 236–299; Charles Stewart III and Barry Weingast, "Stacking the Senate, Changing the Nation: Republican Rotten Boroughs, Statehood Politics, and American Political Development," *Studies in American Political Development* 6 (1992): 223–271; Mathew D. McCubbins, Roger G. Noll, and Barry R. Weingast, "The Political Origins of the Administrative Procedure Act," *Journal of Law, Economics and Organization* 15 (1999): 180–217.

[85] Joanne Brown, "'A is for Atom, B is for Bomb': Civil Defense and American Public Education, 1948–1963," *Journal of American History* 75 (June 1988): 68–90, quoted on 89; for more examples, see the National Defense Education Act, 1958.

[86] Robert Moses, "Civil Defense Fiasco," *Harper's*, November (1957): 29–34, 30.

about what civil defense should do, and who should be doing it, whether states or the national government, help explain why many considered civil defense a failure.

Studies of citizen preparedness criticized the United States effort for being operationally ineffective and superficial. One study estimated the rate of participation in civil defense at only 4.5 percent of the population.[87] Another prominent report noted: "Whether it was looked upon as 'insurance' or as playing a vital role in strategic deterrence, civil defense was never brought to a level of effort that would ensure substantial protection of the population, industry, and the economy in a nuclear assault."[88] Even during the height of the Cold War, policy makers sometimes voiced skepticism publically. At a March 27, 1958 National Security Council meeting, Vice-President Richard Nixon made an impassioned claim that the United States would never survive nuclear war.[89]

These critics overlooked the effort's most profound effects. Civil defense raised the salience of the Cold War whether or not civil defense would have significantly reduced losses during an attack. When President Kennedy made his appeal for family fallout shelters in the Berlin Crisis speech in 1961, he did not need to believe that fallout shelters would actually protect a large number of Americans in order to draw attention to the Soviet threat.[90] Even those people who did not directly participate as a warden, serve as an auxiliary police officer or fireman, or build a shelter in the backyard most likely knew someone who did and were aware of the Cold War home front. Civil defense achieved its goals more by cultivating a sense of shared risk than through active citizen participation. The collective sense of shared risk of attack and of vulnerability to natural disasters and the sense that the federal government could help are examples of social construction. Politicians and administrators pursuing their own goals at various levels of government ended up contributing to organizations and plans that formed a state apparatus to prepare for disaster.

National-level policy makers benefited from the network of policies, plans, and procedures that raised the salience of the Cold War for U.S. citizens by involving individuals on the home front in the war effort.[91] Americans felt connected to the national government through civil defense programs, and even if they did not participate themselves, they realized that they faced a collective, national-level threat to which only the federal government could respond. States and localities had no real choice if they were to prepare for nuclear attack except to cede some

[87] Eric Klinenberg, "Are You Ready for the Next Disaster?" *New York Times Magazine*, July 6, 2008.
[88] Harry B. Yoshpe, *Our Missing Shield: The US Civil Defense Program in Historical Perspective* (Washington DC: FEMA, April 1981), iv.
[89] Guy Oakes, *The Imaginary War: Civil Defense and American Cold War Culture* (New York: Oxford University Press, 1995), 166–167.
[90] Eugene Feingold, "Nuclear Attack and Civil Defense: A Review," *Conflict Resolution* 6 (1962): 282–289.
[91] Feingold, "Nuclear Attack and Civil Defense: A Review," 282–289.

authority to the national government. But if civil defense was politically effective for national policy makers, what did state and local leaders gain? For some communities, participating in civil defense relieved anxiety about nuclear war. For others, participation in civil defense produced anxiety about the future. For still others, civil defense delivered federal government resources for local concerns such as schools, infrastructure, and natural disaster preparedness.

Educators and local communities used FCDA-sponsored programs to shore up their own authority and to argue for more resources. Progressive educational policy was under attack from right-wing anticommunists, and school officials turned to civil defense to demonstrate public schools' commitment to American democracy.[92] The National Education Association's National Commission for the Defense of Democracy was one attempt to link civil defense with support for public schools. In addition to purely political reasons, educators adopted civil defense curricula because they were more serious than the life skills material of the day, which taught children telephone skills and how to dress.[93]

Shelters were part of another effort that produced dubious gains. Many policy makers, including President Eisenhower, doubted the efficacy of shelters. They thought that the cost of sheltering every citizen would be too high and the difficulty too great given the increasing power of nuclear weapons.[94] FCDA administrator Frederick Peterson urged cutting back shelter programs after the 1953 Soviet nuclear test because the blast from one thermonuclear device could destroy an entire American city, shelters and all.[95] Peterson's shift from shelters to evacuation as a civil defense strategy was cheekily referred to as going from "duck and cover" to "run like hell."

Peterson's assessment was correct – the shelters could not withstand Soviet bombs, which were far more destructive (in the megaton range) than the bombs detonated at Hiroshima and Nagasaki that were in the kiloton range. In fact, civil defense and military planners substantially underestimated the effects of fires that would engulf a city after a nuclear blast and cause more complete damage than the blast itself.[96] Very little would be left of a city after a direct strike by a warhead from either the Soviet or American arsenal. Furthermore, even though expanding the shelter program remained the "principal goal of the current civil defense program," according to one 1971 government report,

[92] Clyde W. Meredith, "Civil Defense and the Schools," *School Life* 34 (April 1952): 99–100; Robert A. Luke, "The Educational Requirements of Civil Defense," *Adult Education* 1 (February 1951): 33; Rush Welter, *Popular Education and Democratic Thought in America* (New York: Columbia University Press, 1962); Arthur Bestor, *Educational Wasteland: The Retreat From Learning in Our Schools* (Urbana: University of Illinois Press, 1953).

[93] Brown, "'A is for Atom, B is for Bomb,'" 74, 80; LaVerne Strong, "Helping Children Face a Critical Period," *Childhood Education* 28 (September 1951): 12–16; National Security Resources Board, *Survival under Atomic Attack* (Washington, DC: GPO, 1950).

[94] Kerr, *Civil Defense in the US*, 107–108.

[95] Kerr, *Civil Defense in the US*, 71.

[96] Lynn Eden, *Whole World on Fire: Organizations, Knowledge, and Nuclear Weapons Devastation* (Ithaca, NY: Cornell University Press, 2006).

there were no substantial programs to defend against chemical or biological weapons.[97] The shelter program and civil defense did not arise out of a comprehensive risk assessment taking into account major domestic security threats. The debate over the role of shelters in nuclear strategy led to suboptimal funding from the point of view of shelter advocates, and there were never enough shelters to house the entire population, especially in urban areas where land was relatively expensive and the population dense. Minimal government funding, limited urban space, and reliance on self-help meant that the suburban middle class was most likely to benefit from shelters. Not coincidentally, the new class of suburban voters was an important constituency not yet aligned with either party. Ambitious politicians could win the support of suburban voters by claiming credit for the shelter program.

While the federal government funded offices overseeing the shelter program and provided some seed money, most of the funds and labor for shelters came from cities or civic groups. Public Law 85–606, passed in 1958, authorized federal financial contributions for state and local civil defense personnel and administrative costs. Frank Blazich shows how this allowed North Carolina (and, presumably, other states) to exponentially increase the size of its state civil defense agency, and in turn to increase the public visibility and operational capability for civil defense.[98] Meanwhile, the federal government greatly reduced its shelter funding in the 1970s, although civil defense programs and skeleton shelter programs persisted through the 1980s.[99] By the 1970s, most local offices of civil defense had adopted the phrase *emergency management* to reflect that they spent far more time on preparing for natural disasters than for civil defense emergencies. Most shelter programs had languished by then. For instance, in 1974, the Washington, DC Office of Emergency Preparedness cleaned out the rations in its civil defense shelters and sent them to Bangladesh as food aid.[100] The terms "disaster" and "emergency" morphed into one another in government language, with emergency favoring efforts to prepare for a crisis, often with a security bent, and disaster referring more often to efforts to deal with the consequences of events after they happened.

Why did civil defense survive so long even though its operational effectiveness was dubious? The answer illustrates the stickiness of American political institutions. Once constructed by politicians and bureaucrats swooping in to

---

[97] Report to the Congress, "Activities and Status of Civil Defense in the US," Department of the Army, Comptroller General of the United States, October 26, 1971.

[98] Frank A. Blazich, Jr., *Alert Today, Alive Tomorrow: The North Carolina Civil Defense Agency and Fallout Shelters, 1961–1963* (M.A. thesis, North Carolina Sate University, Raleigh, North Carolina, 2008).

[99] David Monteyne, *Fallout Shelter: Designing for Civil Defense in the Cold War* (St. Paul: University of Minnesota Press, 2011); "Nuclear Fallout Shelters Are Persisting Despite World Détente," *The Washington Post*, November 16, 1972, G6.

[100] "Bangladesh Hungry to Get Biscuits Kept in CD Tunnel," *The Washington Post*, September 14, 1974, D1.

solve a problem but constrained by federalism and democratic politics, the institution of civil defense is not easily unbuilt. The shelter program delivered resources and (in the beginning) credibility to local communities and drew attention to the federal government's Cold War mobilization. Once the government committed to building and improving shelters as a public responsibility to reduce the risk of nuclear war, the government could not easily discontinue the program, however partial and symbolic.

CIVIL DEFENSE AND THE CONSTRUCTION OF DISASTER

The civil defense period beginning after World War II and lasting through the 1980s institutionalized the national government's credit claiming for a number of benefits that fell under the heading of civil defense. The basic logic is this: to achieve duration over time, policies require a mechanism to generate continuous support.[101] In disaster management, politicians can claim credit and win praise from voters if they frame their role as coming to the rescue and distributing relief. During the twentieth century, politicians and bureaucrats generated support by framing disaster management as a public responsibility for which government provided a necessary solution. These structures shaped the meaning of disaster as something for which public organizations bore responsibility on a national level. The national government focused initially on the threat of nuclear attack, but the organizations constructed to prepare for attack and shore up public support came to be used more often to prepare for natural disasters as the threat of attack waned.

Nuclear strategist Herman Kahn emphasized the importance of framing public perception of a problem when he claimed that if the public could see the preparations the government made for nuclear war, they would be more willing to assist in reconstruction and support the governing regime. In a seminal book, he wrote: "It is my belief that if the government has made at least moderate prewar preparations, so that most people whose lives have been saved [by civil defense programs] will give some credit to the government's foresight, then people will probably rally round.... Of course, if there is a fantastic disparity between the government's preparations and the problems to be solved, then none of this would hold."[102]

Kahn assumes that even if a disaster causes extensive damage, people will rally around the flag if the government makes perceptible efforts to prepare for the worst. This thesis was never tested in the nuclear domain, but it undergirds natural disaster policy and is an example of social construction. The plans and programs of the federal government shaped how people thought about disaster. In the twentieth century, politicians and bureaucrats came to believe

---

[101] Paul Pierson, "When Effect Becomes Cause: Policy Feedback and Political Change," *World Politics* 45 (July 1993): 595–628.

[102] Kahn, *On Thermonuclear War*, 90.

preparing for disaster was a responsibility of the federal government, either out of a moral duty or a political calculation to generate support for their activities. To earn the esteem of clients and voters, politicians and bureaucrats sought credit for preparing for disaster, even if the efficacy of these preparations was never tested or, in the case of the shelter program, was dubious.

Beyond the mechanism of credit claiming, the history of civil defense offers other considerations for how social construction shaped disaster management in the context of elections and federalism. Among the broader public, civil defense channeled fear of apocalypse into support for government programs to prepare for the worst. [103] These programs were structured to achieve the maximum possible level of support by appealing to middle-class values. [104] For example, civil defense supported public education and featured middle-class families in its promotional materials. Many of these messages spoke directly to individual citizens rather than being mediated by states and localities. [105] The underlying message of self-help (with federal government support) and patriotic duty was designed to resonate with the white, middle-class, civilian constituency that had the greatest influence in U.S. politics of the day.

Centralization of power in the federal government is often depicted as a uni-directional flow of resources and authority from subnational units of government to Washington, DC. [106] In civil defense, however, centralization occurred through the pull of the federal government *and* the push of states and localities. Political spaces were fragmented across levels of government and federal agencies, which complicated attempts at change. [107]

The use of civil defense plans, equipment, and personnel to prepare for and respond to natural disasters as well as nuclear attack and terrorism came to be known as *dual use*. While the practice had existed in some form since the beginning of civil defense, it was formalized as policy when the president and Congress agreed to liberalize laws relating to natural disasters. After a presidential message to Congress in April 1970 and Office of Management and Budget Review in June 1971, the OMB recommended a closer relationship

---

[103] Grossman, *Neither Dead Nor Red*, 59.

[104] Spencer R. Weart, *Nuclear Fear* (Cambridge, MA: Harvard University Press, 1989), 130.

[105] Once again, the threat was minimized and compared to common experiences and dangers, as in this selection from a comic book: "You have learned to take care of yourself in many ways – to cross streets safely what to do in case of fire BUT the atomic bomb is a new danger Things will be knocked down all over town You must be ready to protect yourself". Brown, "'A is for Atom, B is for Bomb,'" 84.

[106] Ballard C. Campbell, *The Growth of American Government: Governance From The Cleveland Era to the Present* (Bloomington: Indiana University Press, 1995); Robert Higgs, *Crisis and Leviathan: Critical Episodes in the Growth of American Government* (New York: Oxford University Press, 1987); Bruce D. Porter, "Parkinson's Law Revisited: War and the Growth of Government," *The Public Interest* 60 (Summer 1980): 50–68.

[107] Andrew Whitford, "The Pursuit of Political Control by Multiple Principals," *Journal of Politics* 67 (2005): 39–49.

between disaster assistance activities of state and local government and civil defense that could take advantage of dual use.[108]

Cold War civil defense contributed to a mismatch between citizens' expectations of the federal government and the bureaucracy's actual capacity. Civil defense programs implied and sometimes explicitly promised that the government could protect citizens from nuclear war. In reality, the government could not offer absolute protection, and in some cases government actions increased the likelihood of disaster through strategic decisions. Bureaucrats in civil defense agencies were in a tough position. They were charged with managing government disaster preparations, but they did not have much control over the actual causes of disaster, whether nuclear attack or natural disasters.

During the Cold War, the national government ratcheted up its claims for what it could do to protect individual citizens from a host of calamities. Its capacity to prepare for attack, terrorism, fires, floods, and hurricanes did not always keep pace with its promises, however. Increasing claims about what government could do to prepare for disaster posed a danger: with the ratcheting up of central state involvement in a highly complex and unpredictable endeavor, the state risked perpetually underperforming relative to expectations. A moderate underperformance could give citizens a healthy skepticism about government; persistent significant underperformance could lead to a loss of civic capacity and a chronic distrust of public projects.[109]

---

[108] Report to the Congress, "Activities and Status of Civil Defense in the US," Department of the Army by Comptroller General of the US, October 26, 1971, 34.

[109] For a similar problem in social policy, see Edward Banfield, *Government Project* (Glencoe, IL: The Free Press, 1951).

4

The Rise of Emergency Management and FEMA, 1979–2001

Mr. McIntyre: We think the consequences of terrorist acts can be quite similar to the consequences of major natural and manmade disasters. For example, in both instances there will be serious disruptions of essential services or resources, or certainly could be, and I would emphasize the new Agency would be involved only with the consequences of terrorism and not with the incident itself. I want to underscore that point.

Mr. Levitas: That is the point I am most concerned about.

Mr. McIntyre: And so we felt that if you were going to have a broad-based agency to respond to emergency situations, that since the consequences of these terrorist acts could be expected to be similar to other emergencies, that this agency should be in a position to respond.

– From 1978 congressional hearings on the plan to establish FEMA[1]

The modern period in disaster policy and politics, roughly following World War II, is the culmination of a shift in the social construction of disaster organizations.[2] Presidents and government agencies took center stage in the provision of

---

[1] U.S. Congress, "Reorganization Plan No. 3 for 1978" (Washington, DC: House Committee on Government Operations, 1978), 52. Also see Keith Bea, "FEMA's Mission: Policy Directives of the Federal Emergency Management Agency," *CRS Report for Congress*, February 13, 2002, 14.

[2] This chapter draws on thirty interviews conducted between 2003 and 2009. Most of these were "not for attribution," meaning that the source agreed to be identified only in general terms as in "a FEMA official" or a "congressional staffer." Many of the issues they discussed were the subject of ongoing political controversy in which they were still enmeshed. I used "not for attribution" quotations either for illustrative purposes or for information that I confirmed through at least two interviews or through archival and previously reported materials. I report the composition of these interviews in Figure 4.10. Those interviewees who agreed to be quoted directly are cited in the text. Some of the quotations were published in Patrick S. Roberts, "FEMA and the Prospects for Reputation-Based Autonomy," *Studies in American Political Development* 20 (Spring 2006): 57–87. In addition to interviews, I had more informal conversations with many other participants in FEMA's development, including state and local emergency managers, FEMA employees,

disaster aid, and they became increasingly entrepreneurial in finding new roles for government intervention. Before then, disaster victims had asked for ever more aid for a greater range of disasters than before, and politicians, especially in Congress, had been increasingly willing to use the power of government to provide relief to victims whom they saw as part of a national community and therefore deserving of aid. Three things changed in the modern period. First, U.S. government underwent a shift toward presidential, not legislative, dominance. The presidency came to be identified with the policies of government as a whole, and the president gained control over the levers of an expanding bureaucracy through the power of appointment, reorganizations, rhetoric, and a growing White House office.[3] Presidential attempts at control shaped disaster policy, for good and ill.

Second, print and electronic media emerged as a chief mechanism of social and political construction through which political leaders claimed credit and received blame for perceived government actions and inaction. Presidents, members of Congress, and increasingly bureaucrats vied for credit for government achievements by using the media to appeal to citizens and influential social groups.[4] Voters were the audience for the blame game, and they rewarded successes and punished failures through elections.

Third, the onset of the Cold War and the psychology of risk perception led disaster agencies to prepare for two very different kinds of events: natural disasters and deliberate attack from abroad. Domestic agencies such as the Federal Emergency Management Agency (FEMA) juggled responsibility for both, using ideas variously termed *dual use* and *all hazards* as an attempt to give unity to their missions. The ideas at the heart of agency missions are a zone for social and political construction as much as are debates in Congress or presidential campaigns.

In the modern period, FEMA became synonymous with government preparations for disaster. Understanding the shifting meaning of what counts as

FEMA administrators, and other appointees. One product of these discussions is reported in Paul Stockton and Patrick S. Roberts, "Findings from the Forum on Homeland Security after the Bush Administration: Next Steps in Building Unity of Effort," *Homeland Security Affairs* 4 (June 2008): 1–11.

[3] Some of these tools have been used more effectively than others. See David Lewis, *The Politics of Presidential Appointments: Political Control and Bureaucratic Performance* (Princeton, NJ: Princeton University Press, 2008); George C. Edwards, *On Deaf Ears: The Limits of the Bully Pulpit* (New Haven, CT: Yale University Press, 2003).

[4] Thomas A. Birkland, *After Disaster: Agenda Setting, Public Policy, and Focusing Events* (Washington, DC: Georgetown University Press, 1997); Paul C. Light, *Government's Greatest Achievements: From Civil Rights to Homeland Defense* (Washington, DC: Brookings Institution Press, 2002). In one interesting study, the effects of the widely covered school shooting incident in Columbine, Colorado, in 1999 spurred more rapid implementation of policies and tools already available rather than a reevaluation of the general problem. Natural disasters may have a similar relationship with media coverage and policy. See Thomas A. Birkland and Regina G. Lawrence, "Media Framing and Policy Change After Columbine," *American Behavioral Scientist* 52 (June 2009): 1405–1425.

a disaster or an emergency requires putting FEMA at the center of the analysis. A central issue in these developments in disaster policy is the effect of security missions on the performance of natural disaster agencies. Security missions concern preparation for nuclear attack, terrorism, and domestic unrest. When the emergency that FEMA was to prepare for was conceived chiefly as a security one rather than a natural disaster, FEMA operated differently than it did when it was primarily a natural disaster agency. When the agency's security missions were primary, it hired more people with law enforcement and military experience, drew the attention of armed services congressional committees, and had a law-and-order image among the public. When natural disasters were central to the agency's mission, FEMA hired more experienced emergency managers, limited its national security communication with Congress and the White House, and cultivated an image as a natural disaster aid clearinghouse.

DUAL USE, ALL HAZARDS, AND THE BIRTH OF FEMA

Disaster preparedness and relief before the establishment of FEMA, though far more centralized than they had been in the nineteenth century, remained ad hoc and fragmented. Between 1951 and 1973, disaster assistance and relief activities were the responsibility of five different federal agencies and many more programs. A change in the names of an alphabet soup of agencies from civil defense to emergency preparedness is telling: the Federal Civil Defense Administration (1950–1958); the Office of Civil and Defense Mobilization (1958–1961); the Office of Civil Defense (1961–1972); the Office of Emergency Planning (1961–1972); and finally the Office of Emergency Preparedness (1968–1973). From January 1953 to June 1964, these organizations went beyond their mandate to prepare for attacks and coordinated federal disaster assistance for 180 major disasters including 87 floods, 27 hurricanes, 23 severe storms, and 18 tornadoes.[5]

The contemporary, president-centered structure for disaster assistance began formally in 1950, when members of Congress responded to criticism of a weak federal response to floods in the Midwest by enacting the Federal Disaster Relief Act of 1950. The Act provided for "an orderly and continuing means of assistance by the Federal government to the states and local governments in carrying out their responsibilities to alleviate suffering and danger resulting from major disasters."[6] At the time, politicians viewed the Act as an incremental step institutionalizing standard practice. The law was also innovative, however, because it established the first permanent authority for disaster relief

---

[5] Jerry Conley, "The Role of the U.S. Military in Domestic Emergency Management: The Past, Present and Future," *Institute for Crisis, Disaster, and Risk Management Newsletter*, 3 (2003), http://www.seas.gwu.edu/~emse232/emse232jan20030th1full.html (accessed online January 4, 2010).

[6] Pub. L. No. 81–875, 64 Stat. 1109.

without the need for ad hoc presidential or congressional action.[7] The Act invested authority in the president and his staff, and presidents would exploit this authority to claim credit for disaster relief just as some ambitious members of Congress had claimed credit during the nineteenth century.

Risk management scholar Howard Kunreuther claims that a severe earthquake in Alaska in 1964 "marked a turning point in the federal government's role in disaster relief. The severity of the damage caused concern that, unless the SBA [Small Business Administration] liberalized its [loan] policy, many individuals would not qualify for a disaster loan because of their inability to pay off their old mortgages and other debts and still make monthly payments to the SBA."[8] The Alaska earthquake may have loosened the purse strings of the SBA, but federal government aid had been increasing at a high rate for at least a decade. In 1953, Red Cross disaster relief was greater than federal government disaster aid by a ratio of 1.6 to 1. By 1965, federal aid exceeded Red Cross spending by almost 8 to 1.[9]

Media coverage of Lyndon Johnson's trip to a disaster-stricken region in 1965 was typical of how presidents used the Act to their advantage. An Associated Press story began, "President Johnson, misty-eyed at times during a tour of Midwest areas devastated by tornadoes and floods, has declared Indiana, Ohio, and Michigan major disaster areas." The president received immediate coverage and credit for tangible relief and visible sympathy, even though his declaration came in response to requests from governors, and federal agencies would have to wait to survey the region before determining the exact amount of relief aid.[10]

As natural disasters took center stage, civil defense programs declined without being extinguished. Civil defense spending reached a peak of nearly $600 million (in 1977 dollars) after president Kennedy's Berlin Crisis speech in 1961, but in most years between 1951 and 1973, spending was between $100 million and $300 million.[11] (See Figure 3.2 in Chapter 3). After the Kennedy administration, civil defense programs languished, and Congress kept funding levels at about $100 million per year in the 1970s.[12] Most defense policy makers

---

[7] Richard Sylves, *Disaster Policy and Politics: Emergency Management and Homeland Security* (Washington, DC: CQ Press, 2008), 49.

[8] Howard Kunreuther, *Recovery from Natural Disasters: Insurance or Federal Aid?* (Washington, DC: American Enterprise Institute for Public Policy Research, 1973), 9.

[9] Douglas C. Dacy and Howard Kunreuther, *The Economics of Natural Disasters: Implications for Federal Policy* (New York: The Free Press, 1969), 32.

[10] "LBJ Declared Three States As 'Disasters,'" *Ellensburg Daily Record*, April 15, 1965, A1.

[11] See Figure 3.2. For a description of the activities of civil defense programs, see various reports to Congress, including "Activities and Status of Civil Defense in the United States," Report to the Congress by the Comptroller General of the United States, Washington, DC, October 26, 1971. John F. Kennedy, "Radio and Television Report to the American People on the Berlin Crisis," July 1961.

[12] President Carter's reorganization plan creating FEMA in 1979 consolidated civil defense programs in an agency with a natural disaster management mandate at least as large as its civil defense responsibilities.

preferred to fund offensive capabilities rather than passive defenses, and people gradually lost faith in the effectiveness of civil defense efforts as the Soviet nuclear arsenal grew to include intercontinental ballistic missiles that could reach the United States in minutes, not hours.

As the focus of civil defense waned, presidents saw increasing opportunities to palpably improve lives through disaster assistance and relief. On August 17, 1969, category five Hurricane Camille tore through the Mississippi Gulf Coast and continued into Louisiana and Alabama, bringing 20-foot tides and winds in excess of 200 miles per hour. The hurricane caused between 256 and 258 deaths, and an estimated $1.42 billion in damages. Camille's wide swath and its severity made the hurricane a national event covered in the national press, and it drew President Nixon's attention away from the Vietnam conflict abroad and his new federalism programs at home. New federalism was an agenda to transfer some powers previously held by the federal government back to the states, but the hurricane was so devastating that the response could not be left to states and localities alone. The hurricane became a policy actor, at least in a metaphorical sense, because it led to expanded presidential authority in disaster response, which was in tension with new federalism.

Nixon declared south Mississippi as well as portions of western Alabama and Louisiana to be federal disaster areas, and he sent 2,300 Army soldiers and engineers to lead the cleanup effort. Nixon dispatched Vice-President Spiro Agnew to the coast as his personal representative. States and localities mounted their own relief efforts, and, among many private and nonprofit efforts, the entertainer Bob Hope organized a "We Care" telethon in Jackson, Mississippi, to raise money for victims. The federal disaster declaration opened the door to federal relief programs including the Office of Emergency Preparedness's leadership of a relief effort involving twenty-five federal agencies, the Department of Housing and Urban Development's provision of temporary shelters and mobile homes, and Army rescue efforts. The Department of the Treasury established emergency offices in the affected areas that eventually distributed $25 million rehabilitation loans. The Commerce department aided businesses, while the Department of Agriculture contributed loans to help farmers repair their fields, and pesticide to repel swarms of insects that made life difficult in the swampy region. Even the National Aeronautics and Space Administration (NASA) pitched in, its reputation buoyed by the success of a July moon landing. NASA's Mississippi Test Facility became a refugee center for 7,000 storm victims.[13]

The size of the storm and the federal government response spanning multiple agencies marked the beginning of a period in which federal government involvement in disaster relief went beyond declaring a disaster area and setting

---

[13] Philip D. Hearn, *Hurricane Camille: Monster Storm of the Gulf Coast* (Oxford: University of Mississippi Press, 2004), 139–144; R. M. DeAngelis and E. R. Nelson, "Hurricane Camille – August 5–22." *Climatological Data, National Summary* 20 (1969): 5–22.

up temporary shelters to incorporate more targeted aid programs spanning multiple agencies. Following Camille, the president signed the Disaster Relief Act of 1969, which created a federal coordinating officer to represent the president during a relief effort.

With hurricanes on the agenda, Nixon moved civil defense toward a policy of dual use, or use for both natural disasters and terrorist or nuclear attacks. He replaced the Office of Civil Defense with the Civil Defense Preparedness Agency, giving it a mandate broader than defense against attack. He also sponsored a super-reorganization of government, with part of this plan creating FEMA. The intent of the reorganization was to centralize authority for disaster relief programs, but the effect was to spread programs for loans, response, and rebuilding across more than 100 federal agencies.[14] (The Watergate scandal derailed some of Nixon's super-reorganization plans and put FEMA on hold.) The scale of Nixon's reorganization suggests that presidential control over disaster policy was becoming increasingly important. Future presidents would face similar problems as they attempted to balance hierarchical control and bottom-up decentralized approaches to managing emergencies.[15]

At the beginning of the century, presidents responded to disaster by appointing a representative who could take charge at the scene and link local efforts to the federal government. Calvin Coolidge's appointment of Herbert Hoover after the Mississippi River floods was a case in point. What was informally known as the "czar system" functioned adequately when major disasters were rare and the public had lower expectations of the federal government, but high-profile disasters led policy makers to seek fundamental change. Death tolls from disasters fell each decade between the 1930s and the 1970s, but a spate of disasters, notably Hurricane Betsy in 1965 and Camille in 1969, killed thousands and drained state and local relief resources.[16] Subnational governments began to request more federal involvement in disaster relief, although predictably not federal intervention in building codes, zoning, and development plans. See Figures 4.1, 4.2, 4.3, 4.4, and 4.5 for comparisons of disaster declarations and spending over time.

At the same time, congressional armed services committees that oversaw disaster agencies were more concerned with offensive nuclear capability and deterrence than they were with passive defense. The combination of their lagging attention to civil defense, pressure from states and localities to address natural disasters, and emerging technological hazards such as nuclear power led

---

[14] Homeland Security National Preparedness Task Force, *Civil Defense and Homeland Security*, 16.

[15] For a contemporary example of the tension between hierarchical and network forms in emergency management, see a study of incident command systems in Donald P. Moynihan, "Combining Structural Forms in the Search for Policy Tools: Incident Command Systems in U.S. Crisis Management," *Governance* 21 (April 2008): 205–229.

[16] National Oceanic and Atmospheric Administration, "Billion Dollar U.S. Weather Disasters," 2008, available at: http://www.ncdc.noaa.gov/oa/reports/billionz.html#LIST (accessed October 7, 2010).

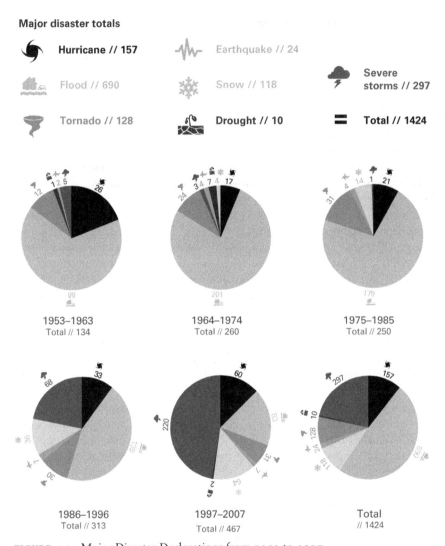

FIGURE 4.1. Major Disaster Declarations from 1953 to 2007.
Sources: The Federal Emergency Management Agency (FEMA), http://www.fema.gov;
The Public Entity Risk Institute (PERI), "All about Presidential Disaster Declarations,"
summary data tables, https://www.riskinstitute.org/peri.

Congress to act. Congress enacted the Federal Disaster Relief Act of 1974 and
along with President Nixon allowed the Department of Defense's Civil Defense
Preparedness Agency (DCDPA) to be officially "dual use" in preparing for
both natural disasters and civil defense emergencies.[17] The Act also authorized

[17] In 1976, Congress amended the Civil Defense Act of 1950 to recognize "that the organizational
structures established jointly by the federal government and several states and their political

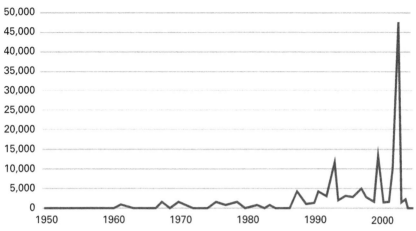

FIGURE 4.2. Presidential Disaster Spending by Year (in thousands) from 1953 to 2008. * No spending was recorded for the years 1950–1953 and 2009. Data for 2008 are incomplete.

Source: The Public Entity Risk Institute (PERI), "All about Presidential Disaster Declarations," summary data tables, https://www.riskinstitute.org/peri.

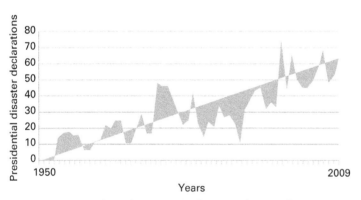

FIGURE 4.3. Presidential Disaster Declarations by Year from 1950 to 2009. * No declarations were issued for the years 1950–1953. Data for 2008 and 2009 are incomplete.

Source: The Public Entity Risk Institute (PERI), "All about Presidential Disaster Declarations," summary data tables, https://www.riskinstitute.org/peri.

subdivisions for civil defense purposes can be effectively utilized, without adversely affecting the basic civil defense objectives of this Act, to provide relief and assistance to people in areas of the United States struck by disasters other than disasters caused by enemy attack." That decision had little immediate impact, but it laid the foundation for policy makers to later expand the dual use and all hazards approaches. Also see Keith Bea, "Proposed Transfer of FEMA to the Department of Homeland Security," *CRS Report*, July 29, 2002.

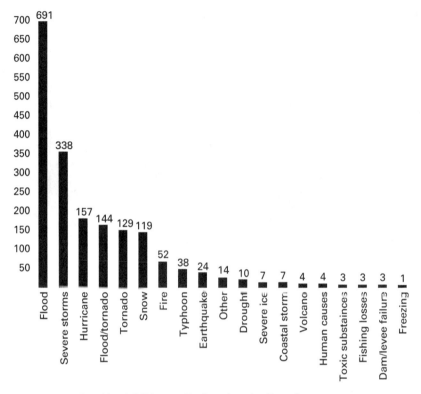

FIGURE 4.4. Presidential Disaster Declarations by Type from 1953 to 2009.
* No declarations were issued for the years 1950–1953. Data for 2008 and 2009 are incomplete.
Source: The Public Entity Risk Institute (PERI), "All about Presidential Disaster Declarations," summary data tables, https://www.riskinstitute.org/peri.

individual and family assistance through state and local governments. A year later, Congress conducted hearings on federal emergency assistance programs, and President Jimmy Carter began to review the issue. Carter eventually submitted Reorganization Plan Number 3 to Congress, which established FEMA in 1979.[18] For the first time, emergency management functions were centralized at the federal level.

The FEMA reorganization rivals the later creation of the Department of Homeland Security in complexity, though not in size. (FEMA's staff is about a sixtieth the size of the DHS). It combined the Department of Defense's DCPA with more than 100 federal disaster response programs that reported to 20 different congressional committees. To appease interest groups and

---

[18] Congress enacted Carter's "Reorganization Plan Number 3" to establish FEMA. The plan took effect April 1, 1979. (See also Executive Order 12127.)

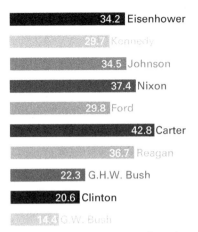

FIGURE 4.5. Percentage of Declaration Requests Turned Down between 1953 and 2009, by Administration.

* No declarations were issued for the years 1950–1953. Data for 2008 and 2009 are incomplete.

Note: A president may turn down a state governor's request for federal assistance following a major natural disaster or emergency.

Source: The Public Entity Risk Institute (PERI), "All about Presidential Disaster Declarations," summary data tables, https://www.riskinstitute.org/peri.

congressional committees, the reorganization plan transferred each program's political appointees to FEMA, which created isolated divisions or stovepiped offices individually connected to relevant congressional committees and interest groups but largely disconnected from each other. One participant in the reorganization recalled that making policy "was like trying to make a cake by mixing the milk still in the bottle, with the flour still in the sack, with the eggs still in their carton."[19]

In addition to stovepipes separating formal divisions and processes, professional cultures divided the agency. At least three distinct cultures combined to create FEMA: the Department of Defense civil defense personnel, who tended to have seniority; the disaster relief program, whose employees had considered themselves so close to the president in the 1970s that they answered the phones with the greeting, "White House"; and a firefighting culture from the scientific and grant-making programs established by the Fire Prevention and Control Act of 1974. Divided by culture and organizational responsibility, the fragmented agency was not able to establish a clear mission. Even so, its first administrator under Carter, John Macy, attempted to put the agency on a path

[19] National Academy of Public Administration, *Coping with Catastrophe: Building an Emergency Management System to Meet People's Needs in Natural and Manmade Disasters* (Washington, DC: NAPA, 1993), 16.

toward an *all hazards* approach by emphasizing the similarities between natural hazards preparedness and civil defense activities.[20] All hazards is a successor to the idea of dual use; it means that the government will use the same plans, procedures, resources, and personnel to address all kinds of hazards and disasters rather than having separate plans and organizations for each kind of hazard.[21] The terms had similar meanings in practice, but all hazards became more widely used, and the language of "all" rather than "dual" opens the concept to many more interpretations. The effect of the all hazards idea was to break down barriers between national security and natural disasters divisions, even though FEMA did not fully embrace all hazards until its 1993 reorganization. Under Macy, FEMA began to develop an Integrated Emergency Management System that included "direction, control and warning systems which are common to the full range of emergencies from small isolated events to the ultimate emergency – war."[22]

All hazards, however, was just one idea in the policy stream, and it drew protests from agency divisions that wanted FEMA to emphasize their own special missions, whether earthquakes, fires, or civil defense. Whereas fire, floods, and even oil spills could rely on identifiable constituencies or stakeholders, terrorism and civil defense had significant support only in the bureaucracy and on congressional committees.[23] Businesses and communities that faced routine flooding, for instance, came together to lobby for federal government intervention to help flood planning and recovery. No such collaborations existed for civil defense, probably because states and localities never experienced major terrorism or foreign attack. The institutional supports for civil defense that were a legacy of top-down national government Cold War plans might have withered away if events had not propelled terrorism and nuclear war back on the national agenda.

TERRORISM ENTERS THE AGENDA

While FEMA's official histories locate the agency as a natural extension of the development of natural disaster programs, we know from records of state governors' concerns at the time that the agency was also created because of public

[20] Macy was administrator from August 1979 to January 1981.
[21] William L. Waugh, Jr., *Living with Hazards, Dealing with Disaster: An Introduction to Emergency Management* (Armonk, NY: M. E. Sharpe, 2000), 48–50.
[22] "FEMA History," available at http://www.fema.gov/about/history.shtm (accessed October 4, 2010).
[23] Thomas A. Birkland and Regina Lawrence, "The Social and Political Meaning of the *Exxon Valdez* Oil Spill," *Spill Science and Technology Bulletin* 7 (2002): 3–4; Thomas A. Birkland, "Scientists and Coastal Hazards: Opportunities for Participation and Policy Change," *Environmental Geosciences* 8 (2001): 61–67; Peter J. May and Thomas A. Birkland, "Earthquake Risk Reduction: An Examination of Local Regulatory Efforts," *Environmental Management* 18 (1994): 923–939.

and media pressure on the government to do something about the nebulous terrorist threat.[24] Terrorism first drew the attention of emergency preparedness planners during the 1972 Munich Olympics; there, television cameras captured the images of hooded Palestinian terrorists who tried to leverage 11 Israeli hostages for the release of 200 Arab guerrillas imprisoned in Israel. The media covered the events from the moments when the terrorists first captured the Israeli athletes to the murder of the hostages the next day. The grisly material and the almost continuous television coverage "turned viewers into voyeurs," and while commentators have remarked on how this prominent coverage changed the nature of television, it was also true that the television coverage changed how Americans perceived terrorism.[25] At the very least, terrorism's greater exposure in the American media put the threat of terrorism on the national agenda.[26]

Terrorism was the subject of several commissions and studies in the late 1970s, one of which resulted in a 1978 National Governors Association report warning that "Little coordinated federal-state planning for terrorist consequence management has been undertaken."[27] The Association hoped that a unitary disaster agency might "provide an important foundation for a comprehensive national emergency response system." And so along with a host of other responsibilities, FEMA was given the task of coordinating what was called, in sanitized language, "terrorism consequence management." FEMA was to plan for what might be done to help victims after a terrorist act occurred, whereas most of the work of immediately responding to terrorism would fall to state and local officials.

Terrorism might have gotten lost in the shuffle of reorganization if it were not for world events and a new president who made national security a priority. During 1979–1980, in the last year of the Carter administration, Americans saw pictures of American hostages blindfolded and marched through the streets of Tehran. Television images of terrorist takeovers of U.S. embassies and the use of American hostages as pawns in a foreign revolution in Iran heightened Americans' awareness of the threat posed by terrorism.

---

[24] As of 2012, FEMA's Web site stressed its roots in natural disaster preparation programs, and in politicians' desire to centralize those programs: http://www.fema.gov/about/history.shtm (accessed October 4, 2012).

[25] Michael Thompson-Noel, "This Televisual Life," *New Statesman*, July 26, 1996.

[26] Nancy Signorielli and George Gerbner, *Violence and Terror in the Mass Media: An Annotated Bibliography* (New York: Greenwood Press, 1988); Alex P. Schmid and Janny de Graaf, *Violence as Communication: Insurgent Terrorism and the Western News Media* (Beverly Hills, CA: Sage, 1982).

[27] National Governors' Association, *1978 Emergency Preparedness Project – Final Report* (Washington, DC: Defense Civil Preparedness Agency, 1978), 107; for another example, see: "The Likelihood of the Acquisition of Nuclear Weapons by Foreign Terrorist Groups for Use Against the United States," United States Intelligence Board, Interagency Intelligence Memorandum, January 8, 1976, available at http://www.fas.org/irp/cia/product/nw-terror-1976.pdf (accessed October 19, 2010).

Concerned about the United States' vulnerability to nuclear attack and terrorism by agents of the Soviet Union, the Ronald Reagan administration took over from Carter in 1981 and briefly reinvigorated civil defense as part of its nuclear deterrence strategy.[28] Civil defense and terrorism preparation merged because one of the uses of civil defense was to protect against attacks from abroad and unrest at home by groups that some might label terrorists (while others might call them criminals or in some cases merely protestors). As governor of California from 1967 to 1975, Reagan had been concerned with terrorism preparation and civil defense. After witnessing riots and student protests, he organized the California Specialized Training Institute in 1971, an emergency management counterterrorism training center. The director of the institute, Louis O. Giuffrida, a former National Guard officer and a general in California's state militia, became Reagan's first FEMA administrator in 1981.[29] Giuffrida's security credentials suited Reagan's larger nuclear deterrence agenda, of which FEMA was a small part.[30]

While the Reagan administration promoted a strong national defense and competition with the Soviet Union, Giuffrida shaped FEMA beyond Reagan's mandate to reflect his own interest in terrorism and national security. Before coming to FEMA, Giuffrida had written articles and memos about the government's responsibilities in the event of a terrorist attack, and according to one colleague of Giuffrida's, "he wanted to be a player in the national security realm" and envisioned the agency as a "junior CIA or FBI."[31] When Giuffrida

---

[28] Amanda J. Dory, *Civil Security: Americans and the Challenge of Homeland Security* (Washington, DC: CSIS Press, 2003), 10–13.

[29] Giuffrida was an expert on domestic terrorism. At the U.S. Army War College in 1970, he wrote a thesis that in part concerned the logistics of interning African Americans in the event of an urban riot. The thesis is reprinted here: Senate Committee on Governmental Affairs, Nomination of Louis O. Giuffrida. Washington, DC, 97th Cong., 1st Sess, Committee Print (1981): 34–83.

[30] In 1980, Congress had amended the 1950 Federal Civil Defense Act, intending to revitalize civil defense; in response, FEMA proposed a seven-year, $4.2 billion plan for new education and evacuation programs, among other initiatives. Two years later, President Reagan affirmed the value of civil defense in the effort to defeat the Soviet Union in a National Security Decision Directive, but the end of the Cold War and the collapse of the Soviet Union rendered such programs unnecessary. Amanda J. Dory, *Civil Security: Americans and the Challenge of Homeland Security* (Washington, DC: CSIS Press, 2003), 10–19; General Accounting Office, "The Federal Emergency Management Agency's Plan for Revitalizing U.S. Civil Defense," GAO/NSIAD-84-11, April 16, 1984, i–iii; National Security Decision Directive 23 on "U.S. Civil Defense Policy," February 3, 1982. In 1994, Congress repealed the Federal Civil Defense Act; Public Law 103–337, October 5, 1994; available at http://www.access.gpo.gov/uscode/title50A (accessed October 10, 2010).

[31] In a memo requested by Giuffrida, FEMA General Counsel George Jett lays out FEMA's authority in civil disturbances, "riots, demonstrations which get out of hand, etc." This memo and others refer to a previous Department of Justice memo that rejects FEMA's authority in "non-natural catastrophes." The FEMA counsels explicitly disagree with Justice and advise that "dual use" provisions and FEMA's authority under executive order 12148 may allow FEMA to recommend declarations and assert authority in nonnatural disasters including Love Canal and "the Cuban influx" as well as in "major civil disturbances." See George Jett, General Counsel,

first took office, he asked the FEMA general counsel whether he had the authority to rename FEMA as the "Office of Civil Defense." (He could not because FEMA was a statutory term).

Yet, while he made progress in bringing together the more than 100 disaster response programs that had been moved under the FEMA umbrella, Giuffrida overreached in his desire to make FEMA the lead agency in responding to terrorist attacks. He possessed a passion for counterterrorism, a confidence that FEMA could implement national security policy, and a swagger; yet none of these were enough to overcome the fact that the agency lacked the budget, the expertise, the manpower, and most importantly the bureaucratic clout to be influential in the national security world. The result was that FEMA's forays into national security were bungling at best and scandalous at worst.

Giuffrida most famously led FEMA to overreach its capacity in national security by developing a secret contingency plan that called for a declaration of martial law and suspension of the Constitution, turning control of the United States over to FEMA during a national crisis. The plan itself did not define national crisis, but it implied nuclear war, massive terrorist attacks, or violent and widespread internal unrest. President Reagan never acted on the plan, but portions of it were controversial enough within the Reagan administration to call FEMA's leadership into question.[32] The martial law portions of the contingency plan are cited in a June 30, 1982 memo written by Giuffrida's deputy for national preparedness programs, John Brinkerhoff.[33] The wide-ranging authority that would potentially be granted FEMA alarmed Attorney General William French Smith, who sent a letter to National Security Advisor Robert

"Memorandum for Louis O. Giuffrida, Responsibilities in Civil Disturbances," July 10, 1981; Craig B. Annear, Assistant General Counsel, "Note for Lee Thomas, The Applicability of the Disaster Relief Act of 1974 to Riots and Civil Disorders," May 21, 1981. The 1992 Los Angeles riots were declared a disaster because of fire damage rather than riots.Giuffrida's desire for FEMA to become a national security agency is reflected in a proposed executive order on intelligence activities, in which Jett writes, "I have suggested that consideration be given to the inclusion of a provision concerning FEMA involvement in intelligence matters in times of national emergency planning and response." See Jett, "Memorandum for Louis O. Giuffrida," November 9, 1981.

[32] It is not clear whether Reagan actually signed an executive order approving the contingency plan; the full facts remain obscured in part because President George W. Bush sealed some 68,000 pages of Reagan's White House records in November 2002. Elements of the draft executive order do appear in E.O. 12656 issued on November 18, 1988.

[33] The scenario outlined in the Brinkerhoff memo resembles the elements of Giuffrida's thesis at the Army War College in Carlisle, PA, in which he advocated martial law in case of a national uprising by black militants. The paper also advocated the roundup and transfer to "assembly centers or relocation camps" of at least 21 million "American Negroes." See Alfonso Chardy, "Reagan Aides the 'Secret' Government," *Miami Herald*, July 5, 1987, A1. Officials during the period accused Chardy of bias and inconsistencies in his analysis of the Reagan White House, but there appears to be little evidence contradicting his general findings about FEMA planning. For a critical view of the Chardy article, see Laurence H. Silberman, "On Honor," *Harvard Journal of Law and Public Policy* 32 (Spring 2009): 503–512; 511–512.

McFarlane on August 2, 1984, urging that Reagan delay signing the draft executive order:

I believe that the role assigned to the Federal Emergency Management Agency in the revised Executive Order exceeds its proper function as a coordinating agency for emergency preparedness. This department and others have repeatedly raised serious policy and legal objections to the creation of an 'emergency czar' role for FEMA.[34]

Yet, Giuffrida did not stop with inserting FEMA into contingency plans. With the memory of the Munich attacks still fresh, Giuffrida claimed a role for FEMA in preparing for a possible crisis at the 1984 Los Angeles Olympics. Giving the agency a role in preparing for a crisis at the games might have seemed reasonable, but Giuffrida's overreach made people so suspicious of FEMA that even good ideas were rejected. In addition, other Reagan officials resented Giuffrida's ambition, and Smith's memo was just one example of the backlash against Giuffrida and FEMA, according to some of Giuffrida's colleagues at the time.

Chastened by the Attorney General and others in the national security community, and the subject of a federal investigation of alleged fraud and mismanagement, Giuffrida resigned in 1985. No subsequent FEMA administrator had the same personal interest in counterterrorism and civil defense as Giuffrida, and his controversial tenure kept FEMA from reemerging as a significant participant in national security.[35] FEMA had become a liability for politicians and a potential source of embarrassment.

THE STAFFORD ACT

By the end of Giuffrida's tenure, as the costs of disasters escalated and botched relief efforts drew media attention, Congress attempted to bring coherence to the system of disaster preparedness and response. The Robert T. Stafford Disaster Relief and Emergency Assistance Act of 1988 was the product of years of committee meetings and study, though the effects of Hurricane Gilbert in the Caribbean that year added urgency to the deliberations. The Act defined

---

[34] William French Smith, Attorney General, letter to Robert C, McFarlane, Assistant to the President for National Security Affairs, Washington, DC, August 2, 1984.

[35] It is notable that Giuffrida is not mentioned in FEMA's online history of the agency, available at http://www.fema.gov/about/history.shtm (accessed October 4, 2010). A number of articles in the 1980s criticized FEMA's secret continuity of government programs, including a much-cited article in *Penthouse* featuring Giuffrida. (See Donald Goldberg and Indy Badhwar, "Blueprint for Tyranny," *Penthouse*, August 1985, 72.) Other critical articles included: Steven Emerson, "America's Doomsday Project," *U.S. News & World Report*, August 7, 1989, 26–31; Alfonso Chardy, "North Helped Revise Wartime Plans," *Miami Herald*, July 19, 1987, A17. For a more judicious evaluation of FEMA's continuity of government programs, see Harold C. Relyea, "Continuity of Government: Current Federal Arrangements and the Future," *CRS Reports for Congress*, Washington, DC, November 7, 2003.

how disasters were to be declared, and it established categories of aid: relief, restoration of public and private infrastructure, and hazard mitigation.

Republican Representative Tom Ridge of Pennsylvania, who would later become the first secretary of the Department of Homeland Security, sponsored the Act. It drew bipartisan support, passing by a vote of 368 to 13 in the House. The Act's major provisions include:

- establishing a 75 percent federal, 25 percent local cost-sharing plan, in which the federal government commits to pay no less than 75 percent of the cost of eligible disaster programs;
- providing federal government assistance for disaster mitigation, response, and recovery, after declared disasters; however, most of the Act concerns immediate response;
- clarifying how Department of Defense resources would be used in disaster assistance.

Although enacted with broad support, the Act omitted several powers that would become important limitations on the federal government. In the first omission, the Act failed to provide for economic recovery, which is important after catastrophic disasters that destroy critical infrastructure. Small businesses lack large capital reserves, and if they close for more than a week, mounting expenses may force them to close permanently. By omitting recovery, the Act broke with the policies of the Federal Disaster Relief Act of 1974, which included provisions for long-term assistance after disaster. In contrast, the Stafford Act authorizes preparedness, response, and limited recovery assistance such as repairing damaged buildings and providing temporary housing, but does not explicitly authorize the president to provide long-term economic recovery assistance to communities.[36]

Policy change usually fixes reigning ideas into place rather than provides an occasion to rethink the premises of federal intervention.[37] The Stafford Act was enacted during a time when an ascendant conservative movement had cast federal government involvement in the economy as paternalism, and conservative and moderate coalitions in government were reluctant to enshrine a federal government role in recovery in law.

In its second omission, the Stafford Act provided that mitigation dollars could be spent only after a disaster – not before – which seems counterintuitive because mitigation activities, by definition, are intended to prevent damage in the first place. The federal government could provide technical assistance to

---

[36] The Secretary of Commerce eventually assumed some long-term recovery responsibilities. Title V of P.L. 93–288, the Disaster Relief Act of 1974 (88 Stat. 160–163), authorized the president to provide economic recovery assistance "after the period of emergency aid and replacement of essential facilities and services." Congress never funded this authority, however. Keith Bea, "Federal Stafford Act Disaster Assistance: Presidential Declarations, Eligible Activities, and Funding," *CRS Reports for Congress*, RL33053, Washington, DC, August 29, 2005.

[37] Thomas A. Birkland, "'The World Changed Today': Agenda-Setting and Policy Change in the Wake of the September 11 Terrorist Attacks," *Review of Policy Research* 21 (2004): 179–200.

states and localities in developing mitigation plans to prepare for disasters, and some subnational governments developed these plans on their own. More extensive and expensive mitigation activities, however, had to wait until after disaster when they could be part of a response or recovery effort. These activities might include relocating communities to less risky areas, or strengthening structures. (Some earthquake mitigation was handled under other programs).

Without the power to aid economic recovery or substantial pre-disaster mitigation, emergency planners lacked access to important tools to reduce the damage caused by disaster. Despite such limitations, the Stafford Act contained the seeds of a powerful shift of authority to the president. The Act clearly allowed the president to direct agencies to support disaster assistance operations:

In any emergency, the President may direct any Federal agency, with or without reimbursement, to utilize its authorities and the resources granted to it under Federal law in support of State and local emergency assistance efforts to save lives, protect property and public health and safety, and lessen or avert the threat of a catastrophe.[38]

The Act also allowed the president to suspend environmental regulations, override a $5 million cap on disaster assistance for almost any reason, and spend money on items that federal law might not have specifically authorized.[39]

Moreover, despite the law's broad language, in practice it narrowed the authority of FEMA bureaucrats. Officials from the Office of Management and Budget, none of them skilled in the new field of emergency management, had to approve FEMA's resource requests.[40] FEMA had to wait to deliver relief until a president made a disaster or emergency declaration, but by then much of the damage had been done. Officials in competing agencies sought to constrain FEMA's authority, and the agency could not fight back without the support and attention of the president, an emergency management profession, or an enterprising agency administrator. The Stafford Act functioned well in delivering federal support for more routine disasters and supplementing state and local efforts. It failed to provide much authority for intervention in catastrophic disasters when state and local resources were overwhelmed and the federal government had to pivot to quickly provide supplemental aid. It is difficult to routinize and plan for catastrophe because, by definition, catastrophe is beyond the routine.

The Stafford Act clarified the federal government's authority in disasters by specifying how the presidential declaration of a disaster area triggers federal

[38] Robert T. Stafford Disaster Relief and Emergency Assistance Act, PL 100–707, signed into law November 23, 1988. Available at: http://www.fema.gov/pdf/about/stafford_act.pdf (accessed October 4, 2010).

[39] 42 USC 68 § 5159; see also Eli Lehrer, "Influence, Presidential Authority, and Emergency Management: FEMA's Rise and Fall," in *Ideas From An Emerging Field: Teaching Emergency Management In Higher Education*, edited by Jessica A. Hubbard (Fairfax, VA: PERI Press, 2009), 51–91.

[40] Lehrer, "Influence, Presidential Authority, and Emergency Management"; NAPA, 1993, 20–28.

government funding – an improvement over the more vague language of the Disaster Relief Act of 1974. The Stafford Act did not solve the problems of defining what kinds of disasters the government was to prepare for, however, or what the role of the national government should be in a federal system. In adding specificity to federal government disaster management, the Act enshrined two unintended consequences. Because of an act of Congress, authority over the disaster bureaucracy shifted to the president. And an act that expanded and clarified the government's disaster relief policies ended up limiting the government's power over long-term recovery.

FEMA'S NADIR

By 1988, the year the Stafford Act was passed, a spate of agency administrators had given FEMA a bad name, and roughly half the agency's employees spent their days worrying about nuclear attack. FEMA made numerous blunders in national security – the sort of blunders Guiffrida was known for. For instance, the agency built a secret 112,544-square-foot bunker under the Greenbrier resort in West Virginia to house Congress during a nuclear war.[41] (The expensive and deluxe shelter is now a tourist attraction.) On top of the reputation for overreaching in national security, FEMA showed poor coordination in responding to major disasters. For large disasters, FEMA's response could be slow and excessively bureaucratic. For small and medium-sized disasters, FEMA was often unclear about whether it should intervene at all, and its equivocation frustrated states and localities. Congress was to blame for some of the agency's schizophrenia – at this point, FEMA still reported to more than a dozen congressional committees, including the Senate Armed Services committee, which confirmed appointees to an associate director position.

Moreover, ambiguity about FEMA's mission and a lack of resources contributed to a string of lackluster responses to high-profile disasters, most notably the Loma Prieta earthquake in 1989 and Hurricanes Hugo in 1989 and Andrew in 1992. Hugo caused $1.6 billion in damage, partly because of a rare case of looting in the American Virgin Islands.[42] Buildings were torn apart and the federal government had to dispatch military police and FBI agents to patrol the streets after 150 prisoners were freed from jail by the storm. The agency's slow response and requests for detailed cost assessments during the aftermath in South Carolina prompted Sen. Ernest Hollings to call FEMA a "bureaucratic jackass."[43]

---

[41] Read more about the bunker complex at http://www.pbs.org/wgbh/amex/bomb/sfeature/floor-plan.html (accessed October 4, 2010). The government now offers tours, for a fee, to help defray the cost of upkeep for a Cold War hotel built for 1,000 persons.

[42] E. L. Quarantelli, "Preliminary Paper #205: Looting and Antisocial Behavior in Disasters," Disaster Research Center, University of Delaware, 1994.

[43] James N. Baker, Howard Manly, and Daniel Glick, "The Storm after Hugo," *Newsweek*, October 9, 1989, 40. *Economist*, "Hurricane Hugo; When the Wind Blows," October, 1989, 22; Hollings said, "Looking back on FEMA's sorry performance after Hugo, I am reminded of the

Similar problems with recovery plagued FEMA's response to Hurricane Andrew, which struck south Florida in 1992. FEMA was determined not to repeat the mistakes made during Hugo; the agency had secured a disaster declaration and sent communications equipment to Dade County well before landfall.[44] But things fell apart when the emergency managers, police, fire departments, and power companies who were supposed to respond to the disaster were themselves victims of the hurricane. With first responders incapacitated, no one was able to mount a damage assessment. According to studies of the response, "Officials in the state EOC [Emergency Operations Center] at Tallahassee kept pleading with local officials to tell them what they needed, and frustrated and equally frantic local officials kept saying they did not know what they needed – 'Send Everything!' To which agonized state officials could only reply, 'We can't send everything!'"[45]

The response was still so disorganized three days after the hurricane that Dade County Director of Emergency Preparedness Kate Hale held a press conference and said: "Where the hell is the cavalry on this one? We need food. We need water. We need people. For God's sake, where are they?"[46] After the firestorm of criticism in the media, FEMA's authority broke down. President George H. W. Bush, in the midst of a reelection campaign, sent nearly 20,000 Navy, Air Force, and Coast Guard troops to Florida.[47] Instead of the FEMA administrator leading the effort, the White House sent Andrew Card, the Secretary of Transportation, and a cadre of generals to take charge of the recovery. This resembled the old czar system more than a contemporary bureaucratized response. A National Academy of Public Administration report summed up the chaotic response: "The best laid plans and procedures are now vulnerable to disruption, indeed destruction, by one dramatic sound bite that the media turns into political shock waves."[48] Despite Bush's response, FEMA lore

old expression that there is no education like the second kick of a mule. Or, in this case, there is no education in the second kick of a bureaucratic jackass." Hollings, "Andrew's Aftermath," *Congressional Record*, 102nd Cong, 2nd. Sess., September 9, 1992.

[44] Fortunately, Andrew did not cause a major loss of life because the warning systems had been effective and the hurricane missed the population center of central Miami. But the storm did destroy property, including buildings that were built after the adoption of the South Florida Building Code. It was later revealed that new construction had been in violation of the code.

[45] NAPA 1993; Gary L. Wamsley, and Aaron D. Schroeder, "Escalating in a Quagmire: The Changing Dynamics of the Emergency Management Policy Subsystem," *Public Administration Review* 56 (1996): 235–246.

[46] Peter Slevin and Dexter Filkins, "We Need Help," *Miami Herald*, August 28, 1992.

[47] Bob Davis, "Brewing Storm," *Wall Street Journal*, August 31, 1992, A1. In addition, political theorist Wendy Brown emphasizes the "popular and media discourse about relevant state and federal agencies (e.g., the Federal Emergency Management Agency [FEMA]), that came close to displacing onto the agencies themselves responsibility for the suffering of victims." Wendy Brown, *States of Injury* (Princeton, NJ: Princeton University Press, 1995), 68–69.

[48] NAPA, 1993, 19.

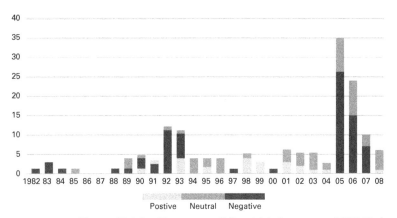

FIGURE 4.6. Tone of Major Newspaper Editorials' Coverage of FEMA from 1982 to 2008.

Note: The most frequent newspaper appearing in the results was *The New York Times*. Tone is easier to establish in an editorial than in a news article because an editorial is, by definition, opinionated. Tone is negative when an editorial criticizes FEMA's ability to achieve some policy goal, such as efficiency, or blames FEMA or its leaders for a political or policy failure. Where there was doubt about the tone, I coded the article as neutral. This graph does not include Op-Eds, Columns, or other commentary.

Source: Data was taken from a Lexis-Nexis search of "Major US Newspaper" mentions of FEMA.

holds that the agency's poor response to fallout from Hurricane Andrew in Louisiana, Georgia, and Florida contributed to his loss in the 1992 presidential race. Politicians depended on the smooth functioning of the disaster bureaucracy to serve constituents and buoy their reputations, yet the development of disaster policy mired FEMA in the pathologies of bureaucracy: conflicting security and natural disasters missions, red tape, and a lack of coordination across programs and levels of government.

FEMA's reaction to major disasters was often slow or piecemeal.[49] The news media routinely held up FEMA as an example of government inefficiency and incompetence; a *Washington Post* article labeled FEMA as "the agency that everybody loves to hate."[50] Most major newspaper editorials during the period cast the agency in a negative light, and almost none were laudatory (see Figure 4.6).

---

[49] Peter J. May, *Recovering from Catastrophes: Federal Disaster Relief Policy and Politics* (Westport, CT: Greenwood Press, 1985); Roy S. Popkin, "The History and Politics of Disaster Management in the United States," in *Nothing to Fear*, edited by A. Kirby (Tucson: University of Arizona Press, 1990), 101–129.

[50] William Claiborne, "'Cultures Being Clubbed,'" *Washington Post*, May 20, 1993, A21.

FEMA UNDER FIRE

Following Hurricane Andrew, Congress commissioned studies of FEMA's shortcomings.[51] The most bold and influential of these, by the National Academy of Public Administration, raised the possibility of a "death penalty" for FEMA, but in the end recommended reorganization along the lines of the original intentions of the agency's creators. One subhead in the report read, "An institution not yet built." FEMA had been created to be a clearinghouse for federal disaster preparation, response, and recovery, but a decade and a half after its birth it still suffered from vague mission statements, an unclear legislative charter, and compartmentalized organization.

The real *bêtes noires* of the NAPA study were FEMA's civil defense and national security programs. The report declared that "the time has come to shift the emphasis from national security to domestic emergency management using an all hazards approach."[52] It charged that FEMA's National Preparedness Directorate was unwilling to use its advanced communications and transportation equipment in rescue efforts for hurricanes, earthquakes, floods, and fires because of concerns that bringing the equipment out into the open might expose national security assets to the enemy. A GAO study and a series of congressional hearings added to the expert consensus for change. U.S. Comptroller General Charles A. Bowsher testified that the national security divisions of FEMA, especially the National Preparedness Directorate, had "significant assets that could be used more effectively to help guide the federal government's response to catastrophic natural disasters, especially in light of the changing nature of national security emergencies."[53]

The NAPA report stated clearly that FEMA must "demilitarize" – at the time of the study, about 38 percent of FEMA's total staff and about 27 percent of its budget (about $100 million, excluding the disaster relief fund) were dedicated to national security emergencies.[54] Of FEMA's 3,000 full-time employees, 1,900 held security clearances, creating (at least) two competing cultures: the security and civil defense personnel, and the disaster relief and fire programs that lacked clearances. Those with security clearances looked down on those without. Two former colleagues remember that, for a time, Giuffrida took to wearing a sidearm.

Not all observers agreed with the NAPA assessment, however. William Cumming, an attorney who retired from FEMA in 1999 after serving in the

---

[51] Thomas W. Lippman, "Hurricane May Have Exposed Flaws in New Disaster Relief Plan," *Washington Post*, September 3, 1992, A21; NAPA 1993; Richard Sylves, "Coping with Catastrophe" (review), *Public Administration Review* 54 (1994): 303–307.

[52] NAPA, 1993, x.

[53] Charles A. Bowsher, "Disaster Management: Recent Disasters Demonstrate the Need to Improve the Nation's Response Strategy." GAO/T-RCED-93-4, January 27, 1993, 13.

[54] NAPA, 1993, 53–54.

general counsel's office since the agency's creation, said that the national security divisions, with their distinct and at times secretive culture, made an easy scapegoat for FEMA's real problem: the agency was insufficiently staffed and funded to both prepare for and respond to disasters as well as to play a role in national security.[55] The FEMA counsel's office advised that defense assets could not be used for natural disasters in a 1992 memorandum: "However, the [Civil Defense] Act does not presently contain any authority for response, at the federal level, to a natural catastrophe."

Regardless of resource constraints and unclear authority, the organizational structure of the agency was bound to create rivalries. FEMA contained two "formless bags": the National Preparedness Directorate that focused on nuclear war and the State and Local Programs Support Directorate that addressed natural disasters.[56] In addition to recommending the breakup of FEMA's national security division, the NAPA and GAO reports concluded that to be effective, FEMA needed greater involvement from the White House so that the "full weight of presidential authority can be brought to bear in managing federal agency work in the aftermath of disasters."[57] In doing so, the reports implicitly signaled a change in how a disaster agency has to relate to its environment if it is to prosper. Gradual expansion of the president's role in U.S. politics, as well as specific legislation such as the Stafford Act, had given the presidency substantial authority to manage disasters. To succeed, FEMA would have to learn to operate in the age of the "plebiscitary" president, or of the "politicized presidency."[58]

In a technocratic model of public administration, an agency might respond to failure by bringing in experts to evaluate its shortcomings and attempting to

---

[55] William Cumming, personal interview, Arlington, VA, December 10, 2003; Patricia M. Gormley, FEMA General Counsel, "Memorandum for Steve Gaddy, Deputy Associate Director, External Affairs Directorate (cc: Grant Peterson)," July 14, 1992. Whatever the correctness of the counsel's advice at that time, Congress amended the FCDA in 1993 to make it "all-hazards." See Public Law 103–160. Other divisions of FEMA saw a greater role for civil defense funds and programs in natural disasters. For example, see Policy Coordinating Committee on Emergency Preparedness and Mobilization Civil Defense Working Group, Dual Use Memo, 1991. In practice, FEMA was used to responding to technological disasters, including the Times Beach, MO dioxin contamination in the early 1980s.

[56] Lehrer, "Influence, Presidential Authority, and Emergency Management"; Albert Gore, "National Performance Review: Federal Emergency Management Agency," Washington, DC: Office of the Vice President, 1993), available at http://govinfo.library.unt.edu/npr/library/reports/fema.html (accessed October 4, 2010).

[57] Richard Sylves, "Ferment at FEMA: Reforming Emergency Management," *Public Administration Review* (May–June 1994): 303–307.

[58] Terry Moe, "Presidents, Institutions, and Theory," in *Researching the Presidency: Vital Questions, New Approaches*, edited by B. A. Rockman (Pittsburgh, PA: University of Pittsburgh Press, 1993), 337–386; Moe, "The Presidency and the Bureaucracy: The Presidential Advantage," in *The Presidency and the Political System*, 7th ed., edited by M. Nelson (Washington, DC: CQ Press, 2003), 425–439; Aaron Wildavsky, *The Beleaguered Presidency* (New Brunswick, NJ: Transaction Publishers, 1991).

fix them by writing new procedures.[59] In a highly visible agency such as FEMA, however, a president could not wait for technocratic remedies to take their course. Ever since 1937, when the President's Committee on Administrative Management (the Brownlow Committee) recommended creating the Executive Office of the President to manage burgeoning government agencies, the presidency has evolved toward a conception of itself as not merely a coequal branch of government or a unit of the executive branch but as the head of a corporation whose job it is to oversee all that is underneath.[60] When something in the factory's machinery goes awry, as in the case of FEMA's response to Hurricane Andrew, it is the president's job to fix it.[61]

In practice, the politicized or corporate model of the presidency resulted in the president's vacillation between ignoring FEMA and micromanaging it, as the NAPA report points out.[62] In addition to ambiguous statutes from Congress, FEMA received ambiguous signals from the president about the level of control or ownership he wanted over FEMA. The result was especially chaotic when mixed with a FEMA political leadership that was relatively inexperienced and un-professionalized – the agency was labeled the "federal turkey farm" by a House committee for its reputation as a dumping ground for political appointees who lacked emergency management qualifications.[63]

BUREAUCRATS STRIKE BACK: PROFESSIONALIZATION

While FEMA was at its nadir, the emergency management profession was ascendant. New associations, higher education degree programs, and journals gave the profession an institutional core that refined a common language of disaster management. A common language, best practices, and institutional homes for emergency management built a profession that could learn from its mistakes and share knowledge across diverse organizations, however imperfectly.

As the Cold War waned, civil defense professional associations gave way to emergency management. The U.S. Civil Defense Council, for example, was founded in 1952 and changed its name to the National Coordinating

[59] David A. Garvin, Amy C. Edmondson, and Francesca Gino, "Is Yours a Learning Organization?" _Harvard Business Review_ 86 (March 2008): 109–116; David A. Garvin, _Learning in Action_ (Boston: Harvard Business School Press, 2000).

[60] Barry D. Karl, _Executive Reorganization and Reform in the New Deal_ (Cambridge, MA: Harvard University Press, 1963); James W. Fesler, "The Brownlow Committee Fifty Years Later," _Public Administration Review_ 47 (August 1987): 291–296.

[61] Moynihan, Donald P. "Extra-Network Organizational Reputation and Blame Avoidance in Networks: The Hurricane Katrina Example," _Governance_ 2 5(2012): 567–588. Christopher Hood, "What Happens When Transparency Meets Blame-Avoidance?" _Public Management Review_ 9 (2007): 191–210; R. Kent Weaver, "The Politics of Blame Avoidance," _Journal of Public Policy_ 6 (1986): 371–398.

[62] NAPA 1993, 21–23.

[63] Larry Van Dyne, "Perfect Places for Those Hard-to-Place Contributors, _Washingtonian_, November, 1992.

(1896–) **National Fire Protection Association**

(1974–) **National Emergency Management Association**
NEMA began as a civil defense organization, but gradually devoted itself to natural hazards and reduced its role in civil defense

(1952–1983) **International Association of Emergency Managers**
(1983–1998) Began as U.S. Civil Defense Council (1952–1983). Then became the National
Coordinating Council on Emergency Management in 1983. Then renamed the
(1998–) International Association of Emergency Managers in 1998

(1962–) **The American Civil Defense Association**
Has refashioned itself as a homeland security and counterterrorism defense association

(1970–) **American Strategic Defense Association**

(1976–) **Natural Hazards Center**

(1979–) **National Voluntary Organizations Active in Disaster**

FIGURE 4.7. Major Professional Emergency Management Associations and Their Founding Dates.

Council on Emergency Management in 1983. In 1998, it began coordinating efforts worldwide as the International Association of Emergency Managers (see Figure 4.7). A slate of conferences, reference materials, and points of contact institutionalized vehicles for debating and developing best practices and common ideas. The growth of an academic discipline of emergency management added to the intellectual resources of the profession. Faculty hired to teach emergency management created journals and organized conferences, and the students trained in newly formed degree programs began to staff federal, state, and local agencies. Gradually, emergency management grew from an occupation whose members entered the field as a third or fourth career and learned on the job to become more of a profession in which members acquired academic and practical credentials.[64] Local and regional associations grew as well, and many began setting up state-regulated exams and licensing procedures.

[64] Information from Wayne Blanchard, FEMA's Higher Education Project file and personal communication, June 4, 2005; Arthur Oyola-Yemaiel and Jennifer Wilson, "Three Essential Strategies for Emergency Management Professionalization in the U.S.," *International Journal of Mass Emergencies and Disasters* 23 (March 2005): 77–84.

As the profession gained more resources, it played a greater role in a continuum of organizations that addressed disasters. As one emergency manager put it, "some emergency management systems are exclusively 'ambulances at the bottom of cliffs', whereas others are also 'fences at the top'."[65] The profession came to understand a disaster as the middle of a longer process of preparation and recovery surrounding the actual event. In addition to *all hazards*, the profession adopted the *all phases* concept, or the idea that emergency management encompasses not just disaster recovery but preparation, response, and long-term mitigation.[66]

The brightest lights in the profession recognized that emergency management lacked coherence. What the 1993 National Academy report said of FEMA held for disaster management at all levels of government: "It has no strategic planning process for developing a mission and goals for the agency as a whole."[67] After analyzing their experiences, emergency managers realized that they could not afford to shut off discussion about one type of disaster from discussion about others. Nor could they examine the response to natural disasters in isolation from all emergency management functions: mitigation, preparedness, response, and recovery. Another panel recommended a solution that would be adopted during the agency's reorganization: "a national emergency management system that is comprehensive, risk-based, and all hazards in approach."[68] The profession's ideas, in addition to the institutional structures it provided, contributed to reorienting FEMA's mission and structure around natural disasters.

The agency had a symbiotic relationship with the profession, and while the profession supplied FEMA with constructive criticism and employees, the agency provided the profession with jobs, visibility, and an institutional home. Emergency management grew exponentially. By 1994, four universities had begun emergency management degree programs.[69] As Figure 4.8 shows, a decade later there were at least 120 college-level programs, from certificates and minors through doctoral degrees.[70] FEMA recognized both a demand and

---

[65] Neil Britton, "Higher Education in Emergency Management: What is Happening Elsewhere," Emergency Management Higher Education Conference, Emmitsburg, Maryland, June 2004, 2.

[66] All hazards refers to the idea that, as much as possible, the same plans, procedures, and personnel should be used to prepare for and respond to all kinds of hazards, including natural disasters, industrial accidents, and attack, rather than having separate organizations responsible for addressing each hazard.

[67] NAPA, 1993, 41.

[68] U.S. Federal Emergency Management Agency, FEMA Renewal, *Federal Emergency Management Agency National Performance Review Report* (Washington 1993), 2–3.

[69] Bachelor's degrees in emergency management were offered at three schools by late 1994 and early 1995: University of North Texas, Thomas Edison University, and Rochester Institute of Technology. In addition, UCLA offered a continuing education certificate program.

[70] Most of these programs reflect content from the emerging discipline of emergency management, which draws on the fields of public administration, sociology, engineering, fire sciences, and criminal justice. A few of the community college programs began as fire sciences programs with

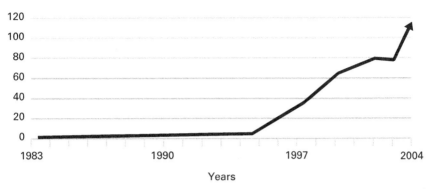

FIGURE 4.8. Growth of Emergency Management Higher Education Programs from 1983 to 2004.
Source: Data provided by Wayne Blanchard, "FEMA Higher Education Project," presentation materials, June 27, 2005.

an opportunity for more academic training and research and established a higher education project in 1995 to foster the growth of college and university programs. The profession as a whole grew accordingly. In 2003, the Bureau of Labor Statistics listed emergency management as one of the fastest-growing occupations in the United States.[71]

The development of an emergency management profession saved lives and property over the long run: in 1969, for example, more than 250 people died when Hurricane Camille struck the Gulf Coast, but only 36 lost their lives when a similar hurricane, Andrew, hit Florida and Louisiana in 1992.[72] Even the response to Camille was an improvement over emergency management in previous generations. When the Great Hurricane hit the Caribbean in 1780, 22,000 people died. A journalist compared its effect with that of Hugo in 1989: "The safety precautions [in 1780], suggested by the authorities, were for residents to put on all their clothes, tie pillows around their heads and hope for the best. By comparison the human toll of Hurricane Hugo was slight. The islanders knew in advance that the wind was coming – though about all they could do was duck."

By 1993, the profession had a strong enough core of prolific academics and experienced practitioners to develop criticism of existing government agencies and a plan for their reform. Although not univocal, the profession's counsel was instrumental in FEMA's reform. The profession provided ideas, training

a new name, but over time they incorporated concepts and experience from the field of emergency management.

[71] The BLS listed occupations with the largest expected increase in employment between 2002 and 2012. Bureau of Labor Statistics, "Tomorrow's Jobs," 2003, available at http://www.bls.gov/oco/pdf/oco2003.pdf (accessed June 8, 2011).

[72] See Figure 4.10. *Economist*, "Hurricane Hugo; When the Wind Blows," October, 1989, 22.

for current and future disaster managers, institutionalization outlasting any particular political leadership, and a common vocabulary waiting to be adopted by an *administrative politician*. The development of a decentralized profession was a necessary precondition for FEMA's reforms that were led from the top in Washington, DC.

FEMA FROM THE ASHES: JAMES LEE WITT AND ALL HAZARDS

After facing the threat of abolition, FEMA underwent a celebrated reorganization in 1993, after which the agency became a valuable asset to politicians and especially the president, rather than an embarrassment. How could a turnaround happen so quickly, especially if FEMA's problems were so deeply rooted? Witt's central accomplishment was to clearly define, articulate, and implement his version of the all hazards approach as the agency's primary mission. The Witt-era FEMA embraced the term "all hazards," which meant that the agency in principle would prepare for and respond to all kinds of hazards, including natural disasters, industrial accidents, and terrorism or nuclear attack. In practice, the all hazards concept allowed Witt to maintain control over national security programs that remained part of the agency's mission, while also transferring many of the resources and much of the attention from national security to natural disasters. The Witt era was never truly all hazards, but the rhetoric caught on and provided an identity for emergency management organizations at all levels of government. Some of his organizational changes improved the agency's performance, and other innovations showed politicians that the agency could perform tasks that would boost citizens' opinions of the federal government.

FEMA's reorganization depended on the collective wisdom of the emergency management profession, which Witt was wise enough to tap. Witt himself was admired most for his political acumen. The former state emergency services director and county judge from Yell County, Arkansas never earned a college degree, but he possessed enough native skill to navigate the political thickets of Washington.

When Witt took office, the agency's reputation was in tatters. After a decade and a half of management scandals, disputes with other agencies, and being blamed for poor disaster response, media accounts portrayed the "long scorned" agency as doomed.[73] One academic study of the agency found that its employees were not sure what the agency actually did.[74] The National Academy of Public Administration study noted earlier quoted one person describing FEMA as "a check-writing agency, an intelligence agency, a social service agency and insurance agency, with a fire administration thrown in."[75]

---

[73] Charles Clark, "Disaster Response," *CQ Researcher* 3 (1993): 891.
[74] Jerry Ellig, *Learning from the Leaders: Results-Based Management at the Federal Emergency Management Agency* (Arlington, VA: The Mercatus Center, 2000), 9.
[75] NAPA, 1993, 42–43.

Witt's first task was to convince members of Congress to give him free rein to reorganize. Senator Barbara Mikulski (D-Maryland), who until 1994 chaired the Senate appropriations subcommittee responsible for FEMA, and Congressman Curt Weldon (D-Pennsylvania) led the charge for reform for him.[76] Mikulski had introduced a bill incorporating most of the suggestions of the NAPA study, and even though the bill died in committee, Witt proceeded to reorganize the agency along the same lines.[77] Winning political support in Congress was not easy – Witt recalls a meeting at which he placated Rep. Pete Stark, who had introduced a bill to abolish the agency: "I went up to the Hill myself and I told [Stark] what I wanted to do to reform, and I said give me one year and if we don't do it I'll tell you."[78]

Witt mollified the agency's critics by promising to refocus its mission from national security to quick response to natural disasters. He also promised more efficient and customer-service-friendly disaster relief. Both of these aims would benefit members of Congress because better, faster disaster relief offered a palpable benefit to citizens, and one for which politicians could claim credit. Witt gave the people what they wanted, but in this case "the people" was Congress. After the Soviet Union collapsed, civil defense lost what credibility it had, and domestic terrorism in 1993 was not a widely feared hazard. Only natural disasters remained on the agenda.

Witt's achievements as FEMA administrator were remarkable because of the hostile political and media environment he initially faced. Before Witt's tenure, members of Congress such as Ernest Hollings won public approval by speaking out against FEMA, reflecting the public's frustration with the agency's slow response in a time of crisis. But Witt convinced politicians that an effective and relatively autonomous FEMA would serve politicians' interests better than a FEMA-as-punching-bag. He pledged that the agency would quickly distribute relief funds, better reassure disaster victims through public relations programs, and increase its role in mitigation. Witt was able to make representatives such as Hollings and Stark realize that FEMA could potentially work to their advantage by providing constituents affected by disaster with an immediate response, one that would be citizens' most palpable and reassuring connection with the federal government.

The potential for aligning FEMA's mission with politicians' reelection goals had been present for some time, but it took active lobbying on Witt's part to make it a reality. Witt spoke to the chairs of the twenty committees that

---

[76] Carla Rivera and Alan C. Miller, "Streamlined FEMA Quake Assistance Seen," *Los Angeles Times*, March 15, 1994, A3, A28.

[77] Witt opposed the Mikulski bill (S.995) because it reduced the power of FEMA by eliminating most political appointees, transferring the continuity of government functions to the Department of Defense, and establishing a domestic crisis-monitoring unit in the White House. See William Claiborne, "Doling Out Praise, FEMA Critic Pressed for Reform at Hearing," *Washington Post*, March 25, 1994, A21.

[78] James Lee Witt, personal interview, Washington, DC, April 15, 2004.

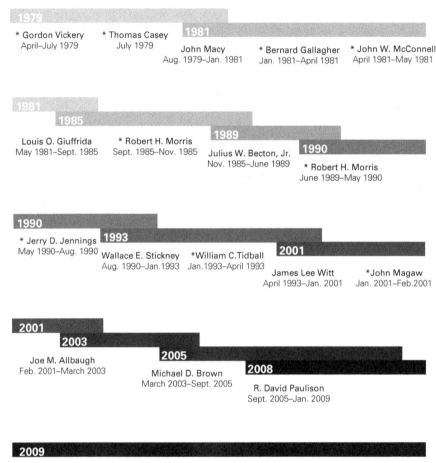

FIGURE 4.9. Federal Emergency Management Agency Administrators.
* Acting administrator
Source: Federal Emergency Management Agency (FEMA), http://www.fema.gov

had a stake in FEMA's reorganization during his first months on the job. And Witt spent two days calling every member of Congress in the nine Midwestern states affected by flooding in the summer of 1993. "You have to reach out," Witt says, "I told them what we were doing, and that if they had a problem, to call me."[79]

His ability to make the case for FEMA's potential effectiveness is remarkable because the legal and operational constraints on FEMA combined with

---

[79] Alasdair Roberts, "The Master of Disaster: James Lee Witt and the Federal Emergency Management Agency," Council for Excellence in Government Conference, April 1997.

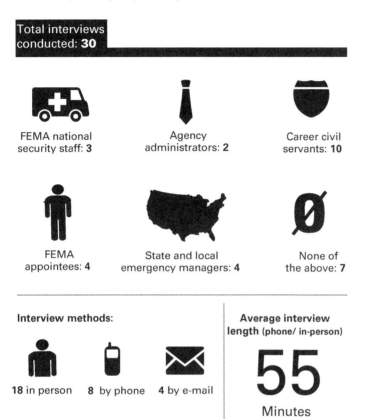

FIGURE 4.10. Interview Summary.

Note: In addition, I had conversations with many other participants in FEMA's development, including state and local emergency managers, FEMA employees, and one additional FEMA administrator. I also learned much by attending emergency management conferences. Interviews were conducted from July 2002 to October 2004. I had subsequent conversations with FEMA staff, including leadership, and with subject matter experts from the end of the interview period until 2012 when the manuscript was submitted for publication.

its high visibility make it easy for politicians to use the agency as a scapegoat. For example, because every jurisdiction faces some kind of potential disaster, many citizens deal with FEMA, either directly or through an intermediary. Vice-President Al Gore's Reinventing Government initiative identified FEMA as one of thirty-two "high impact" agencies that accounted for 80 percent of all federal government contacts with the public.[80] When disasters were averted, FEMA received some of the credit, but when severe disasters occurred, it received much of the blame even though it was only a small piece of a larger

---

[80] Gore, "National Performance Review," 4.

web of events that made communities vulnerable. News cameras contribute to this narrative of blame by filming devastation and personalizing the victims of disaster suffering at the hands of nature and an indifferent and bumbling bureaucracy.[81]

INTERNAL REFORMS

Witt's accomplishments within the agency were as impressive as his success on Capitol Hill. Immediately after becoming FEMA administrator, Witt refocused the agency's mission on the multiple phases of disaster: "to reduce the loss of life and property and protect our institutions from all hazards by leading and supporting the nation in a comprehensive, risk-based emergency management program of mitigation, preparedness, response, and recovery."[82] Witt's tenure compared with other administrators can be found in Figure 4.9. Notably, despite the "all hazards" term, Witt's message was clear: the agency needed to reorganize around natural disasters, not national security. FEMA curtailed national security operations; it remained in charge of a few programs concerned with preserving basic government functions during a time of war, but even these programs were separated from the rest of the agency. At a 1994 congressional hearing on civil defense, Witt spoke about what was wrong with disaster preparedness, not about bomb shelters, spotters, and wardens.[83] Witt's arguments that a reinvigorated FEMA should focus on natural disasters carried the day, and the Civil Defense Act was repealed in 1994, ending Armed Services committee oversight over FEMA. [84] The $146 million in civil defense appropriations in FEMA's budget, as well as $50 million in additional "defense related funds," were transferred to FEMA's all hazards budget, which by this time referred to natural disasters, not terrorism. Defense and security staffs were reassigned, and half of FEMA's staff with national security clearances had their clearances revoked.[85] Previous agency programs had appealed to dual use

---

[81] Saundra K. Schneider, "Government Response to Disaster: The Conflict Between Bureaucratic Procedure and Emergent Norms," *Public Administration Review* 52 (March–April 1992): 135–145.

[82] James Lee Witt and James Morgan, *Stronger in the Broken Places: Nine Lessons for Turning Crisis Into Triumph* (New York: Henry Holt, 2002), 26.

[83] Witt, "Statement Before the Subcommittee on Nuclear Deterrence, Arms Control, & Defense Intelligence, Committee on Armed Services," U.S. Senate, May 25, 1993; Witt, "Hearing on the Civil Defense Budget," Oversight and Investigations Subcommittee, House Armed Services Committee, April 21, 1994.

[84] Lehrer, "Influence, Presidential Authority, and Emergency Management"; Congress deleted a clause from the Civil Defense Act that said civil defense funds could be used for natural disaster purposes only "in a manner that is consistent with, contributes to, and does not detract from attack-related civil defense preparedness." See Amendment to Title II of the Federal Civil Defense Act of 1950, Public Law 97–86-December 1, 1981, Dual-Use Policy, 95 Stat. 1112, 50 USC, app. SEC 207.

[85] Lehrer, "Influence, Presidential Authority, and Emergency Management"; Richard G. Trefry, *Security Practices Board of Review Final Report and Recommendations* (Washington, DC:

or all hazards to justify their actions, but Witt put the concepts at the forefront of FEMA's missions and redefined them to make natural disaster preparedness the centerpiece of the agency.[86]

For Witt, all hazards meant that the agency should give priority to programs that addressed multiple hazards rather than programs that specialized in a single hazard. FEMA still employed earthquake specialists and flood specialists, but the agency limited or merged these programs. All hazards became a mantra that, when combined with organizational changes, turned FEMA into a streamlined, professional natural disasters preparation and response clearinghouse. In the early days of the agency, "you had to be a librarian to keep up with all of the guidelines that were coming from FEMA," said Kay Goss, Associate Director for Preparedness from 1994 to 2001.[87] Having multiple response plans and multiple coordinators did not make sense, according to all hazards proponents, when the same police, fire, and emergency personnel would respond to all types of disasters.

Organizationally, Witt made the changes recommended by the National Academy of Public Administration and GAO studies: he eliminated the National Preparedness Directorate and reduced its role to the Office of National Security Coordination, which became a liaison to the National Security Council and other agencies.[88] He divided the state and local programs section into five directorates: Preparedness, Operations, Mitigation, Response, and Recovery. Each of these was focused around what James Q. Wilson has called a "critical task" – a series of behaviors that shapes an organization's relationship to its environment.[89] In FEMA's case, the agency recruited experienced professionals in each directorate, and told politicians, the public, and state and local officials which part of the agency to turn to for help. Changes in practice accompanied the organizational changes. In the summer of 1993, FEMA used mobile communications vehicles that had been reserved for national security programs for response to floods in the Midwest.[90] To maintain relationships in Washington, DC, Witt established correspondence units to make sure that all letters from members of Congress and governors were answered within ten days.

FEMA, 1992); and Federal Emergency Management Agency, "Which FEMA Personnel Should Be Required to Have Security Clearances to Fulfill Their Emergency Assignments?" (memorandum from the deputy associate director, National Preparedness, December 18, 1986); also see Cumming interview.

[86] Witt's public speeches and internal memos made "all hazards" the centerpiece of FEMA's mission. For example, see Witt, "Memorandum for All FEMA Employees, Organizational Structure and Management," November 5, 1993.

[87] Kay C. Goss, personal interview, Washington, DC, November 20, 2003.

[88] Witt, "Memorandum for All FEMA Employees, Organizational Structure and Management."

[89] James Q. Wilson, *Bureaucracy: What Government Agencies Do and Why They Do It* (New York: Basic Books, 1989), 25.

[90] Roberts, "The Master of Disaster," 1997.

The mitigation directorate, comprised of pre-disaster programs intended to reduce damage, was one of Witt's signature innovations.[91] In the 1990s, only a handful of mitigation programs addressed natural hazards (for instance, bomb-resistant building structures had the added benefit of providing protection against earthquakes).[92] Creating a mitigation directorate was part of the agency's larger move away from national security functions toward natural hazards and it expanded the reach of the agency's grant programs. For example, the "Flood Safe" program encouraged homeowners in flood-prone areas to buy insurance against losses they might incur. It also delivered federal money to states and localities, which pleased constituents.

In concert with the five task-based directorates, the agency had a three-tiered system: a Washington office that provided technical expertise to Congress and the White House; a regional system that provided points of contact for state and local officials; and a national call center that was available to the public.[93] Each of these directorates addressed a major constituency, and each convinced its constituency that FEMA was better as a partner than as an adversary.[94] Washington staffers needed experts available to read and interpret legislation and to advise other agencies on their responsibilities in disaster. States and localities needed regional offices familiar with their particular disasters and institutional contexts (such as hurricanes and the Napoleonic code in Louisiana). Regional offices rarely had more than 100 people, but they provided contextual knowledge to link subnational governments and nonprofits with the rest of FEMA.[95] Citizens seeking relief aid needed an immediate response, and a toll-free number enabled them to mobilize that response.[96]

Procedurally, Witt refocused the agency's mission on quick response to natural disasters; he interpreted statutes so as to allow a response to be set in motion

[91] Patrick S. Roberts, "A Capacity for Mitigation as the Next Frontier in Homeland Security," *Political Science Quarterly* 124 (Spring 2009): 127–142.
[92] Paul F. Mlakar, Donald O. Dusenberry, James R. Harris, Gerald Haynes, Long T. Phan, and Mete A. Sozen, "Findings and Recommendations from the Pentagon Crash," *American Society of Civil Engineers Conference Proceedings* 241 (2003): 43–45.
[93] On the effectiveness of regions see: Patrick Roberts, "Dispersed Federalism as a New Regional Governance for Homeland Security," *Publius: The Journal of Federalism* 38 (Summer 2008): 416–443; James Lee Witt, "The Homeland Security Department's Plan to Consolidate and Co-locate Regional and Field Offices: Improving Communication and Coordination," United Stated Congress, House Committee on Government Reform, Subcommittee on National Security, Emerging Threats, and International Relations. 108th Cong, 2nd sess., March 24, 2004.
[94] Lehrer, "Influence, Presidential Authority, and Emergency Management"; FEMA News Brief, 1:2, September 17, 1993. Letter From James Lee Witt to All FEMA Employees, "FEMA's Reorganization," September 7, 1993. Also see various "Director's Weekly Update," including the one on June 13, 1997.
[95] Roberts, "Dispersed Federalism as a New Regional Governance," 416–421; 426–427.
[96] To provide surge capacity, FEMA entered into agreements with call centers at other agencies such as the IRS. Call center duties, unlike some of FEMA's disaster-specific tasks, are similar enough across agencies to be shared in times of emergency.

even before disaster struck.[97] In August 1993, the agency dispatched twelve tractor-trailer rigs of emergency supplies to North Carolina before Hurricane Emily made landfall. "We made a mistake with Hurricane Andrew by waiting for the states to tell us what they needed first," said Richard Krimm, a FEMA associate director. "Now we go to the state and say, 'Here are the things you need, just tell us if you want them.'"[98] The agency responded similarly well to a flood in the spring and summer of 1993 that caused the Mississippi and Missouri rivers to swell and left millions of acres of farmland underwater. FEMA also silenced the usual chorus of critics after it helped victims of a January 1994 earthquake that killed 61 people in the Los Angeles area.

Some of the Witt reforms involved instilling more efficient management practices by measuring performance. FEMA reduced the time it took for payments to reach disaster victims, going from the 30 days it took for checks to reach victims when Witt first took office to an average of seven. The agency cut the time it took temporary housing assistance to reach the victims it began to call "customers," going from an average of 20 days to 7 to 10, according to FEMA officials.[99]

Witt's mitigation efforts were not without controversy, of course. Critics claimed that mitigation programs were not held accountable for achieving their goals, and that mitigation programs promoted moral hazard.[100] They charged that property owners who had participated in mitigation programs to acquire insurance or to lower their insurance rates had little incentive to avoid risky behavior – through land use, zoning, and development patterns – if they could count on being reimbursed by the federal government. Indeed, despite their early promise, mitigation programs fell into two categories, as either liberally distributed pork barrel grants measured by outputs rather than outcomes, or programs that educated public officials and private citizens about how to protect themselves against disasters and, when absolutely necessary, provided them with financial assistance.

Despite such criticisms, the agency had unusual freedom during the Clinton years. Because it was created by executive order, FEMA could reorganize itself, refocus its mission, and shape its niche if Congress acquiesced. The Stafford Act gave the president a high degree of discretion over disaster funding, so much of FEMA's spending was outside the normal congressional budget process.

---

[97] The Stafford Act and other statutes give FEMA a broad – and vague – mandate (NAPA 1993). Witt did not have to interpret the statutes in the way he did; legally, all FEMA administrators could have been more active in disaster response and even more active in national security matters, but the reason that they had to decline intervention in a number of occasion was that they lacked the resources. See Wamsley and Schroeder, "Escalating in a Quagmire."

[98] Roberts, "The Master of Disaster," 331.

[99] Stephen Barr, "Transforming FEMA," in *Triumphs and Tragedies of the Modern Presidency*, David Abshire, editor, (Westport, CT: Praeger Publishers, 2001), 268–269.

[100] Rutherford H. Platt, *Disasters and Democracy: The Politics of Extreme Natural Events* (Washington, DC: Island Press, 1999), 69–110.

Furthermore, the agency was one of Vice-President Al Gore's reinvention laboratories; Gore's own office provided minimal-oversight Stafford Act regulations rather than delegating the task to persnickety low-level Office of Management and Budget personnel who had reviewed the agency's regulations in the past. [101]

EYES AND EARS OF THE PRESIDENT

FEMA's unusual latitude also depended on Witt's success in persuading Congress, relevant congressional committees, and especially the president to go along with his vision. [102] Witt was personally close to Bill Clinton; he was the only member of Clinton's Arkansas cabinet offered an equivalent position in the federal government. The personal relationship gave Witt's actions the imprimatur of the president, and Witt made certain that he would be given a free hand before he took office. [103] Witt said that upon his nomination as director, "The president knew something had to be done and he said are you going to be able to do it, and I said yes, I'll fix it." [104]

In addition to giving FEMA a new mission, new organization, and new procedure, Witt professionalized its workforce. He added at least half a dozen appointees who had state or local emergency management experience. His associate director, Lacy Suiter, was an experienced professional who led Tennessee's emergency management agency under both Democratic and Republican governors. He made room for these appointments by convincing Clinton to take a gamble and reduce patronage slots in exchange for a more effective agency. Political appointments sometimes go to experienced professionals, but often they reward campaign staff and fundraisers who may be highly capable individuals but lack experience in the policy areas they are assigned to lead. [105] FEMA had long been one of the most heavily politicized agencies. Before Clinton took office, FEMA had an unusually high ratio of 40 political appointees out of 3,000 employees. [106] During the campaign, Clinton pledged to reduce his White House staff by 25 percent, and therefore had fewer jobs to give to campaign staffers than he might otherwise have had. Democratic political operatives valued presidentially appointed positions in agencies as plum jobs for loyal campaign supporters. (The list of such positions published every four years

[101] Gore, "National Performance Review," 4.
[102] Lehrer, "Influence, Presidential Authority, and Emergency Management," 51–58; 88–91.
[103] Lehrer, "Influence, Presidential Authority, and Emergency Management," 51–58.
[104] James Lee Witt, personal interview, Washington, DC, April 15, 2004.
[105] Hugh Helco, *Government of Strangers* (Washington, DC: Brookings Institution, 1977); David E. Lewis, "Revisiting the Administrative Presidency: Policy, Patronage, and Administrative Competence," *Presidential Studies Quarterly* 39 (2009): 60–73.
[106] Office of Personnel Management, *The Plum Book, November 2004* (Washington, DC: U.S. Government Printing Office, 2004), 79–81. Available at: http://www.gpoaccess.gov/plumbook/2004/2004_plum_book.pdf (accessed November 4, 2010).

is informally referred to as the "Plum Book.") Nonetheless, in one of his first acts as administrator, Witt eliminated ten presidentially appointed management posts in the agency. "The White House didn't like that," Witt said, "but the President didn't mind."

Clinton had decided to make FEMA a priority during the campaign after seeing the devastation wrought by Hurricane Andrew in south Florida. He realized that voters could reward or punish a president based on the agency's performance after a disaster. Writing in his autobiography, Clinton remembers concluding during the campaign that:

Traditionally, the job of FEMA director was given to the political supporter of the President who wanted some plum position but who had no experience with emergencies. I made a mental note to avoid that mistake if I won. Voters don't choose a President based on how he'll handle disasters but if they're faced with one, it quickly becomes the most important issue in their lives.[107]

Two points are especially important in Clinton's revelation: the idea that voters reward or punish a president based on the government's performance in the immediate aftermath of a disaster, not its actions in encouraging good zoning, land use, and mitigation before an event; and the implicit recognition that media coverage gives *all* voters access to evaluations of the government's performance, not just voters directly affected by the disaster. (Clinton does not mention the media explicitly here.) Witt, too, was aware that disasters are "political events" because federal politicians receive benefits when emergency managers help the public recover from disasters.[108]

Combined with a close relationship with the president, FEMA's reorganization, procedural changes, professionalization, and increased autonomy led to a much-improved reputation. At the one-year anniversary of the Reinventing Government initiative, Clinton noted that "today [FEMA] may be the most popular agency in the federal government." Witt summed up the success this way: "We took FEMA and made it a brand name and people responded and supported it."[109] Over the long term, Clinton's bargain with Witt paid off because FEMA's newly positive brand name became associated with the president. FEMA's improved disaster response attracted attention, and Witt himself appeared at disaster scenes as the "eyes and ears" of the president (as he described his role during the recovery of the bodies of victims of TWA Flight 800).[110] Before 1993, Associated Press newspaper articles included a description of FEMA's function in any article that mentioned the agency. After 1994, most Associated Press articles dropped the description because the FEMA

[107] Bill Clinton, *My Life* (New York: Alfred A. Knopf, 2004), 428.
[108] Testimony to the U.S. Senate, April 30, 1996.
[109] James Lee Witt, personal interview, Washington, DC, April 15, 2004. Witt mandated that all of FEMA's 4,000 full- and part-time staff receive training in customer service techniques.
[110] Roger W. Cobb and David M. Primo, *The Plane Truth: Airline Crashes, the Media, and Transportation Policy* (Washington, DC: Brookings Institution, 2003).

name was widely recognized. Figure 4.6 shows a graph of the number of major newspaper editorials that mention FEMA in a positive tone compared with the number that mention FEMA in a negative or neutral tone; whereas almost all are negative before 1993, the trend reverses after Witt's reorganization.

In short, FEMA's newly improved reputation depended on a variety of factors: improved response times, professional orientation, customer service, improved relations with states and localities, a deemphasized national security role, and a leader who was an administrative politician linking the potential expertise of civil servants with the needs of elected politicians and, therefore, voters. Witt connected the activities of his agency to the long-term reelection interests of politicians by restructuring the agency and liberally reinterpreting statutes to gain authority where he thought the agency most needed it.

Among FEMA's many missions, the all hazards idea was its signature. In interviews with twenty-three current or former upper-level FEMA employees or emergency managers, all but one mentioned all hazards without my prompting when discussing the agency's mission.[111] Witt repeated the term like a mantra, and it announced the agency's broad mission to address all disasters while implying its deemphasized national security mission. The agency's responsibilities for preserving government functions in secret during a national emergency were deemphasized and separated from the rest of the agency.[112] Most importantly, the all hazards idea gave a common language to professionals in the agency and in states, localities, and emergency management training programs.

BUREAUCRATIC AUTONOMY IN CONTEMPORARY TIMES

Under Witt, the Clinton-era FEMA developed what political scientists call bureaucratic autonomy – the ability of an agency to shape the political environment and influence what politicians and social groups want the agency to do.[113] The concept of bureaucratic autonomy contrasts with a common understanding of bureaucracy that assumes that agencies merely respond to the rules set out for them by the president or Congress.[114] Standard social science models ascribe bureaucratic power either to the structural characteristics

---

[111] See Figure 4.10 for a breakdown of interview subjects.

[112] Harold C. Relyea, "Continuity of Government: Current Federal Arrangements and the Future," *Congressional Research Service Report* (November 7, 2003): 1–6.

[113] Carpenter (*Forging of Bureaucratic Autonomy*, 17) claims that autonomy exists when agencies "can bring their political legitimacy to bear upon the very laws that give them power."

[114] Jonathan Bendor, Amihai Glazer, and Thomas Hammond, "Theories of Delegation in Political Science," *Annual Review of Political Science* 4 (2001): 235–269; David Epstein and Sharyn O'Halloran, *Delegating Powers* (Cambridge: Cambridge University Press, 1999); Samuel Kernell, "Rural Free Delivery as a Critical Test of Alternative Models of American Political Development," *Studies in American Political Development* 15 (2001): 103–112; Roderick Kiewiet and Matthew McCubbins, *The Logic of Delegation* (Chicago: University of Chicago Press, 1991).

of an agency or to a blurring of the lines between the interests of political appointees charged with setting policy and the interests of career civil servants. In these models, characteristics of bureaucratic power include an agency's size, ties to interest groups and congressional committees (*iron triangles*), information asymmetries, political appointees who "marry the natives" and adopt the preferences of career civil servants, and, finally, self-interested behavior such as maximizing agency budgets or shirking unrewarding but necessary work responsibilities.[115] In the case of FEMA, however, many of these conditions for bureaucratic power did not exist. It is not a particularly large agency, with only roughly 3,000 employees, nor are its core tasks top secret and insulated from political meddling, like those of the intelligence agencies. It lacks organized interest groups of the kind that support the Environmental Protection Agency, and it lacks the Department of Defense's connections to private industry. Rather, it was FEMA's reputation among disaster-plagued communities and politicians for effectively addressing natural disasters that won its leaders enormous leverage in defining their mission and core tasks. More specifically, a perfect storm of factors gave the agency sufficient authority to refocus its mission on natural disasters: an enterprising director, the accumulated knowledge of the emergency management profession, and the development of the all hazards organizing idea supported by a malleable authorizing statute and presidential authority. The confluence of these factors into the ingredients for bureaucratic autonomy is best described by the term "social construction." No single actor planned for a relatively autonomous agency focused on natural disasters, and yet actors pursuing their own interests arrived at a security-focused federal government disasters agency, followed by crisis and upheaval, and then an agency that evolved to focus on natural disasters with an unusual degree of autonomy.

To be sure, among public organizations, autonomy does not function in the strict philosophic sense of the term. No agency is entirely self-ruling because each operates under the constraints presented by environmental conditions and organizational structure. Instead, most social science literature employs autonomy as a description of the relative independence of an agency from its political superiors.[116] Herbert Emmerich captured the essence of autonomy

[115] Marissa Martino Golden, *What Motivates Bureaucrats?* (New York: Columbia University Press, 2000); Heclo, *Government of Strangers*; Kenneth J. Meier, *Politics and the Bureaucracy*, 3rd ed. (Pacific Grove, CA: Brooks/Cole, 1993); Kenneth J. Meier, Robert D. Wrinkle, and J. L. Polinard, "Politics, Bureaucracy and Farm Credit," *Public Administration Review* 59 (July–August 1995): 293–302; William A. Niskanen, "The Bureaucrat's Maximand," in *Bureaucracy and Representative Government* (Chicago: Aldine Atherton, 1971), 36–42; James Q. Wilson, *The Revolt Against the Masses, and Other Essays on Politics and Public Policy* (New York: Basic Books, 1971), 36–65.

[116] Barnett and Finnemore define autonomy as multiple periods in which an institution acts independently, albeit not necessarily defiantly, of its political superiors. See Michael Barnett and Martha Finnemore, *Rules for the World* (Ithaca, NY: Cornell University Press, 2004). Carpenter (*The Forging of Bureaucratic Autonomy*, 17) notes that autonomy occurs when

when he noted in a classic study that "[t]here is a persistent, universal drive in the executive establishment for freedom from managerial control and policy direction."[117] Autonomy is simply the desire and ability of an agency to implement its own ideas. In FEMA's case, its reputation as the federal government's central natural disasters agency gave it latitude to respond to disasters and even bend the rules in disaster response by, for example, establishing new aid programs immediately after an event. Such newfound autonomy was impressive because the agency had tried to act independently before and failed.

This does not mean that FEMA secured its autonomy at the expense of politicians' wishes. The agency simply knew how to pursue politicians' interests in reelection and effective government through disaster preparation and response. Aside from the more subtle and general exercises of autonomy, FEMA demonstrated its independence during the 1993 reorganization. The agency's leadership shrewdly reinterpreted statutes to give it broad authority for preparation as well as response to all kinds of disasters.[118] As pivotal segments of Congress wanted to either abolish the agency or shift its responsibility toward human-caused or technological disasters, Witt made the case that a reinvigorated FEMA focused on natural disasters and customer service and not civil defense and security hijinks could serve politicians' interests.[119]

Witt is widely credited with turning FEMA from a bureaucratic backwater into a brand name. The agency had gone from being invisible to the media at its creation, to being heavily criticized, and then under Witt to receiving praise.

---

agencies "can bring their political legitimacy to bear upon the very laws that give them power." These laws, however, still constrain the agency. Also see Anne M. Khademian, *Checking on Banks: Autonomy and Accountability in Three Federal Agencies* (Washington, DC: Brookings Institution, 1996).

[117] Herbert Emmerich, *Federal Organization and Administrative Management* (Tuscaloosa: University of Alabama Press, 1971), 17.

[118] FEMA mostly intervened in natural disasters, but it did play some role in national security policy areas such as terrorism, civil defense, and civil disturbances, including the events from the 1979 Mariel Boatlift of Cuban refugees to security for the Olympic Games. There has been a complicated legal debate throughout the history of emergency management agencies over the degree to which those agencies were either required to or able to address these policy areas. The general consensus is that FEMA in particular was able to address hazards of all kinds on U.S. soil, including terrorism, nuclear attack and civil disturbances. The Federal Civil Defense Act of 1950 (repealed in 1994), for example, gave priority to "attack-related civil defense" over natural disasters. Even through 9/11 there was some confusion in the responsibilities of FEMA and the FBI and law enforcement agencies in the event of an attack. Both bore some responsibility, but the FBI asserted that it would be the lead on-site agency until the Attorney General determined that the immediate threat had subsided. See Keith Bea, "Federal Disaster Policies after Terrorists Strike: Issues and Options for Congress," *CRS Report to Congress*, October 22, 2002. See also John Ashcroft, "Letter to Joseph Allbaugh, FEMA Director," August 2, 2001. For a discussion of FEMA's authority in national security and terrorism, see the unpublished legal appendix to NAPA, 1993.

[119] A 1993 sense of Congress resolution, discussed in the narrative, asks FEMA to focus resources on human-caused or technological disasters; P.L. 103–160, 107 Stat. 1855–56, November 30, 1993.

Yet Witt's turnaround was not an unvarnished success. The agency's rise in popularity corresponded with an increase in federal disaster declarations and allocation of disaster funds to the states, so part of his success stemmed from greater federal spending. Witt was also fortunate that no catastrophic disasters struck during his eight-year term. Furthermore, Witt's deputies and the emergency management profession deserve as much of the credit for the turnaround as Witt himself.

Still, his behavior is instructive. The way in which Witt forged bonds with elected politicians was strikingly different from how Progressive-era bureaucratic entrepreneurs related to political actors. During the early twentieth century, maverick government agency leaders such as Gifford Pinchot and Harvey Wiley staked out their independence from politicians and developed widespread support for their policies.[120] Administrative politicians in FEMA, however, enhanced their agency's reputation through close relationships with politicians. This is the crucial difference between the progressive maverick and the modern administrative figure – Witt did not stake out a position independent of politicians as much as he supported their interests.

IMPLICATIONS OF THE FEMA TURNAROUND FOR THEORIES OF U.S. GOVERNMENT

No one knew it at the time, but FEMA would be at the center of public criticism a decade later during Hurricane Katrina. The brevity of FEMA's success and its ability to shape its own mission says something about the predicament of contemporary agencies. In a study of bureaucratic autonomy in the early twentieth century, Daniel Carpenter locates the roots of bureaucratic autonomy – essentially agencies' sustained discretion – in a strong reputation supported by innovative bureaucratic actors and organized social groups, or "coalitions of esteem."[121] Progressive-era expansion of the Post Office, for example, was

---

[120] Pinchot and Wiley both courted symbolically important politicians just like they courted other symbolically important social leaders. Convincing politicians that their agency's success was crucial to electoral ambitions was less important to Pinchot and Wiley's project, however, than it was to Witt. Timothy Egan chronicles Pinchot's close personal relationship with Theodore Roosevelt, including their frequent White House wrestling matches, as well as the differences in their vision for the American West. See *The Big Burn: Teddy Roosevelt and the Fire that Saved America* (New York: Houghton Mifflin Harcourt, 2009).

[121] Carpenter defines bureaucratic power, and specifically "autonomy," as those occasions in which "elected authorities see it as in their interest to either (1) defer to an agency's wishes for new policy or (2) grant a wide range of discretion to an administrative agency over an extended period of time." My own concern is less with the creation of new programs – after all, much of the radical policy making of the contemporary era involves eliminating programs – than with an agency's ability to define its missions and core tasks. Carpenter defines reputation as an "evolving belief" among the politicians and the public – and especially organized interests – in the ability of an agency to anticipate and solve problems. Reputation may adhere to a single agency, a small set of agencies, or, in part, to a bureaucratic entrepreneur who leads an agency. See Daniel P. Carpenter, "State Building through Reputation Building: Coalitions of Esteem and

supported by moral reform groups, including prohibitionists. These networks outlasted politicians' attempts to co-opt them because they spanned the usual partisan and class boundaries. Today, however, the rich associational life of the progressive era has given way to pervasive individualism, so that the United States is not the nation of joiners it once was.[122] Powerful interest groups located in Washington replaced more organic local associations; belonging to a modern interest group requires no more commitment than writing a check. Whereas Progressive-era communication occurred through printed bulletins, face-to-face meetings, and rallies, the media looms large in contemporary communication for both politicians and bureaucrats.

President Clinton and members of Congress whose districts were struck by disasters were happy to take credit for FEMA's quick response (and not shy to blame the agency for failures during the 1980s and early 1990s). Witt recognized the "electoral connection" between the agency's tasks and politicians' ultimate interest – reelection – when during congressional testimony he said that "disasters are political events."[123] He recognized that his power was ultimately located in the agency's ability to support the interests of politicians and, sometimes, to anticipate those interests better than politicians could do on their own.

Only the president has the power to declare a federal disaster area, making it eligible for federal disaster assistance, and only then at the request of a state's governor. FEMA, however, shaped demand for aid. The agency's improved efficiency and all hazards mission allowed it to respond to more kinds of disasters. FEMA became more effective at responding to hazards and at mitigating their effects, but it also responded to more disasters than ever before and to more kinds of disasters, including "snow emergencies" for which previous Republican administrations had refused aid (see Figures 4.1–4.5). The improved FEMA brand, to use Witt's marketing analogy, increased demand for its product.[124]

Government services do not operate like a market from the perspective of citizens, however, because politicians can regulate how services are used in ways that may not align with public demands. In FEMA's case, social scientists have found that politicians use disaster aid to reward favored constituencies. Andrew Healy and Neil Malhotra show that voters reward the incumbent presidential party for delivering disaster relief, but not for investing in disaster preparedness, at least when measured in the aggregate.[125] They conclude that

Program Innovation in the National Postal System, 1883–1913," *Studies in American Political Development* 14 (2000): 121–155; 122, 124.

[122] Robert D. Putnam, *Bowling Alone: The Collapse and Revival of American Community* (New York: Simon & Schuster, 2000).

[123] Testimony to U.S. Senate, April 30, 1996; David R. Mayhew, *Congress: The Electoral Connection* (New Haven, CT: Yale University Press, 1974).

[124] Birkland, *After Disaster*, 37; Peter J. May, *Recovering from Catastrophes: Federal Disaster Relief Policy and Politics* (Westport, CT: Greenwood Press, 1985); Platt, *Disasters and Democracy*, 11–46.

[125] Andrew Healy and Neil Malhotra, "Myopic Voters and Natural Disaster Policy," *American Political Science Review* 103 (2009): 387–406.

the government underinvests in pre-disaster mitigation activities – evidence consistent with the Witt-era FEMA's role as the "eyes and ears" of the president after disaster. The agency improved its reputation because of its speedy and ample delivery of aid after disaster, not its work behind the scenes in helping communities prepare. Paradoxically, FEMA made greater advances in mitigation under Witt than before or since. Mitigation is less visible than relief, but it can still be used for distributive politics or pork, particularly if it finances infrastructure projects. Mitigation was a new field for disaster managers, and as in any field it would take time to determine which mitigation policies tended to produce greater benefits and which ones had questionable impacts.

During the Witt years, the president and congressional committees appeared to use disaster spending to reward politically important constituencies, but presidents of all parties have been increasingly likely to issue disaster declarations. From 1953 to 1969, Eisenhower, Kennedy, and Johnson averaged about 1.3 major disaster declarations per month; from 1989 to 2005, George H. W. Bush, Bill Clinton, and George W. Bush averaged 3.9 major disaster declarations per month. (See Figure 4.3 for the number of disaster declarations each year and Figure 4.5 for the percentage of requests for disaster assistance turned down by presidents.) The creation of FEMA made it easier for Congress and the president to regularize disaster relief through a single point of contact for states. Moreover, economists Thomas Garrett and Russell Sobel have argued that from 1991 to 1999, states politically important to a president had a higher rate of disaster declaration by the chief executive and that disaster expenditures were higher in states that had congressional representation on FEMA oversight committees.[126] They also find that disaster aid is higher in election years, controlling for the true size of a disaster, which they measure through private property insurance claims and Red Cross assistance levels.

Politics appear to make a difference at the margins. Large disasters always receive federal aid, but political interests determine whether smaller states receive federal dollars or have to make do on their own. For example, in 1994, Bill Clinton refused to provide aid for recovery for floods that caused $6.7 million in damage on the South Side of Chicago. A year later, Clinton did provide aid to residents of New Orleans, where a flood caused $10 million in damage. The difference was that Illinois was considered a solidly Democratic state and therefore not valuable to Clinton's reelection efforts, whereas Louisiana was deemed a competitive state. Because natural disasters are so frequent, politicians in every part of the country use them to deliver federal aid.

As civil defense receded, an ascendant emergency management profession and an enterprising leader had engineered a turnaround of FEMA built on its

[126] Thomas A. Garrett and Russell S. Sobel, "The Political Economy of FEMA Disaster Payments," *Economic Inquiry* 41 (2003): 496–509. Other studies have found that the president's decision to issue a disaster declaration is influenced by congressional and media attention. See Richard T. Sylves, "The Politics and Budgeting of Emergency Management," in *Disaster Management in the US and Canada*, edited by Richard T. Sylves and William H. Waugh, Jr. (Springfield, IL: Charles C. Thomas, 1996), 26–45.

success in the natural disasters realm, and they were determined to limit the agency to a supportive rather than leadership role in addressing terrorism. Witt left FEMA when George W. Bush took office in 2001. The true test of Witt's legacy would come when a new president and a new party sought to remake FEMA according to their agenda.

The tumultuous history of FEMA shows how the process of social construction by which people create institutions and assign them meaning influences the bureaucracy. As an organizational form, bureaucracies are intended to provide predictability and routine over ad hoc arrangements. Even so, the FEMA bureaucracy assumed diverse forms and missions within a brief time span. FEMA is evidence that, as social construction theories predict, the federal government's role after disaster could have taken different forms. Social construction is not simply about institutional forms or facts, however. It also includes beliefs, and FEMA' diverse missions show the ambiguity present in the concept of disaster, which referred to foreign attack as well as natural events such as fires, floods, hurricanes, and even snow.

5

Terrorism and the Creation of the Department of Homeland Security, 1993–2003

The emergence of terrorism on the national agenda in the 1990s brought to the fore issues of what counts as a disaster and how much preparation and response the federal government should engage in. FEMA under James Lee Witt institutionalized the idea that the federal government should lead preparation for natural disasters and coordinate the federal government's response. Witt's FEMA enshrined the all hazards rhetoric, but in practice terrorist attacks and war lay outside FEMA's activities. The White House, Congress, and blue ribbon commissions concerned about global rather than homegrown terrorists pressured FEMA and other government agencies to include terrorism as the primary disaster on the national agenda. FEMA refused new terrorism missions before 2001, however, because the agency's leaders preferred to focus on its competence in natural disaster preparation. After September 2001, terrorist attacks forced the government's hand, and in haste Congress and the president established a new department focused on preventing terrorism. The Department of Homeland Security (DHS) swallowed up FEMA, and less than a decade after Witt reduced the agency's national security missions, FEMA's mission was redefined to include preparing for terrorism.

FEMA's incorporation of terrorism preparedness and response missions sheds light on the process of social construction. After a major attack, the government's role in preparing for disaster shifted to include domestic terrorism. The new prominence of terrorism on the national agenda collided with ongoing government attempts at coordinating a large bureaucracy, and the result was the new DHS. Disaster management is not a concept that can be operationalized, as social scientists say, and made universal. Rather, it is part of a shifting web of beliefs about what counts as a disaster, and how government should prepare. The changing status of terrorism in federal government disaster organizations shows the contestability of security missions. What it means for the government to provide security in general and in disaster management

is not a given. For a decade after the Witt era began in 1993 and punctuated by
the attacks of 2001, terrorism was an uneasy fit for disaster management. After
the DHS was fully operational in 2003, terrorism would become a central part
of disaster management and the new field of homeland security.

HOW FEMA DEALT WITH INCREASING CONCERNS ABOUT TERRORISM

While support for traditional civil defense flickered out at FEMA, terrorism
was increasingly on the national agenda in the 1990s. Some policy makers
urged FEMA to embrace counterterrorism as part of its core mission, but the
agency refused, having just completed a major reorganization. Some parti-
sans of civil defense questioned whether Witt had gone too far in reorganizing
FEMA. According to one longtime FEMA employee, "Some will say he introduced all hazards. I say he reduced the importance of some hazards at the
expense of others." In shifting resources to programs that could be more generally applied to natural hazards and scaling back its national security role, Witt
left the agency ill prepared, they said, to combat the emerging terrorist threat.

Other bureaucratic actors knew that FEMA's national security role would
have to be reduced even further in exchange for a more effective natural disasters response. While recognizing FEMA's new direction, other agencies asked
questions about who, if not FEMA, would be responsible for domestic security
functions outside the purview of the FBI or state and local agencies. A letter
from the Department of Defense to FEMA said, "The relevant question is not
whether we save the name civil defense, whether the [Civil Defense] Act is
amended or replaced, or whether 'all hazards' includes 'attacks.' Instead, the
Congress and the Administration together must focus on stating clearly: What
is the Government's commitment to Federal and State civil preparedness and
military support for that preparedness, and how will they be authorized and
funded after FY 1993?"[1]

In 1993, a Sense of Congress resolution called on the president to:

strengthen Federal interagency emergency planning by the Federal Emergency
Management Agency and other appropriate Federal, State and local agencies for
development of a capability for early detection and warning of and response to:
(1) potential terrorist use of chemical or biological agents or weapons, and (2) emergencies or natural disasters involving industrial chemicals or the widespread outbreak
of disease.[2]

Numerous blue ribbon commissions studied terrorism in the 1990s, spurred by
terrorist incidents in Oklahoma City, at the World Trade Center in New York,
at the Khobar Towers housing complex in Saudi Arabia, and at U.S. embassies

[1] Maxwell Alston, Office of the Undersecretary of Defense, to John McKay, FEMA, and Chris
Heiser, Office of Management and Budget, May 7, 1993.
[2] P.L. 103–160, 107 Stat. 1855–56, November 30, 1993.

in Kenya and Tanzania.[3] The National Security Council also hoped that FEMA would take on additional responsibilities in preparing for a domestic terrorist attack. Richard Clarke, the first National Coordinator for Security, Infrastructure Protection, and Counterterrorism, was worried about the United States' organizational capability to respond to terrorism, but the NSC was not able to persuade FEMA to add counterterrorism responsibilities.[4] FEMA was offered the opportunity to train first responders for weapons of mass destruction (WMD) attacks, but declined; the training programs were eventually run by the Department of Defense and the Department of Justice, which created the Domestic Preparedness Program in 1998.[5] One former civil defense official said that he and others tried to persuade Witt to pay more attention to the growing terrorist threat by taking on programs to train first responders: "I went to Witt twice and asked him, and he refused to do it." In this account, Witt refused to allow the agency to take on a greater role in terrorism because he thought the agency lacked the resources, not the authority, to do an adequate job. Witt's reasoning had some merit if the agency's autonomy from politicians and other agencies stemmed from its reputation for addressing natural disasters. Witt and the agency's leaders were loath to risk the agency's reputation in order to take on a new mission. If FEMA had possessed less autonomy, other agencies would have been able to overcome Witt's objections and force FEMA to take on new responsibilities. The issue was not a high enough priority to attract the attention of the president, and other agencies knew that if Clinton had intervened, he would have sided with his friend, Witt, and the agency that was his eyes and ears during a disaster.

---

[3] *The September 11 Sourcebooks*, Jeffrey Richelson and Michael L. Evans, eds. National Security Archive Electronic Briefing Book No. 55, Washington, DC, September 21, 2001. Available at:http://www.gwu.edu/~nsarchiv/NSAEBB/NSAEBB55/index1.html (accessed February 6, 2013).

[4] Clarke sent a memo on October 16, 1996 to Lacy Suiter, FEMA's Executive Assistant Director for Response and Recovery, asking the agency to clarify its responsibilities in the event of a terrorist incident. Clarke asked FEMA a series of questions about what prevented the agency from taking a greater role in terrorism preparedness and consequence management, especially during the recently completed Atlanta Olympics. The agency responded by saying that FEMA's policy was that it did not generally have the authority to use money for preparedness in advance of disaster threats. It also wrote that "each agency with an emergency preparedness function for terrorist incident consequence management is responsible for requesting funding for its predeployment activities and emergency preparedness." See John P. Carey, FEMA General Counsel, "FEMA's Role in Advance of a Terrorist Incident," Memorandum for Richard A. Clarke, National Security Council, November 21, 1996. Information about Clarke's actions comes from conversations with two of his colleagues in FEMA.

[5] The Office for Domestic Preparedness (ODP), in the Border and Transportation Security Directorate of DHS as of March 1, 2003, was formerly in the Department of Justice. It is assigned by the Homeland Security Act of 2002, Public Law 107–296, as the principal component of the DHS responsible for preparing state and local governments and private entities for acts of terrorism. In carrying out its mission, ODP is the primary office responsible for providing training, funds for the purchase of equipment, support for the planning and execution of exercises, technical assistance, and other support to assist states and local jurisdictions.

Witt told a different story about FEMA's relationship to terrorism. He acknowledged resisting a partnership between the FBI and FEMA to train responders for terrorist attacks, and said it was because the new program was buried in the Department of Justice. He also said that he asked Attorney General Janet Reno to move the Office for Domestic Preparedness to FEMA, and she refused. In both cases, however, natural hazards were a far greater priority for Witt and FEMA than were national security and terrorist hazards. Witt offered informal advice and formal testimony against creating a new White House position responsible for terrorism policy and against adding some terrorism programs to FEMA.[6] In debates over whether to include FEMA in the DHS, Witt often noted that the agency responded to more than 500 emergencies and major disasters during the 1990s, but only two of these were related to terrorism (the Oklahoma City and New York City World Trade Center bombings).[7] While factually correct, his reply neglected the political importance of these two events compared to other disasters. Commission members, White House staff, and former FEMA civil defense personnel were concerned about the problem of terrorism, but no one had the clout to persuade the agency to broaden its mission.

Eventually, an annex of the Federal Response Plan, issued in 1997, delineated responsibility for combating terrorism: crisis management responsibilities were given to the FBI and consequence management was given to FEMA.[8] It was a "kick in the pants" to get the agency to strengthen its terrorism responsibilities, according to one member of FEMA's national security division, but the agency made no major organizational changes in response to the plan. When, from 1998 to 2001, the Hart-Rudman Commission looked for an agency to become the cornerstone for revitalizing domestic security to address the threat of terrorism, it found FEMA lacking. "FEMA was considered a centerpiece, but in need of significant resources and culture shock," according to Frank Hoffman, who directed the Commission's homeland security research.[9] FEMA's history and mission statement allowed for a greater

---

[6] James Lee Witt, "Hearing before the Subcommittees on Oversight, Investigations, and Emergency Management, of the Committee on Transportation and Infrastructure," H.R. 4210, Preparedness Against Terrorism Act of 2000, May 4, 106th Congress, 2nd sess. House of Representatives (Washington, DC: GPO, 2000).

[7] James Lee Witt, personal interview, Washington, DC, April 15, 2004. Also see James Lee Witt and Associates, *Department of Homeland Security and FEMA* (Washington, DC: Witt and Associates, 2002), unpublished.

[8] Terrorism Annex of the Federal Response Plan, issued February 7, 1997. The Federal Response Plan was first published in May 1992 by FEMA pursuant to the authority in the Stafford Act and after a lengthy coordination process with the other signatory agencies. The Plan coordinates delivery of disaster response services among twenty-five federal agencies and the American Red Cross. See Keith Bea, *Overview of Components of the National Response Plan and Selected Issues*, CRS Reports (Washington, DC: Congressional Research Service), December 24, 2003.

[9] Frank G. Hoffman, personal e-mail correspondence, December 11, 2003. FEMA's witnesses before the Hart-Rudman Commission were Lacey Suiter and V. Clay Hollister. Notes of their briefing do not exist.

national security and counterterrorism role, Hoffman said, but by the late 1990s its culture and capabilities were not up to the task. The Hart-Rudman Commission supported the concept of all hazards as a way to maximize federal support for disasters among different kinds of hazards *including* terrorism and minimize bureaucracy, but the Commission also supported restoring security capabilities to FEMA and adding new ones, contrary to the Witt agenda. With a few minor exceptions, then, FEMA insulated itself from terrorism planning elsewhere in government until an event put terrorism back on everyone's agenda.[10]

THE ATTACKS

On September 11, 2001, nineteen Arab men hijacked four American commercial airliners and, with 24,000 gallons of jet fuel aboard each, turned them into flying bombs. Two struck New York City's signature Twin Towers – the buildings of the World Trade Center. One hit the Pentagon and another, intended for Washington, DC, never reached its target and crashed into a field in Pennsylvania after a passenger revolt. Approximately 3,000 people were killed, exceeding the toll of 2,400 dead after the Japanese surprise attack on the United States in 1941. Taking population growth into account, this was a proportionately lower death toll than Pearl Harbor. Nevertheless, the attack was treated as the new century's Pearl Harbor.

By the next day, media the world over had transmitted the now familiar image of the second airplane plowing into the south tower of the World Trade Center and declared it a world-altering moment. The French newspaper *Le Monde*, often critical of the United States, ran a front-page headline reading *"Nous sommes tous Américains."* In London, Buckingham Palace played the U.S. national anthem during the changing of the guard. The world's response brought home the unprecedented nature of the event. The media broadcast an image of firefighters raising the U.S. flag over the rubble, evoking the Iwo Jima flag raising: as with the mentions of Pearl Harbor, the nation was grasping at imagery from "the good war" to make sense of this infamous event.

In the immediate aftermath, the United States placed security forces on a high state of alert and – for the first time – suspended civilian air travel for three days. Shortly after the attacks, al Qaeda, a militant Islamic group, and its leader, Osama bin Laden, claimed responsibility. President George W. Bush ordered a military offensive against the group, the first initiative in what his administration later termed the Global War on Terror. In October 2001, the

---

[10] For a summary of government efforts to combat terrorism written by one of the participants, see Richard A. Clarke, *Against All Enemies: Inside American's War on Terror* (New York: Free Press, 2004). For a more scholarly account, see Timothy Naftali, *Blind Spot: The Secret History of American Counterterrorism* (New York: Basic Books, 2005).

United States invaded Afghanistan, where bin Laden and his conspirators were believed to be hiding.

At home, the media and the government focused attention on government agencies' collective responsibility to prevent and respond to terrorism. Congress and the president chartered commissions to investigate whether the attacks could have been prevented. Foremost among these, the 9/11 Commission published a record of its probe, and the book became a best seller.[11] The commission concluded that the United States was vulnerable to attack because of the failure of intelligence and law enforcement officials to "connect the dots" and piece together signs of a terrorist plot.

The primary governmental response to the terrorist attacks of 2001 was a renewed focus on the threat of foreign terrorism and a reorganization of the federal government that had profound implications for states and localities. Before September 11, Pentagon bureaucrats had used the term *homeland security* to refer to missile defense programs. After September 11, it gave this name to the collection of federal agencies engaged in defense against domestic and international terrorism – and it quickly became a household term. Civil servants in these agencies had never before seen their work as part of a collective counterterrorism enterprise, even though federal agencies had been doing things that now counted as homeland security for at least half a century. The Central Intelligence Agency and FEMA both had ancestors in World War II and Cold War bureaucracies that emerged to defend the United States against foreign attack. Immigration agencies had long been concerned about who was entering the country, even though security missions were often buried under a host of other concerns. Initially, the president created a new White House Office of Homeland Security. When the office proved to be too weak to coordinate agencies across government and the political pressure to take greater action grew stronger, Congress and the president created a cabinet-level department – the DHS.

Many of the most important agencies charged with defending against attacks, including the CIA, FBI, and the visa agency within the Department of State, were not included in the new department. These agencies won the bureaucratic turf battles for self-preservation. Yet FEMA was unique among those who lost such battles, because compared with, say, the Transportation Security Administration or the Secret Service, FEMA lacked champions in Congress and was particularly vulnerable to evisceration by the DHS.

The creation of the DHS raised questions about the efficacy of bureaucratic reorganization and centralization as a means to address changing threats. Can we expect a bureaucracy to adapt to a new environment and anticipate problems before politicians recognize them – before it is too late? Recent

---

[11] National Commission on Terrorist Attacks Upon the United States, *The 9/11 Commission Report: Final Report of the National Commission on Terrorist Attacks Upon the United States* (Washington, DC: Government Printing Office, 2004).

scholarship is pessimistic about the effectiveness of massive reorganizations.[12] Large reorganizations, because of their size, require compromise among competing interests. This compromise can frustrate a new organization's ability to achieve the larger goal it was created for. Still, reorganizations are one way in which agencies adapt. Rather than view the birth of the DHS as new creation, it is better to view it as one reorganization following a long line of others in the history of its component parts.[13]

FEMA AFTER SEPTEMBER 11

Few blamed FEMA for the events of September 11 because the agency had defined its all hazards mission as natural disaster response and relief rather than as assessing the risk of all potential categories of disaster. FEMA's immediate response to the attacks was limited but well regarded.

Actually the entire federal government's role in recovery from the attacks was limited compared to the efforts of states and localities, and FEMA was no exception. In one of the best histories of the immediate aftermath of the attacks in New York, William Langewiesche writes, "[T]he federal government [i.e., FEMA] was poised to intervene [in the recovery process], but agreed to hold off, and then agreed to hold off again."[14] Langewiesche and the 9/11 Commission report barely mentioned FEMA, instead focusing on local authorities or federal government intelligence and law enforcement agencies.[15] According to some formal government plans, FEMA ought to have assumed the lead in recovery, but in practice building engineers from New York City's Department of Design and Construction oversaw cleanup and rebuilding.[16]

Despite not being featured in major histories of the period, FEMA mounted a response widely regarded as effective.[17] FEMA's administrator, Joe Allbaugh, was a close associate of President Bush, and he dispatched search-and-rescue teams and kept relief dollars flowing. FEMA brought in ice-making machines and generators for residents of New York City without power. It provided housing grants for people without work. The notoriously vague Stafford Act does not explicitly authorize FEMA to create new grant programs, but the

---

[12] Moynihan shows how reforms at the DHS in the name of public management hewed closer to the Bush administration's executive-centered and anti-union policy preferences than the broader new public management agenda; Donald P. Moynihan, "Public Management Policy Change in the United States 1993–2001," *International Public Management Journal* 6 (2003): 371–394.

[13] Patrick S. Roberts, "Homeland Security," in *Governing America: Major Policies and Decisions of Federal, State, and Local Government*, edited by William E. Cunion and Paul Quirk (New York: Facts on File Press, 2011), 926–937.

[14] William Langewiesche, *American Ground: Unbuilding the World Trade Center* (New York: North Point Press, 2002).

[15] Langewiesche does, however, mention FEMA's Urban Search and Rescue Teams.

[16] Langewiesche, *American Ground*, 9–10. On FEMA's role in the Oklahoma City bombing recovery, see Witt and Morgan, *Stronger in the Broken Places*, 101–111.

[17] One exception is Lehrer's "Influence, Presidential Authority, and Emergency Management."

agency acted anyway.[18] Allbaugh announced that FEMA would pay $1.7 billion for cleanup in New York City, which was near the total cost to the federal government.[19] In the weeks following the attacks, Allbaugh was a consistent and reassuring figure in the media, giving what one account described as "a breakout performance."[20] He gave credit to local emergency services near the World Trade Center and Pentagon sites, and he furthered the image of FEMA as the federal government's lead agency in times of disaster.[21]

While FEMA was a media darling, its response on the ground was limited. Disaster management scholar Eli Lehrer argues that while many government agencies overreacted to the event by sending more people and resources than could be used, FEMA probably underreacted.[22] FEMA deployed the same number of urban search-and-rescue teams (eight) to New York as it did to Oklahoma City after the bombing there, even though the attacks of 2001 were far more devastating. [23] FEMA eventually sent more search-and-rescue teams, but almost all were gone within two weeks. At the Pentagon site, FEMA never issued an engineering report on the structural damage, something it had done for every major building disaster in the preceding twenty years.[24] FEMA's reluctance might have stemmed from its de-escalation of terrorism response missions or from the Department of Defense's assertion of control. In either case, the agency's response to the attacks was competent but largely rhetorical and administrative.

FEMA's ad hoc and enterprising role after the attacks stands in contrast to its neat hierarchical designation as a lead agency in coordinating terrorism response. In May 2001, President Bush and Allbaugh announced that FEMA would create an Office of National Preparedness to coordinate the government's response to a terrorist attack. President Bush announced the move by making clear the diverse kinds of security threats FEMA would take responsibility for, saying, "It is clear that the threat of chemical, biological or nuclear weapons being used against the United States – while not immediate – is very

[18] Office of Inspector General (OIG), *FEMA's Delivery of Individual Assistance Programs, New York, September 11, 2001* (Washington, DC: FEMA, 2002), 24–25. Quoted in Lehrer, "Influence, Presidential Authority, and Emergency Management," 83.
[19] Government Accountability Office, *Information about FEMA's Post 9/11 Assistance to the New York City Area* (Washington, DC: GAO, 2003), 11.
[20] Chuck Lidell, "Stalwart Bush Adviser Says He Will Leave His FEMA Post," *The Austin American-Statesman*, December 17, 2002.
[21] James Gerstenzang, "Bush Puts FEMA in Charge of Domestic Terrorism Response," *Los Angeles Times*, May 9, 2001, A21.
[22] Lehrer, "Influence, Presidential Authority, and Emergency Management."
[23] Lehrer, "Influence, Presidential Authority, and Emergency Management; FEMA, "FEMA Mobilizes 12 Urban Search and Rescue Teams," September 11, 2001, available at: http://www.fema.gov/nwz01/nwz01_94.shtm (accessed October 15, 2010); Langewische, *American Ground*, 67.
[24] *Arlington Virginia After-Action Report on the Response to the September 11 Terrorist Attack on the Pentagon* (Washington, DC: Titan Systems Corporation, 2002).

real."²⁵ After May 8 and with the support of the vice-president's office in particular, FEMA's National Preparedness division began planning for terrorism. While FEMA reassured the public after the attacks of 2001, its relatively limited response suggests that its capabilities for addressing the effects of terrorism were not comparable to its capacity for responding to natural disasters.²⁶

A study of how other organizations responded to the terrorist attacks on the World Trade Center puts FEMA's role in perspective. A total of 1,607 organizations participated in the response, and of these 1,196 were nonprofits and 149 were private firms.²⁷ Organizations with well-rehearsed plans seemed to perform well, but the event was so unexpected that a large enough response could never have been rehearsed precisely.²⁸ The relevant actors appeared to understand their roles and adapt their response energetically if not spontaneously. Charities, for example, devoted resources to helping victims' families and to helping thousands of New Yorkers cope with the trauma of a direct attack. FEMA was one organization among many.

Allbaugh resigned in March 2003 after the agency was incorporated into the DHS. The reorganization swallowed FEMA, a roughly 3,000-person agency, into a department of approximately 180,000. Expert reports cautioned that the benefits FEMA might bring to the much larger DHS could be outweighed by the costs to the agency's effectiveness, but the FEMA name was too valuable to leave out.²⁹ The agency's brand name and all hazards mantra were valuable enough to be included in the new DHS.

Under the original White House Plan, FEMA was to be part of the DHS and its administrator was to be a cabinet-level appointee (as had been true under Clinton). In the final bill passed by Congress and signed by President Bush, the agency was still part of the DHS but smaller than the White House intended, and its administrator was effectively demoted to a mid-level bureaucrat who reported to the Homeland Security secretary and deputy secretaries.

FEMA's responsibility for terrorism in the new arrangement was contested and contingent on turf wars. The White House's initial proposal included the Justice Department's Office of Domestic Preparedness (ODP) within FEMA. (The ODP distributed counterterrorism grants to police agencies.) But the

---

²⁵ George W. Bush, *Statement on Domestic Preparedness Against Weapons of Mass Destruction*, May 8 (Washington, DC: Government Printing Office, 2001). Available at:http://www.gpo.gov/fdsys/pkg/PPP-2001-book1/pdf/PPP-2001-book1-doc-pg498.pdf (accessed June 17, 2011).
²⁶ Gerstenzang, "Bush Puts FEMA in Charge of Domestic Terrorism Response," A21.
²⁷ Naim Kapucu, "Interagency Communication Networks during Emergencies: Boundary Spanners in Multi-agency Coordination, *The American Review of Public Administration* 36 (2006): 207–225; 213.
²⁸ Government Accountability Office, "September 11: Interim Report on the Response of Charities," GAO-02-1037, Washington, DC, September 3, 2002; GAO, "September 11: Overview of Federal Disaster Assistance to the New York City Area," GAO-04-72, Washington, DC, October 2003, 13–34.
²⁹ Keith Bea, Proposed *Transfer of FEMA to the Department of Homeland Security: Issues for Congressional Oversight* (Washington, DC: Congressional Research Service, 2002).

program's officials remembered Witt's refusal to take the program in 1997, and blocked its inclusion in the DHS, keeping it in Justice.[30] In addition to losing direct access to the president, the FEMA administrator lost the power to reorganize his agency.[31] In response to these changes, many of the agency's most experienced leaders resigned and moved elsewhere within the DHS. Michael Brown was appointed in January 2003 as the first Undersecretary of Emergency Preparedness and Response in the Department of Homeland Security, and he also bore the title of FEMA administrator. Upon taking the job, he said, "I've told Joe [Allbaugh] that the job you held doesn't exist anymore."[32] Neither did FEMA, not in the same form.

FEMA's autonomy and its good reputation were short-lived. The agency's ability to shape its mission and core tasks proved fragile compared to the changes that followed September 11. The agency's all hazards concept remained, but its structure and tasks were not the same. To some degree, the agency had become a victim of its own success. The FEMA brand proved so attractive that politicians wanted to include the agency in a new department in order to lend credibility to homeland security.[33] The reorganization effectively demoted the FEMA administrator and mired the agency in layers of oversight by the new department, limiting the agency's autonomy.

POLITICIZATION

One explanation for why FEMA performed below expectations following Witt's departure is that politicians appointed cronies and politically minded managers rather than experts to agency leadership jobs. Some observers speculated that the Bush administration intended to shrink the non-security missions of homeland security agencies in order to fulfill a long-standing agenda to reduce the federal government's capacity in domestic policy.[34] At the very least, Congress and the executive branch attempted to substitute their policy preferences for those of career civil servants. The chief vehicles for this kind of substitution, often called politicization, are appointments, policy statements, and reorganization. Joseph Allbaugh, the political campaign manager whom President Bush selected to replace Witt as FEMA administrator, began his tenure by reducing mitigation programs and proposing new programs for terrorism preparedness.

[30] Christopher Cooper and Robert Block, *Disaster: Hurricane Katrina and the Failure of Homeland Security* (New York: Times Books, 2006), 79; also interviews.

[31] President Carter's Reorganization Plan Number 3 of 1978 states that the FEMA administrator "shall have the power to designate [the] responsibilities of his ... deputies."

[32] Lehrer, "Influence, Presidential Authority, and Emergency Management."

[33] Though FEMA was officially called EP&R (Emergency Preparedness and Response) in early homeland security documents, agency officials continued to use the FEMA brand in practice because of its cachet.

[34] Bryan D. Jones and Walter Williams, *The Politics of Bad Ideas* (New York: Pearson Longman, 2008).

These were the signature terrorism initiatives sought by the pre-September 11 Bush White House. The attacks catalyzed the trend toward a terrorism-focused mission, and a new class of political appointees at FEMA pushed the agency to prepare for terrorism and to work through the DHS rather than directly with the White House.

FEMA had thirty-eight political appointees by the end of 2002, although it had only twenty-two appointees at the end of Clinton's first term in 1997, down from thirty-eight under President George H. W. Bush in 1989. Under George W. Bush, political appointees filled top management positions, policy development and speechwriting jobs, and some presumably technical jobs in the External Affairs Directorate and Information Technology Services. Whereas many of the Witt-era appointees had long careers in emergency management, the George W. Bush administration filled the agency's upper management with appointees who lacked disaster experience, including Michael Brown, whose previous position was with the International Arabian Horse Association. (To be fair, Brown was as qualified as some other prior FEMA administrators.) The number of qualified professionals just below top management also shrank. According to the Office of Personnel Management, the number of Senior Executive Service members in the agency, the highest civil service designation, fell from sixty-one in 2000 to thirty-nine in 2004.[35]

The remaining careerists were not happy. FEMA ranked last in employee satisfaction among a selection of agencies in a 2003 survey, a decline from the high morale of the Witt years. In 2005, the Partnership for Public Service and the Institute for the Study of Public Policy Implementation ranked the DHS, which absorbed FEMA, twenty-ninth out of thirty agencies in a "best places to work in government" survey.[36] After 2001, FEMA's funding streams and programs shifted in and out of the agency, creating organizational churn that felt like instability to many in the agency, according to a GAO report.[37] Between 2003 and 2004, more than $1.3 billion in funding for new initiatives entered the agency, and by 2005, nearly $1.5 billion left. The balance between money in and money out masked political and budgetary caprice. For example, when FEMA joined the DHS in 2003, it gained $513 million in new programs transferred from the Department of Health and Human Services, but by 2005, the

[35] Office of Personnel Management, *Demographic Characteristics of the Senior Executive Service 2005* (Washington, DC: OPM, 2005), 9.

[36] Stephen Barr, "Morale Among FEMA Workers, on the Decline for Years, Hits Nadir," *Washington Post*, September 14, 2005, available at: http://www.washingtonpost.com/wp-dyn/content/article/2005/09/14/AR2005091401047.html (accessed February 8, 2013); General Accountability Office, "Federal Emergency Management Agency: Status of Achieving Key Outcomes and Addressing Major Management Challenges," GAO–01–832, July 9, 2001.

[37] General Accountability Office, "Budget Issues: FEMA Needs Adequate Data, Plans, and Systems to Effectively Manage Resources for Day-to-Day Operations," GAO-07–139, Washington, DC, January 2007; Kevin Fox Gotham, "Disaster, Inc.: Privatization and Post-Katrina Rebuilding in New Orleans," *Perspectives on Politics* 10 (September 2012): 633–646; 636–637.

White House had transferred most of those programs and their funding out of FEMA and back to Health and Human Services or new agencies within the DHS. By 2005, FEMA was left with only $34 million of the original $513 million in new funding. The agency's mission was diluted, however, having taken on new health emergencies as part of its disasters mission but without the resources or planning capacity to prepare for them.

Thus, during the homeland security era, the agency lost or eliminated many of the elements of its turnaround a decade before. The Witt-era turnaround had drawn on the knowledge of the emergency management profession to expand mitigation programs and develop the all hazards approach. While the agency could never assure protection against literally *all* hazards, during the Witt years the rhetoric of all hazards allowed the agency to get the most out of limited resources by claiming authority for natural disaster preparedness against factions committed to protecting civil defense fiefdoms. By 2005, the conflict between preparation for civil defense and natural disasters had receded, and FEMA faced new challenges. Emergency managers who wanted to improve preparation for disaster and reduce vulnerability faced layers of political management in the DHS and in their own agency as well as entrenched state and local authority over disaster preparedness.

The dissatisfaction among career emergency managers in FEMA grew as the agency incorporated more terrorism missions. Of $1.6 billion in homeland security grants in fiscal year 2007, approximately $1.1 billion went to the Urban Area Security Initiative, the State Homeland Security Program, and the Law Enforcement Terrorism Prevention Program. At the same time, $46 million went to Citizen Corps (the successor to civil defense councils) and the Metropolitan Medical Response System, which were all hazards emergency response programs.[38] Between 2001 and 2005 fiscal years, DHS grant-funding programs focused on terrorism exceeded funding for all hazards programs three to one, and the Witt-era natural disaster mitigation program Project Impact was cancelled.[39] Mitigation programs remained in FEMA, but they were not treated as seriously as they had been under Witt. Shortly before Hurricane Katrina in 2005, a group of five state emergency management directors traveled to Washington to meet with Deputy Secretary of Homeland Security Michael Jackson to voice concern about what was happening to emergency management. Journalists Christopher Cooper and Robert Block report that, "in plain language, the group told Jackson that the Department of Homeland Security's

[38] Office of Grants and Training, *Overview, FY 2007 Grant Programs* (Washington, DC: Department of Homeland Security, 2007); Anne M. Khademian, "Hurricane Katrina and the Failure of Homeland Security," in *Judging Bush*, edited by Robert Maranto et al. (Stanford, CA: Stanford University Press 2009), 195–214.

[39] Khademian, "Hurricane Katrina and the Failure of Homeland Security," 200–201; General Accountability Office, "Homeland Security: DHS' Efforts to Enhance First Responders' All Hazards Capabilities Continue to Evolve," GAO-05–652, Washington, DC, July 11, 2005.

obsession with terrorist attacks had undermined the nation's readiness for natural disasters."[40]

Terrorism complicated FEMA's efforts to respond to natural disasters by adding new considerations to preparedness efforts, not by seizing resources formerly directed to natural disasters as some critics alleged.[41] Congress delivered new money to terrorism preparedness, but could not expand the time and attention of disaster managers who found themselves trying to reconcile security and natural hazards concerns. Authoritative federal response plans invoked the all hazards language, but the language was not reflected in organizational structures at lower levels of government. Most state emergency management offices promptly posted the homeland security color-coded threat advisory and posted antiterrorism notices on their Web sites, crowding out useful information about natural disasters but earning substantial grants-in-aid.[42]

Sufficient resources flowed to natural disaster preparedness, but not enough attention was devoted to how to reconcile the different threats posed by terrorism and natural disasters, especially at the state and local levels. In a terrorist attack, the FBI and law enforcement agencies traditionally take the lead because the disaster is a crime scene. Disaster agencies might assist in search and rescue. In a natural disaster, however, the sole focus is rescue and recovery, tasks best left to emergency managers. When Katrina struck, states and localities had been crafting plans and procedures for terrorist attacks but in many cases had failed to refine plans for natural disaster response. Louisiana and New Orleans officials had conducted an exercise known as Hurricane Pam alongside FEMA in 2004. The fictional but prescient Hurricane Pam produced effects similar to those in Katrina, but the exercise was curtailed because of budget cuts, and its conclusions were never incorporated in state and local plans or DHS plans.

Witt had refused to take on some terrorism-related programs offered to FEMA because he thought the programs were outside of FEMA's area of distinctive competence in natural disaster management, and that terrorism was too unpredictable for government to address effectively. Yet after September 11, it was unrealistic to expect politicians to ignore the terrorist threat, and

---

[40] Cooper and Block, *Disaster*, xiii.

[41] Patrick S. Roberts, "Shifting Priorities: Congressional Incentives and the Homeland Security Granting Process," *Review of Policy Research* 22 (July 2005): 437–450; Ben Canada, "Homeland Security Standards for State and Local Performance," *CRS Report for Congress*, January 2 (Washington DC: Congressional Research Service, 2003).

[42] The color-coded advisory system was intended to communicate with law enforcement officials who needed to know when to escalate their alert levels, but the system was vulnerable to misinterpretation by the public and other government officials. See Jacob N. Shapiro and Dara Kay Cohen, "Color-Bind: Lessons from the Failed Homeland Security Advisory System." *International Security* (2007) 32: 121–154; Susan A. MacManus and Kiki Caruson. "Code Red: Florida City and County Officials Rate Threat Information Sources and the Homeland Security Advisory System." *State & Local Government Review* (2006): 12–22.

FEMA's promise to protect citizens from all hazards proved too tempting for politicians looking for a bureaucratic savior to ignore. FEMA was subsumed by the DHS, but during Katrina, a natural disaster, not a terrorist attack, revealed the limits of its competence.

FROM DISASTER MANAGEMENT TO HOMELAND SECURITY

The quick incorporation of terrorism into FEMA's missions and of FEMA into the DHS shows how, over time, the government's capability to deal with disaster could not keep up with the public's rising expectations. (The public expresses its expectations through the electoral process, where elections guarantee that politicians focus on public concerns.) FEMA claimed a capacious all hazards mission, which gave its employees a sense of pride and which resonated with politicians. FEMA succeeded in defining its operational mission relatively narrowly, primarily supporting states and localities in natural disaster preparation and response, but public demand for protection against the new hazard of terrorism led to the creation of a new department with a broad mission of homeland security. FEMA and the DHS would never offer absolute protection. Nevertheless, FEMA's all hazards mission and the agency's credit claiming in the media gave rise to beliefs among the public, politicians, and blue ribbon commissions that the agency and its parent, the DHS, could come to the rescue after almost any kind of disaster.

Perceptions of the agency's power outstripped its actual capacity, and the ability of the agency to shape its own mission. The agency's all hazards concept remained after the changes that followed September 11, but its structure and tasks were not the same. Bureaucratic autonomy from politicians and other agencies depends on a confluence of factors coming together at the same time.

FEMA shifted terrorism responsibilities to other agencies and used its limited capacity to reassure the public following September 11. The agency's performance in its terrorism missions was not organizational failure as much as a lack of capacity to actually do anything about terrorism and a bit of overreach in its terrorism response mission. Some of the elements for organizational failure emerged after 2001, however. Political cronies rather than experienced emergency managers assumed managerial positions in FEMA, and the agency was hobbled by having to report to multiple management layers within the DHS rather than simply working with Congress, the president, and subnational governments. Furthermore, the mission of preparing for terrorism was so different from preparing for natural disasters that some critics accused the agency of mission conflict and of sacrificing natural disasters efforts at the expense of a focus on the terrorist threat.

6

"Where the Hell Is the Army?": Hurricane Katrina Meets the Homeland Security Era

After well-regarded government responses to the attacks of 2001 and to hurricanes in Florida, Hurricane Katrina showed the fragility of the system of disaster management. Hurricane Katrina is at once an archetypical case of failures in government coordination and a peculiar event that was made worse by a vulnerable location and relatively weak state and local government. Katrina shaped the conceptual category of disaster, reframing it as an event that overwhelms state and local authorities and leaves people asking, "Where was the federal government?"[1] Mention the term "disaster" now, and people think of Katrina and FEMA. Spike Lee's widely circulated documentary showed victims of the storm holding signs that read "Where is FEMA?" and "Where is President Bush?" No similar questions were posed regarding the mayor or local leaders.[2] Images like these both reflected heightened expectations of the federal government and shaped how people outside of the affected region thought about the government's relationship to disaster, and about disaster itself. President George W. Bush's offhand praise of FEMA administrator Michael Brown, "Brownie, you're doing a heck of a job," expressed a reality so far from these kinds of experiences that it became an ironic meme, a shorthand for the popular conversation about the government's miserable performance. The reaction to Hurricane Katrina

[1] Harry Eckstein, "Case Study and Theory in Political Science," in *The Handbook of Political Science*, edited by F. I. Greenstein and N. W. Polsby (Reading, PA: Addison-Wesley, 1975), 79–138; Richard Rose, "Comparing Forms of Comparative Analysis," *Political Studies* 39 (1991): 446–462; 459; Gary Goertz, "Case Studies, Causal Mechanisms, and Selecting Cases," unpublished manuscript, 2012; Gary Goertz and James Mahoney, "Case Selection and Hypothesis Testing," in *A Tale of Two Cultures: Contrasting the Qualitative and Quantitative Research Paradigms*, edited by Gary Goertz and James Mahoney (Princeton, NJ: Princeton University Press, 2012), 177–191.
[2] Douglas Brinkley lays blame on the mayor and local officials in *The Great Deluge: Hurricane Katrina, New Orleans, and the Mississippi Gulf Coast* (New York: William Morrow, 2006).

says as much about the expectations of contemporary disaster management as it does about shortcomings in the government's performance along the hurricane-ravaged Gulf Coast.

A close examination of how Hurricane Katrina unfolded shows what happens when a federal agency assumes responsibility for protecting citizens from all hazards without having the necessary administrative capacity. This chapter begins by describing what happened before, during, and after the storm. Then, it contrasts the prevailing view that either FEMA, the government, or federalism failed during the response with an alternative view that rather than a failure of response, Katrina reveals a political failure of administrative capacity and overpromising. Ultimately, FEMA lacked the capacity to carry out its all hazards mission and to live up to the expanded sense of its responsibility to protect the public.

HURRICANE KATRINA AND THE IMMEDIATE RESPONSE

On Monday, August 29, 2005, Hurricane Katrina made landfall on the coast with high-velocity winds, storm surge, heavy rain, hail, and tornadoes. The storm caused deaths, injuries, property and infrastructure damage, economic loss, and human suffering in coastal Louisiana, Mississippi, and Alabama. The Louisiana Department of Health reported that 1,464 people died as a result of Katrina's effects in Louisiana, mostly in New Orleans Parish.[3] Mississippi reported 238 dead from the storm, and hundreds more in both states were counted as missing. Losses from the storm were estimated at more than $200 billion including all public and private property.[4] Private insurer losses from Hurricane Katrina for damaged, destroyed, or flooded homes and businesses, and for offshore oil and gas platforms that were either damaged, lost, or missing and presumed sunk in the Gulf of Mexico, are estimated to be in the range of $40 billion to $60 billion. This amount would make Katrina the costliest disaster in U.S. history adjusting for inflation, exceeding Hurricane Andrew in 1992 and the terrorist attacks of September 11, 2001.

The hurricane was unusually catastrophic because of its size and because it struck a concentrated urban population. Critical functions such as commerce, health care, and the provision of water and food ceased. State and local governments suspended normal operations. The federal government was not prepared to mount an immediate response, and many people were left on their own. They sought refuge on rooftops, in the Superdome, or in one of Louisiana's 113

[3] Louisiana Department of Health and Hospitals, Deceased Reports, available at: http://www.dhh. louisiana.gov/offices/page.asp?ID=192&Detail=5248 (accessed December 2, 2009); Michelle Krupa, "Presumed Missing," *New Orleans Times-Picayune*, March 5, 2006; "Deaths of Evacuees Push Toll to 1,577," *New Orleans Times-Picayune*, May 19, 2006.
[4] Rawle O. King, "Hurricane Katrina: Insurance Losses and National Capacities for Financing Disaster Risk," *CRS Reports*, RL33086, September 15, 2005.

overcrowded shelters.[5] The hurricane devastated residents of the Louisiana and Mississippi Gulf Coasts, but the government's shortcomings were most evident in New Orleans, where promises and expectations did not match reality.

The Stafford Act provides the statutory authority for most federal disaster response activities, and it is sufficient for most low- to medium-intensity disasters. The government's planning process in general typically addresses smaller and more routine events or creates fantasy documents such as civil defense plans that pretend to prepare for what is really unpredictable and unknown. Plans more easily routinize responses for frequent events, such as a direct hit of a smaller storm or a larger storm that makes landfall in a less densely populated area. It is difficult, however, to make responses to rare and catastrophic disasters routine because written plans, abstract rules, strict hierarchies, and stovepiped roles and responsibilities are rarely written for the worst case. When organizations do account for the worst case, their leaders are accused of crying wolf. Katrina, however, was a worst case. The sustained winds of the hurricane were 125 mph at landfall, officially a category 3 on the Saffir-Simpson scale. The scale combines both wind speed and storm surge, however, and the surge had the strength of a category 5 storm.[6] Where a hurricane hits is as important as its strength, and the storm followed a path into densely populated New Orleans.[7] It was an exceptionally severe event.

The emergency manager's time line of a disaster has three stages: preparedness, including mitigation and preparing to respond; the response itself; and recovery. These refer to humans' actions before and after the event, more than to the event itself. The most common explanations for the Katrina calamity focus on shortcomings during the response period after the hurricane bore down on the Gulf Coast, not the period of preparation beforehand. Some scholars and pundits claim that the official disaster plans were faulty, especially the ballyhooed National Response Plan, the federal government's attempt to coordinate all levels of disaster agencies.[8] The White House "Lessons Learned" report takes the NRP to task and begins by noting that emergency response plans "came up short."[9] David Paulison, who became FEMA administrator

---

[5] Donald Menzel, "The Katrina Aftermath: A Failure of Federalism or Leadership?" *Public Administration Review* 66 (2006): 808–812; U.S. Senate Committee of Homeland Security and Government Affairs, *Hurricane Katrina: A Nation Still Unprepared* (Washington, DC: GPO, 2006).

[6] It was a strong storm, but less than a category 5, which can have sustained winds of 200 mph.

[7] The precise eye of the hurricane made landfall at the Louisiana-Mississippi state line, near but not in New Orleans. See the central Florida Hurricane Center's map at: http://flhurricane.com/googlemap.php?2005s12 (accessed February 10, 2011).

[8] Stephen E. Flynn and Daniel B. Prieto, "Neglected Defense: Mobilizing the Private Sector to Support Homeland Security," Council on Foreign Relations Special Report, no. 14, 2006; Kathleen Tierney, "Social Dimensions of Catastrophic Disasters," February 28, 2006, at Stanford University, Stanford, CA.

[9] White House, *The Federal Response to Hurricane Katrina: Lessons Learned* (Washington, DC: GPO, 2006), 1.

after Katrina, claims that a better plan for coordinating disaster response would have prevented the calamity. "If that had been in place," Paulison said, "in my opinion, during Katrina, we would not have had the situation that we had."[10]

The 427-page response plan (winnowed down from its original 600 pages) is typical of plans written by committee.[11] Its language is overly formal without being precise, and its instructions are repetitive. DHS officials, including the secretary, were confused by the plan's delegation of on-site disaster coordination to two positions, the principal coordinating official and the federal coordinating officer. The one large-scale exercise before Katrina, TOPOFF 3, found "a fundamental lack of understanding of the principles and protocols set forth in the NRP and NIMS" at all levels of government.[12] The TOPOFF 3 scenario simulated a terrorist campaign in the United States as a test of the homeland security system across locations and levels of government. Although it did not involve Louisiana, the scenario called attention to a lack of understanding of coordination and planning processes.

The backbone of coordination in the National Response Plan was a system of incident command first developed for firefighters. When applied to the homeland security system as a whole, however, incident command was vague about who was to take charge.[13] The response plan also drew criticism for not providing enough space for consensus building in unprecedented events such as Katrina, in which emergency responders have not had the opportunity to rehearse responses and are forced to build coalitions on the spot to solve unforeseen problems.

Even if the plans had been perfectly clear, however, the federal government has limited authority over state, local, and private decisions about land use and hazards planning. Federal assistance would have been more effective earlier, in mitigation and response preparations such as enhancing barrier islands, rehearsing evacuation, or providing more detailed plans for vulnerable populations, but the final decisions about these activities are the domain of states and localities. The Director of the Mississippi Governor's Office of Recovery and Renewal from 2006 to 2007, Gavin Smith, speculated that the expectation of federal government aid might have even contributed to suboptimal efforts by the state and localities. "Because we have become so accustomed to the federal

[10] David Paulison, "FEMA Director Paulison Delivers Remarks at National Press Club," *CQ Transcripts*, November 30, 2006, 4. "If that had been in place, in my opinion, during Katrina, we would not have had the situation that we had," Paulison said. "You can't stop the hurricane from coming in, but we would have known very clearly what was going on in the Superdome, we would have known very clearly what was happening at the convention center, and we would have known clearly what was going on with the levees. But we did not. And that's the type of system we have to have in place."

[11] The plan originally contained 600 pages.

[12] U.S. Senate Committee of Homeland Security and Government Affairs, *Hurricane Katrina: A Nation Still Unprepared* (Washington, DC: GPO, 2006), 10–12.

[13] Donald Moynihan, "The Use of Networks in Emergency Management," *American Political Science Association*, Philadelphia, PA, August 30, 2006.

government coming in with lots of resources, state and local governments have come to expect that and not to rely on themselves," Smith said. "We are penalizing all players by becoming over reliant on federal resources."[14]

A REVISIONIST VIEW OF THE GOVERNMENT'S PERFORMANCE IN KATRINA

The focus on problems with the National Response Plan, FEMA, and its leadership obscures the broader point that the size and scale of the response was unprecedented. Compared to the government's response to the San Francisco earthquake of 1906, the 1927 Mississippi River floods, Hurricane Andrew in 1992, and countless other events, the federal government's response to Katrina was both speedy and massive. Wherever one comes down on the trade-offs between hierarchy and consensus building, the National Response Plan provides sufficient authority for a "push" of federal resources into a potential disaster zone before disaster strikes. The initial draft plan was written in a hurry after September 11 by outside consultants, but subsequent drafts incorporated the concerns of local emergency managers that the plan address natural disasters as well as terrorism.[15]

One of the most effective preparatory tactics for hurricanes is evacuation, and on that score the residents of New Orleans, aided by the local government's evacuation planning, performed well. The evacuation was larger than any previous effort and more effective than planners thought possible before the storm.[16] In one study of evacuations, Charles Ruch and Greg Schumann estimated a 90 percent evacuation rate for a medium-sized Texas city threatened by a hurricane based on a survey of people's intentions.[17] Studies of actual evacuation rates, however, lead to lower estimates, between 20 and 40 percent.[18] By comparison, during Katrina, approximately 1.2 million people – 92 percent of the affected population – evacuated in a 40-hour period.[19]

[14] Gavin Smith, "Untitled Presentation," *Natural Hazards Center Annual Workshop*, Broomfield, CO, July 15, 2008.

[15] Department of Homeland Security, *Catastrophic Incident Annex in National Response Plan*, Draft 7 (Washington, DC: GPO, 2004); *The Federal Response to Hurricane Katrina*, 1; Patrick Roberts, "FEMA and the Prospects for Reputation-Based Autonomy," *Studies in American Political Development* 20 (Spring 2006): 57–87.

[16] The second-largest rescue operation in terms of resources required since the creation of FEMA was the Mariel boatlift. Between April and October 1980, approximately 125,000 Cubans attempted to enter southern Florida, and the U.S. Coast Guard and FEMA participated in search-and-rescue operations. Alex Larzelere, *The 1980 Cuban Boatlift* (Washington DC: National Defense University Press, 1988).

[17] Charles Ruch and Greg Schumann, *Corpus Christi Study Area Hurricane Contingency Planning Guide* (College Station: University of Texas Press, 1997).

[18] E. J. Baker, "Hurricane Evacuation Behavior," *International Journal of Mass Emergencies and Disasters* 9 (1991): 287–310.

[19] Governor Kathleen Blanco, written statement for a hearing on Hurricane Katrina: Preparedness and Response by the State of Louisiana, on December 14, 2005, submitted to the U.S. House

By most accounts, the evacuation order from New Orleans Mayor Ray Nagin came later than it should have. By Friday, August 26, Mayor Nagin and other officials such as governor Kathleen Blanco and meteorologist Max Mayfield, director of the National Hurricane Center, were issuing increasingly stark warnings to residents, and suggesting evacuation. Nagin did not issue an official mandatory evacuation order until Sunday morning, and by then many residents without means for transportation or adequate shelter sought refuge in the city's shelter of last refuge, the Superdome sports stadium, or in a makeshift shelter in the city's Convention Center.[20] The incomplete evacuation combined with the scale of the disaster contributed to a loss of life, especially in New Orleans. New Orleans Parish had only approximately 25 percent of the population of the three surrounding Mississippi Parishes, but the death toll in New Orleans Parish was three times higher than in the more sparsely populated Mississippi counties where the storm hit with greater force.[21] In some cases, people simply refused to leave, or refused to believe that the storm could be deadly. Some residents lacked private cars, and response plans did not provide the means for all of them to leave the city in time, or the legal authority to force them to leave against their will. An estimated 40,000–70,000 people remained in New Orleans during the flood. The House's *Failure of Initiative* report found that more than 250,000 cars were in the city during the storm, and that cars were found parked in the driveways of many of the dead.[22] The report acknowledges that individuals who did not leave the city "share the blame" for the incomplete evacuation.[23] Political scientist Marc Landy goes further: "Those car owners who failed to evacuate in the face of mandatory evacuation orders that, however tardy, still left them plenty of time to leave, do not *share* in the blame, they *are* to blame."[24]

The evacuation was too late and not comprehensive enough for victims of the storm, but the government and nonprofit response as a whole was

Select Committee to Investigate the Preparation for and Response to Hurricane Katrina, 109th Congress, 1st session.

[20] FEMA Director Michael Brown criticizes Nagin for issuing an evacuation order too late in Michael Brown and Ted Schwarz, *Deadly Indifference, The Perfect (Political) Storm: Hurricane Katrina, The Bush White House, and Beyond* (Lanham, MD: Taylor Trade Publishing 2011), 80–88.

[21] U.S. House of Representatives, *A Failure of Initiative: Final Report of the Select Bipartisan Committee to Investigate the Preparations and Response to Hurricane Katrina* (Washington, DC: GPO, 2006), 115, available at: http://katrina.house.gov/full_katrina_report.htm (accessed March 8, 2010). "Death Toll from Katrina Likely Higher than 1,300," *MSNBC.com*, February 10, 2006, available at: http://www.msnbc.msn.com/id/11281267 (accessed March 8, 2010); Martha Derthick, "Why Federalism Didn't Fail," *Public Administration Review* 67 (2007): 36–47.

[22] U.S. House, *A Failure of Initiative*, 116.

[23] U.S. House, *A Failure of Initiative*, 114.

[24] Marc Landy, "Review Essay of *A Failure of Initiative* and *The Federal Response to Hurricane Katrina Lessons Learned*," *Publius: The Journal of Federalism*, 38.1: (2008): 152–165, 157; U.S. House, *A Failure of Initiative*, 116.

more effective than planners had estimated. In the week after Katrina struck, 563 American Red Cross or state emergency shelters in Louisiana housed 146,292 people who lacked adequate food, water, medical services, and toilets.[25] The Red Cross organized a $2 billion, 220,000-person effort in the year following Katrina, 20 times larger than any previous mission, serving 3.7 million victims.[26] FEMA also organized an unprecedented temporary housing program, with 62,000 trailers housing victims by January 2006.[27] The Department of Defense issued the largest domestic military deployment since the Civil War, and the National Guard deployment of 50,000 troops was its largest ever. Nongovernmental organizations responded on a similar scale.

Despite the valiant efforts of many, including members of the Coast Guard and Fish and Wildlife agencies who conducted heroic rescues from rooftops, the response was judged not swift enough.[28] FEMA and the federal government endured criticism for months after the disaster. It is worth asking what size federal response, if any, would have been large enough? The federal government authorized $75 billion in aid within three weeks of Katrina's landfall, and in March 2007, a Senate committee approved a $122 billion emergency spending bill that waived a requirement that Louisiana pay only 10 percent of the cost of FEMA assistance to Katrina victims.[29] Congress authorized unprecedented amounts of disaster relief, and the evacuation worked better than most people expected. Nevertheless, FEMA was unable to live up to its all hazards mission in the eyes of the public. The agency failed to meet expectations, but expectations for all hazards protection were impossibly high. FEMA and the DHS lacked the capacity to force the Army Corps to improve the levees before the storm, to move all citizens out of risky locations as the storm approached, and to return the city after the storm to its pre-storm population level and condition.

FEMA AND FEDERALISM

Although FEMA bore the brunt of the blame, it was only one of many federal, state, and local agencies involved in the Katrina response. Individuals and community groups also assisted friends and neighbors after the storm. At the very least, a multiplicity of formal organizations and informal networks sprang up to save lives, spare property, and assuage victims. FEMA was only loosely connected to most of these efforts. Daniel Smith, a young architect, told Columbia

---

[25] U.S. House, *A Failure of Initiative*, 312.
[26] U.S. House, *A Failure of Initiative*, 315; Martha Derthick judges the evacuation a mixed success. See Derthick, "Why Federalism Didn't Fail," 37–38.
[27] U.S. House, *A Failure of Initiative*, 314.
[28] Derthick, "Why Federalism Didn't Fail," 40–41.
[29] Bruce Alpert, "Senate Committee Approves Spending Bill," *New Orleans Times-Picayune*, March 23, 2007.

University's oral history interviewer that New Orleans residents spontaneously organized mutual assistance efforts even after professionals arrived:

Everyone was in charge when the National Guard came. They were in charge. The army came. They were in charge. There wasn't – on the upper levels, there wasn't a lot of coordination in a lot of ways. In some ways, that may sound like it was frustrating, but actually, what it enabled us to do is cut through all the red tape and get work done, since we weren't connected with FEMA or the OEM (New York's Office of Emergency Management) or the Red Cross, the Salvation Army, the National Guard. We were able to just go in and do work.[30]

Improvised response and recovery were important, because formal plans for housing, feeding, and caring for remaining residents broke down.[31] The Superdome, the primary site for displaced residents, grew hot and overcrowded, and its plumbing failed. It became uninhabitable. Thousands fled to an alternative site – the city's convention center – which had not been stocked with food, water, or medical supplies. Others left behind in the city fled to dry land and assembled on bridges and overpasses in the summer heat. Neighbors, friends, and strangers foraged for food, water, and medical care.

The emergency management system authorized by the Stafford Act, of which FEMA was a part, assumed that mayors and governors would ask for federal help, and then FEMA would step in. Yet requests for help took too long to make their way up the chain of command, and FEMA was not sure how to coordinate a massive response. Rather than account for improvisation, the system ossified. Disaster planning had developed many of the worst elements of the Weberian model. In German sociologist Max Weber's seminal account of "bureaucracy," he explains that in a bureaucracy, jurisdictional arenas are clearly specified, hierarchy reigns rather than collaboration, abstract rules and written documents govern decisions, organizations have a unity of command, and civil servants are career experts.[32] At its best, the Weberian ideal type of bureaucracy has clear lines of authority and accountability and detailed specializations and divisions of labor that promote efficiency and effectiveness. At its worst, the ideal type devolves in practice into bureaus with separate lines of authority that do not communicate, layers of hierarchy that are impenetrable, and the sluggishness that comes with following detailed procedures.

[30] Rebecca Solnit, *A Paradise Built in Hell: The Extraordinary Communities that Arise in Disaster* (New York: Viking, 2009), 206–207.

[31] David Mendonça, "Decision Support for Improvisation in Response to Extreme Events," *Decision Support Systems* 43.3 (2007): 952–967; David Mendonça and William A. Wallace, "Studying Organizationally-Situated Improvisation in Response to Extreme Events," *International Journal of Mass Emergencies and Disasters* 22 (2004): 5–29; John R. Harrald, "Achieving Agility in Disaster Management," *International Journal of Information Systems for Crisis Response and Management* 1 (2009): 1–11.

[32] Max Weber, "Bureaucracy," in *From Max Weber: Essays in Sociology*, edited and translated by H. H. Gerth and C. Wright Mills (New York: Oxford University Press, [1946 orig.] 1958), 196–244.

FEMA's difficulty in delivering buses to the city illustrates some of the problems with coordinating a large response bureaucratically. On Tuesday, August 30, FEMA Administrator Brown, Louisiana Governor Blanco, and Louisiana's two senators toured the devastation by helicopter. The governor saw the city under water and asked for buses; everyone agreed that buses were urgent. Brown declared, "If there's one thing FEMA's got, it's buses."[33] Brown then made the first of several calls to Washington asking for hundreds of buses, and FEMA headquarters forwarded the request to the Department of Transportation. At some point the number requested had been limited to 455. Louisiana officials were told the buses would arrive by the next morning, so they stopped requests for buses from local schools, churches, and private firms. Some buses arrived from the federal government on Wednesday, and these evacuated the sick and disabled, but the majority of buses did not arrive until Friday.[34] Blue ribbon commissions and reporters investigating what happened during the storm never found an adequate explanation for what happened to the buses. The miscommunication surrounding them shows the problems with a fragmented, multilayered bureaucracy, where lines of control and authority are unclear and implementation sometimes depends on chance rather than on fixed plans.

Sometimes clear rules and routines also stood in the way to moving people to safety. Brown reports pleading with Transportation Security Administration (TSA) officials to help load evacuees onto a commercial aircraft and move them to safety. "'But we have to screen them,' I was told [by TSA officials in Washington]. 'The law requires us to screen them before they can board a plane.'"[35] Brown was livid, and the plane eventually took off with passengers, but much later than it should have because of protests by TSA officials who, following their job requirements, could not find adequate security screeners at the airport and therefore delayed the plane's departure. The TSA was part of the same DHS that housed FEMA, but both agencies were stuck in their silos, each focused on their own missions and priorities, at least until the TSA relented.

Most government officials recognized that FEMA was overmatched, including FEMA's own staff. FEMA officials intended that the Department of Defense would step in, although FEMA was slow to send formal requests for assistance to Defense, which resists intervening in domestic affairs without legal authority because of deference to civilian control and the difference between military culture and civilian norms.[36] In particular, many in the military believe that

[33] Cooper and Block, *Disaster: Hurricane Katrina and the Failure of Homeland Security*, 2006, 162.

[34] U.S. Senate, *Hurricane Katrina: A Nation Still Unprepared*, 70; Cooper and Block, *Disaster: Hurricane Katrina and the Failure of Homeland Security*, 2006, 172, 184–187, 210; Derthick, "Why Federalism Didn't Fail," 42; Brown and Schwarz, *Deadly Indifference*, 73–74.

[35] Brown and Schwarz, *Deadly Indifference*, 151–152.

[36] Cooper and Block, *Disaster*, 161, 166–167; U.S. Senate, *Hurricane Katrina: A Nation Still Unprepared*, 482.

the Posse Comitatus Act of 1878, passed after Reconstruction, prohibits the military from exercising police powers domestically in all but the most extreme situations. Yet these worries did not prevent Brown from pleading for military intervention in the crisis.

Perhaps because of a combination of FEMA's limited capacity, the crisis atmosphere, and media-fueled rumors of rape, murder, and pillaging (most of which were unfounded), Brown went as far as to request that the president invoke a law to give the military authority to restore domestic order during insurrection. "I requested that the Insurrection Act be invoked on Tuesday," Brown said, "and discussed [this] up until Friday when I emailed the White House and said 'where the hell is the army?'"[37]

Saying no to Brown's request for military intervention might have been one of the wisest decisions the president made during the disaster. The military's shooting at suspected looters during the 1906 San Francisco earthquake provides an object lesson in the need to separate local police forces and national militaries. Furthermore, had authorities focused even more on chasing ghosts during Katrina and less on search and rescue, hundreds of people would have been lost. By law, the president may invoke the Insurrection Act to quell "insurrection, domestic violence, unlawful combination, or conspiracy."[38] The Act gives the military authority for domestic law enforcement and, presumably, the authority to shoot to kill. While most of the public believes the military is doing its job when it shoots enemies on foreign soil, news of the U.S. military shooting U.S. citizens could have provoked a crisis even greater than the Katrina catastrophe. One Defense official blanched at the thought of "American military guns going off in the Superdome," the temporary shelter for thousands of displaced New Orleanians.[39] That even the FEMA administrator would ask for military intervention shows how ill prepared the disaster agency was to meet the expectations of politicians and the public. In his 2011 memoir, Brown praised Mississippi Governor Haley Barbour for announcing that anyone who was caught looting would be shot. "Loot in Mississippi and you would take a bullet ...," Brown wrote. "He [Barbour] further announced that anyone who shot a looter would not be prosecuted. It was hard nose, clear, and decisive." Brown favorably compared Barbour's announcement with Louisiana Governor Kathleen Blanco's more moderate statements that "Everyone should work

[37] Michael Brown, personal interview, July 12, 2006; Brown confirms that he recommended that the president "waive the Insurrection Act and the Posse Comitatus Act and take over the National Guard, law enforcement, and other emergency response agencies in New Orleans and Louisiana." Brown reports that Louisiana Governor Kathleen Blanco resisted the idea. Brown, *Deadly Indifference*, 154.

[38] Jennifer K. Elsea, "The Use of Federal Troops for Disaster Assistance: Legal Issues," *Congressional Research Service Report*, Washington, DC, August 14, 2006; Jeff Stein, "Fine Print in Defense Bill Opens Door to Martial Law," *Congressional Quarterly*, December 1, 2006, available at: http://public.cq.com/public/20061201_homeland.html (accessed December 12, 2010).

[39] Defense official, personal interview, Boulder, CO, July 12, 2006.

together in the crisis," and found Blanco to be too tepid.⁴⁰ It is plausible that, in the heat of the moment, Brown encouraged the White House to use the military in ways that approximated conduct in a war zone. The local police in New Orleans behaved regretfully enough, firing unnecessarily on unarmed civilians in the chaotic aftermath of the storm. In 2011, a federal jury convicted five current or former New Orleans police officers in connection with the Danziger Bridge shootings that left two citizens dead and four injured.⁴¹

FEMA AND THE DHS

It is tempting to blame shortcomings in the government's response to Katrina on the creation of the DHS – the behemoth, 180,000-person department created after September 11, ostensibly to improve the nation's defense against terrorism. The department further entrenched disaster management in rules upon rules, a shell of hierarchy and management layers, and metaphorical stovepipes in which civil servants have rigid and narrowly defined responsibilities. Largely because of homeland security activities, government regulatory staffing levels were 43 percent larger in 2008 than in 2000, and regulatory spending increased by $13.2 billion over the same period.⁴²

The number of layers of administrators in the DHS delayed the government's response, as did the varying levels of their understanding of the situation. The secretary of homeland security, Michael Chertoff, was a member of the president's cabinet, whereas the FEMA administrator was merely an undersecretary reporting to Chertoff. In practice, managers within FEMA worked through their agency's bureaus, which then reported to the DHS. The Department developed its own disaster operations center, which delivered information to the White House and Congress, and the DHS formed a bottleneck between experienced disaster managers and politicians. In particular, Gen. Matthew Broderick, head of the recently created Homeland Security Operations Center charged with monitoring crises, did not believe that New Orleans's devastation was unusual.⁴³ His hesitation may have been part of the reason that the White

⁴⁰ Brown, *Deadly Indifference*, 130–131.
⁴¹ A. C. Thompson, "Five New Orleans Cops Convicted for Their Role in Post-Katrina Shootings," *ProPublica*, August 5, 2011, available at: http://www.propublica.org/nola/story/five-new-orleans-cops-convicted-for-their-role-in-post-katrina-shootings (accessed November 12, 2012).
⁴² Jerry Brito and Melinda Warren, "Growth in Regulation Slows: An Analysis of the US Budget for Fiscal Years 2007 and 2008," in *Regulators' Budget Report* 29 (Arlington, VA and St. Louis, MO: Mercatus Center and Weidenbaum Center, 2008); Jonathan Rauch, "Flying Blind in a Red-Tape Blizzard, How George Bush Became the Regulator-in-Chief," *Reason*, July 18, 2007, available at: http://reason.com/archives/2007/07/18/flying-blind-in-a-red-tape-bli (accessed January 7, 2011).
⁴³ Cooper and Block, *Disaster*, 131–133, 145–151; Andrew Campbell, Jo Whitehead, and Sydney Finkelstein, "Why Good Leaders Make Bad Decisions," *Harvard Business Review* (February 2009): 60–68.

House took so long to respond to the storm. Broderick ignored reports and e-mails about breached levees and instead used a CNN video clip of crowds partying on Bourbon Street to prove that the city was not in crisis. Before going home for the night, Broderick issued a report that the levees had not been breached. (The Army Corps of Engineers had also reported that it had no evidence of levee breaches.) Broderick appeared to exhibit confirmation bias – the tendency to accept evidence that confirms prior expectations and discount contradictory evidence.[44] Furthermore, his frame of reference for what counts as a crisis might have been military combat zones; his previous experience in operations centers was in Vietnam and other military engagements.[45]

Miscommunication and misunderstanding in the middle management of the DHS delayed the government's response to Katrina.[46] Because the supply chain for how rescue supplies such as food, ice, and shelters were supposed to reach a disaster area was not clear, it took longer than expected for relief to arrive. Even before Katrina, FEMA had a record of having an insufficient number of trained procurement professionals. Immediately after the storm, the agency asked for logistics help from the Department of Defense, but that request took time to flow through interagency processes.[47] Even though Defense's Northern Command monitored the progress of the storm before it made landfall, many deployments of rescue teams and supplies did not reach the disaster area until days later. Analyses of the government's response blame Defense processes as well as overly complicated layers of communication within the DHS for the slow response.[48]

Bureaus within the DHS failed to tell the political appointees and operations managers who could ask for help from other agencies how severe the storm was, and the Bush administration and its appointed managers within the Department failed to take action. As the House's *Failure of Initiative Report* put it, "Passivity did the most damage."[49]

The DHS's response to Katrina shows the problem with agencies that have stovepipes, which in the organizational context occur when managers and civil servants have rigid and narrowly defined responsibilities that prevent communication and improvisation outside formal channels. Stovepipes and their attendant hierarchies are common organizational forms because they can offer

---

[44] Daniel Kahneman, *Thinking, Fast and Slow* (New York: Farrar, Strauss, and Giroux, 2011), 80–81.

[45] Campbell, Whitehead, and Finkelstein, "Why Good Leaders Make Bad Decisions," 67–68.

[46] Cooper and Block, *Disaster*, 131–133, 145–151.

[47] Amy K. Donohue and Robert V. Tuhy, "Lessons We Don't Learn: A Study of the Lessons of Disasters, Why We Repeat Them, and How We Can Learn from Them," *Homeland Security Affairs* 2 (July 2006): 1–28; Russell Sobel and Peter Leeson, "Government's Response to Hurricane Katrina: A Public Choice Analysis," *Public Choice* 127 (2006): 55–73.

[48] Steve Bowman, Lawrence Kapp, and Amy Belasco, "Hurricane Katrina: DOD Disaster Response," RL 33095, Washington, DC: Congressional Research Service, September 19, 2005.

[49] U.S. House, *A Failure of Initiative*, 359.

advantages: they allow for specialization, division of labor, and a clear chain of accountability. The DHS, however, had conflicting missions that prevented the efficiencies of hierarchy from being realized; some organs of the department existed to prevent terrorism, others to prevent natural disasters, and others to engage in routine security and protect commerce.[50] It was not always clear what a FEMA employee charged with flood preparations should do to prevent terrorism and secure the homeland. And if a FEMA manager had to attend meetings with other managers to construct plans to prepare for terrorism, that was time away from natural disasters–related activities.

In general, the diversity and unpredictability of disasters are a poor match for stovepiped organizations. A major hurricane may strike one year, and forest fires may cause more alarm in another. One state may be more prepared in a given year than another. As a bipartisan congressional committee put it, "The preparation and response to Hurricane Katrina show we are still an analog government in a digital age."[51] The staffer's pithy phrase may be a little too cute, but it draws attention to an important point: the DHS was both overly hierarchical in that it put diverse agencies under a single terrorism-focused mission, and not hierarchical enough in that it had limited authority over disaster preparations at the state and local levels.

Many federal government programs, in areas from housing to energy and the environment, shaped the Gulf Coast's vulnerability to disaster, but no federal government agency monitored the cumulative effects of these programs. In the most famous example, the city's heralded levee system had been built by the Army Corps of Engineers at the request of Congress to protect the city from no more than a category 3 hurricane.[52] The Corps' New Orleans region budget had been reduced by $80 million in 2005 alone, and much of the region's wetlands – previously a natural impediment to storm surges – had been sacrificed to industrial and commercial development. The levees were structurally deficient, and repair budgets promised more than they delivered.[53] The levees protecting

---

[50] Anne M. Khademian, "Hurricane Katrina and the Failure of Homeland Security," in *Judging Bush*, edited by Robert Maranto, Tom Lansford, and Jeremy Johnson (Stanford, CA: Stanford University Press, 2009), 195–214; 198.

[51] U.S. House, *A Failure of Initiative*, 1

[52] Some levees were partly built and maintained by the Orleans levee board after a 1983 cost-sharing agreement. The Louisiana legislature established the Orleans Levee District in 1890. The District is primarily responsible for the operation and maintenance of levees, embankments, seawalls, jetties, breakwaters, water basins, and other hurricane and flood protection improvements surrounding New Orleans, including the southern shores of Lake Pontchartrain and along the Mississippi River. The District and the U.S. Corps of Engineers participate and share costs in several joint flood protection projects. For more information on the Army Corps projects in the district, see: http://www.mvn.usace.army.mil/hps/pdf/numbers_and_statistics.pdf and http://www.mvn.usace.army.mil/hps/pdf/Updated_Cost_Estimates_and_Appropriations-Authority.pdf (accessed December 11, 2010).

[53] Cooper and Block, *Disaster*, 13, 29; Ivor L. Van Heerden and Mike Bryan, *The Storm: What Went Wrong and Why During Hurricane Katrina* (New York: Viking, 2006); U.S. Army Corps

the suburbs mostly held, however. They were built by contractors who were not connected to New Orleans's political class, and they were not maintained by the notoriously lax Orleans Parish Levee Board. Federal authorities bore responsibility for New Orleans's predicament, too. New Orleans would not have been as vulnerable to storm surges without federal government and especially Army Corps assistance in clearing wetlands for development. Yet the Army Corps was never part of FEMA or the DHS.

Debate over the purpose of homeland security and uncertainty about the status of FEMA led to the departure of FEMA's most experienced professionals before the storm. Some retired, some became consultants, and others were reassigned within the DHS. The agency's all hazards mission suffered when preparedness grant programs were moved out of FEMA into a separate office in the DHS. Representative Bill Shuster, a Republican from Pennsylvania, said that the department's leaders allowed FEMA's capacities to deteriorate "because its disaster mission cannot compete with DHS' terrorism prevention mission."[54] States, localities, and citizens expected FEMA to take the lead in response to Katrina, but FEMA could not lead because of its weakened capacity and legal and organizational constraints.

DISASTER AND DEVELOPMENT

Hurricane Katrina exposed problems with disaster management that run deeper than the response phase. Government agencies designated to protect cities located in highly vulnerable areas such as New Orleans are being asked to manage the unmanageable. Areas with extreme physical vulnerability, such as dense populations below sea level, and social vulnerability, such as a concentration of poor and marginalized populations, will not bounce back immediately from a major event. Public administrators charged with protecting the public from hazards wield legal tools designed to cope with more routine disasters, not catastrophes.

Commercial pressures to develop coastal land and the short time horizons of politicians focused on elections limit what FEMA civil servants can do to prepare for major disasters. Political scientist Brian Gerber notes that emergency preparedness experts have long understood how to prepare for disaster by building protections or not building at all in risky areas,

of Engineers, *Performance Evaluation of the New Orleans and Southeast Louisiana Hurricane Protection System: Draft Final Report of the Interagency Performance Evaluation Task Force* (Washington, DC: US Army Corps of Engineers, 2006), available at: https://ipet.wes.army.mil/(Accessed October 8, 2010), http://biotech.law.lsu.edu/katrina/ipet/ipet.html (Accessed April 15, 2013); Raymond Seed et al., *Investigation of the Performance of the New Orleans Flood Protection Systems in Hurricane Katrina on August 29, 2005* (Berkeley: University of California Press, 2006), available at: www.ce.berkeley.edu/~new_orleans/ (accessed December 8, 2010); Brig. Gen. Stuart Leavenworth, "Will We Ever Learn?" *Sacramento Bee*, July 2, 2006.
[54] Bill Shuster, U.S. Congress, Press Release, April 27, 2006, available at: http://www.house.gov/list/press/pa09_shuster/whyfemafailed.html (accessed December 8, 2010).

issuing warnings in advance of an event, and carrying out a well-rehearsed, bottom-up response. The problem is that experts have trouble persuading citizens and policy makers to act on that knowledge.[55] Local leaders face pressure from citizens and developers to build in vulnerable areas or divert institutions, such as levee boards, from their original purpose to more short-sighted activities that provide immediate benefits to constituents and carry electoral benefits. (The New Orleans levee boards assumed responsibility for parks, policing, and recreational profit-making enterprises in addition to the levees themselves.) Renters and homeowners still settle in flood-prone areas and fail to rehearse evacuation plans. The knottiest problems are not scientific but political.

Zoning regulations in the United States are sparse and uneven, and they typically succeed only after a major disaster, if even then. The closest thing the United States has to a national zoning code is the community rating system portion of the National Flood Insurance Program. The rating system provides favorable, federal-government-backed insurance rates to communities that engage in activities under four categories: Public Information, Mapping and Regulations, Flood Damage Reduction, and Flood Preparedness. As of 2009, only 1,095 communities participated in the community rating system out of approximately 20,000 covered through the national flood insurance program.[56]

Even after Katrina, Mississippi did not adopt a statewide building code, and coastal counties adopted a code that was only voluntary.[57] Even though strict building codes reduce the consequences of disasters, it is understandable why they are not more common in the Gulf Coast. The benefits of building codes are too diffuse and far off in the future to offset the short-term costs of lost potential development and of bringing a building up to code. Studies of post-disaster reform highlight the role of major focusing events, or large-scale disasters with similar characteristics, in calling attention to the need for reform to prepare for the future.[58] Rare events by definition have so little precedent, however, that relying on one to structure preparation could be irrelevant or

[55] Brian J. Gerber, "Disaster Management in the United States: Examining Key Political and Policy Challenges," *Policy Studies Journal* 35 (2006): 236–237.

[56] National Flood Insurance Program, Community Rating System data sheet, 2009; *Information on Proposed Changes to the National Flood Insurance Program*, GAO-09-420R, Washington, DC, February 27, 2009; *Challenges Facing the National Flood Insurance Program: Testimony Before the Subcommittee on Housing and Community Opportunity, Committee on Financial Services, House of Representatives*, GAO-03-606T, Washington, DC, April 1, 2003; *Challenges Facing the National Flood Insurance Program*, GAO-06-174T, Washington, DC, October 18, 2005.

[57] Gavin Smith, "Recovery After Hurricane Katrina," talk given at *Natural Hazards Center Workshop*, Boulder, CO, July 12, 2006.

[58] Thomas A Birkland, *After Disaster: Agenda Setting, Public Policy, and Focusing Events* (Washington, DC: Georgetown University Press, 1997); Erik J. Dahl, "Preventing Terrorist Attacks: Intelligence Warning and Policy Response," Ph.D. thesis, Fletcher School of Law and Diplomacy, Tufts University, Somerville, MA, 2008.

misleading in thinking about the next disaster. Preparing for the next Katrina does not necessarily help FEMA prepare for the next big earthquake or help residents of vulnerable areas – think about Miami Beach – recognize that they too should prepare.

The private market does not prepare well for catastrophic disasters, either. Insurance helps prevent some kinds of disasters: for example, some people add fire-resistant features to their homes to qualify for fire insurance.[59] The insurance industry cooperates with government regulators to develop standards to make homes safer and enforce adoption of building codes. Flood insurance, however, is not adopted widely enough to have the same beneficial effects as fire insurance. The private insurance market does not provide affordable insurance for most large-scale rare events because the true probabilities of these events are unknown, and the market rate for insurance would be too high. Most people would simply take the risk and not buy insurance.[60] Even with the National Flood Insurance Program's favorable rates, the majority of homes in coastal counties affected by Katrina did not have flood insurance, ranging from 57.7 percent of homes with insurance in St. Bernard Parish, Louisiana, to 3.9 percent in Mobile, Alabama.[61] In other regions, the number is even lower. Ninety-nine percent of Wisconsin residents lacked flood insurance in 2006, even though the state's rivers and lakes routinely overflow.[62] However, the fact that few people have flood insurance is not enough to blame individuals. Insurance rates can send a signal not to build in certain areas provided that insurance rates reflect a true market price that takes into account the risk of disaster losses. If insurance rates are set by political means, however, all bets are off. Insurance rates in Louisiana did not reflect the true risk, and organizations were allowed to build in vulnerable areas or degrade regions important for flood protection.

Other fragmented and short-sighted local decisions put communities at risk. The bodies responsible for land use policies were fragmented and concerned with other matters beside disaster risk. For instance, the levee system that protected New Orleans was a system in name only (like FEMA itself). In truth, it was a collection of loosely affiliated local levee boards that worked with the Army Corps of Engineers at the federal level, and very rarely with FEMA. Gulf Coast towns had experienced enough large hurricanes to know that they

[59] The development of fire insurance occurred in fits and starts, only after many costly disasters and unsustainable arrangements. See Scott Gabriel Knowles, *The Disaster Experts: Mastering Risk in Modern America* (Philadelphia: University of Pennsylvania Press, 2011), 1–161.

[60] Robert Meyer, "Why We Under-Prepare for Hazards," in *On Risk and Disaster: Lessons from Hurricane Katrina*, edited by Ronald J. Daniels, Donald F. Kettl, and Howard Kunreuther (Philadelphia: University of Pennsylvania Press 2006), 153–174.

[61] Insurance Information Institute, "Hurricane Season of 2006: Impacts on US P/C Instance Markets in 2006 & Beyond," New York, 2006, 54, 156.

[62] Federal Emergency Management Agency, "99 Percent of Wisconsin Residents Don't Have Flood Insurance," (Washington, DC: FEMA, 2006).

should have prepared for the next one, yet for multiple reasons they continued to put lives and property at risk.

In many cases, the federal government's land use policies also contributed to vulnerability. For example, the Army Corps of Engineers completed a 76-mile canal, the Mississippi River Gulf Outlet ("Mr. Go"), in the 1960s as a short-cut for ships traveling from the river to the gulf. Studies of Hurricane Katrina show that it served as a funnel increasing the velocity of storm surges into New Orleans.[63] Federal, state, and local players contributed to increasing vulnerability, but FEMA was expected to come to the rescue.

DISASTER MANAGEMENT AFTER KATRINA

By the twenty-first century, the public expected the federal government to lead response to and recovery from disaster. Politicians responsible for creating the DHS were eager to claim an expansive portfolio for the new department, and emergency managers in government were eager to claim more responsibility for their organizations.

But public expectations and FEMA's broad all hazards mandate were disproportionate to the bureaucracy's capacity to deal with rare catastrophes. Katrina overwhelmed FEMA and the federal government, and the government lacked the resources and the organizational acumen to mount a sufficient response. Most importantly, the federal government did little to shape the underlying causes of increased disaster losses in urbanization and development patterns.

Advocates of centralization and advocates of decentralization both had ideas for reform. President George W. Bush's response to the crisis was typical of the former. He said, "It is now clear that a challenge on this scale requires greater federal authority and a broader role for the armed forces – the institution of our government most capable of massive logistical operations on a moment's notice."[64] The logic of centralization holds that disaster response will be improved when the federal government organizes more of the response to a disaster, and the only government agency with the capability to mount a massive, centralized response is the military. The military, however, has resisted intervening in domestic affairs since it ceded civil defense functions to domestic agencies in the 1950s.

States and localities, meanwhile, resisted greater centralization that would strip them of authority and reduce their budgets. Florida Governor Jeb Bush's remarks are typical of a state official, but remarkable on the heels of the recommendation of his brother, the president: "I can say with certainty that federalizing emergency response to catastrophic events would be a disaster as bad as Hurricane Katrina," Governor Bush said. "The current system works when

---

[63] Christopher Cooper and Robert Block, *Disaster: Hurricane Karina and the Failure of Homeland Security* (New York: Times Books, 2006), 26–28.

[64] George W. Bush, televised address, New Orleans, September 15, 2005.

everyone understands, accepts, and is willing to fulfill their responsibilities
... the bottom-up approach yields the best results."⁶⁵ State and local officials
resented federal government aggrandizement, but they welcomed federal funds
for disaster management and federal agencies as a scapegoat during crisis.

At the same time, there is a symbiotic relationship between public expectations and federal government activity. Ambitious politicians and bureaucrats
welcome more authority, and the public and the members of Congress who
represent them are willing to expect more of government. The capacious idea
of homeland security, a department devoted to securing the nation against
a range of threats, was a logical extension of James Lee Witt's all hazards
paradigm, which itself extended the federal government's promise of civil
defense. Asking the federal government to radically devolve disaster response
to the states is an unrealistic solution because disaster response has become an
unquestioned responsibility of the federal government and of citizens' obligations to one another.

Federal government intervention was once controversial, and as late as
1886, business leaders in Charleston, South Carolina, rebuffed federal offers of
assistance for fear that the city would be labeled as earthquake prone.⁶⁶ Today,
even conservatives, who bill themselves as advocates of smaller government,
accept the constitutionality and necessity of federal government intervention
in disaster management. Writing during Katrina, conservative Jonah Goldberg
pronounced hyperbolically that, "When a city is sinking into the sea and rioting runs rampant, government should probably saddle-up."⁶⁷ A CBS News
poll of a national sample six months after Katrina asked, "In New Orleans,
after the Hurricane, hundreds of thousands of people were unable to evacuate
the flooded city and they lacked food, water and shelter. Who would you say
was most to blame for those conditions?" ⁶⁸ (The poll's claim that hundreds
of thousands of people were unable to evacuate is overstated.) Twenty-seven
percent of respondents said FEMA or the federal government was to blame,
another 11 percent said President Bush, and another 11 percent blamed government in general. State and local officials were blamed less often, despite the
fact that the federal government had no formal responsibility for planning and
issuing evacuation orders.

While the contemporary consensus holds the federal government responsible for coming to the rescue after disaster, the federal government lacks the
capacity and the legal authority to be the first responder. As Katrina showed,

⁶⁵ Jeb Bush, "Think Locally on Relief," *Washington Post*, September 30, 2005, A19, available at:
   http://www.washingtonpost.com/wp-dyn/content/article/2005/09/29/AR2005092901636.html
   (accessed December 8, 2010).
⁶⁶ Steinberg, *Acts of God*, 22–24.
⁶⁷ Jonah Goldberg, "The Feds," The Corner Blog, *National Review Online*, August 31, 2005,
   available at: http://corner.nationalreview.com/post/?q=YjM3YTY5MTNiMTNmMDI1ZjFlYm
   E1NzIyYWJkMDUoY2Q= (accessed December 8, 2010).
⁶⁸ CBS News Poll, "Hurricane Katrina: Six Months Later," February 27, 2006.

residents of disaster-stricken areas are inevitably the first ones to help one another, and they provide mutual assistance after the government leaves. Nevertheless, the federal government can play an important role if it breaks deadlocks over reducing vulnerability at the local level, such as when local officials are too myopic or too fragmented to take action to prepare for disaster. The federal government can also provide some unique expertise in long-term mitigation and long-term recovery because these tasks require planning and mapping expertise that subnational governments lack. Yet the government's role in economic recovery is hampered by the Stafford Act's omission of agency authority for economic development and widespread suspicion about tampering with the economy. Disaster managers' attempts to construct how people think about disasters by encouraging them to appreciate spending now to avert a flood or hurricane later run up against limits imposed by the nature of these rare events.[69] Mitigation is difficult to defend because its benefits are not easily appreciated. It is hard to claim credit for mitigating a disaster by erecting flood barriers if a disaster never happens.

[69] In actor network theory, disasters can be "actants" in a process of social construction. For an overview, see Anne Taufen Wessells, "Reassembling the Social: An Introduction to Actor-Network-Theory by Bruno Latour," *International Public Management Journal* 10.3 (2007): 351–356.

7

Administrative Evil and Elite Panic in Disaster Management

Hurricane Katrina shows what happens when compound catastrophes overwhelm bureaucracies best suited for routine floods and hurricanes. While disasters kill fewer people today than in the past, the bureaucratic form of contemporary disaster management produces its own pathologies. Bureaucrats and politically appointed managers plan for security threats in secrecy and work under time pressure. In some cases, their imaginations may unconsciously tap fears about marginalized groups. In a few instances, security hawks in FEMA and elsewhere shaped what counted as disasters and emergencies by naming citizens and marginalized groups as opposing categories. Citizens were to be protected from the marginalized, even though the marginalized were citizens. Thus, contemporary disaster management offers the unfortunate possibility that administrative processes for planning for the worst case may ignite deep fears in policy makers, leading them to engage in discriminatory practices.

The culture of disaster management assumes irrational characteristics as it bureaucratizes. As Cold War security organizations transform into homeland security, it is worth paying attention to how arguments in the name of security during a crisis overstate objective levels of threat and harm marginalized groups. Large disasters tap fears and the imagination, and these desires and fantasies manifest at moments of social construction when they shape planning processes to prepare for the worst. The dominant mode of social science analysis that assumes conscious, goal-seeking rational behavior does not provide much guidance to understanding where paranoid fantasies about marginalized groups might come from.[1] Appreciating these irrational elements of contemporary disaster management requires taking a dip into psychoanalytic theory and

---

[1] There are plausible rational explanations for discriminatory practices in disaster and crisis management, but these explanations do not account for the source of discrimination. See Gabriel Almond, "Rational Choice Theory and the Social Sciences," in *A Discipline Divided* (Newburg Park, CA: Sage Publications, 1990), 117–137.

modes of analysis usually found in literary studies, anthropology, and public administration theory, not political science.

In three cases in recent history, members of disaster and security organizations singled out marginalized groups in moments of crisis. In one case during the early 1980s, FEMA developed plans to quarantine members of the public, likely African Americans, during riots, believing them to be the instigators of civil disorder. In another case, FEMA kept lists of gays and lesbians in the agency as late as 1988 because agency leaders believed that homosexuals posed a security threat. In the final case, public officials spread tales of bestial conduct by residents of New Orleans (again, presumably poor African Americans) during Hurricane Katrina. In each case, the stories turned out to be rumors and wild exaggerations.

The three cases of discriminatory practices are a caution to the federal government's growing role in disaster and domestic security because they occurred in a late-twentieth-century, post–civil rights bureaucratic culture officially committed to antidiscrimination and subject to equal opportunity law and procedure. Rather than write off these abuses as exceptions or aberrations, one should read them as manifestations of unconscious bigotry only muted and mollified by multiculturalism and by the Herculean efforts of civil right movements, but reactivated by a sense of crisis and social upheaval. These cases do not show that all disaster planning overreaches, but they do illustrate potential dangers in state disaster and security planning. The state engages in social construction of disaster when it categorizes what counts as a disaster and who counts as a victim or a potential perpetrator.

ADMINISTRATIVE EVIL

The classic sociological explanation for organizational deviance – the amoral calculating manager – locates the source of wrongdoing in the calculations of individual leaders.[2] It is tempting to dismiss plans and rumors that vilify a marginalized group as the bizarre behavior of a single leader and thus an exception to the reigning liberal consensus. Yet discriminatory practices also emerge not from a single individual but through formal organizations and informal networks during fear of a crisis. As the three examples in this chapter show, individuals make judgments with discriminatory effects by relying on existing procedures and echoing and enhancing the judgments of others about which individuals or groups pose a threat. The knowledge and fantasy that exist in the realm of the mind find a home in existing patterns and routines for

[2] Robert A. Kagan and John T. Scholz, "The Criminology of the Corporation and Regulatory Enforcement Strategies," in *Enforcing Regulation*, edited by Keith Hawkins and John M. Thomas (Boston: Kluwer-Nijhoff, 1984), 67–96; Diane Vaughan, "The Challenger Space Shuttle Disaster," in *Corporate and Government Deviance*, 6th ed., edited by M. David Ermann and Richard J. Lundman (New York: Oxford University Press 2002), 306–333; 308.

identifying security threats during crisis and disaster. Although the language of psychoanalysis and unconscious fantasy is not common in contemporary social science, the idea of collective fantasy helps explain the repeated excesses of crisis planning better than standard accounts of deviant behavior.

Before examining the details of the three instances of discriminatory behavior, it is worth considering how the theories of administrative evil and elite panic provide a framework to understand the similarities among the cases. Planning for crisis and disaster can tend toward what some scholars call *administrative evil* – a provocative term that describes how otherwise responsible civil servants commit evil acts while pursuing bureaucratic routines.[3] Administrators may act efficiently in terms of their responsibilities within an organizational hierarchy, perhaps by interdicting a person who might pose a security threat. Their acts become evil, or at least unjust, when they are discriminatory and out of proportion with the ends they serve when judged in retrospect or when seen by an outsider. Disaster and security organizations often keep their procedures secret, however, and closed organizational loops make it all too easy for an administrator or public official to commit an act he or she thinks is good in the context of the organization but which seems extreme and unjust from other perspectives.

The idea of administrative evil stems from Hannah Arendt's account of the banality of evil during the German prosecution of the Holocaust.[4] Arendt did not mean that evil itself was banal, but rather that some German officials showed no capacity for reflection about the morality of their acts. Singling out minorities as security risks may not seem comparable to the horrors of Nazi death camps, but the gulf between the two is evidence of Arendt's point. The pervasive unthinkingness at every level of an organization is "evil" to her. It is easy to vilify the war criminals, but it is more difficult to talk about an institutional, bureaucratic evil, and so people create monsters.

Contemporary scholars of public administration use the term "evil" in a rather elastic fashion. Some scholars have criticized the term as "nonsensical" because it is difficult to separate individuals who commit evil or at least morally wrong acts from the influence of organizations.[5] The term is useful, however, for drawing attention to situations where people behave according to social norms in most cases, but overreact when put in charge of crisis planning.

A culture of technical rationality enables the emergence of administrative evil, and by the late twentieth century the institutionalized and professionalized

[3] Guy Adams and Danny Balfour, *Unmasking Administrative Evil* (Armonk, NY: M. E. Sharpe, 2006).

[4] Hannah Arendt, *Eichmann in Jerusalem: A Report on the Banality of Evil* (New York: Viking Press, 1963).

[5] Mel J. Dubnick, Jonathan Justice, and Dominic A. Bearfield, "Imagining and Managing Organizational Evil," in *The Foundations of Organizational Evil*, edited by Carole L. Jurkiewicz (Armonk, NY: M.E. Sharpe, 2012), 249–281; Mel J. Dubnick, "The Case for Administrative Evil: A Critique," *Public Administration Review* 60 (2000): 464–474.

world of emergency management had fostered the creation of such a culture. Technical rationality privileges a scientific and analytic view of the world and assumes technological progress.[6] Actions that conform to scientific rationality and technological progress by reducing risk, such as plans to increase security during crisis, are less likely to be criticized. The language of technical rationality in disaster organizations tends to be arcane, which makes it more difficult for outsiders even within the organization to understand and criticize security procedures until after the fact.

Sociologists offer similar explanations for how seemingly well-meaning people can commit acts in an organizational context that are later judged to be evil. Scholars sometimes invoke "culture" to explain deviant behavior. Specifically, people may see their own cultural understandings as conforming to behavioral norms even when they deviate from larger social norms or explicit goals of organizational design. Diane Vaughan summarizes this explanation: "One line of thought is that by drawing on largely unconscious cultural knowledge, individuals make the problematic nonproblematic by formulating a definition of the situation that makes sense of it in cultural terms, so that in their view their action is acceptable and non-deviant prior to an act."[7] Individuals or groups within a large organization can draw on available cultural scripts to legitimate an action that violates standards held up elsewhere in the organization. Sometimes these scripts may come from a faction within an organization or within society; at other times scripts may be buried deep inside individual or collective consciousness.[8] For example, security procedures may require giving extra scrutiny to groups that pose a threat. Ideas about which groups pose a threat come from past discrimination, conflicts, and unconscious ideas (what psychoanalysts call "fantasies") buried deep inside the mind.[9] For managers of

[6] Guy Adams and Virginia Hill Ingersoll, *The Tacit Organization* (Greenwich, CT: JAI Press, 1992); Adams and Balfour, Unmasking Administrative Evil, 2006, 29–36.

[7] Diane Vaughan, "The Dark Side of Organizations," *Annual Review of Sociology* 25 (1999): 271–305; 273, 281; Calvin Morril, Ellen Snyderman, and Edwin J. Dawson, "It's Not What You Do, But Who You Are," *Sociological Forum* 12 (2004): 519–543; Diane Vaughan, *The Challenger Launch Decision* (Chicago: University of Chicago Press, 1996); Lynn Zucker, "The Role of Institutionalization in Cultural Persistence," *Annual American Sociological Review* 42 (1977): 726–743.

[8] Rather than analyzing the features of organizational culture, historians prefer to examine the "patterns of conduct and spirals of escalation" that over time lead to extreme practices. Conduct and practices, rather than ideology, are at the center of such studies. Members of organizations resort to extreme practices to solve a problem or address a threat that absorbs so much attention that they do not see the practice itself as problematic. Isabel Hull shows how the deeply embedded assumptions and practices, unchecked by civilian control, drove the Imperial German Army to seek not simply victory but the absolute destruction of its enemies beyond strategic necessity. She provides a historical-institutional rationality to seemingly irrational outcomes. See Isabel V. Hull, *Absolute Destruction: Military Culture and the Practices of War in Imperial Germany* (Ithaca, NY: Cornell University Press, 2005), 3.

[9] Jacques Lacan, *The Four Fundamental Concepts of Psychoanalysis*, edited by Jacques-Alain Miller, translated by Alan Sheridan (London: Hogarth Press, 1977), 56; Jean Laplance and

crisis and disaster, ideas about who posed a threat were shaped by the crisis situation, the Cold War and post-9/11 milieus, fears of the worst case and of losing control, and images about transgressive and bestial human behavior that could not be expressed openly.

PLANNING FOR THE WORST CASE

Soon after FEMA was created in 1979 to respond to natural and industrial disasters, policy planners within the agency developed secret contingency plans that considered interning citizens in the event of a riot. In hindsight, planning for the highly improbable event of civil disorder appears extreme because the costs to civil liberties far outweighed the benefits for security. When viewed through the lens of Cold War practices and assumptions, however, the contingency plans conform to the norms of security procedures. The federal government had institutionalized contingency planning; with the threat of nuclear war on the wane, mass rioting posed a conceivable, though by no means likely, replacement as a threat to national security.

When President Carter created FEMA as an amalgam of agencies responsible for natural, industrial, and deliberate disasters, he included in it programs for civil defense and continuity of government, or the operation of government in a protected location if Washington, DC were attacked by a nuclear bomb. Programs to maintain continuity of government and civil defense programs, both long past their heyday, retained substantial influence within the agency because of the insulation offered by secrecy. Much of their work was classified and they controlled a large portion of the budget that, being classified, was difficult to compare to the open FEMA budget.

Civil defense concerns came to the fore when President Reagan appointed Giuffrida as FEMA administrator in 1981.[10] Giuffrida, a former National Guard officer and a general in California's state militia who insisted that he be called "general" while at FEMA, took a greater interest in domestic security than any other FEMA administrator before or since. According to one colleague of Giuffrida's, "He wanted to be a player in the national security realm," and envisioned the agency as a "junior CIA or FBI."[11]

Jean-Baptiste Pontalis, "Fantasy and the Origins of Sexuality," in *Formations of Fantasy*, edited by Victor Burgin, J. Donald, and C. Kaplan (London and New York: Methuen 1986), 5–27; Victor Burgin, "Fantasy," in *Feminism and Psychoanalysis: A Critical Dictionary*, edited by Elizabeth Wright (Oxford: Blackwell, 1992), 84–88.

[10] Giuffrida was an expert on domestic terrorism. At the U.S. Army War College in 1970, he wrote a thesis that in part concerned the logistics of interning African Americans in the event of an urban riot. The thesis is reprinted here: Senate Committee on Governmental Affairs, Nomination of Louis O. Giuffrida. Washington, DC, 97th Cong., 1st Sess (1981), 34–83.

[11] See George Jett, General Counsel, "Memorandum for Louis O. Giuffrida, Responsibilities in Civil Disturbances," July 10, 1981; Craig B. Annear, Assistant General Counsel, "Note for Lee Thomas, The Applicability of the Disaster Relief Act of 1974 to Riots and Civil Disorders," May 21, 1981. Other disasters cross multiple categories. The 1992 Los Angeles riots were declared

FEMA was created to prepare for worst-case disasters, the ones that states and localities could not handle alone, but the Giuffrida regime's ideas about what constituted worst cases emphasized security threats – an example of how the media, public managers, and organizational environments socially construct what a disaster is. What if antiwar protests morphed into violence, or what if African Americans demonstrated against discrimination? Giuffrida had seen student protests and the 1965 Watts riots as an emergency manager in California. As governor, Reagan appointed him to be director of the California Specialized Training Institute, an emergency management counterterrorism training center, in 1971. As soon as he took office at FEMA, Giuffrida asked his general counsel to clarify the agency's authority in "riots, demonstrations which get out of hand, etc."[12] The counsel reassured Giuffrida that FEMA had a role in national emergencies and that the agency could exercise intelligence tasks in planning for crisis.[13]

Taking its civil defense mission to heart, Giuffrida's FEMA began planning for nuclear attacks, riots, industrial accidents, and direct strikes on government officials. From 1982 to 1984, officials at FEMA met with Lt. Col. Oliver North, an enterprising National Security Council staffer who led an interagency group devoted to crisis planning. North operated in the NSC during a period that Zbigniew Brzezinski termed a "mid life crisis."[14] The NSC had lost its sense of direction, and the overuse of interagency working groups allowed ambitious staffers to build their own policy domains with little oversight from above.

a presidential disaster because of fire damage rather than riots. Giuffrida's desire for FEMA to become a national security agency is reflected in a proposed executive order on intelligence activities in which Jett writes, "I have suggested that consideration be given to the inclusion of a provision concerning FEMA involvement in intelligence matters in times of national emergency planning and response." See Jett, "Memorandum for Louis O. Giuffrida," November 9, 1981. In a memo requested by Giuffrida, Jett laid out FEMA's authority in civil disturbances, "riots, demonstrations which get out of hand, etc." This memo and others referred to a previous Department of Justice memo that rejected FEMA's authority in "nonnatural catastrophes." The FEMA counsels explicitly disagreed with Justice and advised that "dual use" provisions and FEMA's authority under executive order 12148 allowed FEMA to recommend declarations and assert authority in nonnatural disasters like Love Canal and "the Cuban influx" as well as in "major civil disturbances."

12 See George Jett, General Counsel, "Memorandum for Louis O. Giuffrida, Responsibilities in Civil Disturbances," July 10, 1981; Craig B. Annear, Assistant General Counsel, "Note for Lee Thomas, The Applicability of the Disaster Relief Act of 1974 to Riots and Civil Disorders," May 21, 1981

13 See Jett, "Memorandum for Louis O. Giuffrida," November 9, 1981. Jett adds: "I have suggested that consideration be given to the inclusion of a provision concerning FEMA involvement in intelligence matters in times of national emergency planning and response."

14 Douglas T. Stuart, *Creating the National Security State: A History of the Law That Transformed America* (Princeton, NJ: Princeton University Press, 2008), 230–273; Office of the Historian, U.S. Department of State, August 1997, available at: http://www.whitehouse.gov/nsc/history.html (accessed November 20, 2010).

An early-1980s working group including FEMA and NSC officials crafted a secret contingency plan that assigned emergency power to FEMA during a "national crisis" and provided for the possibility of martial law.[15] The contingency plan was part of a crisis package that included an executive order and legislation that was written but would not be made into law until a severe crisis occurred.

The most heavy-handed parts of the plan advocated imposing martial law in the event of a national uprising. The plan was meant to remain secret, but the *Miami Herald* obtained a copy of a June 30, 1982, memo in which Giuffrida's acting associate director for national preparedness, John Brinkerhoff, mapped it out. The *Herald* reported that the plan drew on a master's thesis Giuffrida wrote in 1970 at the Army War College in Carlisle, Pennsylvania, about the government's response during an uprising by black militants.[16] The thesis estimated the resources needed to transfer at least 21 million "American Negroes" (approximately the entire black population at the time) to "assembly centers or relocation camps" and assumed that rioting by black militants and counteroffensives by whites were, judging by past treatment of Native Americans and Japanese, almost inevitable.

To be fair, Giuffrida explicitly condemned prejudice and discrimination during his career. At his nomination hearing, Giuffrida spoke about feeling the sting of prejudice as an Italian Protestant growing up in predominately Catholic Little Italy. Although his thesis predicts violent racial antagonism, it ends by condemning racial prejudice. Giuffrida's mindset is different than either traditional racism or "symbolic" racism that employs ideology as a mask for prejudice.[17] Giuffrida took steps to combat bias; while in the Army, he initiated racial and ethnic sensitivity training, not the actions of an outright racist.[18] His public concern for reducing prejudice, however, was apparently mixed with a private fear of social disorder and Cold War practices that assumed the federal government must surveil the population. Emergency situations appeared to justify extreme measures against groups he feared might revolt, most especially African Americans.

---

[15] When the working group first met is uncertain. Alfonso Chardy, "North Helped Revise Wartime Plans," *Miami Herald*, July 9, 1987, A17. The Giuffrida-Jett communication supports the claim that such planning was taking place.

[16] Giuffrida's thesis can be found in Senate Committee on Governmental Affairs, Nomination of Louis O. Giuffrida. Washington, DC, 97th Cong., 1st Sess (1981), 34–83.

[17] Donald Kinder and David O. Sears, "Prejudice and Politics: Symbolic Racism versus Racial Threats to the Good Life," *Journal of Personality and Social Psychology* 40 (1981): 414–431. Nils Gilman summarizes the view that "racial discrimination takes place not merely through intentional (though perhaps unselfconscious) interactions between individuals, but also as a result of deep social and institutional practices and habits." See Gilman, "What Katrina Teaches About the Meaning of Racism," Social Science Research Council, available at: http://understandingkatrina.ssrc.org/Gilman/ (accessed July 8, 2011).

[18] For other cases in which organizational forms permit racially discriminatory outcomes, see Lilia M. Cortina, "Unseen Injustice: Incivility as Modern Discrimination in Organizations," *Academy of Management Review* 33 (2008): 55–75.

During his nomination hearing, Giuffrida repeatedly assured senators concerned about the racial content of his thesis that his job was to prepare for a "worst case scenario." Like the meaning of disaster itself, what counts as a worst case is a product of changing social and political meanings. Cold War civil defense practices shaped what counted as a worst case: it was an event the federal government and not just states alone was responsible to plan for, it involved mass panic, and it assumed the existence of groups that intended to overthrow or undermine the regime.

In Giuffrida's mind, the worst usually involved social disorder that could be addressed only through federal control. In the thesis, he defends the notion that the government might need to intern its citizens:

The Government has historically had the right to protect itself. A Government faced with prolonged, simultaneous, apparently coordinated riots disrupting the entire Nation to the point where the Government feared its very existence was in jeopardy would take many actions which in calmer times would never be considered.[19]

While at FEMA, Giuffrida never spoke publicly about race war or antagonism, but he made preparing for domestic unrest a priority. Brinkerhoff and his preparedness staff feared a looming crisis.[20] In the early 1980s, they considered a Soviet attack to be the most likely scenario. "Unless the Soviet Union dismantles every nuclear missile, our population will remain at risk," John Brinkerhoff told the *New York Times*.[21] Brinkerhoff's imaginative preparations for crisis led him to consider a proposal to revoke Posse Comitatus, a law and associated doctrine in place since 1878 that prevents the military from acting as a domestic police force. In a worst-case security threat, regular law enforcement would be overwhelmed, and it might take the heavy guns of the military to quell violence. Worst cases usually require an enemy of the state, and after the racial strife of the 1960s, African Americans were likely candidates. Black disobedience and sometimes violence were reactions to the structural and literal violence against black people that preceded it.[22] Justifying further violence against black people because of their violent reactions requires weak logic that security hawks also

---

[19] Louis O. Giuffrida, "National Survival – Racial Imperative" (Carlisle Barracks, Pennsylvania: US Army War College, 1970), 42. Quoted in: Senate Committee on Governmental Affairs, Nomination of Louis O. Giuffrida. Washington, DC, 97th Cong., 1st Sess (1981).

[20] George Edmonson, "Law Restricting Domestic Use of Military Could Get Review Under President's Plan," Cox News Service, July 19, 1992. John Brinkerhoff, a retired Army officer and former federal official who has studied and written about the Posse Comitatus Act, labels as "an urban myth" the widespread view that it prohibits the military from any involvement in domestic law enforcement. "We ought to start fresh," he said, "and have a commission or a study where people of all persuasions can consider what is the appropriate role of armed forces when you have a terrorist threat inside the United States."

[21] Judith Miller, "Despite Foes and Skeptics Administration Presses Ahead on Civil Defense," *New York Times*, June 10, 1982, B20.

[22] Doug McAdam, *Political Process and the Development of Black Insurgency, 1930–1970* (Chicago: University of Chicago Press, 1999); Stuart C. Gilman, "Black Rebellion in the 1960s: Between Non-violence and Black Power," *Ethnicity* 8 (December 1981): 452–475.

used against gays and lesbians, erasing the context in which minority groups behaved differently than the majority and penalizing the victim. The process was a moment of social construction, where individuals pursuing their own interests changed the meaning and effects of security practices.

Any meetings about the logistics of interning Americans took place deep inside the bureaucracy, in FEMA or in its working group with the NSC rather than at the upper echelons of the White House. The gist of a crisis plan made its way across the desks of the president's principal advisors until Attorney General William French Smith protested that the plan gave far too much authority to FEMA. In an August 2, 1984 letter to McFarlane, Smith wrote:

> I believe that the role assigned to the Federal Emergency Management Agency in the revised Executive Order exceeds its proper function as a coordinating agency for emergency preparedness. This department and others have repeatedly raised serious policy and legal objections to the creation of an 'emergency czar' role for FEMA.[23]

As previously mentioned, the executive order might not have actually been signed; if it was, it remains secret and obscured, in part because President George W. Bush sealed some 68,000 pages of Ronald Reagan's White House records in November 2002.[24] But a few years later, FEMA's crisis planning seeped out of the bureaucracy and into the media when the *Miami Herald* ran a front page article in 1987 titled "REAGAN AIDES AND THE 'SECRET' GOVERNMENT."[25] This article, along with many others critical of the excesses of FEMA's national security endeavors, tarnished the image of the agency and its supporters in Congress and the White House.[26] Giuffrida, meanwhile, had resigned in 1985 after being the subject of a federal investigation for alleged fraud and mismanagement. Even though he was the longest-serving administrator after James Lee Witt, he is not mentioned in the online history of the agency.[27]

---

[23] William French Smith, Attorney General, letter to Robert C. McFarlane, Assistant to the President for National Security Affairs, Washington, DC. August 2, 1984.

[24] Elements of the draft executive order do appear in E.O. 12656 issued on November 18, 1988. Smith may have also been reacting against Giuffrida's attempts to direct security and contingency plans for the 1984 Los Angeles Olympics.

[25] Alfonso Chardy, "North Helped Revise Wartime Plans," *Miami Herald*, July 9, 1987, A17.

[26] A number of articles in the 1980s criticized FEMA's secret continuity of government programs designed to preserve government functions during a nuclear attack, including a much-cited article in *Penthouse* featuring Giuffrida. See Donald Goldberg and Indy Badhwar, "Blueprint for Tyranny," *Penthouse*, August 1985, 72–90. Other critical articles include: Steven Emerson, "America's Doomsday Project," *U.S. News & World Report*, August 7, 1989, 26–31; Chardy, "North Helped Revise Wartime Plans," *Miami Herald*, July 9, 1987, A17. For a more judicious evaluation of FEMA's continuity of government programs, see Harold C. Relyea, "Continuity of Government: Current Federal Arrangements and the Future," *Congressional Research Service Report*, November 7, 2003.

[27] "FEMA History," at http://www.fema.gov/about/history.shtm (accessed November 12, 2010). The count does not include Craig Fugate, the director at the time of this book's publication.

FEMA's plans for civil disorder appear bizarre when placed in historical context. FEMA was a new and relatively small agency that rarely had more than 3,000 employees, and it lacked the resources and bureaucratic clout of the other players in national security. It had a mandate to prepare for and respond to a range of disasters, from fires, hurricanes, and chemical spills to war and domestic attack.[28] Natural disasters, however, struck far more frequently, and FEMA could do far more to shore up building codes and hone evacuation plans in preparation for natural disasters than it could do to prepare for a protean enemy that would cause domestic unrest.

FEMA's overreaching in national security and its siloed security organizations were a form of bureaucratic inefficiency built into an agency cobbled together in haste. The agency's inefficiencies rose to the level of administrative evil when they drew on malicious and covert stereotypes or fantasies about marginalized groups to enact plans and policies that were out of proportion with the ends they served. Riots and unrest by marginalized groups were less of a threat than the threat security planners posed to civil liberties and the equal protection of citizens under the law. FEMA participated in social construction of disaster by naming groups of citizens as threats to be protected against, and by imagining riots and unrest as an emergency for which the government should prepare.

THREATS FROM WITHIN: GAYS AND LESBIANS

In 1992, FEMA pressured a gay employee to reveal the names of other homosexuals in the agency and, when he finally revealed the names, added them to a list of people the agency deemed security risks. Although the incident concerns singling out people by sexuality rather than race, it fits an organizational-historical process similar to the one that governed in the previous case. The agency's organizations, routines, and practices were part of a process of social construction when they found that groups not conforming to social norms posed a risk to the social order. These groups needed to be monitored, the logic holds – and in a Cold War period of prolonged crisis, separated from the rest of society – so as not to breed greater unrest. Other civilian agencies had long since stopped inquiring about their employees' sexuality, and a year earlier Secretary of Defense Richard Cheney dismissed the idea that gays posed a security risk as "a bit of an old chestnut."[29] By 1992, homosexuality was no longer viewed as a reason for denying or revoking security clearances

---

[28] FEMA's first administrator, John Macy, began development of an Integrated Emergency Management System that included "direction, control and warning systems which are common to the full range of emergencies from small isolated events to the ultimate emergency – war." "FEMA History," at http://www.fema.gov/about/history.shtm (accessed November 12, 2010)

[29] Barton Gellman, "Cheney Rejects Idea That Gays Are Security Risk," *Washington Post*, August 1, 1991, http://www.highbeam.com/doc/1G1-156226237.html (accessed January 2, 2012).

in the federal government, with the exception of the Pentagon, which excluded gays on entirely different grounds, claiming that they would harm morale.

Yet FEMA remained in the mode of a Cold War security agency even after the fall of the Berlin Wall, and it targeted gays and lesbians as security risks long after other agencies thought such a policy was reasonable. The highest levels of the agency approved a policy of ferreting out gays and lesbians, and the policy was not abandoned until it created a scandal that drew the ire of major editorial pages.[30] In the agency's defense, Administrator Wallace Stickney lamely explained that "FEMA has not violated any law or regulation" in keeping tabs on gays and lesbians, but refused to consider how agency routines and security procedures might be immoral while not being illegal.[31]

FEMA's practice of identifying suspected gays and lesbians came to light when an agency management analyst, Jerald Johnson, testified before Congress during an investigation into an unrelated topic: employees' use of agency vehicles for personal business. During the hearing, FEMA Administrator Wallace Stickney made a vague reference to a discussion with Johnson about an agency "national security requirement."[32] Senators pressed Johnson on what Stickney meant, and Johnson admitted that in order to receive a security clearance he was asked to provide a list of FEMA officials who were homosexual.[33] When he first applied for the clearance, Johnson disclosed his sexuality as well as the names and employers of his former partners. He drew the line, however, at naming names within FEMA.

After his testimony, Johnson's security clearance was withheld, and he claims that supervisors tried unsuccessfully to remove him from the agency. Johnson held firm until supervisors refused to approve his participation in a sought-after scientific consulting project in Poland. Once again, FEMA senior management officials, one of whom Johnson said was gay, asked Johnson to provide a list of gay employees and assured him that the list would be kept confidential.[34] Johnson turned over a list of names and was given the plum assignment.

Johnson first complained about the request from FEMA's Office of Security to his immediate supervisors and then to the upper echelons of the agency, including the chief of staff and Administrator Wallace Stickney, who initially

[30] "Witch Hunt at FEMA," *New York Times*, May 15, 1992, available at: http://www.nytimes.com/1992/05/15/opinion/witch-hunt-at-fema.html. (accessed February 10, 2013); "Big Brother Is Still Alive, Spying," *Sun Sentinel*, Ft. Lauderdale, Florida, May 19, 1992, available at: http://articles.sun-sentinel.com/1992–05–19/news/9202090265_1_fema-officials-security-clearance-security-risk (accessed February 12, 2012).
[31] "Witch Hunt at FEMA."
[32] Jerald Johnson, Hearing Before the Legislation and National Security Subcommittee of the Committee on Government Operations, House of Representatives, 102nd Congress, 2nd sess. April 30, 1992, 67; Jerald Johnson, phone interview with the author, March 16, 2006.
[33] Some FEMA employees are issued security clearances to work on top-secret programs to develop contingency plans for major disasters, including terrorism and nuclear war.
[34] Jerald Johnson, phone interview with the author, March 16, 2006.

refused to reverse the decision by the security office. Under scrutiny by the press and the public, Stickney released a statement saying that security officials became "concerned that any FEMA employees concealed their sexual preference and were vulnerable to coercion."[35] Stickney's explanation received little sympathy outside the agency. The *New York Times* and the *Washington Post* penned critical editorials, and openly gay member of Congress Barney Frank (D-Mass.) threatened to hold hearings on the matter. In the end, FEMA relented. Stickney reassigned his chief of staff, whom Johnson called "the fall guy," and announced a review of its security procedures.[36]

FEMA's security clearance procedures dated from the Cold War, when security officials displaced fears of communists onto gays and lesbians. In psychological theories of displacement, the mind displaces aggression from one group to another more acceptable or more available group. Anger at one's parents might be directed toward coworkers. In the case of the Cold War, anger toward and anxiety about communism and nuclear war found new targets in homosexuals who populated the military and civil service. As McCarthyism fell into disrepute, Republicans charged that the Roosevelt and Truman administrations were "honeycombed with homosexuals," and they held hearings to rid the government of gays and lesbians.[37] Eisenhower issued an executive order in 1953 to dismiss federal workers for "any behavior that suggests the individual is not reliable or trustworthy," including "sexual perversion."[38] The order created a personnel security program for the federal government that provided guidelines for security clearances and investigations into possible security compromises, which ranged from financial fraud to intimate behavior. In the end, several thousand gay men and women lost their jobs and many more resigned so that they would not have to endure the shame of an investigation.

Beginning during the 1950s and 1960s, federal officials feared that closeted gays and lesbians would be candidates for blackmail. In addition, some officials suspected that homosexuality was a sign of weak character and yet somehow also contagious: if it spread, it could put the country at a disadvantage in the Cold War. Military and civilian agencies purged gays and lesbians from their ranks in the name of security from blackmail and organizational cohesion, and by the 1970s the civil service refused to employ gays or lesbians.[39] Aside from

[35] James Rowley "FEMA Destroys List of Purportedly Gay Officials," Associated Press, May 19, 1992.

[36] James Rowley, "Homosexual Worker Says Agency Just Saving Face on Gay List," Associated Press, May 19, 1992.

[37] David K. Johnson, *The Lavender Scare: The Cold War Persecution of Gays and Lesbians in the Federal Government* (Chicago: University of Chicago Press, 2004); "Interview with David K. Johnson," University of Chicago Press, 2004, available at http://www.press.uchicago.edu/Misc/Chicago/404811in.html (accessed March 3, 2010).

[38] E. O. 10450, April 27, 1953.

[39] Margot Canaday, *The Straight State: Sexuality and Citizenship in Twentieth Century America* (Princeton, NJ: Princeton University Press, 2009), 174–177; Johnson, *The Lavender Scare* 44–60, 117, 160, 172–180; Gregory Lewis, "Lifting the Ban on Gays in the Civil Service: Federal

these public reasons for employment discrimination, homosexuality became associated with Cold War security practices that demanded security from some threat. With communists hard to find, gays and lesbians filled the void.

The Cold War practices used against suspected domestic communists were similar to the ones used against homosexuals from the 1950s through at least the 1980s. The Veteran's Administration, for example, established a "Little FBI" to root out fraud, suspected communists, and gays and lesbians.[40] The government targeted both groups through guilt-by-association and through forcing the accused to name names. Through secret lists and public shaming, elites thought they could limit the reach of these allegedly subversive groups. Finally, political attacks against both groups had similar political payoffs. Politicians found they could tarnish their enemies as both Red and Lavender.

The civil service was not immune to the climate of suspicion. It barred gays and lesbians from employment and, when explicit bans fell out of favor, simply refused to make their dismissal illegal. By 1975, however, after court cases had chipped away at exclusion, the Civil Service Commission removed "immoral conduct" from its list of disqualifications for federal employment. The official press release explained that the Civil Service Commission would apply "the same standards in evaluating sexual conduct, whether heterosexual or homosexual."[41]

FEMA's bizarre concern with identifying homosexuals – it was a disaster agency after all, not the CIA – stemmed from Cold War personnel security practices that were a type of administrative evil in the sense of the term used by scholars. Administrators of the program were given culturally outdated guidelines about the dangers posed by gays and lesbians and a great deal of autonomy, and they performed their work efficiently given budget constraints. Yet when brought to light by a congressional hearing, critical observers found the program to be unnecessary at best and perverse at worst.

The issuance of security clearances was the most widespread form of government security practice during the Cold War. To analyze the practice of security clearances after FEMA's catalog of homosexuals came to light, a commission produced what became known as the Trefry report. The 1992 report found that of 2,604 employees at FEMA, 1,501 possessed top-secret clearances and 381 had secret clearances.[42] The report recommended slashing the number of clearances at the agency to 300, roughly the number required for administrators in the secret continuity of government programs who planned for preserving government functions in case of nuclear attack. The report blamed the agency's

---

Policy Towards Gay and Lesbian Employees since the Cold War," *Public Administration Review* 57 (September/October 1997): 387–395.

[40] Canaday, *The Straight State*, 155.

[41] Johnson, *Lavender Scare*, 210.

[42] Final Report and Recommendations, Federal Emergency Management Agency Security Practices Board of Review (Trefry Report), Richard G. Trefry, Chairman, Washington, DC, November 1992, 9.

extensive security practices on a "culture" and a "social standard" that said security clearances were required for career advancement and prestige within the agency.[43] Years before, the Stillwell report, submitted to the secretary of Defense in 1985 to review security practices, also recommended reducing security clearances in defense agencies and observed that administrators valued security clearances for their prestige. Both reports described what social scientists call *institutional isomorphism*: agencies adopt the practices of the leaders in their field even if the practices are not useful.[44] In the classic case of institutional isomorphism, landlocked nations establish military navies simply because great powers have navies. Similarly, many of FEMA's personnel measured the agency by whether it conformed to the security norms of leading defense and security agencies. The Trefry report found that "in the matter of homosexual employees the requirements of outside agencies have been applied to FEMA."[45]

If an employee requested a clearance or held a position that required a clearance, or if an employee occupied a position with the murky designation of "public trust," and if that employee was suspect of being homosexual, FEMA conducted a background investigation.[46] FEMA's behavior was unusual because by 1992 other government agencies and reports had concluded that homosexuality should not be grounds for denial or revocation of security clearances. At the time, the Department of Defense was revising its personnel security guidelines to remove references to homosexuality and sodomy but retaining references to protecting against blackmail or coercion.[47]

One influential government report on the subject, "Homosexuality and Personnel Security," was cited in the Trefry report as saying:

The PERSEREC [Defense Personnel Security Research and Education Center] data bank currently includes 117 cases of American citizens who between 1945 and the present committed or attempted to commit espionage. Only six have been identified as homosexuals. Their motives appear to be the same as for persons not identified as homosexuals: primarily money, secondarily resentment. All were volunteers except one, who was recruited by a heterosexual friend. None was a target of blackmail although one offender claimed to have been coerced.[48]

---

[43] The FEMA inspector general made similar pronouncements. See the Trefry Report, 9–10.

[44] Paul J. DiMaggio and Walter Powell, "The Iron Cage Revisited: Institutional Isomorphism and Collective Rationality in Organizational Fields," *American Sociological Review* 48 (1983): 147–160.

[45] Trefry report, 9–10.

[46] Trefry report, 13.

[47] For example, the Department of Defense National Industrial Security Program Common Adjudicative Standards, issued April 30, 1992 and provided in an appendix to the Trefry report, states: "Sexual behavior is a security concern only if it involves a criminal offense, indicates a personality disorder, exposes the individual to undue influence or coercion, or is blatant to the point that it reflects a lack of judgment or discretion." The standards establish the category of sexual behavior but do not mention sodomy or homosexuality. See Trefry report, 7.

[48] Theodore R. Sarbin, *Homosexuality and Personnel Security* (Monterey, California: Defense Personnel Security Research and Education Center, 1991), 30.

The report's explanation for the mismatch between the objective threat posed by homosexuals and the agency's policing of homosexuality conforms to the definition of administrative evil as a practice in which those who commit the acts behave efficiently according to their organizational role but, when seen in retrospect or from another context, appear to have behaved disproportionately. Security personnel performed their jobs according to outdated Cold War security procedures toward gays and lesbians. As the report notes, "The Board believes strongly that the problems in the system should not be attributed to security personnel in particular, either as individuals or in groups of individuals in FEMA, or elsewhere in the civil service. They are required to administer a bureaucratic nightmare."[49] The Trefry report points to the diffusion of responsibility that is the essence of what Arendt meant by the banality of evil.

Yet FEMA's security practices were slow to change. Security personnel had a high degree of autonomy, and they operated in an environment in which FEMA leadership implied that agency administrators should follow the norms of leading security and defense agencies that were FEMA's competitors.[50] The agency's career leadership wanted to adopt security practices maintained by larger and more established security agencies. Yet the personnel security system was too complex for political appointees at the top of the agency to change because appointees serve only between two and three years on average. Furthermore, some appointees, such as Giuffrida, explicitly wanted FEMA to be a national security agency.

In FEMA, deep-seated ideas about gays and lesbians were institutionalized as security practices and produced discrimination that far outweighed the objective benefits of policing homosexuality for the agency's mission. In addition to the simple fact that FEMA's security clearance program and practices dated from the early Cold War, discussion among members of the Trefry report's board fixed on the fear of a classic worst case, another Pearl Harbor – but this time potentially nuclear – as a reason for vigilance in background checks to make certain that public administrators were not vulnerable to coercion:

COLONEL DABROWSKI: Isn't another reason because you found that some of the enemy intelligence instructions that you were able to get hold of did mention certain sexual or people who were closet homosexuals as people that could be targeted?[51]

---

[49] Trefry report, 16
[50] Trefry report, 16. The board found that problems within FEMA were similar to problems in other agencies. Report to the Committee on Government Operations of the House of Representatives, August 22, 1992, "Investigating the Investigators: Justice Department Background Reviews Break Down," House Report 102–854; Lori L. Jean, Memo to Security Practices Board, Adjudication Standards and Sexual Orientation, August 6, 1992, on file with author and included as an appendix to the Trefry report.
[51] Excerpt from Official Transcript of FEMA Security Practices Review Board, July 24, 1992, Colloquy between Peter R. Nelson, Deputy Director of Personnel Security at the Department of Defense and various members of the Board. Appendix A of the Trefry report, 48.

DR. KUPPERMAN: Yes, but now that the sexual mores and standards are changing, it just becomes irrelevant.

GENERAL TREFRY: But you see, you pursue this. At the same time they might have targeted homosexuals, they also targeted other people, femme fatales –

MR. NELSON: Sure, oh, absolutely. In fact, there are obviously far more cases where there was a heterosexual inducement. There is no question about that. That's certainly of concern.

It's just that we're saying we can't afford to ignore any possibility because the consequences could be so dire.

GENERAL TREFRY: Well, that's right, but Pearl Harbor has been a very expensive experience for the United States I can tell you that. We're going to make sure that never happens again. So, we have millions of clearances, you see, and thousands of people on alert 24 hours a day.

Robert Kupperman, a longtime government official, noted that social mores had changed, but public officials were stuck thinking in terms of the worst case, framed by Cold War security practices and the memory of Pearl Harbor. General Trefry did not support policing homosexuals in particular, but he framed FEMA's obligations in terms of its responsibility to maintain security to prevent a catastrophic event whose nature is uncertain but whose consequences are devastating. Historians mark the end of the Cold War in 1991 with the fall of the Soviet Union, but as this exchange demonstrates, the Cold War lives on as national security: a set of practices designed to defend against a catastrophic, apocalyptic attack from a protean enemy from abroad operating within the U.S. borders.

In a policy area that still prepared for the Cold War and in agency divisions that existed to ferret out security risks, homosexuals provided a convenient threat. Had FEMA's leaders asked larger questions about what the agency existed to do after the Cold War, and had they expanded their notion of risk beyond groups of people to include organizational risks such as weak evacuation plans or levee failures, they might have recognized the folly of their security procedures. FEMA lacked the resources and the expertise to be a national security agency, and yet its leaders insisted on adopting the practices of national security agencies. This also meant they were ill prepared to respond to natural disasters.

ELITE PANIC IN HURRICANE KATRINA

In contrast to the previous two instances of planning for a worst case that never materialized, Hurricane Katrina was an actual catastrophe. Whereas FEMA should have done less planning for race riots and homosexual blackmail, it could have done much more in actual practice during a massive hurricane in New Orleans. Despite these differences, Katrina brought to the fore the same assumptions about mass panic and the need for security that distorted emergency management in the previous cases.

In the days after Hurricane Katrina struck New Orleans, fears of rape, looting, pillaging, and murder fueled by the media drove residents indoors and rescue workers away. The city's police chief told the national media that tourists were being robbed and raped on the streets. The public assumed that the city had descended into anarchy. Most of the tales turned out to be nothing more than lurid rumors spread by panic, a media frenzy, and a breakdown in communications. Contrary to initial reports, it was the elite, not the general public, who panicked and spread rumors. Sociologists Lee Clarke and Caron Chess coined the term "elite panic" to describe how elites overreact to the fear of crisis, social breakdown, and challenges to their authority.[52] Hurricane Katrina appears to be a paradigmatic case in which elites – in this case public officials – panicked.

The lurid tales of a city turning on itself began when officials lost their cool in a crisis and performed far worse than expected – they panicked – and behaved in the maniacal way that they supposed citizens themselves would behave. In isolation, individual rumors might have been excusable but, like other examples of administrative evil, cumulatively the rumors formed "patterns of conduct and spirals of escalation" that led to a system failure.[53]

Why would city leaders (including the police chief) charged with helping rebuild New Orleans spread lurid tales of a city descended into chaos? These rumors slowed recovery efforts and tarnished the city's reputation in the eyes of the world. City leaders may have exaggerated stories as a cry for help, and these stories were stoked by the media, but most of all elites responded to a deep-seated fear of social breakdown. City leaders' fears were in some sense rational; recovery would not be immediate, and they could be held responsible and their careers would be ruined. The poorest areas of the city were hit the hardest; 71 percent of destroyed housing units were lost by people in "affordable housing" or the lower income range.[54] Race, though in the background, played a role in the recovery. New Orleans was one of the largest

[52] Lee Clarke, "Panic: Myth or Reality," *Contexts* 1 (2002): 21–26; Lee Clarke, "Systems Fail, Not People," *New York Daily News*, February 20, 2003, available at http://leeclarke.com/docs/dailynews_oped.pdf (accessed October 9, 2011).

[53] Isabel V. Hull uses the term "extreme practices" rather than administrative evil to describe abusive behavior by the Germany military in *Absolute Destruction: Military Culture and the Practices of War in Imperial Germany* (Ithaca, NY: Cornell University Press, 2005), 3.

[54] Prema Katari, "Housing Helps," in *Multifamily Trends* (Washington, DC: Urban Land Institute, November–December 2005). "Lower income" is defined as earning less than 80 percent of the area median income. A number of authors have examined how government policies before and after Hurricane Katrina had disproportionally negative consequences for the poor and for African-Americans. See Robert D. Bullard and Beverly Wright, *The Wrong Complexion for Protection: How the Government Response to Disaster Endangers African American Communities* (New York: New York University Press, 2012), 73–99; Michael Eric Dyson, *Come Hell or High Water: Hurricane Katrina and the Color of Disaster* (New York: Basic Books, 2006).

majority-African-American cities in the country, and the city's identity was shaped by its prominent black cultures.[55]

Rather than focus on the devastation, however, media stories in the days following the hurricane turned to reports of rape, murder, assaults, and pillaging. Fox News anchor John Gibson anticipated a likely confrontation between the crazed public and law and order: "All kinds of reports of looting, fires and violence. Thugs shooting at rescue crews. Thousands of police and National Guard troops are on the scene trying to get the situation under control. Thousands more on the way. So heads up, looters." MSNBC's Tucker Carlson told the Rev. Al Sharpton, "People are being raped. People are being murdered. People are being shot. Police officers are being shot."[56]

The media's tendency to exaggerate is lamentable but well known. During the media "feeding frenzy" surrounding a crisis, reporters on a twenty-four-hour news cycle are rewarded for being first with a story, not for being right.[57] Unfortunately, people get information in a crisis from the media rather than emergency managers, and even local civil servants appeared to be caught up in the rumor explosion in New Orleans.[58] In Katrina, public officials reported rumors that began in the media rather than in a careful professional assessment of the conditions.

On September 4, Police Superintendent Eddie Compass told the *New York Times*, "The tourists are walking around there, and as soon as these individuals see them, they're being preyed upon. They are beating, they are raping them in the streets."[59] The city's two primary shelters, the Convention Center and the Superdome, really did become miserable places without air conditioning or light. The squalor may have fed rumors about the Superdome like the ones Eddie Compass spread on September 6 in an appearance on the television show "Oprah." The police chief told the audience, "We had little babies in there, some of the little babies getting raped." Mayor Ray Nagin painted a similar picture: "They have people standing out there, have been in that frickin' Superdome for five days watching dead bodies, watching hooligans killing people, raping people."

In some cases, local authorities provided apparently sober eyewitness accounts that the media simply repeated. In one broadcast, Fox News' Greta

55 Kevin Fox Gotham, *Authentic New Orleans: Tourism, Culture, and Race in the Big Easy* (New York: New York University Press, 2007).

56 David Carr, "More Horrible Than Truth: News Reports," *New York Times*, September 19, 2005, available at: http://www.nytimes.com/2005/09/19/business/media/19carr.html?oref=login&_r=0 (accessed October 11, 2010).

57 Doris S. Graber, *Mass Media and American Politics*, 7th ed. (Washington, DC: CQ Press, 2005); Larry Sabato, *Feeding Frenzy: Attack Journalism & American Politics* (New York: Free Press, 1993).

58 Spike Lee, "When the Levees Broke: A Requiem in Four Acts," HBO Films, 2006.

59 Jim Dwyer and Christopher Drew, "Fear Exceeded Crime's Reality In New Orleans," *New York Times*, September 29, 2005, A1.

Van Susteren interviewed Dr. Charles Burnell, an emergency room physician who provided medical care in the Superdome. "Well, we had several murders," he told Van Susteren. "We had three murders last night. We had a total of six rapes last night. We had the day before I think there were three or four murders. There were half a dozen rapes that night." Arthel Neville, of the renowned Louisiana musical family, told Van Susteren that she heard that a man was beaten to death by an angry mob in the Dome after he raped and killed a seven-year old.[60] National guardsmen told tales of bodies being stored in freezers in the Superdome.

Many of the more outlandish rumors, of mothers tossing babies out of towers and of men fighting in the streets, came from evacuees, afraid, desperate, and faced with dark nights and hot, humid days. Major daily newspapers quoted these purported witnesses to rapes and beatings both while in New Orleans and after they had fled to neighboring cities. Media reports filtered throughout the world and, in a process familiar to every elementary schoolchild, became exaggerated. British commentator Timothy Garton Ash declared in the *Guardian* that New Orleans had descended into "a Hobbesian state of nature, a war of all against all."[61] On September 2, golfer Tiger Woods, at a tournament in Boston, said, "[I]t's just unbelievable ... how people are behaving, with the shootings and now the gang rapes and the gang violence and shooting at helicopters who are trying to help out and rescue people."[62]

The *Los Angeles Times* reported that National Guard troops "took positions on rooftops, scanning for snipers and armed mobs as seething crowds of refugees milled below, desperate to flee. Gunfire crackled in the distance."[63] A Houston TV station reported a cholera outbreak and "sexual assaults ... occurring daily" among the 16,000 Katrina evacuees housed in Houston's Astrodome.[64]

All of these rumors later proved false. The hurricane devastated the city, and conditions were grim, but the city did not devolve into a Hobbesian war of all against all. Ten people died while in the Superdome and Convention Center, but only one appeared to have been murdered. The week after first making his claims, Compass clarified that there were no confirmed rapes in the city. Before Katrina, New Orleans had the unwelcome distinction as the most violent city in the United States, and violence and predation during the storm did

---

[60] Timothy Garton Ash, "It Always Lies Below," *The Guardian* (London), September 8, 2005.

[61] Garton Ash, "It Always Lies Below."

[62] Matt Welch, "They Shoot Helicopters, Don't They? How Journalists Spread Rumors during Katrina," *Reason*, December 2005.

[63] Susannah Rosenblatt and James Rainey, "Rita's Aftermath," *Los Angeles Times*, September 27, 2005, A16.

[64] Donna Britt, "In Katrina's Wake, Inaccurate Rumors Sullied Victims," *The Washington Post*, September 30, 2005, B1. Rumors and fear spread to neighboring towns. "We do not want to inherit the looting and all the other foolishness that went on in New Orleans," Kip Holden, the Baton Rouge mayor, told the *Baton Rouge Advocate*. "We do not want to inherit that breed that seeks to prey on other people."

not appear to be worse than normal. The city's police department in particular had a long history of civil rights abuses.[65] During the storm, video cameras at a Wal-Mart showed police themselves leaving with merchandise, and the department's Public Integrity Bureau and state attorney general's office investigated officers for removing about 200 cars from a Cadillac dealership. Worse, in 2011, five current and former New Orleans police officers were convicted of shooting six citizens unnecessarily in the aftermath of the storm, and other police engaged in a cover-up. The vast majority of police, however, put aside concerns about their immediate well-being to help keep order in the city and help rescue those stranded.[66]

Many of the apparent cases of looting were actually reasonable attempts to gather necessities during a time of need. Grocery stores were not open for business, after all, and emergency services were slow to bring aid to flooded areas. The jewelry and antique stores of the French Quarter were untouched. In Jefferson County, prosecutors declined to press charges against 84 of the 290 people charged with looting from August 27 through November 30.[67] These were crimes of opportunity rather than crimes of vengeance. The city's criminal element took advantage of the chaos but, contrary to rumor, the rest of the citizenry did not descend into violence.[68]

There are many local reasons for the spread of rumors. The traumatic conditions made some people exaggerate out of fear. "It was urban myth," according to New Orleans Lieutenant Benelli, who also heads the police union. "Any time you put 25,000 people under one roof, with no running water, no electricity and no information, stories get told."[69] In addition, the lack of communications and even the darkness at night may have contributed to people's disorientation and fed their worst imaginings. Police, too, exaggerated the threat in order to draw attention to their contributions to safety. In one incident, Compass claimed that he and other officers wrestled thirty weapons away from criminals. Officers later denied the story.[70]

[65] "Investigation of the New Orleans Police Department," Civil Rights Division, United States Department of Justice, March 16, 2011, available at: http://www.justice.gov/crt/about/spl/nopd_report.pdf (accessed July 9, 2012).

[66] Michael Perlstein and Trymaine Lee, "The Good & the Bad," *New Orleans Times Picayune*, January 19, 2006, A4.

[67] Paul Purpura, "'Survival' Looters Get Leniency from DA," *New Orleans Times-Picayune*, February 7, 2006, available at: http://blog.nola.com/kenner/2006/02/survival_looters_get_leniency.html (accessed October 18, 2010).

[68] Historians have long known that rumors of violence and mayhem can cause a crowd to exercise real violence. See George Rudé, *The Crowd in the French Revolution* (Oxford, UK: Clarendon Press, 1959).

[69] Jim Dwyer and Christopher Drew, "Fear Exceeded Crime's Reality in New Orleans," *New York Times*, September 29, 2005, A1.

[70] "Hurricane-force rumors," Weblog, New Orleans Times-Picayune, September 27, 2005, available at: http://www.nola.com/newslogs/opinion/index.ssf?/mtlogs/nola_opinion/archives/2005_09_27.html (accessed October 9, 2010).

The lurid tales had consequences. The rumor of social breakdown as much as the reality of the hurricane and flood-wrought devastation delayed emergency response. The National Guard refused to enter the Convention Center until September 2, 100 hours after the hurricane, because, as Gen. H. Steven Blum put it, "We waited until we had enough force in place to do an overwhelming force."[71] The awkward repetition of "force" in Blum's phrase underscores what was on security officials' minds. Paramedics were prevented from entering Slidell, a town near New Orleans, for ten hours because state troopers reported that armed mobs were raiding anyone who entered. The reports later turned out to be false.[72] There were similar tales of ambulances refusing to leave the hospital and rescue supplies being diverted because of a fear of armed groups. In one telling example, National Guard soldiers were sent to rescue a St. Bernard Parish deputy sheriff who requested help because he was pinned down by a sniper. When soldiers arrived with a SWAT team, they found that a relief valve on a gas tank made a gunshot-like sound every few minutes.[73]

Taken alone, the rumors spread by New Orleans community leaders and citizens seem bizarre, but when viewed alongside other major catastrophes, they reveal a pattern. Elites *assume* mass panic during a disaster, and they often take grave steps to maintain order. In 1871, a firestorm swept Chicago for twenty-six hours, killing approximately 300, injuring thousands, and destroying a fourth of the structures in the city. Irish, Scandinavian, and German immigrants were unjustly suspected of looting and marauding. Newspapers published rumors of "heartless killers, vigilante mobs, and miscellaneous looters, incendiaries, thieves, and extortionists" roaming the streets. Chicago's Anglo-Protestant elite thought the municipal government was too weak to handle a crisis so they formed citizens committees as an ersatz local government. In her study of the fire's aftermath, Karen Sawislak shows how "a native-born urban elite presented their own beliefs and preferences as those that best served all of the people of the city."[74] The governor opposed giving power to the military, but Chicago business leaders were eager to surrender authority for keeping the peace. As a result, soldiers patrolled the streets for two weeks. In an arrangement that foreshadowed contemporary pleas for contracting out federal services, Allen Pinkerton's for-hire security force assumed it had orders to shoot looters.

While disaster routinely produces rumors of panic and predation, social scientists have shown that people almost never display behavior that could be interpreted as panic. In most cases, people act rationally and humanely; they

[71] Steven Blum, "Lt. Gen. Steven Blum's Assessment of the Guard/N.O. Situation," Defense Department Briefing, Washington, DC, September 5, 2005. Transcript available at: http://www.rense.com/general67/blum.htm (accessed October 12, 2010).

[72] Dwyer and Drew, "Fear Exceeded Crime's Reality In New Orleans."

[73] Dwyer and Drew, "Fear Exceeded Crime's Reality In New Orleans."

[74] Karen Sawislak, *Smoldering City, Chicagoans and the Great Fire, 1871–1874* (Chicago: University of Chicago Press, 1995), 1–17; Philip Fradkin, *The Great Earthquake and Firestorms of 1906* (Berkeley: University of California Press, 2005), 14–15.

may leave an area quickly, but in an orderly fashion. In a book about altruism in the wake of disaster, Rebecca Solnit writes that "many fear that in disaster we become something other than we normally are – helpless or bestial and savage in the most common myths – or that is who we really are when the superstructure of society crumbles. We remain ourselves for the most part, but freed to act on, most often, not the worst but the best within. The ruts and routines of ordinary life hide more beauty than brutality."[75] Solnit offers many examples of altruism and solidarity during a disaster, but in New Orleans, public officials and city leaders were all too willing to believe the worst. While the idea that people panic in a crisis is largely a "myth," more recent research has fixed upon the idea that elites do panic during a crisis.[76] Public officials, administrators, and media figures panic because they fear for their safety and loss of power, or they fear that the public will panic, and sometimes elite panic causes panic among the public.[77] Yet media attention focuses on panic and predatory behavior among the public rather than among elites.[78]

A similar story could be told about other major catastrophes. A third of the burgeoning city of Galveston, Texas was destroyed during a 1900 hurricane. As the wind and rain receded, the fear of violence and looting moved in. Philip Fradkin quotes a letter from a Galveston mother to her out-of-town daughter repeating rumors that circulated in newspapers and by word of mouth. "Ears and hands have been cut off the dead, because of ear-rings and rings," she wrote. "Fingers have been found in the pockets of looters, mostly Negroes, one of whom had sixteen and another eleven."[79] Rumors characterized blacks as well as Mexicans and southern Europeans as ghouls who roamed the streets lopping off limbs to steal jewelry. The military was called in to patrol the streets, along with a semiofficial vigilante force. Yet, the stories of looting were probably as exaggerated as the stories of ghouls.

---

[75] Rebecca Solnit, *A Paradise Built in Hell: The Extraordinary Communities that Arise in Disaster* (New York: Viking, 2009), 70.

[76] Lee Clarke, "Panic: Myth or Reality," *Contexts* 1 (2002): 21–26.

[77] Lee Clarke and Caron Chess "Elites and Panic: More to Fear Than Fear Itself," *Social Forces* 87 (December 2008): 993–1014. Examples include the 2001 anthrax attacks and the 2004 "lemongate" incident. See Paul Blustein and Brian Byrnes, "Lemons Caught in a Homeland Security Squeeze," *Washington Post*, September 10, 2004, available at http://www.nbcnews.com/id/5960478/ns/business-washington_post/t/lemons-caught-homeland-security-squeeze/#.URmFpqXiiR8 (accessed January 14, 2012).

[78] The visual economy of disaster highlights distressed members of the public roaming the streets in search of food or, often, presumed to be looting, in a media frame that assumes Hobbesian motivations of greed and self-interest. Disaster researchers have found, however, that people are more given to cooperation than predation, even in the pursuit of self-preservation. See Thomas E. Drabek, "Community Processes: Coordination," in *Handbook of Disaster Research*, edited by Havídan Rodríguez, Enrico L. Quarantelli, and Russell Dynes (New York: Springer, 2007), 217–233.

[79] Fradkin, *Great Earthquake*, 20.

The 1906 earthquake and subsequent fire left San Franciscans with a similar fear of social breakdown. On their own initiative, Army commanders stationed in the area ordered troops to protect the Treasury and essential services during the chaos after San Francisco burned. The mayor issued 5,000 handbills telling citizens that he had (illegally) ordered federal troops and local police to shoot looters.[80] Rumors spread even after less catastrophic disasters. After every major hurricane, reports circulate about looting, and in almost every case these reports are false or greatly exaggerated.[81] The media echo chamber present by the time of Katrina propelled the same kind of rumors that emerged during other disasters to a wider, international audience.

REASON AND FANTASY

One might wonder how, in our purportedly multicultural, tolerant, and politically correct age, large organizations charged with protecting the public became sites of discriminatory thought, practice, and planning. Imputing discriminatory practices and aberrant behavior to egomaniacal individuals, renegade bureaucrats, or kooky cabals is tempting, but in all three cases, the overwrought anxieties of elites threatened groups they had already marginalized. Treating these cases as exceptions mutes their implicit message about residual discrimination in a post–civil rights public sphere that professes antidiscrimination in law and mores; furthermore, it forestalls consideration of policies to prevent future discriminatory practices in disaster and security policy.

The practices themselves might not have been exceptional – elite panic and secret security planning occurred repeatedly – but the social milieus in which these practices arose were extraordinary. In all three examples, political elites suspended fair treatment of marginalized groups in times of crisis – or in planning for crisis scenarios where mayhem seemed likely. Egalitarian in other contexts, these administrators and public officials resorted to paranoid fantasies when they imagined the worst. Elite panic, the structures that make possible administrative evil within an organization, and existing security practices allowed administrators and local leaders to resort to stereotypes about marginalized groups.

When taken together, however, the exceptional appears to be a norm. Italian political philosopher Giorgio Agamben famously claimed that exceptional

---

[80] Simon Winchester, *A Crack in the Edge of the World* (New York: Harper Collins 2006), 307–310; Doris Muscatine, *Old San Francisco: From Early Days to the Earthquake* (New York: Putnam and Sons 1975), 428.

[81] E. L. Quarantelli, "Sociology of Panic," in *International Encyclopedia of the Social and Behavioral Sciences*, edited by Neil J. Smelser and Paul B. Baltes (Oxford: Elsevier Science Ltd., 2002): 11020–11023. In one recent exception, looters roamed St. Croix immediately after Hurricane Hugo struck the island in 1989. The wind and storm helped free inmates from a prison, the police force was corrupt, and the society was highly unequal; yacht owners lived next to people barely above subsistence level.

treatment of foreign peoples and nations during crisis was the norm for twentieth-century Western democracies.[82] Agamben thought that political elites framed claims for exceptions to liberal democratic norms as pragmatic modifications when in fact they were part of the normal operation of purportedly liberal states. Whereas Agamben emphasized the actions of national-level political elites, the three cases presented here show how civil servants and local leaders exempt themselves from liberal norms when planning for and responding to crisis.

While emergency managers and local elites committed discriminatory acts, they need not themselves be racist or antigay in the sense of believing in the superiority of one race or one type of sexuality. Social scientists distinguish between manifest racism, outward expressions of racist sentiment, and latent racism, the latter being assumptions and attitudes that frequently produce, without insidious intent, racist outcomes.[83] Harder to quantify, latent racism eludes detection and frequently masquerades as a different ideology – individualism or regionalism, for example. Yet crisis, or the fear of crisis, provides occasions for racist ideas to reemerge. If individuals repress such ideas under social pressure, they may nevertheless retain them, subconsciously or otherwise, and redeploy them in periods of crisis or planning for crisis where they feel vulnerable, threatened, and powerless. Trust, respect, and tolerance toward marginalized groups oscillate over time. Abandoned stereotypes can renew their representational force in periods of social unrest. Individuals might resuscitate misconceptions of blacks as innately prone to violence and antisocial behavior, or homosexuals as innately deceitful, in a social climate where civil upheaval appears likely. Crisis not only occasions these anxieties and discriminatory practices; it legitimates them. People who devise such plans and promulgate such views can attribute their extreme behavior to caution and concern for public safety, or to preventing a Pearl Harbor–like bolt from the blue.

Social science that assumes conscious, goal-seeking rational behavior does not provide much guidance about where these fantasies originated or why they targeted African Americans and gays and lesbians. There are plausible rational explanations for discriminatory practices in disaster and crisis management: Administrators and public officials might target marginalized groups as threats in order to build support among the public for their organizations, or administrators at FEMA might have focused on security threats in order to prove to

[82] Giorgio Agamben, *State of Exception*, translated by Kevin Attell (Chicago: University of Chicago Press, 2005).

[83] Jennifer A. Richeson, A. A. Baird, H. L. Gordon, T. F. Heatherton, C. L. Wyland, S. Trawalter, and J. N. Shelton, "An fMRI Examination of the Impact of Interracial Contact on Executive Function," *Nature Neuroscience* 6 (2003): 1323–1328; Jennifer A. Richeson and R. J. Nussbaum, "The Impact of Multiculturalism versus Color-Blindness on Racial Bias," *Journal of Experimental Social Psychology* 40 (2004): 417–423; Donald R. Kinder, "The Continuing American Dilemma: White Resistance to Racial Change 40 Years after Myrdal," *Journal of Social Issues* 42 (1986): 151–171.

themselves and others that FEMA was a national security agency in the same league as the FBI. But these explanations do not account for the source of discrimination, either.[84]

While discriminatory practices may be in some sense rational, psychoanalytic claims about the existence of the unconscious provide a plausible supplement to explain behaviors toward marginalized groups that are otherwise puzzling.[85] The idea of unconscious motivation rejects the claim that people always know what they are doing.[86] In the realm of visual perception, the idea of unconscious motivation seems obvious. People see a tree or a lake but they are unconscious of the process by which the eye and the brain process information from the world. The common assumption about the existence of unconscious processes through which humans relate to the natural world becomes radical when it is applied to how humans relate to one another.

The theory of unconscious motivation assumes that there are cognitive systems we are not aware of, not just for visual perception and sensory features, but for how human beings think about the world and decide what to value and what actions to take. Sigmund Freud famously categorized the unconscious into the id, the ego, and the superego, but his central point was that the unconscious is a realm of conflicting motivations, and these motivations do not always provide clear benefits. Human beings have certain desires they would rather not know, so they hide them. *Sublimation* describes how humans can direct sexual or aggressive desires toward art, and *displacement* describes how humans refocus shameful desires onto an "other," essentially category of person with whom a person does not explicitly identify.[87]

Theories of sublimation and displacement are most useful in describing harmful drives and passions that people would rather cloak than acknowledge. Public officials may claim that they acted to prevent a threat, but the reasons why they thought a group was a threat may have little to do with objective threat and a lot to do with their unconscious attraction or repulsion to certain groups. For instance, a study of homophobic men in Georgia found that homoerotic pictures led to high levels of sexual arousal in many of the most homophobic men. These men expressed negative attitudes toward gays

[84] Gabriel Almond, "Rational Choice Theory and the Social Sciences," in *A Discipline Divided* (Newburg Park, CA: Sage Publications, 1990), 117–137.

[85] While out of favor in much of social science, psychoanalytic insights have contributed to foundational work in political science and sociology. Harold Lasswell's work is particularly influential. See William Ascher and Barbara Hirschfelder-Ascher, "Linking Lasswell's Political Psychology and the Policy Sciences," *Policy Sciences* 37 (2004): 23–36.

[86] John A. Bargh and Tanya L. Chartrand, "The Unbearable Automaticity of Being," *American Psychologist* 54 (1999): 462–479; Drew Westen, "The Scientific Status of Unconscious Processes: Is Freud Really Dead?" *Journal of the American Psychoanalytic Association* 49 (1999): 1–30.

[87] Roy F. Baumeister, Karen Dale, and Kristen Sommer, "Freudian Defense Mechanisms and Empirical Findings in Modern Social Psychology: Reaction Formation, Projection, Displacement, Undoing, Isolation, Sublimation and Denial," *Journal of Personality* 66 (1998): 1081–1124.

and lesbians, but physiological measures showed that they were aroused by homosexual images, although they either consciously suppressed the arousal, or were themselves unaware and interpreted arousal as disgust, or in rejecting arousal in themselves also had to reject the people doing what they secretly wanted.[88] Organizations can amplify individual displacement of disgust onto marginalized groups.[89]

Discriminatory ideas about marginalized groups gather force through the repetition of stories.[90] Individuals who heard or read tales of bestial conduct subsequently contrived their own narratives. As storytellers, they resembled the government officials who spun tales of minority malfeasance in crafting security measures – for example, Giuffrida's thesis – in case of social upheaval. The original author of this document, Giuffrida was also its reader, and he spun a tale in conformity with his expectations of what blacks might do during periods of unrest.

FEMA's plans, like the universe of memos and documents that make up the history of disaster management, are examples of social and not solely individual authorship. In general, governmental memos and plans appear to emanate from organizations, not from individuals, making it difficult to impute motives or intentions to a specific author or set of authors. And yet individuals, both alone and in groups, construct these documents and necessarily infuse them with their biases and fantasies. Cultural prejudices, albeit perhaps in muted form, will appear in government documents, which we must consequently not read as the rational output of disembodied minds, but rather as a process of social construction.

One might argue that the three incidents described in this chapter demonstrate the continued necessity of multicultural discourse, promoting tolerance and cultural sensitivity. New Orleans preserves celebrated African-American cultures, and the DHS now has an organization for its gay and lesbian civil servants. But to the extent that these multicultural values underscore difference – indeed, make difference a value unto itself – they can enable envy and suspicion on the part of dominant groups. During peaceful times, these differences underscore our national diversity, convey satisfying feelings of cosmopolitanism, and provoke intellectual and cultural curiosity. Emphasizing alterity,

---

[88] Henry E. Adams, Lester W. Wright, Jr., and Bethany A. Lohr, "Is Homophobia Associated With Homosexual Arousal?" *The Journal of Abnormal Psychology* 105 (August 1996): 440–445; Robert Trivers, "Rethinking Productivity Speaker Series," University of Regina, Regina, Canada, October 3, 2007.

[89] Jacques Lacan describes an individual tendency toward sadistic behavior that attaches to the use of institutional authority, which is similar to the concept of administrative evil. See David Farmer, *The Language of Public Administration* (Tuscaloosa: University of Alabama Press, 1995), 228.

[90] Judith Hubback, "The Changing Person and Unchanging Archetype," in *Carl Gustav Jung: Critical Assessments*, edited by Renos K. Papadopoulos (London: Routledge, 1992): 398–410; 424.

however, comes at a cost, because when we grant the other his singularity and refuse the colonizing gesturing of reading his practices and beliefs through a mainstream or secularizing lens, we simultaneously preserve the distance between us that makes possible fantasies and projections. In times of crisis, this distance widens, rendering multiculturalism more a problem than a solution. Perhaps emphasizing citizenship, which unites diverse groups with shared national rights and obligations, is a better approach than emphasizing differences, which security planners can all too easily take to extremes.

DISCRIMINATORY PRACTICES AND DISASTER PLANNING

The September 11 and Katrina catastrophes brought to the fore the idea that worst cases can and do happen, even in relatively risk-free modern societies. U.S. citizens certainly perceive risk, as reflected in headline news about a range of dangers from swine and avian flu to nuclear proliferation. Faced with so many dangers, some policy experts call for "more creative thinking and organization for worse cases" and for the need to balance probabilistic thinking with "possiblistic" thinking.[91] The September 11 Commission blamed the bureaucracy for a "failure of imagination" because federal agencies could not conceive that airplanes might be used as bombs. The recent history of discriminatory practices in disaster management provides a caution to those who would goad the bureaucracy into imagining the worst. Worst-case thinking does not occur in a vacuum; rather, it affixes to existing routines and practices and might tap deep-seated fears about the threat posed by groups that seem visibly different. Any attempt at routinizing worst-case thinking in a bureaucracy charged with contingency planning must also routinize self-criticism so that consideration of the possible rather than the merely probable does not lead to unreasonably discriminatory plans. These are present concerns. In 2008, a U.S. Army War College report proposed that the economic crisis could cause riots and domestic unrest that would require the military to maintain domestic peace. Treasury secretary Henry Paulson alluded to martial law, and the fear of panic filtered down to police in Phoenix, Arizona, who prepared for civil unrest.[92]

Examining discriminatory practices in disaster management has implications for public policy. One sensible method of restricting these practices is to limit the activities that can be justified on security or worst-case grounds. Security seems to swallow up everything and justify activities that do not necessarily make people more secure in the long run. Security can become co-opted by people seeking to maintain power and, perhaps, by unconscious fantasies.

---

[91] Lee Clarke, *Worst Cases: Inquiries Into Terror, Calamity, And Imagination* (Chicago: University of Chicago Press 2005), 178.

[92] Mike Sunnucks, "Ariz. Police Say They Are Prepared as War College Warns Military Must Prepare for Unrest; IMF Warns of Economic Riots," *Phoenix Business Journal*, December 17, 2008, quoted in Solnit, *A Paradise Built in Hell*, 310.

Legislation can outlaw discrimination, but however noble, it is not sufficient. The abuses chronicled in this chapter occurred after the Civil Service Reform Act of 1978 that barred discrimination for any attribute that does not affect job performance.

Reagan-era officials stumbled on a solution when they spoke out against FEMA's overreaching. Bureaucratic competition provides a built-in safeguard to administrative abuses as each agency seeks to protect its own turf. FEMA's abuses might have been worse had it extended its authority without challenge from other agencies or, as the previous chapter showed, from a nascent emergency management profession suspicious of the agency's secret programs. The flipside of bureaucratic competition, however, is fragmentation and bureaucratic infighting, which plagued the government's efforts in Katrina. Within each disaster agency, crisis planning needs to be less insular, incorporate ideas from a broad section of a community, including the obvious demographic representation, and recognize local experts as able to contribute outside the formal hierarchy of disaster management plans and routines. Examining significant cases in which public officials and administrators used claims about security during a crisis or potential crisis to justify discrimination against marginalized groups should temper expectations about what government can and should do in a crisis.

8

Government's Increasing Role in Disaster Management

The Mississippi River Flood of 1927 was, at the time, the most destructive river flood in U.S. history, and the federal government responded with an unprecedented effort at recovery that built the reputations of future President Herbert Hoover and future Louisiana Governor Huey Long.[1] Hurricane Katrina, in 2005, was the most destructive hurricane in U.S. history, but the government's response at all levels drew criticism. Rather than being propelled to higher office, politicians deflected blame for the slow and inadequate government response onto civil servants and appointed managers, particularly the FEMA administrator, Michael Brown.

Two things had changed since the early twentieth century. First, voices across the political spectrum and the public at large expected the federal government to respond quickly to a wide array of hazards and to allay nearly all grievances. After 2012's Hurricane Sandy, New Jersey Governor Chris Christie, usually an acid-tongued critic of President Obama, greeted the president warmly and toured flooded regions with him. Soon after, Christie asked the federal government for $38.6 in disaster relief funds.[2] The request was remarkable because two years earlier Christie made headlines for turning down federal government funding to build a transit tunnel under the Hudson River. Christine explained that his fiscally conservative principles would not allow him to accept federal money for the project, telling an audience of prominent Republicans, "You have to be willing to say no to those things that compromise your principles."[3]

---

[1] Risk Management Solutions, *The 1927 Great Mississippi Flood: An 80-Year Retrospective* (San Francisco: RMS Special Report, 2007).
[2] Joelle Farrell, "Christie Asks the Federal Government for More Storm Recovery Money," Philadelphia Inquirer, November 30, 2012, available at: http://articles.philly.com/2012–11–30/news/35437131_1_christie-storm-recovery-federal-funds (accessed February 14, 2013).
[3] Kate Zernike, "Report Disputes Christie's Basis for Halting Tunnel," *New York Times*, April 10, 2012, A18.

While transit infrastructure was in tension with conservative principles, providing billions of dollars in disaster relief was a core responsibility of the federal government.

During Katrina, conservative writer Jonah Goldberg, usually a crusader against federal government intrusions, wrote that, "When a city is sinking into the sea and rioting runs rampant, government should probably saddle-up."[4] (Reports of rioting were vastly overstated, as Chapter 7 discusses.) In Spike Lee's documentary about the hurricane, *When the Levees Broke*, New Orleans residents are shown holding signs that read, "Where Is FEMA?" and asking why the federal government was not more prepared. None of those interviewed asked the same questions of state and local governments or nonprofits and community associations. Six months after the disaster, a CBS News/*New York Times* poll queried a random sample of U.S. citizens: Who was to blame for conditions in New Orleans after Katrina? Twenty-seven percent of respondents said FEMA and the federal government were most to blame, while another 11 percent blamed the president – even though FEMA and the federal government have no formal authority to conduct evacuations.[5]

The second major change was the expansion of disaster agencies and programs, as well as an inflation in politicians' promises to constituents, all of which fed public expectations of the federal government in disaster.[6] The arc of this study traces the development of the government's claims and the public's expectations expressed through the media and public documents. Yet these goals, promises, and expectations did not match agencies' actual capacity to prepare for and respond to disasters. The federal government could never deliver absolute protection against all disasters, from extreme weather events to the unknown consequences of nuclear war.

FEMA's response to Katrina – which exemplifies the complexity of the government environment of the twenty-first century – was limited by the degree to which other agencies responded to its requests. The agency existed in a network of multiple, overlapping authorities, rather than a hierarchy – although many of the plans governing disaster management assumed hierarchical relationships. While communicating among disaster management agencies became more cumbersome as the network became more dense, the public learned about disasters ever more quickly through electronic media, and people were quicker to find fault and lay blame. In Katrina, images of suffering and chaos were broadcast around the world as they happened, and viewers did not wait

---

[4] Jonah Goldberg, "The Feds," The Corner Blog, *National Review Online*, August 31, 2005.

[5] CBS News Poll, "Hurricane Katrina Six Months Later," February 27, 2006. Nationwide random telephone sample of 1,018 adults, February 22–26, 2006. The poll added the factually questionable statement, "Hundreds of thousands of people were unable to evacuate."

[6] Nuclear energy professional organizations pledged to do the opposite: to diminish public expectations of nuclear power in order to be less likely to disappoint their audiences. See Brian Balogh, *Chain Reaction: Expert Debate and Public Participation in American Commercial Nuclear Power, 1945–1975* (New York: Cambridge University Press, 1991), 171–235.

as long as it took Hoover to arrive on the scene in 1927 to assess whether the response was a government success or a failure. As terrible as the suffering during Katrina was, any large-scale disaster is likely to cause harm, and ambitious politicians and angry citizens can use the media to blame federal agencies for the calamity. By 2005, federal agencies, and FEMA in particular, had become the locus of responsibility for preparing for disaster and the target of blame when things went poorly.[7]

SHAPING DISASTER MANAGEMENT

The difference in the expectations and reactions surrounding these events frames this book's central puzzle: what is the role of the federal government in addressing disasters, and how has it changed? The answer is that citizens, members of Congress, disaster managers, presidents, and the media inadvertently shape what counts as a disaster and how much responsibility the federal government has in addressing it. This process of social construction occurs while various actors pursue their own interests, whether winning reelections, making promises to voters, managing organizations, reporting the news, or preparing for disasters.

While the standard scholarly explanations for organizational failure consider crucial moments in agency design, structure, or implementation, this book has examined agencies over time to show how evolving expectations and political opportunities shape the missions of public organizations.[8] An agency's design is open to interpretation by the bureaucrats who run it and the professions and social groups it serves. A central claim of this study is that by the late twentieth century, entrepreneurial bureaucrats began claiming credit for successes their agencies did not deserve and were being blamed for failures beyond their control.[9] New interventions created precedents and established organizations

---

[7] For example, some nonprofit organizations criticized FEMA for being part of an exploitative recovery process. One study claimed that "a quarter of the workers rebuilding the city were immigrants lacking papers, almost all of them Hispanic, making far less money than legal workers." Judith Browne-Dianis, Jennifer Lai, Marielena Hincapie, and Saket Soni, *And Injustice for All: Workers' Lives in the Reconstruction of New Orleans, Advancement Project*, July 6, 2006, 29, available at www.advancementproject.org (accessed September 17, 2011); Naomi Klein, *The Shock Doctrine: The Rise of Disaster Capitalism* (New York: Picador, 2007), 521–522.

[8] This is a highly contextual version of reputational theories of organizations, whose most famous expositors include: Daniel Carpenter, *Reputation and Power: Organizational Image and Pharmaceutical Regulation at the FDA* (Princeton, NJ: Princeton University Press, 2010); Mary Douglas, *How Institutions Think* (Syracuse, NY: Syracuse University Press, 1986); and John Meyer and Brian Rowan, "Institutionalized Organizations: Formal Structure as Myth and Ceremony," *American Journal of Sociology* 83 (1977): 340–363.

[9] Kent Weaver argued that politicians tend to prefer avoiding blame over taking credit, although they seek to do both. See R. Kent Weaver, "The Politics of Blame Avoidance," *Journal of Public Policy* 6 (1986): 371–398. Christopher Hood extends the argument to public administrators in *The Blame Game: Spin, Bureaucracy, and Self-Preservation in Government* (Princeton, NJ: Princeton University Press, 2010), 14–15.

and administrative cultures that accumulated over time to produce a general trend. Citizens, politicians, and bureaucrats expected the government to provide more security from more kinds of disasters over time. The trend reached its apex when FEMA adopted "all hazards, all phases" as its mantra.[10] The all hazards idea implies that the agency uses similar plans and people to prepare for many kinds of hazards, from hurricanes and floods to earthquakes and even industrial hazards or attack. The all phases idea means that unlike, say, Hoover's ad hoc flood response in 1927, the agency runs disaster programs at all times. FEMA prepares for disasters before they occur, seeks to mitigate the effects of disasters that do happen, responds to major events, and helps communities recover, covering all phases of the disaster timeline.

Despite the rhetoric, the federal government's increasingly bold claims and heightened public expectations are disproportionate to the ability of the federal government to prevent or reduce the damage caused by disaster. Most of the authority over zoning, development, and land use, all of which contribute to disaster losses, is in the hands of state and local governments and private citizens. The federal government's primary disaster organization, FEMA, is a small coordinating agency that does not own most of the resources it relies on to respond to disaster. The agency has frequently been at the center of political battles over patronage appointments, pork barrel spending, and the status of terrorism and security missions. Its predecessors in civil defense endured similar fates.

Finally, the uncertainty inherent in many catastrophic disasters should humble those who claim to be prepared. For most events serious enough to be called disasters, we observe the effects of a generator of probability, not the generator itself. In a game of chance, we know that a die has six sides, but for some events such as a severe disaster we may observe historical data that show a world that appears to have a six-sided die until one day it is suddenly governed by a sixteen-sided die. The upshot of this reality is that risk models or memory of the recent past convey a false sense of certainty. The inherent uncertainty involved in preparing for the worst contrasts with politicians' and bureaucrats' increasingly bold promises to protect citizens from all hazards.

The trajectory of disaster policy over time provides a window into the construction of basic categories of the state, including the role of the president, Congress, and civil servants. Particularly at issue has been the question of who counts as a citizen. Disaster managers were no more discriminatory than anyone else, but the sense of security threat and the organizational routines of crisis planning sometimes led to singling out already marginalized groups as threats. In the civil defense and homeland security eras, disaster agencies named some people as citizens to be protected and others as threats, even though the

---

[10] Chapter 4 examines the emergence of the all hazards concept in FEMA during the 1980s and 1990s.

purportedly dangerous African Americans, gays and lesbians, or poor people in hurricane-stricken New Orleans were citizens, too.

The mechanism of social construction through which the federal government intervenes more and more over time and shapes disaster management cannot be measured by journalists or chroniclers of the latest disaster; it occurs over the *longue durée* and requires the initially incongruous welding of nineteenth-century congressional arguments about disaster relief and twenty-first-century bureaucratic wrangling. With attention to history and the basic institutions of political power, however, disaster management appears as a construction of democratic politics. Politicians, bureaucrats, and citizens articulate and repeat claims about what the government should be doing. As Stephen Skowronek puts it, "Whether a given state changes or fails to change, the form and timing of the change, and the governing potential in the change – all of these turn on a struggle for political power and institutional position, a struggle defined and mediated by the organization of the preestablished state."[11] Social construction, in this view, is a basic mechanism of politics over time.

THE DRIVERS OF INCREASING INVOLVEMENT AND THE LIMITS
TO GOVERNMENT CAPACITY

The venues for credit and blame games, and for deliberation about the nature of government involvement, changed over time. In the nineteenth century, elected politicians debated on the floor of Congress the federal government's obligations to citizens in the wake of disaster. In the twentieth century, the president emerged as a locus of responsibility; later, more responsibility fell to the bureaucracy. In each period, the process of increasing federal government involvement in disaster assumed common characteristics.

Three features shaped federal involvement in most cases. They are elections, particularly the incentive structure for elected officials, federalism, and – in the twentieth century – bureaucracy. The structure of Congress emphasizes geographically based constituencies, and members work to obtain benefits for their districts, sometimes by going along with other members' requests. A member who seeks hurricane relief may be more likely to support earthquake relief because he expects reciprocal favors for his district. Presidents also use disaster agencies as a tool to receive credit for government initiatives. While the performance of disaster agencies added luster to the presidency during the James Lee Witt era and in the aftermath of September 11, Calvin Coolidge and Hoover had reaped the political benefits of disaster intervention long before. Crises and disasters provided opportunities for presidential leadership and a tempting object for political ambition. The accumulation of

---

[11] Stephen Skowronek, *Building a New American State, The Expansion of National Administrative Capacities, 1877–1920* (Cambridge: Cambridge University Press, 1977), 285.

precedent for presidential and national-level intervention contributed to an expanding disaster policy state.

Politicians, however, are in a hurry. They need to deliver results before the next election, and they do not want to risk blame. As a result, politicians have incentives to offload difficult long-term problems such as how to cope with disaster losses onto administrative agencies. While politicians respond to the short timelines of the news cycle or of elections every two, four, or six years, disaster vulnerability takes place over a longer period during which humans build in risky environments. The disconnect between the time horizon of politicians and the slow unfolding of disasters over decades or hundreds of years complicates efforts to prepare for disaster. A devastating hurricane or flood might occur regularly every few hundred years, but it appears to be a bolt from the blue compared to the human lifespan or the political cycle. The difference between political lifespans and disaster frequencies has consequences for how people perceive risk. Earthquakes in Missouri and South Carolina were violent enough to ring church bells in neighboring states during the nineteenth century, but today these areas are considered relatively safe compared to San Francisco – even though California has superior building codes and evacuation procedures and may be relatively safer on average. The difference is that Missouri and Charleston were spared major earthquakes in the last century.

Federalism further constrains government involvement in disaster by limiting the federal government's power over states and localities. FEMA relies on state resources for much of its disaster planning and relief efforts. And cities control one important aspect of disaster vulnerability, which is land. Unfortunately, if cities can find someone to certify valuable but vulnerable land as safe, they will likely develop it, no matter the risk.[12]

The term "federalism" as I use it here implies the multiplication and fragmentation of government powers separated vertically and horizontally, not just the original constitutional design. Any given area affected by a disaster has dozens or even hundreds of overlapping and conflicting jurisdictions: cities, counties, school districts, fire districts, levee districts, public utilities, and mosquito abatement districts. Each of these has elected or appointed supervisors who may not communicate with one another often, especially about hazards and disaster. The number of governments in a geographic region confounds reformers seeking to rationalize preparation and response through a bureaucratic structure. Fragmented political structures allow politicians and government agencies to claim credit for successes that stem from collective efforts and attempt to escape blame for failures to which they contributed. At the same time, no single actor in fragmented political space has responsibility for all of the facets of disaster preparation and response, even though formal plans for disaster management assume a Weberian bureaucratic structure. Attempts at comprehensive reform usually end up being only partially successful.

---

[12] Paul E. Peterson, *City Limits* (Chicago: University of Chicago Press, 1981).

Finally, bureaucratic forms shape disaster management through routines, hierarchies, and a security culture. Routines can provide efficiencies, but they can also blind people to new situations that demand improvisation. Hierarchy also offers efficiencies, but it runs the risk of devolving into isolated stovepipes that separate groups within an organization from potential collaborators, as in the case of mitigation activities' distance from economic recovery programs, or from necessary criticism of their actions, as in the case of FEMA's security culture. Sometimes security cultures justify discriminatory treatment, but other times security cultures wall themselves off from others and become just another excuse for turf wars. Cooperation between security and non-security divisions can produce shared gains, such as when FEMA used satellite equipment designed for national security to identify flooded areas in need of disaster relief. But sometimes agencies are locked in zero-sum games that distort shared missions, as in the miscommunication among agencies and within the DHS that occurred during Katrina.

INCREASING EXPECTATIONS AND PROMISES VERSUS LIMITED CAPACITY

The federal government has been involved in disaster relief from the beginning of the republic, which suggests that it is an enduring feature of the social contract, itself a form of social and political construction. Yet it is up to each generation to define exactly what the role of government should be in relation to disaster and catastrophe and what role the national government should play compared to subnational governments. Judgments about collective and governmental obligation vary over time.[13] For Plato, the raising of children was a central public responsibility, but in the contemporary United States and in most places in the industrialized world, it is a private one. The United States once had a public bank, but today the banking system is, on the face of it, largely private. Similarly, the government's role in disaster has waxed and waned, although the role of federal bureaucracies responsible for protecting citizens from disaster has mostly waxed.

The term "disaster" comes from the sixteenth-century use of the Italian *disastro*, meaning ill-starred, in the sense of a calamity that occurs because the stars are in an unfavorable alignment. What falls into the category of a disaster for which the federal government has an obligation to provide relief has varied over time to include fires, floods, earthquakes, hurricanes, nuclear attack, snow emergencies, and riots. The federal government did not create a unitary national disaster agency until 1979. Before then, sympathetic members of Congress, bureaucrats, interest groups, and eventually presidents argued for aid. Sometimes their requests were heeded, and sometimes they were

---

[13] Paul C. Light, *The True Size of Government* (Washington, DC: Brookings Institution, 1999), 149–151; Barry Bozeman, *Public Values and Public Interest* (Washington, DC: Brookings Institution, 2007).

ignored. Over time, the accumulation of federal intervention in disaster policy established a precedent. Politicians became increasingly likely to support the idea that a community owed victims of disaster, and they were increasingly receptive to the palpable benefits of disaster aid provided to their constituents. Expectations about the federal government's role in preparing for disaster increased until they collided with events: North-South divisions stalled the increase in federal government involvement in disaster relief before the Civil War. Shifting from expectations to practice, expansion continued apace after the war. Disaster aid also spread to new areas, such as the Gulf Coast, which was vulnerable to frequent hurricanes.

The Cold War altered the path of expanding government intervention in disasters toward a more national system in which security threats were a preeminent concern. Fear of nuclear attack from the Soviet Union and appeals to patriotism broke down resistance to federal government intervention in preparing for the worst, and a civil defense program crafted by defense intellectuals became the heart of national-level disaster preparedness. The federal government provided strategic plans and policy, and states and localities implemented the programs, sometimes shifting national-level civil defense programs toward local concerns. Writing in *Harper's* in 1955, Eric Larabee expressed surprise at the close relationship between preparing for attack and preparing for natural disasters, and at politicians and bureaucrats who supported both. "Surely it is a curious argument for preparing ourselves against the H-bomb that the preparations might also be handy in a hurricane," he wrote.[14] The federal government's policy of allowing civil defense programs to be used for natural disasters grew out of the combination of a political imperative to ramp up the Cold War domestically through civil defense and a local operational imperative to obtain more resources to prepare for natural disasters. Civil defense programs implied and sometimes explicitly promised that government could protect citizens from nuclear war, and some local officials extended the promise to natural disasters. In reality, the government could not offer absolute protection from either.

By the 1970s, states and localities had grown frustrated with the byzantine network of federal agencies responsible for disaster relief, and terrorism abroad led the National Governors' Association to request that the federal government coordinate domestic preparation for terrorist attack. Building on a chorus of state and local demands and following a nuclear accident at Three Mile Island, President Carter and Congress created FEMA in 1979 as an amalgam of disaster relief, hazard mitigation, fire protection, and civil defense agencies. FEMA struggled to unite its diverse missions, which ranged across the timeline of a disaster, from mitigation to response to recovery, and across diverse professional communities and types of hazards. The success the agency enjoyed under administrator Witt was the exception, not the rule. Witt's all hazards paradigm gave the agency a coherent mission that united its work with that

[14] Eric Larrabee, "Running for Cover," *Harper's*, October 1955, 24–26.

of states and localities, but many of the Witt reforms did not stick. The agency deemphasized its mitigation programs and emphasized security during a new a presidential administration and the aftershock of the attacks of September 11. The agency performed well in response to the attacks, but compared to other agencies and nongovernmental organizations, FEMA's greatest achievements after the September 11 attacks were rhetorical, assuring the public that the government was in control of the response. The creation of the DHS in 2003 demoted FEMA and shifted resources toward terrorism. FEMA's administrator lost direct access to the president, and the agency lost many of its experienced professionals to retirement or lateral moves within the DHS.

Before the department was fully up and running, Hurricane Katrina exposed the chinks in the country's disaster armor. The United States was not prepared for a major disaster in an urban area with relatively low government capacity, and many poor citizens died because of miscommunication and negligence, especially poor communication among the levels of government. The loss of between 1,400 and 2,000 people and hundreds of billions in damages ranked as one of the more costly disasters in U.S. history. Increasing federal involvement had not spared citizens from disaster, although some argued that the federal government was not involved enough and that the military should preempt weak states and localities. Yet debates over whether to centralize or decentralize disaster functions missed two important causes of disaster losses: increased development in vulnerable areas and urbanization. (For an illustration of urbanization, see Figure 8.1). Without radically rewriting zoning laws, insurance regulations, or the Constitution's limits on federal power, the federal government has little power over either of these trends.

At the same time, twenty-first-century disaster management had made clear advances over its predecessors. Improvements in storm track forecasting, for example, gave communities better advance warning about approaching hurricanes. The government's response to Hurricanes Ivan and Dennis, which struck the Florida panhandle just before Katrina in 2004 and 2005, was judged a success – in no small measure because of Florida's excellent state and local emergency managers.[15] The federal government's increasingly bureaucratized and rationalized approach to preparing for and responding to hazards and disasters spared lives and property during routine fires, floods, earthquakes, and hurricanes, even as it overpromised what it could do during unusual and extreme events such as Katrina in which local improvisation was key to saving lives. (See Figures 8.2, 8.3, and 8.4 to put losses from Katrina in historical perspective.)

Yet the government's attempts to prepare for disaster verged into discrimination when security concerns became paramount. FEMA planned to intern

[15] Kenneth J. Meier, Laurence J. O'Toole, Jr., and Alisa Hicklin, "I've Seen Fire and I've Seen Rain: Public Management and Performance after a Natural Disaster," *Administration & Society* 41 (January 2010): 979–1003; Joseph B. Treaster, "Hurricane Dennis: The Response," *New York Times,* July 11, 2005, available at: http://query.nytimes.com/gst/fullpage.html?res=9C01E0DE1 23DF932A25754C0A9639C8B63 (accessed January 19, 2011).

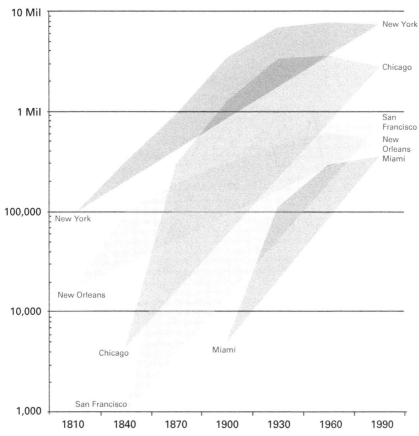

FIGURE 8.1. Population Growth in Major U.S. Cities from 1870 to 1990.
* San Francisco had an estimated population of 1,000 in 1848.
Sources: The U.S. Census Bureau, "Population of 100 Largest Urban Places," Tables 4, 7, 10, 13, 16, 19, 22; the population of Miami in 1900 was taken from Rumler Internet Services, http://www.rumler.com/miami/; Rand Richards, *Historic San Francisco: A Concise History and Guide*, San Francisco: Heritage House Publishers, 1992.

citizens during riots in the early 1980s, and it kept lists of gays and lesbians in the agency that it deemed security risks long after most other domestic agencies had abandoned the practice. Not all disaster planning is discriminatory, but planning for crisis has the potential to awaken fears of disorder and tap unconscious fantasies about marginalized groups. While discrimination is as old as disaster, the bureaucratized, procedural, and rational government response to disaster is new. The development of permanent state agencies devoted to preparing for disaster makes possible new forms of discrimination. Administrators who identify a security threat may act efficiently or rationally according to their duties within an organizational hierarchy. Yet security policies can be discriminatory in a larger context, or they can be out of proportion with the

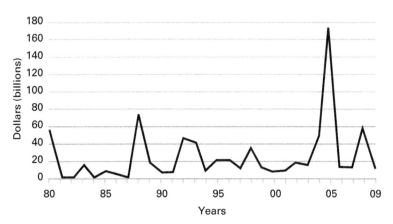

FIGURE 8.2. Billion-Dollar Disaster Losses from 1980 to 2009.
* Adjusted to 2007 constant dollars.
Notes: Monetary figures are estimates by the National Center for Disease Control (NCDC) and the National Oceanic and Atmospheric Administration (NOAA), and are based on costs in terms of property that would not have been lost had the disaster not occurred. Although it is impossible to calculate the precise total of losses resulting from major natural disasters, it is possible to arrive at reasonable estimates using a variety of data sources from insurance companies, local and state governments, and FEMA, among others. The data in this chart were taken primarily from NCDC and NOAA reports, and supplemented with additional information to arrive at the most comprehensive estimate of losses.

Definition of a billion-dollar disaster: According to the NCDC report on "Billion Dollar U.S. Weather Disasters," the United States has sustained ninety-six natural disasters since 1980 in each of which overall damages and costs reached or exceeded $1 billion. Damage and cost estimates include public and private property as well as insured and uninsured losses.

Sources: Wayne Blanchard, "Billion Dollar U.S. Disasters," 2008, http://www.gadr. giees.uncc.edu/PPT_SLIDES/Billion_Dollar_Disasters.pdf; The Federal Emergency Management Agency (FEMA), http://www.fema.gov; NCDC and NOAA data from 1980 to 2009 on billion-dollar disasters, http://www.ncdc.noaa.gov/oa/reports/billionz. html#chron

security goals they fulfill. As civil defense security organizations transform into homeland security, it is worth paying attention to whether arguments in the name of security during a crisis overstate objective levels of threat and harm marginalized groups.

PUZZLES IN CONTEMPORARY DISASTER POLICY

Although disaster agencies in the United States provide more public assistance for a greater range of disasters than ever before, damage from disasters

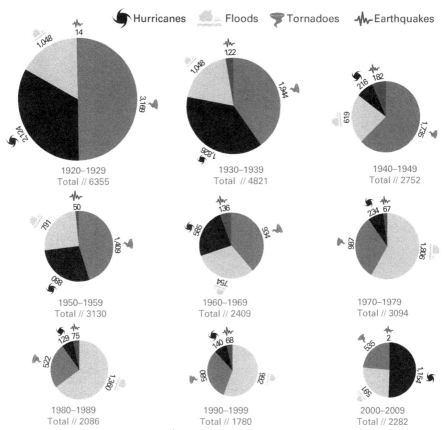

FIGURE 8.3. Natural-Disaster-Related Deaths from 1920 to 2009.

* Death totals for 2009 are incomplete.

** Some estimates for fatalities in Hurricane Katrina exceed 1,800, but many of those estimates do not differentiate between hurricane- and flood-related deaths. Still, the number represented here is relatively low.

Note: This table is a compilation of sources that calculate death totals from the best available data. Disaster deaths are difficult to establish, especially those that strike major metropolitan areas. Numbers for these disasters typically include estimates for the homeless, and the number of missing persons, resulting in a wide range of possible numbers. Some government officials may also dispute the number of disaster deaths for political reasons, or to downplay the effects of a disaster. For many of the earliest recorded disasters, and even those in more recent times, the actual number of deaths may be lost to history.

Sources: Ted Steinberg, *Acts of God: The Unnatural History of Natural Disaster in America*, 2nd ed., Oxford: Oxford University Press, 2006 (table on p. 74); the NWS and NOAA data on weather-related disasters and the "69-Year List of Severe Weather Fatalities," http://www.weather.gov/os/hazstats.shtml; the United States Geological Survey (USGS), "Deaths in the United States from Earthquakes," http://earthquake.usgs.gov/earthquakes

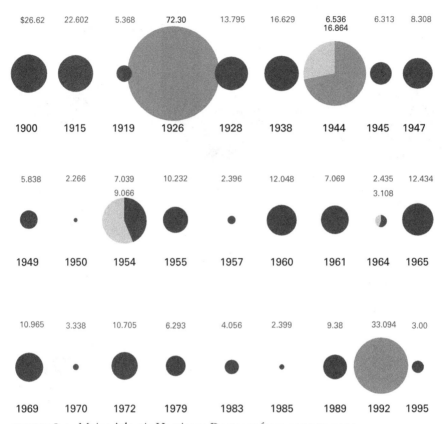

FIGURE 8.4. Major Atlantic Hurricane Damages from 1900 to 1995.

Note: The dollar figures (in billions) are normalized to 1995 dollars by inflation, personal property increases, and population changes. Losses reflect direct impacts resulting from hurricanes, such as wind damage to personal property. Two figures for one year indicate two major hurricanes for that year.*Source*: R. A. Pielke, Jr. and C. W. Landsea, "Normalized Hurricane Damages in the United States: 1925–1995," *Weather and Forecasting* 13 (1998): 621–631.

has increased over the past six decades.[16] Fatalities have decreased, but they remain a problem. One of the paradoxes of disaster policy is that as authorities and citizens become better at saving lives, they put more people and property at risk. This occurs because as technologies and organizations improve to save lives, more people choose to live and build in risky areas. Many of the causes of disaster losses in individual behavior are outside the control of the

---

[16] For data on the increase in federal government assistance, see Figures 4.2 and 4.3 in Chapter 4. For data on the increasing cost of disasters, see Swiss Reinsurance Company, "Natural Disasters and Manmade Catastrophes in 2008," *Sigma* (Zurich, Switzerland: Swiss Reinsurance Company Ltd, 2009).

federal government, but preparing for disaster has become the government's unquestioned responsibility.

The relationship of public expectations to the state is also paradoxical. As public expectations of the federal government's responsibility in times of disaster grow, citizens become more distant from state decision-making institutions. Whereas in the nineteenth century, members of Congress debated the merits of citizens' requests for aid, by the twentieth century, citizens' claims were more likely to be filtered through the bureaucracy and the media. FEMA vacillates between being a scapegoat for politicians and a tool that politicians use to claim credit for helping citizens. Finally, among the paradoxes, an expanded state did not result in a more coordinated state. The former fueled politicians' overpromising; the latter ensured that the government would fall short of expectations.

Several political trends amplify the difficulty of preparing for disaster. Political influence over the bureaucracy, the proliferation of management layers, deference to states and localities, privatization, social heterogeneity, and tensions between security and non-security missions complicate efforts to prepare for the shifting category of disaster.[17] The success FEMA enjoyed in coordinating preparation and response efforts during the 1990s was the exception, not the rule. FEMA and its predecessors have always been small agencies without the capacity to govern by command.

Despite limited governing capacity, the dynamics of democratic politics lead citizens to demand assistance from government after disaster, and politicians and bureaucrats are eager to provide it. Speaking after hurricane Katrina in New Orleans, Republican President George W. Bush portrayed massive federal government aid to help citizens rebuild as an American tradition: "Every time, the people of this land have come back from fire, flood, and storm to build anew – and to build better than what we had before. Americans have never left our destiny to the whims of nature – and we will not start now."[18] Even relatively conservative politicians promise abundant government resources to victims of disaster in a democratic media age.

If disaster relief is a democratic imperative, why have the government's efforts in Hurricane Katrina and other disasters of the past century fallen so woefully short of expectations? Social science offers several explanations. The management literature on high-reliability organizations emphasizes the need for better organizational coordination.[19] High-reliability organizations, like the Federal Aviation Administration's Air Traffic Control system, are highly

[17] E. L. Quarantelli, ed., *Disasters: Theory and Research* (Beverly Hills, CA: Sage Publications, 1978).

[18] George W. Bush, "President Discusses Hurricane Relief in Address to the Nation," New Orleans, September 15, 2005.

[19] Karl E. Weick and Kathleen Sutcliffe, *Managing the Unexpected* (New York: Jossey-Bass, 2001).

reliable because they are tightly coupled, which means that their parts and processes are interdependent. Delays and mechanical failures do not shut down the entire system of commercial aviation. But a tightly coupled system could break down at *any* weak point.[20] The disaster relief system, however, is loosely coupled, and there is usually sufficient redundancy so that if one organization breaks down, the entire system does not fail. The multiple, overlapping, and sometimes confusing nature of authorities is a strength of the system because precisely where and when disaster will happen is unpredictable. In an alternate account, sociologists explain some large-scale disasters as "normal accidents" – normal because they are to be expected in highly complex systems.[21] Yet telling the public to expect calamity is not politically feasible. Finally, political scientists propose that some organizations are "designed to fail" because the coalitions that created them disagreed about their purposes and compromised long-term performance goals for short-term political credit.[22]

While the standard explanations examine crucial moments in agency design, structure, or implementation, this book has examined agencies over time to show how evolving expectations and political opportunities shape the missions of public organizations. An agency's design is open to interpretation by the bureaucrats who run the agency and the professions and social groups it serves. A central claim here is that by the late twentieth century, entrepreneurial bureaucrats were claiming credit for successes that their agencies did not deserve and being blamed for failures beyond their control.

There are enlightening ways to examine the relationship between disasters and the state other than the perspective presented here. Presidents use disaster policy as an important tool for achieving their objectives.[23] Disasters bring out the best and the worst in people, and sometimes they shape people's understanding of what it means to be a citizen.[24] Decentralized, networked responses to disasters seem to be more effective than purely hierarchical plans and responses.[25] Finally, studies of the expansion of state capacity in the United

---

[20] Scott Snook, *Friendly Fire: The Accidental Shootdown of U.S. Black Hawks over Northern Iraq* (Princeton, NJ: Princeton University Press, 2002).

[21] Charles Perrow, *Normal Accidents, Living with High Risk Technologies* (Princeton, NJ: Princeton University Press, 1999).

[22] Amy Zegart, *Flawed by Design: The Evolution of the CIA, JCS, and NSC* (Stanford, CA: Stanford University Press, 1999); Terry Moe, "The New Economics of Organization," *American Journal of Political Science* 28 (1984): 739–777.

[23] Andrew Reeves, "Political Disaster? Presidential Disaster Declaration and Electoral Politics," unpublished manuscript, March 4, 2009; Richard Sylves, *Disaster Policy and Politics: Emergency Management and Homeland Security* (Washington, DC: CQ Press, 2008).

[24] Peter Alexander Meyers, *Civic War and the Corruption of the Citizen* (Chicago: University of Chicago Press, 2008).

[25] Donald P. Moynihan, "Combining Structural Forms in the Search for Policy Tools: Incident Command Systems in U.S. Crisis Management," *Governance* 21 (2008): 205–229; Moynihan, "Learning under Uncertainty: Networks in Crisis Management," *Public Administration Review* 68 (2008): 350–361; Naim Kapucu, "Interagency Communication Networks during

States offer explanations useful for understanding the federal government's increasing role in disasters.[26] Many works in the field of American political development focus on the link between the presidency or Congress and the public. In these works, the link between the public and government is visible through opinion polls and elections. Focusing on the development of disaster management bureaucracy, however, obscures the link between the public and government, or at least makes it harder to measure. Public expectations are filtered through the news media, the rare elections in which disasters are a major issue, and sometimes politicians' comments in anticipation of public reactions.[27]

DISASTERS AND DEMOCRACY: HOW TO BETTER PLAN FOR THE FUTURE

Federal government intervention in disasters has had high points: the James Lee Witt years, the early days of civil defense (which featured a relatively high level of public engagement compared to other eras), Hoover's response to the Mississippi Valley Flood (though it was characterized by bigotry worse than the Katrina rumor mill), and competent nineteenth-century responses to restore commercial hubs. During many less prominent disasters, federal agencies performed important but unheralded work, as when, for example, they arranged for the construction of flood barriers or persuaded cities not to locate critical functions in areas prone to fires or flooding. Although these are valuable services, it is difficult for officials to take credit for disasters that did not happen.

Yet the problems disaster agencies face are political rather than purely managerial. As public administration scholar Dwight Waldo observed, the United States is both Greek and Roman.[28] It has the tumult of Greek democratic politics, but it also depends on Roman features of administration, such as professional conduct and expertise. It is the job of disaster agencies to "straighten the path" of government by bringing expertise to bear on democratically arrived-at

Emergencies: Boundary Spanners in Multi-Agency Coordination," *The American Review of Public Administration* 36 (2006): 207–225; Louise K. Comfort, Arjen Boin, and Chris Demchak, *Designing Resilience for Communities at Risk: Sociotechnical Approaches* (Pittsburgh, PA: University of Pittsburgh Press, 2010).

[26] Stephen Skowronek, *Building a New American State, The Expansion of National Administrative Capacities* (New York: Cambridge University Press, 1982).

[27] David Twigg finds that Hurricane Andrew in 1992 privileged state and local incumbents, who were seen helping constituents during the response to and recovery from the storm. See David K. Twigg, *The Politics of Disaster: Tracking the Impact of Hurricane Andrew* (Gainesville, FL: University of Florida Press, 2012). In a comparative study, Governing After Crisis finds that disasters sometimes upset the political status quo, but skillful politicians often emerge more powerful after a disaster. See *Governing after Crisis: The Politics of Investigation, Accountability, and Learning*, edited by Arjen Boin, Allan McConnell, and Paul 'T Hart. (New York: Cambridge University Press, 2008).

[28] Dwight Waldo, "Politics and Administration: A Profound Disjunction," working paper, national conference, American Society for Public Administration, Honolulu, HI, March 21–25, 1982.

questions. Planning for a hurricane in New Orleans, for instance, should not simply consider the wishes of the New Orleans levee boards or even of the present citizens of New Orleans itself, but also the needs of future residents of New Orleans and of citizens of the nation who will inevitably be asked to rescue and restore the city after the next big hurricane. The government's role in disaster reflects the nation's obligation toward its members.

The problems of disaster agencies are a microcosm of problems with the contemporary administrative state. FEMA was held responsible for preparing the nation for all hazards, even though its legal authority flows from an ambiguous law, the Stafford Act, and a hodgepodge of presidential executive orders. Disaster agencies, including civil defense and emergency management agencies, are criticized for costing too much, for not being politically responsive, or for not adapting to new problems. Yet most efforts at reform do not address the core responsibilities of government. Reforms usually retreat to ideas of scientific management – that administrators must be controlled, administration is about implementation, and administrative legitimacy is defined and limited by politicians. The creation of FEMA and the DHS as well as post-Katrina reforms reflect the assumptions of scientific management. Yet efforts to centralize and bureaucratize disaster agencies end up giving them unmanageable tasks while constraining what they can do, and thereby often set disaster agencies up to fail.

Federal government intervention in disaster takes place against the backdrop of the development of an American state that delegates problems to administrative agencies through ambiguous authority. The national government became more powerful over time and assumed greater regulatory powers. In the past, states did most of the regulation, zoning, and mitigation, as well as response. After the New Deal and Cold War, Congress turned over much of its power to the executive branch by delegating powers to agencies without making clear what rule of law the agency was operating under. Congress performs more oversight through committee hearings, reports, and budgeting, and less common deliberation about the purposes of policy, than it once did. In 2011, House Foreign Affairs Committee ranking member Howard Berman expressed exasperation about Congress's tendency to delegate policy decisions to the executive or to administrative agencies with the bitter jab, "We declare ourselves to be one big, constitutionally created potted plant."[29]

In the textbook account of a liberal state, the legislature makes clear what a law is supposed to do, and executive agencies carry out the law. In the real world of disaster policy (and many other areas), the legislature debates how to distribute resources according to malleable, socially constructed categories, such as civil defense or homeland security. Once resources are allocated, administrative agencies argue about the purposes they exist to serve, and the

---

[29] Pete Kasperowicz, "House Passes Boehner Libya Resolution, Votes Down Kuchinich's," *The Hill*, June 3, 2011.

most intrepid agencies forge new missions while the laggards remain in place past their useful lifespan.

The expansion of government authority during crisis is nothing new. In 1794, James Madison famously warned against "the old trick of turning every contingency into a resource for accumulating force in government."[30] Government accumulates power and responsibility after a major disaster, but government's power rarely recedes after the crisis has passed. The federal government accumulates tools of power, including new agencies, regulatory authority, and grants-in-aid programs, to influence state and local government behavior, but these powers are not necessarily focused on long-term goals.

In contemporary disaster policy, members of Congress demanded assistance for their districts, and presidents sought recognition on the national stage. The rise of national media allowed presidential intervention in a single geographically specific disaster to resonate throughout the nation. Some critics of the federal government's handling of disaster praise communitarian or civic republican alternatives, but these are either idealized or workable only on a small scale.[31] Rather than replace democracy, it may be better to amend it. Democracy is a fine system, but under certain circumstances it creates incentives to do bad things. People fail to plan for the future, or they act on narrow, short-sighted interests. Organizations become politically efficient and serve the electoral or bureaucratic interests of their members, but they may not improve policy outcomes.

A large, heterogeneous democracy such as the United States governs through a system of laws, procedures, administrative agencies, and expert civil servants collectively known as "the state." Americans tend to think that the modern democratic state does not need to be managed, but will simply run itself.[32] The history of disaster policy shows this is not the case. By the measures of public assessments in the media, the criticism of expert reports, and employees' evaluations of their own organizations, disaster agencies often perform poorly. Shortcomings in their performance are attributable to more than managerial lapses; they stem from the limits of what federal government disaster agencies can do to prepare for extreme events.

An analysis of historical development does not automatically lead to policy recommendations, but there are a few possible ways to address overpromising and inflated expectations in disaster management. A first step toward improving the federal government's interventions in disaster is the fostering of a greater historical consciousness beyond the last disaster.

For policy makers, the payoff from a greater historical consciousness is an appreciation of the degree to which they can achieve policy change through the

[30] Ezra Taft Benson, *The Red Carpet* (Salt Lake City, UT: Bookcraft, 1962), 142.
[31] Solnit, *A Paradise Built in Hell.*
[32] Dwight Waldo, *The Administrative State: A Study of the Political Theory of American Public Administration* (Toronto: Wiley and Sons, 1988), 99.

political process. Policy change includes passing laws and reorganizing agencies, but also creating new ideas about what government should be doing. The idea of social construction refers to the role that policy makers and the media have in shaping what counts as a disaster or who should be responsible. Over time, several actors participated in increasing expectations of government by expanding the number and kinds of disasters for which the federal government bore responsibility.

Unfortunately, expectations outstripped capacity, and reform of disaster management reorganizations usually focused on the last disaster rather than on a comprehensive view on what the government should prepare for. Major reorganizations followed the Civil War in the form of the Freedman's Bureau; the Cold War with the expansion of civil defense; after hurricanes in the 1970s, the creation of FEMA; FEMA's reorganization in 1993 after hurricane Andrew; and the creation of the DHS after the attacks of September 11. By better understanding the history of disaster management, politicians, bureaucrats, and the public might be less willing to adopt a radical reorganization focused on the last disaster. Instead, they might recognize the wide range of disasters for which the government could provide assistance and the degree of choice that people have in deciding what counts as a disaster that the government should prepare for.

The social construction of disasters reminds scholars that disasters, like other concepts such as bureaucracy or democracy, do not have intrinsic properties that researchers observe. Instead, disasters are inventions of particular times and political cultures with meanings that change gradually over time. Social scientists often search for universal laws, and in doing so they operationalize concepts such as disaster into categories that can be measured, such as "reported disaster losses." Scholars with a greater historical consciousness about disaster management would be less willing to put forward general claims about disasters as a comprehensive account and more willing to acknowledge how historical context shapes meaning in particular cases that are related to one another but not subject to universal regulative laws. With a greater focus on relating cases to concepts rather than finding universal laws, scholars might stumble on solutions. For example, disaster management appears to work best in the United States when separated from security concerns, and the security programs that do exist can be held in check by bureaucratic competition.

The challenge of contemporary disaster management is to balance competition for resources and attention among a greater number of hazards preparation tasks than ever before, and to weigh improvements in saving lives with other trends such as increasing development that contributes to rising property losses. The federal government has always been responsible for national-level problems, but over time a greater number and diversity of disasters became national concerns. Despite increasing government intervention and scientific and technological advances, disaster losses remain a problem in the twenty-first century. The impact of disasters on property has trended higher, depending on how one calculates losses, while the number of deaths caused by large-scale disasters has decreased.[33] Improvements in warning and evacuation have saved lives, but they have not spared property. Analyzing the development of the disaster state suggests some avenues for improvement. Citizens might prepare more for disaster on their own if politicians toned down their rhetoric. Even conservative politicians assume that the federal government has a duty to build back every region laid low by disaster even bigger and better than before. And if FEMA is to be something other than a scapegoat or a tool, it needs a cadre of experienced emergency managers. It remains to be seen, however, where a reduction in political credit claiming and an increase in administrative capacity might come from, aside from policy change after disaster.

Congress and the president shaped the initial development of the federal government's role in disaster management. Today, however, administrative agencies are an important source of innovation, as in the ideas that fueled the Witt reorganization of FEMA. The role of the national government, including administrative agencies, is not merely managerial but constitutive because it participates in shaping its own purposes.[34] The federal government is in some measure responsible for constituting and shaping a people as well as for defining what counts as a disaster. By circumstance and the accretion of history rather than by design, administrative agencies have become a site for deliberating about their own purposes and the role of states and localities relative to the federal government. Neither Congress, presidents, the public, nor the media has sufficient incentive to match disaster agencies' capacities to their goals, leaving it up to the agencies themselves to make the case for what they should be doing and what they will require.

---

[33] See Figure 8.3 in this chapter.
[34] Brian J. Cook, *Bureaucracy and Self-Government: Reconsidering the Role of Public Administration in American Politics* (Baltimore: Johns Hopkins University Press, 1996).

Bibliography

Ackroyd, Stephen. "Organizational Failure". *Blackwell Encyclopedia of Sociology*, Ritzer, ed., Oxford: Blackwell, 2007, 576–580.

Adams, Guy and Danny Balfour. *Unmasking Administrative Evil*. Armonk, NY: M. E. Sharpe, 2006.

Adams, Guy and Virginia Ingersoll. *The Tacit Organization*. Greenwich, CT: JAI Press, 1992.

Adams, Henry, Lester Wright, and Bethany Lohr. "Is Homophobia Associated with Homosexual Arousal?" *The Journal of Abnormal Psychology* 105 (1996): 440–445.

Abridgement of the Debates of Congress, From 1789 to 1856. New York: D. Appleton & Company, 1858.

Agamben, Giorgio. *State of Exception*. Chicago: University of Chicago Press, 2005.

Almond, Gabriel. *Rational Choice Theory and the Social Sciences*. Newburg Park, CA: Sage Publications, 1990.

American National Red Cross. *The Mississippi Valley Flood Disaster of 1927: Official Report of the Relief Operations*. Washington, DC: Red Cross, 1929.

Arendt, Hannah. *Eichmann in Jerusalem: A Report on the Banality of Evil*. New York: Viking Press, 1963.

Arnold, R. Douglas. *The Logic of Congressional Action*. New Haven, CT and London: Yale University Press, 1990.

Ascher, William and Hirschfelder-Ascher, Barbara. "Linking Lasswell's Political Psychology and the Policy Sciences." *Policy Sciences* 37 (2004): 23–36.

Baker, E.J. "Hurricane Evacuation Behavior." *International Journal of Mass Emergencies and Disasters* 9 (1991): 287–310.

Balogh, Brian. "Americans Love Government, as Long as They Can't See It." *History News Network*, June 15, 2009. http://www.hnn.us/articles/88154.html

  Chain Reaction: Expert Debate and Public Participation in American Commercial Nuclear Power, 1945–1975. New York: Cambridge University Press, 1991.

  A Government Out of Sight: The Mystery of National Authority in Nineteenth-Century America. New York: Cambridge University Press, 2009.

Banfield, Edward. *Government Project*. Glencoe, IL: The Free Press, 1951.

Bannard, Henry C. "The Oleomargarine Law: A Study of Congressional Politics," *Political Science Quarterly* 2 (December 1887): 545–557.

Bargh, John and Tanya Chartrand. "The Unbearable Automaticity of Being." *American Psychologist* 54 (1999): 462–479.

Barnett, Michael and Martha Finnemore. *Rules for the World*. Ithaca, NY: Cornell University Press, 2004.

Barr, Stephen. "Transforming FEMA," in *Triumphs and Tragedies of the Modern Presidency*. David Abshire, editor. Westport, CT: Praeger Publishers, 2001: 268–269.

Barry, John M. *Rising Tide: The Great Mississippi Flood of 1927 and How it Changed America*. New York: Simon & Schuster, 1997.

Baumeister, Roy, Karen Dale, and Kristen Sommer. "Freudian Defense Mechanisms and Empirical Findings in Modern Social Psychology: Reaction Formation, Projection, Displacement, Undoing, Isolation, Sublimation and Denial." *Journal of Personality* 66 (1998): 1081–1124.

Baumgartner, Frank and Bryan Jones. *Agendas and Instability in American Politics*. Chicago: The University of Chicago Press, 1995.

Bea, Keith. "Proposed Transfer of FEMA to the Department of Homeland Security: Issues for Congressional Oversight." *CRS Report*, Washington, DC, July 29, 2002.

  "Federal Stafford Act Disaster Assistance: Presidential Declarations, Eligible Activities, and Funding." *CRS Report*. Washington DC, August 29, 2005.

  "FEMA's Mission: Policy Directives of the Federal Emergency Management Agency." *CRS Report*, Washington, DC, February 13, 2002.

Beckman, Norman. "Limiting State Involvement in Foreign Policy: The Governors and the National Guard in Perpich v. Defense." *Publius* 21 (1991): 109–123.

Bendor, Jonathan, Amihai Glazer, and Thomas Hammond. "Theories of Delegation in Political Science." *Annual Review of Political Science* 4 (2001): 235–269.

Bensel, Richard F. *The Political Economy of American Industrialization*. New York: Columbia University Press, 2000.

  "Sectionalism and Congressional Development." In *Oxford Handbook of the American Congress*, Eric Schickler, Frances E. Lee, eds. New York: Oxford University Press, 2011: 761–786.

Bestor, Arthur. *Educational Wasteland: The Retreat From Learning in Our Schools*. Urbana: University of Illinois Press, 1953.

Bimes, Terri and Stephen Skowronek. *Speaking for the People: The Rhetorical Presidency in Historical Perspective*. Amherst: University of Massachusetts Press, 1998.

Birkland, Thomas. *After Disaster: Agenda Setting, Public Policy, and Focusing Events*. Washington, DC: Georgetown University Press, 1997.

  "Scientists and Coastal Hazards: Opportunities for Participation and Policy Change." *Environmental Geosciences* 8 (2001): 61–67.

  "'The World Changed Today': Agenda-Setting and Policy Change in the Wake of the September 11 Terrorist Attacks." *Review of Policy Research* 21 (2004): 179–200.

Birkland, Thomas and Regina Lawrence. "The Social and Political Meaning of the Exxon Valdez Oil Spill." *Spill Science and Technology Bulletin* 7 (2002): 3–4.

Birkland, Thomas and Regina Lawrence. "Media Framing and Policy Change after Columbine." *American Behavioral Scientist* 52 (2009): 1405–1425.

Blanchard, Wayne. *American Civil Defense 1945–1975*. PhD diss., University of Virginia, 1980.

Blazich, Frank. "Alert Today, Alive Tomorrow: The North Carolina Civil Defense Agency and Fallout Shelters, 1961–1963." M.A. thesis, North Carolina Sate University, 2008.

Boardman, Mabel. *Letters of Theodore Roosevelt, The Big Stick*, Vol. 5. Cambridge, MA: Harvard University Press, 1954.

Boin, Arjen, Allan McConnell, and Paul 't Hart, editors. *Governing after Crisis: The Politics of Investigation, Accountability, and Learning*. New York: Cambridge University Press, 2008.

Bolles, Albert. *Industrial History of the United States*. Norwich, CT: The Henry Bill Publishing Company, 1879.

Bowsher, Charles. *Disaster Management: Recent Disasters Demonstrate the Need to Improve the Nation's Response Strategy*. Washington, DC: Government Accounting Office, 1993.

Bozeman, Barry. *Public Values and Public Interest*. Washington DC: Brookings Institution, 2007.

Brands, H.W. *TR: The Last Romantic*. New York: Perseus, 1997.

Breen, William. *Uncle Sam at Home: Civilian Mobilization, Wartime Federalism, and the Council of National Defense, 1917–1919*. Westport, CT: Greenwood Press, 1984.

Brinkley, Douglas. *The Great Deluge: Hurricane Katrina, New Orleans, and the Mississippi Gulf Coast*. New York: William Morrow, 2006.

Bronson, William. *The Earth Shook, the Sky Burned*. Garden City, NY: Doubleday, 1959.

Brown, Joanne. "A is for Atom, B is for Bomb: Civil Defense and American Public Education, 1948–1963." *Journal of American History* 75 (1988): 68–90.

Brown, Michael and Ted Schwarz. *Deadly Indifference, The Perfect (Political) Storm: Hurricane Katrina, The Bush White House, and Beyond*. Lanham, MD: Taylor Trade Publishing, 2011.

Brown, Wendy. *States of Injury*. Princeton, NJ: Princeton University Press, 1995.

Bullard, Robert D. and Beverly Wright. *The Wrong Complexion for Protection: How the Government Response to Disaster Endangers African American Communities*. New York: New York University Press, 2012.

Burgin, Victor. *Fantasy*. Oxford: Blackwell, 1992.

Campbell, Andrew, Jo Whitehead, and Sydney Finkelstein. "Why Good Leaders Make Bad Decisions." *Harvard Business Review* (2009): 60–68.

Campbell, Ballard. *The Growth of American Government: Governance from the Cleveland Era to the Present*. Bloomington: Indiana University Press, 1995.

Canaday, Margot. *The Straight State: Sexuality and Citizenship in Twentieth Century America*. Princeton, NJ: Princeton University Press, 2009.

Caplan, Bryan. *The Myth of the Rational Voter: Why Democracies Choose Bad Policies*. Princeton, NJ: Princeton University Press, 2007.

Cardoszier, V.R. *The Mobilization of the United States in World War II: How the Government, Military, and Industry Prepared for War*. Jefferson, NC: McFarland, 1995.

Carpenter, Daniel P. *The Forging of Bureaucratic Autonomy*. Princeton, NJ: Princeton University Press, 2001.

 Reputation and Power: Organizational Image and Pharmaceutical Regulation at the FDA. Princeton, NJ: Princeton University Press, 2010.

"State Building through Reputation Building: Coalitions of Esteem and Program Innovation in the National Postal System, 1883–1913." *Studies in American Political Development* 14 (2000): 121–155.

Cathcart, Arthur. "The Supreme Court and the New Deal." *Southern California Law Review* 9 (1935): 328–330.

Ceaser, James W. *Presidential Selection.* Princeton, NJ: Princeton University Press, 1979.

Chun, Young H. and Hal G. Rainey. "Goal Ambiguity in U.S. Federal Agencies." *Journal of Public Administration Research and Theory* 15 (2005): 1–30.

"Goal Ambiguity and Organizational Performance in U.S. Federal Agencies." *Journal of Public Administration Research and Theory* 15 (2005): 529–557.

Clarke, Lee. *Mission Improbable, Using Fantasy Documents to Tame Disaster.* Chicago: University of Chicago Press, 1999.

"Panic: Myth or Reality." *Contexts* 1 (2002): 21–26.

Worst Cases: Inquiries Into Terror, Calamity, And Imagination. Chicago: University of Chicago Press, 2005.

Clarke, Richard. *Against All Enemies: Inside American's War on Terror.* New York: Free Press, 2004.

Clinton, Bill. *My Life.* New York: Vintage, 2004.

Clymer, Kenton. "U.S. Homeland Defense in the 1950s: The Origins of the Ground Observer Corps." *Journal of Military History* 75 (2011): 835–859.

Cobb, Roger and David Primo. *The Plane Truth: Airline Crashes, the Media, and Transportation Policy.* Washington DC: Brookings Institution, 2003.

Coffman, Edward M. *The Regulars, The American Army, 1898–1941.* Cambridge, MA: Belknap Press, 2004.

Cohen, Wilbur and Evelyn Boyer. "Federal Civil Defense Act of 1950: Summary and Legislative History." *Social Security Bulletin* (1951): 14.

Collier, Stephen and Andrew Lakoff. "Distributed Preparedness: The Spatial Logic of Domestic Security in the United States." *Environment and Planning D: Society and Space* 26 (2008): 7–28.

Comfort, Louise, Arjen Boin, and Chris Demchak. *Designing Resilience for Communities at Risk: Sociotechnical Approaches.* Pittsburgh, PA: University of Pittsburgh Press, 2010.

"Comprehensive Policies and Procedures Are Needed to Ensure Appropriate Use of and Accountability for International Assistance." Washington, DC: Government Accountability Office, 2006.

Conley, Jerry. "The Role of the U.S. Military in Domestic Emergency Management: The Past, Present and Future." Institute for Crisis, Disaster, and Risk Management Newsletter, George Washington University, 2003.

Conn, Stetson, Rose Engelman, and Byron Fairchild. *Guarding the United States and its Outposts.* Washington, DC: Center of Military History: the United States Army, 2000.

Cook, Brian R. *Bureaucracy and Self-Government: Reconsidering the Role of Public Administration in American Politics.* Baltimore: Johns Hopkins University Press, 1996.

Cooling, Franklin. "US Army Support of Civil Defense: The Formative Years," *Military Affairs* 35 (1971): 7–11.

Cooper, Christopher and Robert Block. *Disaster: Hurricane Katrina and the Failure of Homeland Security.* New York: Times Books, 2006.

Cortina, Lilia M. "Unseen Injustice: Incivility as Modern Discrimination in Organizations." *Academy of Management Review* 33 (2008): 55–75.

Corwin, Edward. "The Spending Power of Congress – Apropos the Maternity Act." *Harvard Law Review* 36 (1922–1923): 548–582.

Costello, Augustine E. *Our Firemen: A History of the New York Fire Departments.* New York: Costello, 1887.

Croley, Stephen P. *Regulation and Public Interests: The Possibility of Good Regulatory Government.* Princeton, NJ: Princeton University Press, 2008.

Cuéllar, Mariano-Florentino. "'Securing' the Nation: Law, Politics, and Organization at the Federal Security Agency, 1939–1953." *University of Chicago Law Review* 76 (2009): 587–717.

    Governing Security, The Hidden Origins of American Security Agencies. Stanford, CA: Stanford University Press, 2013.

Currie, David P. "The Constitution in the Supreme Court: The New Deal, 1931–1940." *University of Chicago Law Review* 54 (1987): 504–555.

Dacy, Douglas and Howard Kunreuther. *The Economics of Natural Disasters: Implications for Federal Policy.* New York: The Free Press, 1969.

Dahl, Eric. *Preventing Terrorist Attacks: Intelligence Warning and Policy Response.* Ph.D. diss., Tufts University, Somerville, MA, 2008.

Dahl, Robert and Charles Lindblom. *Politics, Economics, and Welfare.* New York: Harper & Row, 1958.

Daniel, Pete. *Deep'n As It Come: The 1927 Mississippi River Flood.* New York: Oxford University Press, 1977.

Dauber, Michele Landis. "Fate, Responsibility, and Natural Disaster Relief: Narrating the American Welfare State." *Law and Society Review* 33 (1999): 257–318.

    "Helping Ourselves: Disaster Relief and the Origins of the American Welfare State." PhD diss., Northwestern University, 2003.

    "Let Me Next Time Be 'Tried by Fire': Disaster Relief and the Origins of the American Welfare State, 1789–1874." *Northwestern Law Review* 92 (1998): 967–103.

    "The Real Third Rail of American Politics." In *Catastrophe: Law, Politics, and the Humanitarian Impulse.* Austin Sarat and Javier Lezau, eds. Amherst, MA: University of Massachusetts Press, 2009: 60–82.

    "The Sympathetic State." *Law and History Review* 23 (2005): 387–442.

    "The War of 1812, September 11, and the Politics of Compensation." *DePaul Law Review* 53 (2003): 289–354.

Davies, Gareth. *See Government Grow: Education Politics from Johnson to Reagan* Lawrence: University of Kansas Press, 2007.

DeAngelis, R. and E. Nelson. "Hurricane Camille-August 5–22." *Climatological Data, National Summary* 20 (1969): 5–22.

The Debate on the Constitution: Federalist and Antifederalist Speeches, Articles, and Letters During the Struggle over Ratification Part Two: January to August 1788, Bernard Baylin, ed. New York: Library of America, 1993.

Derthick, Martha. "Why Federalism Didn't Fail." *Public Administration Review* 67 (2007): 36–47.

Devine, Edward. *The Principles of Relief.* New York and London: Macmillan, 1904.

Diamond, Martin. "The Federalist's View of Federalism." In *Essays in Federalism,* George C. Benson, ed. Claremont, CA: Institute for Studies in Federalism, 1962: 21–64.

Die Katastrophe von San Francisco: Mit einer kurzen illustrierten Vorgeschichte der Stadt. St. Louis, MO: Louis Lange, 1906.

DiMaggio, Paul and Walter Powell. "The Iron Cage Revisited: Institutional Isomorphism and Collective Rationality in Organizational Fields." *American Sociological Review* 48 (1983): 147–160.

Dory, Amanda. *Civil Security: Americans and the Challenge of Homeland Security.* Washington, DC: CSIS Press, 2003.

Douglas, Mary. *How Institutions Think.* Syracuse, NY: Syracuse University Press, 1986.

Drabek, Thomas. "Community Processes: Coordination." In *Handbook of Disaster Research,* Havídan Rodríguez, Enrico L. Quarantelli, and Russell Dynes, eds. New York: Springer, 2007: 217–233.

"The Evolution of Emergency Management." In *Emergency Management: Principles and Practice for Local Government.* Thomas E. Drabek and Gerard J. Hoetmer, eds. Washington, DC: International City Management Association, 1991: 3–29.

Dubnick, Mel. "The Case for Administrative Evil: A Critique." *Public Administration Review* 60 (2000): 464–474.

Dubnick, Mel, Jonathan Justice, and Dominic Bearfield. "Imagining and Managing Organizational Evil". In *The Foundations of Organizational Evil.* Edited by Carole L. Jurkiewicz. Armonk, NY: M.E. Sharpe, 2012.

Dull, Matthew and Patrick S. Roberts "Continuity, Competence, and the Succession of Senate-Confirmed Agency Appointees, 1989–2009." *Presidential Studies Quarterly* 39 (2009): 432–453.

Dulles, Foster Rhea. *The American Red Cross.* New York: Harper and Brothers, 1950. http://www.redcross.org/museum/history/sanfranquake.asp

Dynes, Russell. "Community Emergency Planning: False Assumptions and Inappropriate Analogies." *International Journal of Mass Emergencies and Disasters* 12 (1994): 141–158.

Dyson, Michael Eric. *Come Hell or High Water: Hurricane Katrina and the Color of Disaster.* New York: Basic Books, 2006.

Eckstein, Harry. "Case Study and Theory in Political Science." In *The Handbook of Political Science, Vol. 7: Strategies of Inquiry,* edited by Fred I. Greenstein and Nelson W. Polsby. Reading, PA: Addison-Wesley, 1975, pp. 79–137.

Eden, Lynn. *Whole World on Fire, Organizations, Knowledge, and Nuclear Weapons Devastation.* Ithaca, NY: Cornell University Press, 2004.

Edwards, George. *On Deaf Ears: The Limits of the Bully Pulpit.* New Haven, CT: Yale University Press, 2003.

Egan, Timothy. *The Big Burn: Teddy Roosevelt and the Fire that Saved America.* New York: Houghton Mifflin Harcourt, 2009.

Eiler, Keith. *Mobilizing America: Robert P. Patterson and the War Effort, 1940–1945.* Ithaca, NY: Cornell University Press, 1997.

Ellig, Jerry. *Learning from the Leaders: Results-Based Management at the Federal Emergency Management Agency.* Arlington, VA: The Mercatus Center, 2000.

Ely, John. *Democracy's Distrust, A Theory of Judicial Review.* Cambridge, MA: Harvard University Press, 1980.

Emmerich, Herbert. *Federal Organization and Administrative Management.* Tuscaloosa: University of Alabama Press, 1971.

Epstein, David and Sharyn O'Halloran. *Delegating Powers.* Cambridge: Cambridge University Press, 1999.

Eskridge, William and John Ferejohn. *A Republic of Statutes: The New American Constitution*. New Haven, CT: Yale University Press, 2010.

Fairman, Charles. "The President as Commander-in-Chief." *The Journal of Politics* 11 (1949): 145–170.

"Government Under Law in Time of Crisis." In *Government Under Law*. Arthur E. Sutherland, Ed. Cambridge, MA: Harvard University Press, 1956.

Farmer, David. *The Language of Public Administration*. Tuscaloosa: University of Alabama Press, 1995.

Feingold, Eugene. "Nuclear Attack and Civil Defense: A Review." *Conflict Resolution* 6 (1962): 282–289.

Feldman, Jay. *When the Mississippi Ran Backwards: Empire, Intrigue, Murder, and the New Madrid Earthquakes*. New York: Free Press, 2005.

Feldman, Martha. *Order without Design: Information Production and Policymaking*. Stanford, CA: Stanford University Press, 1989.

Feldman, Martha and Anne Khademian. "The Role of the Public Manager in Inclusion: Creating Communities of Participation." *Governance* 20 (2007): 305–324.

Fesler, James. "The Brownlow Committee Fifty Years Later." *Public Administration Review* 47 (1987): 291–296.

Fiorina, Morris. *Congress: Keystone of the Washington Establishment*. New Haven, CT: Yale University Press, 1989.

Fleming, A.S. "The Impact of Disasters on Readiness for War." *American Academy of Political and Social Science* 309 (1957): 65–70.

Fleming, Thomas. *The New Dealers' War: FDR and the War Within World War II*. New York: Basic Books, 2001.

Flynn, Stephen E. and Daniel B. Prieto. "Neglected Defense: Mobilizing the Private Sector to Support Homeland Security." Council on Foreign Relations Special Report, no. 14, New York, 2006.

Foster, Gaines. *The Demands of Humanity: Army Medical Disaster Relief*. Washington, DC: Center of Military History, United States Army, 1983.

Fradkin, Philip. *The Great Earthquake and Firestorms of 1906*. Berkeley: University of California Press, 2005.

Friedberg, Aaron. *In the Shadow of the Garrison State: America's Anti-Statism and Its Cold War Grand Strategy*. Princeton, NJ: Princeton University Press, 2000.

American Antistatism and the Founding of the Cold War State. Princeton, NJ: Princeton University Press, 2002.

Galvin, Daniel and Colleen Shogan. "Executive Authority and the Bureaucracy: The Analytical Shortcomings of the Modern Presidency Construct." *Polity* 36 (2004): 477–504.

Garrett, Thomas and Russell Sobel. "The Political Economy of FEMA Disaster Payments." *Economic Inquiry* 41 (2003): 496–509.

Garrison, Dee. *Bracing for Armageddon: Why Civil Defense Never Worked*. New York: Oxford University Press, 2006.

Garvin, David, Amy Edmondson, and Francesca Gino. "Is Yours a Learning Organization?" *Harvard Business Review* 86 (2008): 109–116.

Learning in Action. Boston: Harvard Business School Press, 2000.

Gellman, Benet. "Planning for a National Nuclear Emergency: The Organization of Government and Federal-State Relations." *Virginia Law Review* 52 (1966): 435–462.

General Accountability Office. "Budget Issues: FEMA Needs Adequate Data, Plans, and Systems to Effectively Manage Resources for Day-to-Day Operations." GAO-07-139, Washington, DC: Government Accountability Office, 2007.

Gerber, Brian. "Disaster Management in the United States: Examining Key Political and Policy Challenges." *Policy Studies Journal* 35 (2006): 236–237.

Gerring, John. "Causal Mechanisms: Yes, But..." *Comparative Political Studies* 43 (2010): 1499–1526.

Gillman, Howard. "Disaster Relief, 'Do Anything' Spending Powers, and the New Deal." *Law and History Review* 23 (2005): 443–450.

Gilman, Stuart. "Black Rebellion in the 1960s: Between Non-violence and Black Power." *Ethnicity* 8 (1981): 452–475.

Glaeser, Edward. "Urban Colossus: Why Is New York America's Largest City?" *FRBNY Economic Policy Review* (2005): 7–24.

Goertz, Gary and James Mahoney. *Case Selection and Hypothesis Testing – A Tale of Two Cultures: Contrasting the Qualitative and Quantitative Research Paradigms.* Princeton, NJ: Princeton University Press, 2012.

Goldberg, Chad. *Citizens and Paupers: Relief, Rights, and Race, from the Freedmen's Bureau to Workfare.* Chicago: University of Chicago Press, 2007.

Golden, Marissa. *What Motivates Bureaucrats? Politics and Administration During the Reagan Years.* New York: Columbia University Press, 2000.

Goodwin, Doris. *No Ordinary Time.* New York: Simon & Schuster 1995.

Gore, Albert. *National Performance Review: Federal Emergency Management Agency.* Washington, DC: Office of the Vice President, 1993. http://govinfo.library.unt.edu/npr/library/reports/fema.html.

Gotham, Kevin. *Authentic New Orleans: Tourism, Culture, and Race in the Big Easy.* New York: New York University Press, 2007.

"Disaster, Inc.: Privatization and Post-Katrina Rebuilding in New Orleans." *Perspectives on Politics* 10 (2012): 633–646.

Gould, Lewis. *The Presidency of William McKinley.* Lawrence: University of Kansas Press, 1981.

Gould, Lewis and Richard Smith. *The Modern American Presidency.* Lawrence: University of Kansas Press, 2004.

Government Accountability Office. Information about FEMA's Post-9/11 Assistance to the New York City Area. Washington, DC, 2003.

Grant, Rebecca. "The Long Arm of the US Strategic Bombing Survey." *Air Force Magazine* (2008): 64–67.

Gray, Jane and Elizabeth Wilson. *Looting in Disaster: A General Profile of Victimization.* Disaster Research Center, Ohio State University, 1984. http://dspace.udel.edu:8080/dspace/bitstream/19716/1295/1/WP71.pdf

Greenstein, Fred I. *The Presidential Difference: Leadership Style from FDR to Clinton.* New York: The Free Press, 2000.

Grossman, Andrew. *Neither Dead nor Red: Civilian Defense and American Political Development during the Early Cold War.* New York: Routledge, 2001.

Guthman, L. *Warplane Spotter's Manual.* Washington, DC, 1943.

Hacking, Ian. *The Social Construction of What?* Cambridge, MA: Harvard University Press, 2000.

A Handbook for Fire Watchers. Washington, DC: United States Office of Civil Defense, 1941.

Harrald, John. "Achieving Agility in Disaster Management." *International Journal of Information Systems for Crisis Response and Management* 1 (2009): 1–11.

Healy, Andrew and Neil Malhotra. "Myopic Voters and Natural Disaster Policy." *American Political Science Review* 103 (2009): 387–406.

Hearn, Philip. *Hurricane Camille: Monster Storm of the Gulf Coast.* Oxford: University of Mississippi Press, 2004.

Hedström, Peter and Petri Ylikoski. "Causal Mechanisms in the Social Sciences." *Annual Review of Sociology* 36 (2010): 49–67.

Heerdon, Ivor and Mike Bryan. *The Storm: What Went Wrong and Why During Hurricane Katrina.* New York: Viking, 2006.

Helco, Hugh. *Government of Strangers.* Washington, DC: Brookings Institution, 1977.

Heymann, Philip B. *The Politics of Public Management.* New Haven, CT: Yale University Press, 1987.

Higgs, Robert. *Crisis and Leviathan: Critical Episodes in the Growth of American Government.* New York: Oxford University Press, 1987.

Historical Development of Organized Efforts to Plan for and Respond to Disasters. Newark, DE: Disaster Research Center, University of Delaware, 2000.

Hobsbwam, Eric and Terence Ranger. *The Invention of Tradition.* New York: Cambridge University Press, 1992.

Hofstadter, Richard. "Herbert Hoover and the Crisis of American Individualism," in *The American Political Tradition and the Men Who Made It"* New York: Vintage, 1948.

Hollings, Ernest. "Andrew's Aftermath." *Congressional Record*, 102nd Cong, 2nd. Sess., September 9, 1992.

Holmes, William. "William Alexander Percy and the Bourbon Era in Mississippi Politics." *Mississippi Quarterly* 26 (1972–1973): 71–87.

Hood, Christopher. "What Happens When Transparency Meets Blame-Avoidance?" *Public Management Review* 9 (2007): 191–210.

The Blame Game: Spin, Bureaucracy, and Self-Preservation in Government. Princeton, NJ: Princeton University Press, 2010.

Hubback, Judith. *The Changing Person and Unchanging Archetype.* London: Routledge, 1992.

Hull, Isabel. *Absolute Destruction: Military Culture and the Practices of War in Imperial Germany.* Ithaca, NY: Cornell University Press, 2005.

John, Richard. *Spreading the News: The American Postal System from Franklin to Morse.* Cambridge, MA: Harvard University Press, 1998.

Johnson, David. *The Lavender Scare: The Cold War Persecution of Gays and Lesbians in the Federal Government.* Chicago: University of Chicago Press, 2004.

Jones, Bryan. *Politics and the Architecture of Choice: Bounded Rationality and Governance.* Chicago: University of Chicago Press, 2001.

Jones, Bryan and Walter Williams. *The Politics of Bad Ideas.* New York: Pearson Longman, 2008.

Jordan, Nehemiah. *US Civil Defense Before 1950: The Roots of Public Law 920*, Study S-212 (1966): 56–57.

Kagan, Robert and John Scholz. "The Criminology of the Corporation and Regulatory Enforcement Strategies." In *Enforcing Regulation*, Keith Hawkins and John M. Thomas, eds. Boston: Kluwer-Nijhoff, 1984: 67–96.

Kahneman, Daniel. *Thinking, Fast and Slow.* New York: Farrar, Strauss, and Giroux, 2011.

Kapucu, Naim. "Interagency Communication Networks during Emergencies: Boundary Spanners in Multi-agency Coordination." *The American Review of Public Administration* 36 (2006): 207–225.

Karl, Barry. *Executive Reorganization and Reform in the New Deal*. Cambridge, MA: Harvard University Press, 1963.

Katari, Prema. *Housing Helps*. Washington, DC: Urban Land Institute, 2005.

Katznelson, Ira and Martin Shefter. *Shaped by War and Trade: International Influences on American Political Development*. Princeton, NJ: Princeton University Press, 2002.

Keller, Morton. *Affairs of State: Public Life in Late Nineteenth Century America*. Cambridge, MA: Harvard University Press, 1977.

   America's Three Regimes: A New Political History. New York: Oxford University Press, 2007.

Kennedy, John. *The Great Earthquake and Fire, San Francisco*. New York: Morrow, 1963.

Kernell, Samuel. "Rural Free Delivery as a Critical Test of Alternative Models of American Political Development." *Studies in American Political Development* 15 (2001):103–112.

Kerr, Thomas. *Civil Defense in the US, Band-Aid for a Holocaust?* Boulder, CO: Westview Press, 1983.

Khademian, Anne. *Checking on Banks: Autonomy and Accountability in Three Federal Agencies*. Washington, DC: Brookings Institution, 1996.

   "Hurricane Katrina and the Failure of Homeland Security." In *Judging Bush*, Robert Maranto, ed. Stanford, CA: Stanford University Press, 2009: 195–214.

Kiewiet, Roderick and Matthew McCubbins. *The Logic of Delegation*. Chicago: University of Chicago Press, 1991.

Kinder, Donald and David Sears. "Prejudice and Politics: Symbolic Racism Versus Racial Threats to the Good Life." *Journal of Personality and Social Psychology* 40 (1981): 414–431.

   "The Continuing American Dilemma: White Resistance to Racial Change 40 Years after Myrdal." *Journal of Social Issues* 42 (1986): 151–171.

Kingdon, John. *America the Unusual*. New York: Worth Publishers, 1999.

Kingsley, J. Donald. *Representative Bureaucracy: An Interpretation of the British Civil Services*. Yellow Springs, OH: Antioch Press, 1944.

Klein, Naomi. *The Shock Doctrine: The Rise of Disaster Capitalism*. New York: Picador, 2007.

Klinenberg, Eric. "Are You Ready for the Next Disaster?" *New York Times Magazine*, July 6, 2008.

Knowles, Scott. "Defending Philadelphia: A Historical Case Study of Civil Defense in the Early Cold War." *Public Works Management & Policy* 11 (2007): 1–16.

   The Disaster Experts: Mastering Risk in Modern America. Philadelphia: University of Pennsylvania Press, 2011.

Kosar, Kevin. *Disaster Response and the Appointment of a Recovery Czar: The Executive Branch's Response to the Flood of 1927*. Washington, DC: Congressional Research Service, 2005.

Krebs, Ronald R. and Patrick T. Jackson. "Twisting Tongues and Twisting Arms. The Power of Political Rhetoric." *European Journal of International Relations* 13 (2007): 35–66.

Kuklick, Bruce. *Blind Oracles: Intellectuals and War from Kennan to Kissinger*. Princeton, NJ: Princeton University Press, 2006.

Kunreuther, Howard. *Recovery from Natural Disasters: Insurance or Federal Aid?* Washington, DC: American Enterprise Institute for Public Policy Research, 1973.

Lacan, Jacques. *The Four Fundamental Concepts of Psychoanalysis*, Jacques-Alain Miller, ed. London: Hogarth Press, 1977.

Landis, James. "The Central Problem of Civilian Defense: An Appraisal." *State Government* 23 (1950): 236.

Landy, Marc, "Review Essay of *A Failure of Initiative* and *The Federal Response to Hurricane Katrina Lessons Learned*," *Publius: The Journal of Federalism*, 38.1: (2008): 152–165.

Landy, Marc, Marc Roberts, and Stephen Thomas. *The Environmental Protection Agency: Asking the Wrong Questions*. New York: Oxford University Press, 1990.

Langewische, William. *American Ground: Unbuilding the World Trade Center*. New York: North Point Press, 2002.

Laplance, Jean and Jean Pontalis. *Fantasy and the Origins of Sexuality*. London and New York: Methuen 1986.

Larson, John. *Internal Improvement: National Public Works and the Promise of Popular Government in the Early United States*. Chapel Hill: University of North Carolina Press, 2000.

Larzelere, Alex. *The 1980 Cuban Boatlift*. Washington, DC: National Defense University Press, 1988.

Lash, Joseph. *Eleanor and Franklin*. New York: W.W. Norton & Company, 1971.

Latour, Bruno. *Reassembling the Social: An Introduction to Actor-Network-Theory*. New York: Oxford University Press, 2007.

Law, John and John Hassard. *Actor Network Theory and After*. Hoboken, NJ: Wiley-Blackwell, 1999.

Lehrer, Eli. "Influence, Presidential Authority, and Emergency Management: FEMA's Rise and Fall." In *Ideas From An Emerging Field: Teaching Emergency Management In Higher Education*, Jessica A. Hubbard, ed. Fairfax, VA: PERI Press, 2009: 51–91.

Levinson, Sanford. *Constitutional Faith*. Princeton, NJ: Princeton University Press, 1989.

Lewis, David. "The Politics of Agency Termination: Confronting the Myth of Agency Immortality." *Journal of Politics* 64 (2002): 89–107.

The Politics of Presidential Appointments: Political Control and Bureaucratic Performance. Princeton, NJ: Princeton University Press, 2008.

"Revisiting the Administrative Presidency: Policy, Patronage, and Administrative Competence." *Presidential Studies Quarterly* 39 (2009): 60–73.

Lewis, Gregory. "Lifting the Ban on Gays in the Civil Service: Federal Policy Towards Gay and Lesbian Employees since the Cold War." *Public Administration Review* 57 (1997): 387–395.

Light, Paul. *The True Size of Government*. Washington, DC: Brookings Institution Press, 1999.

Government's Greatest Achievements: From Civil Rights to Homeland Defense. Washington, DC: Brookings Institution Press, 2002.

Lim, Elvin T. *The Anti-Intellectual Presidency*. New York: Oxford University Press, 2008.

The Lovers' Quarrel: The Two Foundlings in American Political Development. New York: Oxford University Press, 2013.

Linthicum, Richard, Trumbull White, and Samuel Fallows. *Complete Story of the San Francisco Horror*. Chicago: n.p., 1906.
http://www.gutenberg.org/files/26380/26380-8.txt
Lohof, Bruce. "Herbert Hoover, Spokesman of Humane Efficiency: The Mississippi Flood of 1927." *American Quarterly* 22 (1970): 690–700.
   Hoover and the Mississippi Valley Flood of 1927. A Case Study of the Political Thought of Herbert Hoover. Syracuse, NY: Syracuse University Press, 1968.
Lukacs, John. *George Kennan: A Study of Character*. New Haven, CT: Yale University Press, 2007.
Luke, Robert. "The Educational Requirements of Civil Defense." *Adult Education* 1 (1951): 33.
Majewski, John. *Modernizing a Slave Economy: The Economic Vision of the Confederate Nation*. Chapel Hill: University of North Carolina Press, 2009.
Mauck, Elwyn. *Civilian Defense in the United States: 1940–1945*. Washington, DC: Office of Civilian Defense, 1946.
May, Peter. *Recovering from Catastrophes: Federal Disaster Relief Policy and Politics*. Westport, CT: Greenwood Press, 1985.
May, Peter and Thomas Birkland. "Earthquake Risk Reduction: An Examination of Local Regulatory Efforts." *Environmental Management* 18 (1994): 923–939.
May, Peter and Walter Williams. *Disaster Policy Implementation. Managing Programs under Shared Governance*. New York: Plenum Press, 1986.
MacManus, Susan A. and Kiki Caruson. "Code Red: Florida City and County Officials Rate Threat Information Sources and the Homeland Security Advisory System." *State & Local Government Review* (2006): 12–22.
McAdam, Doug. *Political Process and the Development of Black Insurgency, 1930–1970*. Chicago: University of Chicago Press, 1999.
McCubbins, Matthew D., Roger Noll, and Barry Weingast. "The Political Origins of the Administrative Procedure Act." *Journal of Law, Economics and Organization* 15 (1999): 180–217.
McCubbins, Matthew D. and Thomas Schwartz. "Congressional Oversight Overlooked: Police Patrols versus Fire Alarms." *American Journal of Political Science* 28 (1984): 165–179.
McCullough, David. *The Johnstown Flood*. Gloucester, MA: Peter Smith Publisher, 1968.
McEnaney, Laura. *Civil Defense Begins at Home: Militarization Meets Everyday Life in the Fifties*. Princeton, NJ: Princeton University Press, 2000.
McGuire, O.R. "The New Deal and the Public Money." *Georgetown Law Journal* 23 (1935): 155–190.
McQuaid, John and Mark Schleifstein. *Path of Destruction: The Devastation of New Orleans and the Coming Age of Superstorms*. New York: Little, Brown, 2006.
McPherson, James. *Lincoln and the Second American Revolution*. New York: Oxford University Press, 1991.
Meier, Kenneth. *Politics and the Bureaucracy*. 3rd ed. Pacific Grove, CA: Brooks/Cole, 1993.
Meier, Kenneth, Laurence O'Toole, and Alisa Hicklin. "I've Seen Fire and I've Seen Rain: Public Management and Performance after a Natural Disaster." *Administration & Society* 41 (2010): 979–1003.
Meier, Kenneth, Robert Wrinkle, and J.L. Polinard "Politics, Bureaucracy and Farm Credit." *Public Administration Review* 59 (1995): 293–302.

Mendonça, David. "Decision Support for Improvisation in Response to Extreme Events." *Decision Support Systems* 43 (3): 952–967.

Mendonça, David and William Wallace. "Studying Organizationally-Situated Improvisation in Response to Extreme Events." *International Journal of Mass Emergencies and Disasters* 22 (2004): 5–29.

Menzel, Donald. "The Katrina Aftermath: A Failure of Federalism or Leadership?" *Public Administration Review* 66 (2006): 808–812.

Meredith, Clyde. "Civil Defense and the Schools." *School Life* 34 (1952): 99–100.

Meyer, John and Brian Rowan. "Institutionalized Organizations: Formal Structure as Myth and Ceremony." *American Journal of Sociology* 83 (1977): 340–363.

Meyer, Robert. "Why We Under-Prepare for Hazards". In *On Risk and Disaster: Lessons from Hurricane Katrina.* edited by Ronald J. Daniels, Donald F. Kettl, and Howard Kunreuther. Philadelphia: University of Pennsylvania Press, 2006.

Meyers, Peter. *Civic War and the Corruption of the Citizen.* Chicago: University of Chicago Press, 2008.

Miller, Geoffrey P. "Public Choice at the Dawn of the Special Interest State: The Story of Butter and Margarine. *California Law Review* 77 (January 1989): 83–131

Miller, Robert. "The War That Never Came: Civilian Defense, Mobilization, and Morale during World War II," Ph.D. diss., University of Cincinnati, 1991.

Mlakar, Paul, Donald Dusenberry, James Harris, Gerald Haynes, Long Phan, and Mete Sozen. "Findings and Recommendations from the Pentagon Crash." *American Society of Civil Engineers, Conference Proceedings* 241 (2003): 43–45.

Moe, Terry. "The New Economics of Organization." *American Journal of Political Science* 28 (1984): 739–777.

"Interests, Institutions, and Positive Theory: The Politics of the NLRB." *Studies in American Political Development* 2 (1987): 236–299.

Presidents, Institutions, and Theory. Pittsburgh, PA: University of Pittsburgh Press, 1993.

"The Politicized Presidency." In *The New Direction in American Politics*, John E.Chubb and Paul E. Peterson, eds. Washington DC: Brookings, 1995.

"The Presidency and the Bureaucracy: The Presidential Advantage." In *The Presidency and the Political System*, Michael Nelson, ed. Washington, DC: CQ Press, 2003: 425–439.

Monteyne, David. *Fallout Shelter: Designing for Civil Defense in the Cold War.* Minneapolis: University of Minnesota Press, 2011.

Morison, Eting E., ed. *The Letters of Theodore Roosevelt*, vol. 5, *The Big Stick, 1905–1907.* Cambridge, MA: Harvard University Press, 1952.

Morril, Calvin, Ellen Snyderman, and Edwin Dawson. "It's Not What You Do, But Who You Are." *Sociological Forum* 12 (2004): 519–543.

Morris, Charles. *The San Francisco Calamity.* Champaign: University of Illinois Press, 2002.

Moss, David. "Courting Disaster? The Transformation of Federal Disaster Policy since 1803." In *The Financing of Catastrophe Risk*, Kenneth A. Froot, ed. Chicago: University of Chicago Press, 1999: 307–315.

Moynihan, Donald P. "Extra-Network Organizational Reputation and Blame Avoidance in Networks: The Hurricane Katrina Example." *Governance* 25 (2012): 567–588.

"Combining Structural Forms in the Search for Policy Tools: Incident Command Systems in U.S. Crisis Management." *Governance* 21 (2008): 205–229.

"Learning under Uncertainty: Networks in Crisis Management." *Public Administration Review* 68 (2008): 350–361.

"Public Management Policy Change in the United States 1993–2001." *International Public Management Journal* 6 (2003): 371–394.

"The Use of Networks in Emergency Management." APSA, Philadelphia, PA, 2006.

Muscantine, Doris. *Old San Francisco: From Early Days to the Earthquake.* New York: Putnam and Sons, 1975.

Naftali, Timothy. *Blind Spot: The Secret History of American Counterterrorism.* New York: Basic Books, 2005.

National Academy of Public Administration. *Coping with Catastrophe: Building an Emergency Management System to Meet People's Needs in Natural and Manmade Disasters.* Washington, DC: NAPA, 1993.

National Research Council. *Facing Hazards and Disasters: Understanding Human Dimensions.* Washington, DC: National Academies Press, 2006.

National Security Resources Board. *Survival under Atomic Attack.* Washington, DC: NSRB 1950.

Nichols, David. *The Myth of the Modern Presidency.* State College: Pennsylvania State University Press, 1994.

Niskanen, William. *Bureaucracy and Representative Government.* Chicago: Aldine Atherton, 1971.

Novak, William J. *People's Welfare: Law and Regulation in Nineteenth-Century America.* Chapel Hill: University of North Carolina Press, 1996.

Oakes, Guy. *The Imaginary War: Civil Defense and American Cold War Culture.* New York: Oxford University Press, 1995.

Ordóñez, Lisa, Maurice Schweitzer, Adam Galinsky, and Max Bazerman. "Goals Gone Wild: How Goals Systematically Harm Individuals and Organizations." *Academy of Management Perspectives* 23 (2009): 6–16.

Oren, Ido. *Our Enemies and US: America's Rivalries and the Making of Political Science.* Ithaca, NY: Cornell University Press, 2003.

Orren, Karen and Stephen Skowronek. *The Search for American Political Development.* New York: Cambridge University Press, 2004.

Penick, James. *The New Madrid Earthquakes.* Columbia: University of Missouri Press, 1982.

Percy, William A. *Lanterns on the Levee: Recollections of a Planter's Son.* Baton Rouge: Louisiana State University Press, 1942.

Perrow, Charles. "The Analysis of Goals in Complex Organizations." *American Sociological Review* 26 (1961): 854–866.

Normal Accidents, Living with High Risk Technologies. Princeton, NJ: Princeton University Press, 1999.

Perry, James and Hal Rainey. "The Public-Private Distinction in Organization Theory: A Critique and Research Strategy." *Academy of Management Review* 13 (1988): 182–201.

Peterson, Paul. *City Limits.* Chicago: University of Chicago Press, 1981.

Pierson, Paul. "When Effect Becomes Cause: Policy Feedback and Political Change." *World Politics* 45 (1993): 595–628.

Platt, Rutherford. *Disasters and Democracy: The Politics of Extreme Natural Events.* Washington, DC: Island Press, 1999.

Popkin, Roy. "The History and Politics of Disaster Management in the United States." In *Nothing to Fear*, edited by A. Kirby, ed. Tucson: University of Arizona Press, 1990: 101–129.

Porter, Bruce. "Parkinson's Law Revisited: War and the Growth of Government." *The Public Interest*, 60 (1980): 50–68.

Powell, Christine A. "Review of Disaster Deferred: How New Science Is Changing Our View of Earthquake Hazards in the Midwest." *Seismological Research Letters* 82 (2011): 238–239.

Prentiss, Augustin. *Civil Air Defense*. New York: McGraw Hill, 1941.

Putnam, Robert. *Bowling Alone: The Collapse and Revival of American Community*. New York: Simon & Schuster, 2000.

Quarantelli, E.L. *Disasters: Theory and Research*. Beverly Hills, CA: Sage Publications, 1978.

"Preliminary Paper #205: Looting and Antisocial Behavior in Disasters." Disaster Research Center, University of Delaware, 1994.

"Sociology of Panic." In *International Encyclopedia of the Social and Behavioral Sciences*, Paul B. Baltes and Neil Smelser, eds. Oxford: Elsevier Science, 2002: 11020–11023.

Radford, Benjamin. *Media Mythmakers*. New York: Prometheus Books, 2003.

Rainey, Hal G. "Goal Ambiguity and the Study of American Bureaucracy," in Robert Durant, ed., *The Oxford Handbook of American Bureaucracy*. Oxford, UK: Oxford University Press, 2010: 231–252.

Relyea, Harold. "Continuity of Government: Current Federal Arrangements and the Future." *CRS Report*. Washington, DC, 2003.

Richeson, Jennifer, A. Baird, H. Gordon, T. Heatherton, C. Wyland, S. Trawalter, and J. Shelton. "An FMRI Examination of the Impact of Interracial Contact on Executive Function." *Nature Neuroscience* 6 (2003): 1323–1328.

Richeson, Jennifer and R. Nussbaum. "The Impact of Multiculturalism versus Color-blindness on Racial Bias." *Journal of Experimental Social Psychology* 40 (2004): 417–423.

Riper, Paul. *History of the United States Civil Service*. White Plains, NY: Row Peterson, 1958.

Roberts, Alasdair. "The Master of Disaster: James Lee Witt and the Federal Emergency Management Agency." Council for Excellence in Government Conference, 1997.

Roberts, Patrick S. "A Capacity for Mitigation as the Next Frontier in Homeland Security." *Political Science Quarterly* 124 (2009): 127–142.

"Dispersed Federalism as a New Regional Governance for Homeland Security." *Publius: The Journal of Federalism* 38 (2008): 416–443.

"FEMA and the Prospects for Reputation-Based Autonomy." *Studies in American Political Development* 20 (2006): 57–87.

"Homeland Security." In *Governing America: Major Policies and Decisions of Federal, State, and Local Government*. William E. Cunion and Paul Quirk, eds. New York: Facts on File Press, 2011: 926–937.

"Shifting Priorities: Congressional Incentives and the Homeland Security Granting Process." *Review of Policy Research* 22 (2005): 437–450.

Rose, Richard. "Comparing Forms of Comparative Analysis." *Political Studies* 39 (1991): 446–462.

Rubin, Claire. "Local Emergency Management: Origins and Evolution." In *Emergency Management: Principles and Practice for Local Government*, William L. Waugh, Jr. and Kathleen Tierney, eds. Washington, DC: International City/County Management Association, 2007, 25–38.

    Emergency Management: The American Experience 1900–2010. Boca Raton, FL: Taylor & Francis, 2012.

Ruch, Charles and Greg Schumann. *Corpus Christi Study Area Hurricane Contingency Planning Guide*. College Station: Texas A&M University Hazard Reduction & Recovery Center, 1997.

Rude, George. *The Crowd in the French Revolution*. New York: Oxford University Press, 1959.

Sabato, Larry. *Feeding Frenzy: Attack Journalism & American Politics*. New York: Free Press, 1993.

Sanders, Elizabeth. *Roots of Reform: Farmers, Workers, and the American State*. Chicago: University of Chicago Press, 1999.

Sarbin, Theodore. *Homosexuality and Personnel Security*. Monterey, CA: Defense Personnel Security Research and Education Center, 1991.

Sawislak, Karen. *Smoldering City, Chicagoans and the Great Fire, 1871–1874*. Chicago: University of Chicago Press, 1995.

Schmid, Alex and Janny Graaf. *Violence as Communication: Insurgent Terrorism and the Western News Media*. Beverly Hills, CA: Sage, 1982.

Schneider, Anne and Helen Ingram. "The Social Construction of Target Populations: Implications for Politics and Policy." *American Political Science Review* 87 (1993): 334–348.

Schneider, Saundra. "Government Response to Disaster: The Conflict between Bureaucratic Procedure and Emergent Norms." *Public Administration Review* 52 (1992): 135–145.

Schweig, Eugene, Joan Gomberg, and James W. Hendley. *The Mississippi Valley – Whole Lotta Shakin' Goin' On*. Washington, DC: U.S. Geological Survey Fact Sheet, 1995.

Scott, James. *Seeing Like a State: How Certain Schemes to Improve the Human Condition Have Failed*. New Haven, CT: Yale University Press, 1998.

Shapiro, Jacob N. and Dara Kay Cohen. "Color-Bind: Lessons from the Failed Homeland Security Advisory System." *International Security* (2007) 32: 121–154

Siebel, Julia. *Soldiers on the Homefront*. Armonk, NY: M.E. Sharpe, 2003.

Signorielli, Nancy and George Gerbner. *Violence and Terror in the Mass Media: An Annotated Bibliography*. New York: Greenwood Press, 1988.

Silberman, Laurence. "On Honor." *Harvard Journal of Law and Public Policy* 32 (2009): 503–512.

Silbey, Joel H. *The American Political Nation*. Stanford, CA: Stanford University Press, 1991.

Simpson, Christopher. *Science of Coercion: Communication Research and Psychological Warfare, 1945–1960*. New York: Oxford University Press, 1994.

Skowronek, Stephen. *Building a New American State, The Expansion of National Administrative Capacities*. New York: Cambridge University Press, 1982.

Snook, Scott. *Friendly Fire: The Accidental Shootdown of U.S. Black Hawks over Northern Iraq*. Princeton, NJ: Princeton University Press, 2002.

Sobel, Russell and Peter Leeson. "Government's Response to Hurricane Katrina: A Public Choice Analysis." *Public Choice* 127 (2006): 55–73.

Solnit, Rebecca. *A Paradise Built in Hell: The Extraordinary Communities That Arise in Disaster*. New York: Viking, 2009.

Stein, Seth. *Disaster Deferred: How New Science Is Changing Our View of Earthquake Hazards in the Midwest*. New York: Columbia University Press, 2010.

Steinberg, Theodore. *Acts of God: The Unnatural History of Natural Disasters in America*. New York: Oxford University Press, 2000.

Stewart III, Charles and Barry Weingast. "Stacking the Senate, Changing the Nation: Republican Rotten Boroughs, Statehood Politics, and American Political Development." *Studies in American Political Development* 6 (1992): 223–271.

Stewart, David and Ray Knox. *The Earthquake America Forgot*. Marble Hill, MO: Gutenberg-Richter Publications, 1995.

Stockton, Paul and Patrick Roberts. "Findings from the Forum on Homeland Security after the Bush Administration: Next Steps in Building Unity of Effort." *Homeland Security Affairs* 4 (2008): 1–11. http://www.hsaj.org/?article=4.2.4.

Story, Joseph. *Commentaries on the Constitution of the United States*. Boston: Hilliard, Gray & Co., 1833.

Strong, LaVerne. "Helping Children Face a Critical Period." *Childhood Education* 28 (1951): 12–16.

Strupp, Christoph. *Dealing with Disaster: The San Francisco Earthquake of 1906*. Berkeley, CA: Institute of European Studies, 2006. http://escholarship.org/uc/item/9gd2v192

Stuart, Douglas. *Creating the National Security State: A History of the Law That Transformed America*. Princeton, NJ: Princeton University Press, 2008.

Sturges, Wesley A. "The Legal Status of the Red Cross." *Michigan Law Review* 56 (1957): 1–32.

Sylves, Richard T. "Coping with Catastrophe." Public Administration Review 54, 1994: 303–307.

Disaster Policy and Politics: Emergency Management and Homeland Security. Washington, DC: CQ Press, 2008.

"Ferment at FEMA: Reforming Emergency Management." *Public Administration Review* (1994): 303–307.

"The Politics and Budgeting of Federal Emergency Management." In *Disaster Management in the U.S. and Canada: The Politics, Policymaking, Administration, and Analysis of Emergency Management*, 2nd ed., Richard T. Sylves and William L. Waugh, eds. Springfield, IL: Charles C. Thomas Publisher, Ltd., 1996: 26–45.

Thomas, Gordon and Max Witts. *The San Francisco Earthquake*. New York: Stein and Day, 1971.

Thompson, Nicholas. *The Hawk and the Dove: Paul Nitze, George Kennan, and the History of the Cold War*. New York: Henry Holt, 2009.

Trivers, Robert. "Rethinking Productivity Speaker Series." Public lecture, University of Regina, Regina, Canada, 2007.

Tulis, Jeffrey. *The Rhetorical Presidency*. Princeton, NJ: Princeton University Press, 1987.

Twain, Mark. *Life on the Mississippi*. New York: Harper and Brothers, 1901.

Twain, Mark and Charles D. Warner. *The Gilded Age*. Stillwell, KS: Digireads.com Publishing, 2007.

Twigg, David K. *The Politics of Disaster: Tracking the Impact of Hurricane Andrew.* Gainesville, FL: University of Florida Press, 2012.

Tyler, Lyon. *Civil Defense: The Impact of the Planning Years, 1945–1950.* PhD diss., Duke University, Durham, NC, 1967.

United States Army Corps of Engineers. *Annual Report of the Chief of Engineers for 1926: Mississippi River Commission.* Washington, DC: Government Printing Office, 1926.

United States Senate Committee of Homeland Security and Government Affairs. *Hurricane Katrina: A Nation Still Unprepared.* Washington, DC: Government Printing Office, 2006.

Valencius, Conevery Bolton. "Accounts of the New Madrid Earthquakes: Personal Narratives across Two Centuries of North American Seismology." *Science in Context* 25 (2012): 17–48, 32–33.

Vaughan, Diane. *The Challenger Launch Decision.* Chicago: University of Chicago Press, 1996.

    "The Challenger Space Shuttle Disaster." In *Corporate and Government Deviance*, 6th ed., M. David Ermann and Richard J. Lundman, eds. New York: Oxford University Press, 2002: 306–333.

    "The Dark Side of Organizations." *Annual Review of Sociology* 25 (1999): 271–305.

Walch, Timothy. "We Could Use Another Man Like Herbert Hoover." *History News Network*, October 17, 2005.

Waldo, Dwight. *The Administrative State: A Study of the Political Theory of American Public Administration.* Toronto: Wiley and Sons, 1988.

Wamsley, Gary and Aaron Schroeder. "Escalating in a Quagmire: The Changing Dynamics of the Emergency Management Policy Subsystem." *Public Administration Review* 56 (1996): 235–246.

Warren, Charles. *Congress as Santa Claus.* Charlottesville, VA: Michie Company, 1932.

Waugh, William. *Living with Hazards, Dealing with Disaster, An Introduction to Emergency Management.* Armonk, NY: M.E. Sharpe, 2000.

    "Terrorism, Homeland Security, and the National Emergency Management Network." *Public Organization Review* 3 (2003): 373–385.

Weart, Spencer. *Nuclear Fear.* Cambridge, MA: Harvard University Press, 1989.

Weaver, Kent. "The Politics of Blame Avoidance." *Journal of Public Policy* 6 (1986): 371–398.

Weber, Max. "Bureaucracy." In *From Max Weber: Essays in Sociology*, H.H. Gerth and C. Wright Mills, eds. and trans. New York: Oxford University Press, 1958 [1946]: 196–244.

Weick, Karl and Kathleen Sutcliffe. *Managing the Unexpected.* New York: Jossey-Bass, 2001.

Weingast, Barry R. and Mark J. Moran. "Bureaucratic Discretion of Congressional Control?: Regulatory Policymaking by the Federal Trade Commission." *Journal of Political Economy* 91 (1983): 765–800.

Welter, Rush. *Popular Education and Democratic Thought in America.* New York: Columbia University Press, 1962.

Wessells, Anne T. "Reassembling the Social: An Introduction to Actor-Network-Theory by Bruno Latour." *International Public Management Journal* 10 (2007): 351–356.

Westen, Drew. "The Scientific Status of Unconscious Processes: Is Freud Really Dead?" *Journal of the American Psychoanalytic Association* 49 (1999): 1–30.

White House. *The Federal Response to Hurricane Katrina: Lessons Learned.* Washington, DC: Government Printing Office, 2006.

Whitford, Andrew. "The Pursuit of Political Control by Multiple Principals." *Journal of Politics* 67 (2005): 39–49.

Wildavsky, Aaron. "Practical Consequences of the Theoretical Study of Defense Policy." *Public Administration Review* 25 (1965): 90–103.

The Beleaguered Presidency. New Brunswick, NJ: Transaction Publishers, 1991.

Wilson, James Q. *The Revolt Against the Masses, and Other Essays on Politics and Public Policy.* New York: Basic Books, 1971.

Bureaucracy: What Government Agencies Do and Why They Do It. New York: Basic Books, 1989.

Winchester, Simon. *A Crack in the Edge of the World. America and the Great California Earthquake of 1906.* New York: Harper Collins, 2006.

Witt, James and James Morgan. *Stronger in the Broken Places: Nine Lessons for Turning Crisis Into Triumph.* New York: Henry Holt, 2002.

Woodruff, Nan E. *As Rare as Rain: Federal Relief in the Great Southern Drought of 1930–31.* Urbana: University of Illinois Press, 1985.

Yemaiel, Arthur and Jennifer Wilson. "Three Essential Strategies for Emergency Management Professionalization in the U.S." *International Journal of Mass Emergencies and Disasters* 23 (2005): 77–84.

Yoshpe, Harry. *Our Missing Shield: The US Civil Defense Program in Historical Perspective.* Washington, DC: FEMA, 1981.

Zegart, Amy. *Flawed by Design: The Evolution of the CIA, JCS, and NSC.* Stanford, CA: Stanford University Press, 1999.

Zucker, Lynn. "The Role of Institutionalization in Cultural Persistence." *Annual American Sociological Review* 42 (1977): 726–743.

Index

abuses in relief camps, 3
Aceh tsunami, 4–5
actor network theory, 11, 145
Ad Council, 55
administrative evil, 147–150
African Americans
    discriminatory contingency plans, 150
    fear of racial uprising, 82, 83, 147, 151,
        152–154
    latent racism toward, 169, 171
    Mississippi River Flood, 2–3
Agamben, Giorgio, 168–169
agenda-setting, 10
Agnew, Spiro, 74
Agriculture, Department of, 74
Air Traffic Control system, 187
al Qaeda, 117
Alaska earthquake (1964), 73
Alexandria, VA fire (1827), 24, 25
all hazards policy
    about, 11, 94
    and counterterrorism activities, 114–115
    failure of, 128, 176–177
    FEMA and, 80, 106, 113–117, 176–177,
        181–182
    public perception of, 126
all phases concept, 94
Allbaugh, Joseph (Joe), 119–120, 121,
    122–123
altruism, 166–167
American Legion, 45–46
American political development, 14, 16–17,
    24–27, 189
Andrew, Hurricane, 87, 88–89, 95, 105

antiwar protests, 151
Arendt, Hannah, 148
Arkansas National Guard, 49
army, 33–34, 42–47, 74, 134. See also military
Army Corps of Engineers
    and FEMA, 133
    Flood Control Act, 44
    and levees, 5, 138, 142–143
    Mississippi River Gulf Outlet, 143
    Mississippi River Valley, 1
    and vulnerability of New Orleans, 139–140
Ash, Timothy Garton, 164
associational life, 110
Astrodome (Houston), 164
autonomy. See bureaucracy: bureaucratic
    autonomy

Baker, Henry, 2
Balogh, Brian, 28, 31
banality of evil, 148
Barbour, Haley, 136
Barry, John, 2
Benelli, David, 165
Berman, Howard, 190
Betsy, Hurricane, 75
bin Laden, Osama, 117–118
Blanco, Kathleen, 132, 135, 136
Blazich, Frank, 66
Block, Robert, 124
Blum, H. Steven, 166
Bonner, John W., 54
Borah, William, 36
Bovard, James, 40
Bowsher, Charles A., 90

Brinkerhoff, John, 83, 152, 153
Broderick, Matthew, 137–138
Brown, Michael
  appointment of, 122, 123
  Bush on, 127
  and FEMA failures, 135, 174
  and Hurricane Katrina evacuation, 6
  request for military intervention, 136–137
Brown, Wendy, 88
Brownlow Committee, 92
Brzezinski, Zbigniew, 151
building codes, 141–142
Bull Board, 47–49
Bull, Harold, 48
Bureau of Public Roads, 44
Bureau of Refugees, Freedmen, and
    Abandoned Lands, 29, 40
bureaucracy
  and administrative evil, 147–150
  bureaucratic autonomy, 12–13, 38,
    106–109, 112
  competition as safeguard, 173
  and disaster management, 10, 138–139, 180
  discriminatory actions of, 182–184
  and emergency management professionals,
    92–96
  failures of, 134–135, 137–140, 175–177,
    187–188
  of FEMA, 80, 86
  and Stafford Act, 86
Burnell, Charles, 164
buses, 135
Bush, George H.W., 88, 111, 123
Bush, George W.
  disaster declarations, 111
  Global War on Terror, 117–118
  on government responsibilities, 187
  Office of National Preparedness, 120–121
  political appointments, 123
  on post-Katrina reforms, 143
  praise for Brown, 127
  sealing of Reagan's records, 154
Bush, Jeb, 143–144

California Specialized Training Institute, 82,
    151
call centers, 102
Cambreleng, Churchill C., 25
Camille, Hurricane, 74, 75, 95
Cannon, Joseph, 36
Card, Andrew, 88
Carlson, Tucker, 163
Carpenter, Daniel, 109

Carter, Jimmy, 73, 78, 81, 150, 181
centralization of civil defense, 44–46
Chaney, Mayris, 45
Chardy, Alfonso, 83
Charleston, SC, 144
Cheney, Richard (Dick), 155
Chertoff, Michael, 137
Chess, Caron, 162
Chicago fire (1871), 166
CIA, 118
Citizen Corps, 124
citizens groups, 12
Civil Defense Act (1950), 55–56, 76, 100
Civil Defense Corps, 45
Civil Defense Preparedness Agency, 75, 76
civil defense programs
  about, 41–42
  appropriations for, 51
  Bull Board, 47–49
  Cold War, 46, 47–52, 54–60, 181
  counterterrorism activities, 114–115,
    117–118
  decline of, 73–74
  development of, 42–47
  and disaster management, 66–67
  and disaster policy, 11, 14
  and education policy, 65
  and electoral politics, 67–69
  and elite panic, 161–168
  and FEMA, 82, 90
  films and manuals, 41, 55
  and Giuffrida, 150–155
  goal ambiguity, 60–63
  groups seen as threats, 177–178
  Hopley Report, 49–50
  and infrastructure, 47, 52
  and interstate cooperation, 55–56
  and local authorities, 49, 60–63, 66–69, 163
  and the military, 42–47, 50–51
  pre- and post-attack periods, 49
  preparedness plans, 52–54
  presidents and, 42, 60–63
  primacy of federal government, 58–60
  in Reagan era, 82
  and self-help principle, 52, 68
  and sense of shared risk, 64–65
  social construction of, 42, 63–67
  and states, 49, 60–63, 66–69
  strengths and shortcomings of, 63–67
  universities and foundations, 55
  unrealistic expectations of, 69
  worst case planning, 150–155. *See also* all
    hazards policy. dual use policy

civil disorder, fear of, 82, 83, 147–148, 150, 151, 152–154
Civil Service Commission, 158
Civil War, 27, 29
Civilian Defense Board, 45
Clarke, Lee, 57, 162
Clarke, Richard, 115
Clay, Henry, 25
Cleveland, Grover, 30
Clinton, Bill, 104–105, 110–112, 115, 123
Coast Guard, 6, 133
coastal land development, 140–143
Cold War
    civil defense programs, 46–47, 47–52, 54–60, 181
    disaster policy, 14
    discriminatory contingency plans, 150, 152–155
    homosexuals seen as threats, 155–161
    risk perception, 71
collective fantasy, 148
Collins, Susan, 5
Colored Advisory Commission, 3
Columbine school shooting, 71
Commerce, Department of, 74
communications, failures of, 49–50, 134–135, 138
Compass, Eddie, 163, 165
confirmation bias, 138
Congress
    and compensation for losses, 21
    and delegation of authority, 190
    and disaster policy, 9, 16–17, 24–27, 28–31, 76–78
    and disaster relief, 17, 21, 35–39
    and economic and humanitarian aid, 36
    and FEMA, 87, 97–98
    foreign disaster aid, 22
    and general welfare clause, 37–38
    and 9/11 Commission, 118, 119
    political considerations, 178
    and private relief bills, 21, 25
    public pressure on, 39
    taxing power of, 22–23. *See also* federal government
conservative movement, 85
Constitution, U.S.
    and disaster policy, 10, 11
    on disaster relief, 25–26
    general welfare clause, 22–23, 36, 37–38
    preamble, 22–23
contingency plans. *See* disaster planning
contraflow, 6

Convention Center (New Orleans), 132, 134, 163
Coolidge, Calvin, 1, 3–4, 75
Cooper, Christopher, 124
Corwin, Edward, 37
costs and losses
    Alexandria, VA fire, 24
    annual flood costs, 9
    historical perspective, 51, 75, 76–79, 184, 186
    Hurricane Camille, 74
    Hurricane Katrina, 5, 128, 133, 182
    Mississippi River Flood, 2–3
    New York City Fire, 26–27
    and Stafford Act, 84–87
Cota, Norman D., 56–57
cotton farmers, 36
counterterrorism activities, 114–115, 117–118, 124–125
crisis management. *See* disaster management
Crockett, Davy, 26
Crozier, Michael, 62
cultural bias, 171
cultural scripts, 149–150
Cumming, William, 90–91
Currie, David P., 26
"czar system," 75

dairy industry lobby, 30
damage estimates. *See* costs and losses
Danziger Bridge shootings, 137
Dauber, Michele Landis, 30, 43
deaths
    Great Hurricane, 95
    historical perspective, 185
    Hurricane Andrew, 95
    Hurricane Camille, 74, 95
    Hurricane Katrina, 5, 128, 182
    Mississippi River Flood, 2
    San Francisco earthquake and fire, 32
Defense, Department of, 115, 133, 135–136, 138, 159. *See also* military
democracy, 12, 189–193
Dennis, Hurricane, 182
development, 182
DHS (Department of Homeland Security). *See* Homeland Security, Department of
Diane, Hurricane, 53
disaster management
    bureaucratic failures, 10, 138–139, 180
    civil defense programs, 66–67
    civilian responsibility for, 48

disaster management (*cont.*)
  contradictions within, 7
  coordination failures, 187–188
  and electoral politics, 67–69, 105, 178
  and local authorities, 143–144, 179
  and the military, 143
  post-Katrina, 143–145
  professionals, 92–96, 104
  public perception and expectations of, 126,
    127–128, 144, 154, 175, 184–187, 189
  and security missions, 14–15, 71–72, 180
  and technical rationality, 148–149
  and terrorism, 113–114
  vs. development of coastal land, 140–143
  See also Stafford Act (1988)
disaster planning
  civil defense programs, 52–54
  coordination, 130
  and discrimination, 168–173, 177–178
  by the federal government, 52–54, 55–56,
    58, 69, 129, 130
  by local authorities, 52–54
  risk models, 177
  by states, 52–54, 55–56, 58, 125
  worst case planning, 150–155, 172
disaster policy
  civil defense programs, 11, 14
  Cold War, 14
  Congress and, 9, 16–17, 24–27, 28–31
  and cultural scripts, 149–150
  development of, 11, 35–40
  disasters as actors, 11
  and electoral politics, 10, 38–39, 71,
    178–179, 187
  evolution of, 189–193
  and the federal government, 174–178,
    189–193
  and historical consciousness, 191–192
  and the media, 10, 11, 71
  paradoxes of, 184–189
  presidents and, 17, 32–35, 71, 75, 188
  and security fears, 146–147
  setting boundaries, 9–10
  shaped by social construction, 8–9, 176
  and terrorism, 11
disaster relief
  Congress and, 17, 35–39
  economic and humanitarian aid, 36
  FEMA focus on, 97, 100–101
  government agencies and spending, 9, 72,
    73, 175
  historical perspective, 51, 75, 76–79

Hurricane Katrina, 133
  improvised response and recovery, 133–134
  increase of through precedent, 37
  manipulation of, 40
  technological limitations of, 34.
    See also FEMA. Red Cross. Stafford Act
    (1988)
Disaster Relief Act (1950), 52
Disaster Relief Act (1969), 75
disaster state, building of, 16–17
disasters
  as actants, 11, 145
  altruism, 166–167
  definition of, 7–8, 127–128, 180
  disaster declarations, 52, 76–79, 86–87, 111
  domestic *vs.* foreign, 4–5
  Hurricane Katrina as definition of, 127–128
  long term vulnerability, 179
  manipulation of, 40
  nonnatural, 82
  social construction of, 145, 192
discrimination and security fears
  fear of civil unrest, 147–148, 151, 152–154
  and marginalized groups, 146–147,
    168–173, 177–178, 182–184
displacement theory, 157, 170–171
domestic law enforcement, 135–137, 153
Domestic Preparedness Program, 115
Douglas, Melvyn, 45
Driscoll, Alfred, 53
dual use policy, 11, 55, 57, 68, 75, 76–78
"Duck and Cover" film, 55
Duff, James, 56

earthquakes. *See specific earthquakes*
economic assistance, 36, 85. *See also* disaster
    relief
education policy, 10, 65
Eisenhower, Dwight D., 49, 65, 111, 157
electoral politics
  and civil defense programs, 67–69
  and disaster management, 67–69, 105, 178
  and disaster policy, 10, 38–39, 71,
    178–179, 187
  and FEMA, 97–98, 110–112
  and goal ambiguity, 62
  and homeland security, 126
  and shelter program, 66
elite panic, 161–168
embassy bombings, 114
emergency management. *See* disaster
    management

Emily, Hurricane, 103
Emmerich, Herbert, 107
evacuation, 2, 6, 65, 131–133
evil. *See* administrative evil *and* banality of evil

fallout shelters. *See* shelter program
FBI, 108, 116, 118
FCDA (Federal Civil Defense Administration),
    53, 54–56, 58, 72
Federal Aviation Administration, 187
Federal Civil Defense Act, 108
Federal Civil Defense Administration.
    See FCDA
Federal Disaster Relief Act (1950), 72–73
Federal Disaster Relief Act (1974), 76
Federal Emergency Management Agency.
    See FEMA
federal government
    centralization of disaster management,
        143–145
    contingency plans, 150, 152
    as coordinator, 50
    disaster planning, 52–54, 55–56, 58, 69,
        129, 130
    disaster policy, 174–178, 189–193
    disaster relief, 9, 72, 73, 175
    discriminatory practices, 146–147
    federalism, 9, 10, 17, 22–23, 44–46, 179
    financial help for state and local programs,
        66–67
    Hurricane Katrina spending, 133
    and infrastructure, 52
    and land use policies, 140–143
    and legibility, 62–63
    over-reliance on, 130–131
    public perception and expectations of,
        127–128, 175, 177, 180–187
    and routine disasters, 182. *See also* civil
        defense programs. electoral politics.
        FEMA
Federal Response Plan, 116
Federal Security Agency, 14, 44
Feldman, Martha, 61
FEMA (Federal Emergency Management
    Agency)
    all hazards policy, 96–106, 128, 176–177
    and Army Corps of Engineers, 133
    bureaucracy of, 80, 86, 106–109
    and civil defense, 82, 90
    Congress and, 87, 97–98
    creation of, 42, 75, 181
    critiques of, 90–92

directors, 98
as disaster clearinghouse, 6
discriminatory practices of, 146–147
and electoral politics, 13, 110–112
and elite panic, 161–168
exploitative recovery process, 176
failures of, 87–89, 134–135, 175–176
fear of homosexuals, 155–161
fear of racial uprising, 152–154
funding, 123–124
goal ambiguity, 79, 87, 90, 96, 112
Hurricane Katrina, 6–7, 132–133, 137–140
incorporation in DHS, 121–122, 182
increasing demand for, 110
lack of capacity, 133, 140, 177
Mariel Boatlift, 131
and the media, 89, 98–100, 105–106
and the military, 79, 90, 100
and mitigation programs, 102–103,
    124–125
and national security, 83–84, 87, 90, 97,
    100–101, 108, 150–155
and natural disasters, 97, 100–101
and 9/11 attacks, 119–121, 126, 182
organization of, 75, 96–100
politicization of, 12–13, 122–126
and presidential authority, 91–92, 104–106
public expectations and perception of, 126,
    127–128, 133, 154, 175, 177
resources of, 103
search and rescue, 120
and terrorism, 80–84, 113–117, 126
and worst case planning, 150–155.
    See also Giuffrida, Louis O.
films, civil defense, 41, 55
Fire Prevention Control Act (1974), 79
fires. *See specific fires*
first responders, 115, 119–120
Fish and Wildlife agencies, 133
Flood Control Act (1936), 44
floods and flooding, 9, 53, 72, 80, 102, 142,
    146. *See also* specific floods
foreign disaster aid, 4–5, 22, 23, 27
foreign disaster aid to U.S., 33
forest management, 53
foundations, 55
Fourteenth Amendment, 17
Fradkin, Philip, 167
Frank, Barney, 157
Freedmen's Bureau, 29, 40
Freud, Sigmund, 170
Funston, Frederick, 33, 34

Galveston Hurricane, 167
GAO (Government Accountability Office), 90,
    91, 101
Garrett, Thomas, 111
gays, 147, 155–161, 171, 177–178
general welfare clause, 22–23, 36, 37–38
geographic devastation, 47
Gerber, Brian, 140
Gibson, John, 163
Gilbert, Hurricane, 84
Gilman, Nils, 152
Giuffrida, Louis O., 82–84, 90, 150–155, 171
Global War on Terror, 117–118
Goldberg, Jonah, 144, 175
Gore, Al, 99, 104
Goss, Kay, 101
Government Accountability Office (GAO), 90,
    91, 101
Great Depression, 43–44
Great Hurricane (1780), 95
Greenbrier bunker, 87
Grossman, Andrew, 54
Ground Observers Corps, 54

Hale, Kate, 88
Hart-Rudman Commission, 116–117
Healy, Andrew, 110
historical consciousness, 191–192
Hobbesian state, 164, 167
Hoffman, Frank, 116
Holden, Kip, 164
Hollings, Ernest, 87–88, 97
Holocaust, 148
Homeland Security, Department of (DHS)
    creation of, 78, 113–114, 118–119,
        182
    failures of, 135, 137–140
    FEMA incorporation, 121–122, 182
    lack of capacity, 133
    organizational development of, 13
homosexuals, 147, 155–161, 169, 171,
    177–178
Hoover, Herbert, 1–2, 31, 31, 75, 174
Hopley Report, 49–50
housing, emergency, 53
Housing and Urban Development, Department
    of, 74
Houston, TX, 164
Hugo, Hurricane, 87, 95, 168
Hull, Isabel, 149
humanitarian aid, 27
hurricanes, 72, 182, 186. *See also* names of
    specific hurricanes

ice storms, 63
ideology, 10
immigration agency, 118
incorporation doctrine, 17
individualism, 110
infrastructure, 47, 52
institutional isomorphism, 159
insurance, flood, 102, 142, 146
Insurrection Act, 136
Integrated Emergency Management System,
    80, 155
International Association of Emergency
    Managers, 93
Iran hostage crisis, 81
Ivan, Hurricane, 182

Jackson, Michael, 124
Jefferson, Thomas, 38
Jett, George, 82, 151
John, Richard, 28
Johnson, Andrew, 29
Johnson, Francis, 25
Johnson, Jerald, 156–157
Johnson, Lyndon, 73, 111
Johnstown, PA floods, 17
judges, 9
Justice, Department of, 115, 121–122

Kahn, Herman, 67
Kansas-Missouri Floods (1951), 53
Katrina, Hurricane
    about, 128–129
    costs and losses, 5, 128, 133, 182
    criticism of government response,
        174
    deaths, 5, 128, 182
    as definition of disaster, 127–128
    and elite panic, 161–168
    evacuation, 6, 131–133
    failures of disaster response, 4–7, 125,
        137–140, 182
    federal spending on, 133
    and FEMA, 6–7, 132–133, 137–140
    and the media, 136, 162–166
    refusal of foreign assistance, 33
Keller, Morton, 27
Kennedy, John F., 64, 111
Kenya embassy bombing, 115
Khobar Towers bombing, 114
Klein, Naomi, 40
Knowles, Scott, 57
Korean War, 53
Krimm, Richard, 103

Kunreuther, Howard, 73
Kupperman, Robert, 161

Lacan, Jacques, 171
LaFollette, Robert, 43
LaGuardia, Fiorello, 44–45, 49, 50
land use policies, 140–143
Landis, James, 45, 51
Langewiesche, William, 119
Larabee, Eric, 181
Larson, John, 28
latent racism, 169
Law Enforcement Terrorism Prevention
    Program, 124
Lee, Spike, 127, 175
legibility, 62–63
Lehrer, Eli, 120
lesbians, 147, 155–161, 171, 177–178
levees
    Army Corps of Engineers, 5, 138, 142–143
    construction of, 53
    Orleans Parish Levee Board, 139, 140
    responsibility for in New Orleans, 5
    system policies, 142–143
loans, 74
lobbyists, 12, 30, 80
local authorities
    civil defense programs, 49, 60–63, 66–69
    decentralization of disaster management,
        143–144, 179
    and Hurricane Andrew, 88–89
    implementation of preparedness plans,
        52–54, 55–56, 58
    and land use policies, 140–143
    and levee system policies, 142–143
    New Orleans police, 137, 165
    9/11 response, 119–120
    over-reliance on federal government,
        130–131
    request for federal coordination, 50
Loma Prieta earthquake (1989), 87
Long, Huey, 174
looting, 162–166, 167–168
losses. *See* costs and losses
Louisiana Department of Wildlife and
    Fisheries, 6

MacArthur, Douglas, 45
Macy, John, 79, 155
Madison, James, 23, 191
Majewski, John, 28
Malhotra, Neil, 110
Margarine Tax Act (1886), 30

marginalized groups and security fears,
    146–147, 168–173, 177–178, 182–184
Mariel Boatlift, 108, 131
martial law, 83–84, 152
May, Peter, 25
Mayfield, Max, 132
McFarlane, Robert, 84
McGuire, O.R., 37
McKinley, William, 32
McPherson, James, 29
McQuaid, John, 5
media
    and disaster policy, 10, 11, 71
    effects of, 71
    and FEMA, 89, 98–100, 105–106
    Hurricane Katrina, 136
    and Munich Olympics, 81
    and 9/11 attacks, 117, 118
    rumors of looting, rape and murder,
        162–166
Metcalf, Victor, 33
Metropolitan Medical Response System, 124
Michigan Great Fire (1881), 17
Mikulski, Barbara, 97
military
    Brown request for, 136
    and civil defense, 48
    and disaster management, 143
    domestic law enforcement, 135–137,
        153
    and FEMA, 79, 90, 100. *See also* army.
        Defense, Department of. National Guard.
        Stafford Act (1988)
Mississippi, 141
Mississippi River Commission, 1
Mississippi River Floods, 1–4, 30, 75, 174
Mississippi River Gulf Outlet, 143
Missouri earthquakes, 23
mitigation
    FEMA programs, 102–103, 124–125
    local efforts, 25
    and Stafford Act, 85–86
    underinvestment in, 110–111
    vs. development of coastal land, 140–143.
        See also disaster planning
morale building, 47
Munich Olympics (1972), 81
murder, rumors of, 162–166
Murphree, Dennis, 1

Nagin, Ray, 132, 163
NAPA (National Academy of Public
    Administration), 90, 96, 101

National Aeronautics and Space
Administration, 74
National Coordinating Council on Emergency
Management, 92–93
national crisis, 83–84
National Education Association, 65
National Fallout Shelter Survey, 59–60
National Flood Insurance Program,
141, 142
National Guard, 49, 133, 134
National Preparedness Directorate, 90,
91, 101
National Response Plan, 129–130, 131
national security
counterterrorism activities, 114–115,
124–125
and FEMA, 83–84, 87, 90, 97, 100–101,
108, 150–155
and foreign disaster aid, 23. *See also* civil
defense programs. Homeland Security,
Department of (DHS)
National Security Council, 101, 115, 151
National Security Resources Board, 41
natural disasters, 18, 42, 97, 100–101,
124–125. *See also* disaster planning.
specific disaster
Neville, Arthel, 164
New Deal, 43–44
New England Hurricane (1938), 43
new federalism, 74
New Madrid, MO earthquakes, 23
New Orleans, LA
police, 137, 165
violent reputation of, 164
vulnerability of, 5, 129, 139–140, 143.
See also Katrina, Hurricane. levees
New York City Fire, 22, 26–27
9/11 attacks, 117, 119–121, 126, 182
9/11 Commission, 118, 119, 172
Nitze, Paul, 47
Nixon, Richard, 64, 74–75
nonnatural disasters, 82
Norfolk, VA fire, 22
North, Oliver, 151
Novak, William, 28
nuclear attack
contingency plans, 150
fear of, 46, 47, 75, 181
Nixon on, 64
underestimation of severity, 65. *See also* civil
defense programs
nuclear power, 75, 175

Office for Domestic Preparedness, 115
Office of Civil and Defense Mobilization, 72
Office of Civil Defense, 72
Office of Civil Defense Planning, 41
Office of Civilian Defense, 41, 44–46, 50–51
Office of Domestic Preparedness, 116, 121–122
Office of Emergency Management, 44
Office of Emergency Planning, 72
Office of Emergency Preparedness, 72, 74
Office of Management and Budget (OMB),
68, 86
Office of National Preparedness, 120–121
Office of National Security Coordination, 101
Oklahoma City bombing, 114, 120
Olympic games, 81, 108, 115, 154
OMB (Office of Management and Budget),
68, 86
organizational deviance, 147–148
Orleans Parish Levee Board, 139, 140

Pam, Hurricane, 125
Paulison, David, 129–130
Paulson, Henry, 172
Pearl Harbor, 117
Pentagon 9/11 attack, 117
Peterson, Frederick, 65
Peterson, Val, 58
Philadelphia Civil Defense Council, 56–57
Pinchot, Gifford, 109
Pinkerton, Allen, 166
Plato, 180
political appointments, 7, 12–13, 104–105,
122–123
political construction, 8–9. *See also* social
construction
politicization of FEMA, 122–126
politics of disaster management, 178
Polk, James K., 25
poor, 177–178
population growth, 183
Portsmouth, NH Fires, 21, 21
Posse Comitatus Act (1878), 136, 153
Post Offices, 28, 109
Post-Attack Resource Management Act
(VA), 59
preamble to U.S. Constitution, 22
pre- and post-attack periods, 49
precedent, 35–39
preparedness plans. *See* disaster planning
presidents
authority of, 38
and civil defense, 42, 60–63

credit for disaster relief, 72–73
disaster declarations, 52, 76–79, 86–87, 111
and disaster policy, 17, 32–35, 71, 75, 188
and FEMA, 91–92, 104–106
and increased federal government
  involvement, 178–179
and the National Guard, 49
and Stafford Act, 86
private organizations, 31. *See also* Red Cross
progressive era, 109–110
Project Impact, 124
Public Law 85–606 (1948), 66–67
public organizations, 13
public perception and expectations
  of all hazards policy, 126
  of disaster management, 126, 127–128, 144,
    154, 175, 184–187, 189
  of federal government, 127–128, 133, 177

race war, fear of, 152–154
racism, 169
rape, rumors of, 162–166
Reagan, Ronald, 82, 150, 154
Reconstruction, 29–32
Reconstruction Finance Corporation, 43–44
recovery, governmental assistance, 3–4
Red Cross
  and disaster relief, 17, 52, 73
  expanded mission of, 31
  Hurricane Katrina, 133
  Mississippi River Flood, 1–2
  San Francisco earthquake and fire, 33,
    34–35
Reed, Stanley, 43
Reinventing Government initiative, 99, 104
Reno, Janet, 116
Republicans, 17
Ridge, Tom, 85
Rio Grande flood (1897), 37
riots, fear of, 150, 151
risk models, 177, 186
Robert T. Stafford Disaster Relief and
  Emergency Assistance Act. *See* Stafford
  Act (1988)
Roosevelt, Eleanor, 44–45, 51–52
Roosevelt, Franklin D., 14, 32, 43–45, 47
Roosevelt, Theodore, 32–33, 35, 40
Ruch, Charles, 131

Samuel, Bernard, 57
San Francisco, CA earthquake and fire (1906),
  32–34, 40, 136, 168

Sawislak, Karen, 166
SBA (Small Business Administration), 73
Schleifstein, Mark, 5
Schumann, Gregg, 131
search and rescue, 120
secrecy and administrative evil, 148
security missions
  and cultural scripts, 149–150
  and disaster management, 71–72, 180
  and disaster policy, 146–147
  and electoral politics, 126
  as justification for discrimination, 158,
    172–173, 177–178, 182–184
  vs. emergency management, 14–15.
    See also FEMA. Homeland Security,
    Department of (DHS)
self-help principle, 52, 68
September 11 attacks, 117, 119–121, 126, 182
September 11 Commission, 118, 119, 172
shared risk, 64–65
Sharpton, Al, 163
shelter program, 59–60, 64, 66, 67
Shuster, Bill, 140
Skowronek, Stephen, 17, 178
slave insurrection, Haiti, 21
Slidell, LA, 166
Small Business Administration (SBA), 73
Smith, Daniel, 133
Smith, Gavin, 130
Smith, Melancton, 23
Smith, William French, 83, 154
Sobel, Russell, 111
social construction
  about, 12
  of civil defense, 42, 63–67
  of Congress and disaster relief, 39
  and cultural bias, 171
  and disaster policy, 8–9
  and disaster preparedness, 67
  and disaster relief expectations, 176
  of disasters, 7–8, 145, 192
  and goal ambiguity, 112
  labeling of groups as threats, 155
  politics over time, 178
  and security fears, 146–147, 154
  and sense of shared risk, 64–65
  and social contracts, 180
  and terrorism preparedness, 113–114
social welfare, 45, 50–51
Solnit, Rebecca, 167
Soviet Union, fear of, 46, 73–74, 153, 181
spotter system, 54

St. Croix, 168
Stafford Act (1988), 84–87, 103, 129,
    134, 145
Stark, Pete, 97
State, Department of, 118
State and Local Programs Support
    Directorate, 91
state-building, 27–28
State Homeland Security Program, 124
states
    authority of, 58
    civil defense programs, 49, 60–63, 66–69
    decentralization of disaster management,
        143–144
    implementation of preparedness plans,
        52–54, 55–56, 58
    natural disaster preparedness, 125
    over-reliance on federal government, 130–131
Stickney, Wallace, 156
Stillwell Report, 159
storms, 63, 72. *See also* hurricanes. tornadoes.
    specific storm names
Story, Joseph, 22
stovepipes, failures of, 78–79, 138–139
Strategic Bombing Surveys (USSBS), 47
sublimation, 170–171
Suiter, Lacy, 104
Superdome (New Orleans), 6, 132, 134, 163
supply chain, failures of, 138
Supreme Court, 22, 38

Taft, William Howard, 34
Tanzania embassy bombing, 115
taxation, 22–23
technical rationality, 148–149
terrorism
    and disaster management, 113–114
    and disaster policy, 11
    and the FBI, 116
    and FEMA, 80–84, 113–117, 126.
    See also counterterrorism activities.
    Homeland Security, Department of
TOPOFF 3 scenario, 130
tornadoes, 63, 72
Transportation Security Administration (TSA),
    135
Treasury, Department of, 74
Trefry report, 158–161
Truman, Harry, 41, 46, 50

TSA (Transportation Security
    Administration), 135
tsunamis, 4
Tulis, Jeffrey, 32
Twain, Mark, 4, 8

unconscious motivation, 170–171
United States Army War College, 172
universities and civil defense programs, 55
Urban Area Security Initiative, 124
urbanization, 182
US Civil Defense Council, 92
U.S. Constitution. *See* Constitution
US Strategic Bombing Surveys (USSBS), 47

Van Susteren, Greta, 163–164
Vaughan, Diane, 149
Venezuela earthquake (1812), 22
Veteran's Administration, 158
Virginia, 58

Waldo, Dwight, 189
War Department, 45. *See also* Defense,
    Department of
warden program, 54–55, 57–58
weapons of mass destruction, 115
Weather Bureau, 2–3
Weber, Max, 134
Weldon, Curt, 97
wetlands, 139, 140
When the Levees Broke (film), 127, 175
Whiskey Rebellion, 21
White House Office of Homeland
    Security, 118
Wiley, Harvey, 109
Wilson, James Q., 101
Witt, James Lee, 5
    all hazards policy, 96–106, 113–117,
        181–182
    and electoral politics, 110
    successes of, 108–109
    use of political connections, 13
Woods, Tiger, 164
World Trade Center bombing, 114
World War II, 44–45, 46
worst case planning, 150–155, 172.
    See also disaster management

zoning regulations, 141, 182